Tibet

a Lonely Planet travel survival kit

Chris Taylor

Tibet

3rd edition

Published by

Lonely Planet Publications

Head Office: PO Box 617, Hawthorn, Vic 3122, Australia
Branches: 155 Filbert St, Suite 251, Oakland, CA 94607, USA
10 Barley Mow Passage, Chiswick, London W4 4PH, UK
71 bis rue du Cardinal Lemoine, 75005 Paris, France

Printed by

Colorcraft Ltd, Hong Kong

Photographs by

Richard I'Anson (RI), Inge Bollen (IB), Chris Taylor (CT)
Black & White Photograph on page 207, Jann Subiaco (JS)
Front cover: Yumbulagang, Yarlung Valley (CT)
Title page: The Potala, Lhasa (CT)

First Published

April 1986

This Edition

April 1995

Although the authors and publisher have tried to make the information as accurate as possible, they accept no responsibility for any loss, injury or inconvenience sustained by any person using this book.

National Library of Australia Cataloguing in Publication Data

Taylor, Chris
Tibet – a travel survival kit.

3rd ed.
Includes index.
ISBN 0 86442 289 X.

1. Tibet – Guidebooks. I. Strauss, Robert. Tibet.
II. Title. (Series: Lonely Planet travel survival kit).

915.1504

text & maps © Lonely Planet 1995
photos © photographers as indicated 1995
climate charts compiled from information supplied by Patrick J Tyson, © Patrick J Tyson, 1995

Chris Taylor

Chris Taylor spent his early years in England. He emigrated to Australia with his family in the '70s. After frittering away his youth in a variety of fruitless occupations, travelling and working on a useless BA, Chris joined Lonely Planet to work on the phrasebook series. He has since coauthored *China* and *Japan*. Chris Taylor is also author of the city guides to Tokyo and Seoul, and the *Mandarin Chinese phrasebook*.

From the Author

I bumped into innumerable travellers – Westerners, Tibetans and Chinese – while wandering around Tibet, and all of you helped out in some way. I'd like to say a special word of thanks to Michel Rooijackers, computer science doctorate, world traveller and mean drinking companion, who kept me up late on too many occasions and joined me on the 'no-shave-to-Base-Camp' expedition. Hi also to Richard 'Tears-in-Heaven' Newman, who taught me much in the dying art of talking absolute bollocks. Avida of Israel (sorry, I've forgotten your surname) should also not be forgotten.

Alex Gabbay, fashion designer turned student of Buddhism and aspiring script/novel writer, joined me on the trip to Kailash and, along with my truck driver, deserves something of an apology for my sometimes explosive sense of urgency to keep the show on the road. I enjoyed the trip and the endless conversations on literature, fashion design, Tibetan Buddhism and the decline of Western civilisation, Alex.

I'd like to say hello to the Lhasa crowd whose brains I picked: Tibet old hand Steve (sorry, I've forgotten your surname); Gary McCue and Kathy Butler; Geoff 'where's-the-nearest-airport' Greenwald; and Richard & Alison. Claudio Perotti of the Lhasa Holiday Inn treated me to the best dinner I had in Tibet and was generous with his time and inside knowledge of life in Lhasa. Thanks Claudio – you deserve a posting in Tahiti next time round.

Unfortunately the current situation in Tibet makes it impossible to thank the

numerous Tibetans and Chinese who helped me with information and gave me insight into the tragedy of contemporary Tibet.

At lower altitudes I'd like to extend my gratitude to John Ashburne (once again) for lending me his Mamiya m645 so that I could spend my whole trip worrying about light exposures. Ron Gluckmann gave me invaluable contacts and kept me up with the latest developments in Tibet while I was writing this book. Robert Walker and Christine Jones generously opened the doors of their Lamma Island home whenever I passed through Hong Kong. Thanks as always to the Phoenix crew for organising my tickets. And thanks again to Wen-ying for bearing the brunt of the peculiar life style of a guidebook writer, taking care of home while I was away and taking care of me while I was here.

Lastly, I'd like to dedicate my work on this book to the memory of Paul Butler, whose travels came to a tragically premature conclusion while I was away in Tibet. We miss you, Paul.

This Edition

The first edition of this book was researched and written by Michael Buckley and Robert Strauss and the second edition, by Robert Strauss. This, the third edition, was researched and rewritten completely by Chris Taylor.

From the Publisher

This book was edited in Melbourne, Australia by Frith Pike and proofed by Susan Noonan. Richard Stewart produced the maps and designed the book, while Valerie Tellini and Tamsin Wilson produced the illustrations and Valerie designed the cover. Thanks to David Christensen for the Tibetan script and to Chris Taylor for the Chinese script. Thanks also to Dan Levin and Rob Flynn for computer assistance with the Tibetan script and to Dan for producing the fonts used in the Chinese romanisations.

Warning & Request

Things change – prices go up, schedules change, good places go bad and bad places go bankrupt – nothing stays the same. So if you find things better or worse, recently opened or long since closed, please write and tell us and help make the next edition better.

Your letters will be used to help update future editions and, where possible, important changes will also be included in a Stop Press section in reprints.

We greatly appreciate all information that is sent to us by travellers. Back at Lonely Planet we employ a hard-working readers' letters team to sort through the many letters we receive. The best ones will be rewarded with a free copy of the next edition or another Lonely Planet guide if you prefer. We give away lots of books, but, unfortunately, not every letter/postcard receives one.

Thanks

Thanks must go to the following travellers and others (apologies if we've misspelt your name) who used the last edition and wrote to us with information, comments and suggestions. To those whose names have been omitted through oversight, apologies – your time and efforts are appreciated.

John Ackerly (USA), G Bennett, Mirielle Boisson (F), Inge Bollen (D), Greg Buckman (Aus), Tom Camara (USA), Dr Lance Eccles (Aus), Dave Edwards (UK), Stanton Etzi (USA), Mary Gan (Sin), Howard Gethin (UK), Celeste Q Graham (USA), Manuel Guillen (USA), Jonathan Hibbs (UK), Erik Horenberg (D), Tommy Jensen (Dk), David Kula (USA), Mary Lerps (USA), Doris Lie (USA), Jan Magnusson (S), Fiona Marchbanks (UK), Rafaela Mottram (UK), Monika Mueller (USA), Danilelle O'Loughlin (Aus), Ian Pollitt (UK), Mason Risko, Raymond Rose (USA), Stefan Seidel (D), Hal Sharpe (USA), Jane Sillman (F), Stewart Smith (UK), Dr Isaac Sobol (C), Karen Stobbs Aderer (USA), Steve & Joanie Tibbetts (USA), Jia-shu Xu, and Katy Youel (USA).

Aus – Australia, F – France, C – Canada, D – Germany, Dk – Denmark, Sin – Singapore, S – Sweden, UK – United Kingdom, USA – United States of America

Contents

WESTERN TIBET 211

GLOSSARY 228

APPENDIX – Place Names (Chinese) 235

INDEX 237

Map Legend

BOUNDARIES

.... International Boundary

.... Regional Boundary

ROUTES

.... Freeway

.... Highway

.... Major Road

.... Unsealed Road or Track

.... City Road

.... City Street

.... Railway

.... Underground Railway

.... Tram

.... Walking Track

.... Walking Tour

.... Ferry Route

.... Cable Car or Chairlift

AREA FEATURES

.... Park, Gardens

.... National Park

.... Forest

.... Built-Up Area

.... Pedestrian Mall

.... Market

.... Cemetery

.... Beach or Desert

.... Rocks

HYDROGRAPHIC FEATURES

.... Coastline

.... River, Creek

.... Intermittent River or Creek

.... Lake, Intermittent Lake

.... Canal

.... Swamp

SYMBOLS

✪ CAPITAL		National Capital
◉ Capital		Regional Capital
CITY		Major City
● City		City
● Town		Town
● Village		Village
■		Place to Stay
▼		Place to Eat
▯		Pub, Bar
✉	☎	Post Office, Telephone
❶	❸	Tourist Information, Bank
◗	ℙ	Transport, Parking
🏛	⌂	Museum, Youth Hostel
⚏	⚎	Caravan Park, Camping Ground
† ⬛	✝	Church, Cathedral
☪	⚎	Mosque, Hindu Temple
⚊		Buddhist Temple & Monastery

✚	★	Hospital, Police Station
✈	✈	Airport, Airfield
▭	☕	Swimming Pool, Cafe
❖	🐘	Shopping Centre, Zoo
⚘	⊼	Winery or Vineyard, Picnic Site
←	A25	One Way Street, Route Number
	∴	Archaeological Site or Ruins
🏛	🛆	Stately Home, Monument
⛩	▣	Fort, Tomb
⌒	⌂	Cave, Hut or Chalet
▲	☼	Mountain or Hill, Lookout
⚱	⚮	Lighthouse, Shipwreck
)(	⚲	Pass, Spring
		Ancient or City Wall
		Rapids, Waterfalls
		Cliff or Escarpment, Tunnel
		Railway Station

Note: not all symbols displayed above appear in this book

Introduction

Shangrila, the Land of Snows, the Roof of the World; for centuries the mysterious Buddhist kingdom of Tibet, locked away in its mountain fastness of the Himalayas, exercised a unique hold on the imagination of the West. The Jesuits, hearing rumours of Tibet in far away Goa, believed it to harbour a long-lost community of Christians, the Land of Prester John. For adventurers and traders it was a land of treasure and riches. And the dreamers whispered of a lost land of magic and mystery.

But as Tibetans woke to the sound of foreign travellers prying at the closed doors of their kingdom, they then slipped the lock and threw away the keys. Lhasa, the ultimate prize for countless prosletisers, adventurers and dreamers, became the 'Forbidden City'. Until recently, very few Westerners were privileged to lay eyes on the Holy City.

It is all the more the pity that when the doors finally were flung open in the mid-1980s, Tibet was no longer the hidden Buddhist kingdom that had so intoxicated early Western travellers. In 1950, the newly established People's Republic of China (PRC) decided to make good a long-held Chinese claim on the strategically important high plateau that straddled the Himalaya between China and the subcontinent. It made no difference that the Chinese claim was made on highly dubious historical grounds: between 1950 and 1970, the Chinese 'liberated' the Tibetans of their independence, drove their spiritual leader and some 100,000 of Tibet's finest into exile (admittedly a side-effect rather than a goal of Chinese policy), caused some 1.2 million Tibetan deaths (again largely a side-effect) and destroyed most of the Tibetan cultural and historical heritage (deliberate policy).

When the Chinese allowed the first tourists into Tibet in the mid-1980s, they came to a devastated country. Most of Tibet's finest monasteries lay in ruins; monks who, under a recent thaw in Chinese ethnic chauvinism, were once again donning their vestments, cautiously folded them back to display the scars of 'struggle sessions'; and the Tibetan quarter of Lhasa, the Holy City, was now dwarfed by a sprawling Chinatown. The journalist Harrison Salisbury referred to it as a 'dark and sorrowing land'.

The fact that travellers and tourists still come to Tibet is a mark of the fascination that the place continues to exercise on the Western imagination. It is also a tribute to the spirit of the Tibetans themselves, who remain unbroken and are busy restoring the freedoms that were taken from them – chiefly, freedom of worship.

Throughout Tibet, Tibetans are rebuilding their world. Some observers have compared this to the Tibetan renaissance of the 11th century, when Buddhism returned to the land after two centuries of persecution. And to be sure, a walk around Lhasa's Barkhor pilgrimage circuit and a visit to the Jokhang, holiest of Tibet's temples, is proof enough that all the efforts of the Chinese to build a Brave New World have foundered on the remarkable faith of the Tibetan people.

At the same time, however, there is little point in pretending that visiting the Land of Snows is a Disneyland adventure. The Tibetans are a resilient, devout and wonderfully friendly people. But recent history has left its scars. Most Tibetans are only too happy to have foreign visitors in their country and are eager for news of happenings outside Tibet – particularly with regard to the Dalai Lama and the Government in Exile. But do not expect smiles all the way. In mid-1994 travellers complained of being stoned by monks at Rongbuk Monastery, near Everest Base Camp; theft occasionally occurs in Tibetan villages; and many Tibetan tour operators are no more honest than their Chinese counterparts.

Tibet is one of the most remarkable places to visit in Asia: it is also a country under occupation. It offers fabulous monastery

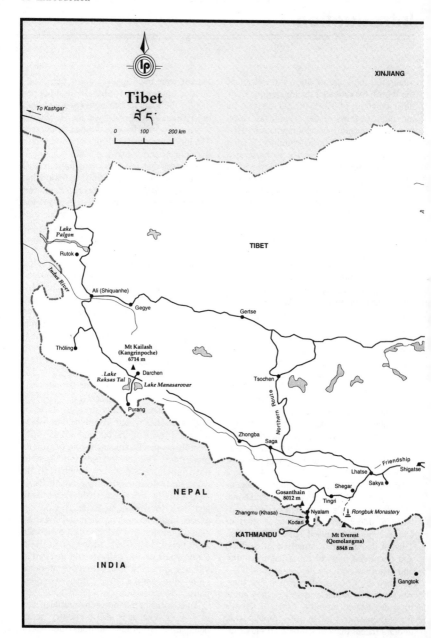

Tibet

 བོད་

XINJIANG

To Kashgar

0   100   200 km

TIBET

Lake Palgon

Rutok ●

Indus River

Ali (Shiquanhe) ●

Gegye ●

Gertse ●

Thöling ●

Mt Kailash (Kangrinpoche) 6714 m ▲

Darchen

Lake Raksas Tal

Lake Manasarovar

Tsochen ●

Purang ●

Zhongba ●

Saga ●

Northern Route

NEPAL

Gosanthain 8012 m ▲

Zhangmu (Khasa)

Nyalam ●

Kodari ●

KATHMANDU ✛

Tingri

Rongbuk Monastery

Mt Everest (Qomolangma) 8848 m ▲

Shegar ●

Lhatse ●

Friendship

Sakya ●

Shigatse ●

INDIA

Gangtok ●

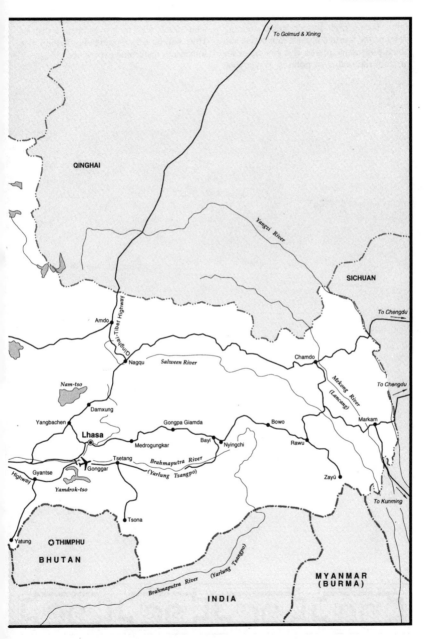

sights, taxing high-altitude treks, stunning views of the world's highest mountains and fabled pilgrimage routes. But you are never far from the reality of politics. For anyone who travels with their eyes open, a visit to Tibet will be a memorable, fascinating, but sometimes disturbing experience.

Facts about Tibet

HISTORY
Mythological Beginnings

Little is known of the beginnings of the Tibetan people. They originated from nomadic, warlike tribes known as the Qiang. Chinese records of these tribes, which harried the borders of the great Chinese empire, date back as far as the 2nd century BC. The people of Tibet were not to emerge as a politically united force to be reckoned with until the 7th century AD, however.

Like all peoples, the Tibetans have a rich corpus of myths concerning the origin of the world and themselves. In the beginning, according to a Tibetan creation myth, the void was filled with a wind that gathered in force until storm clouds brewed and unleashed a torrential rain, forming in time the primeval ocean. After the cessation of the rains, the wind continued to blow over the ocean, churning it like milk, until lands, like butter, came into existence.

According to myth, the Tibetan people owe their existence to the union of an ogress and a monkey on Mt Gangpo Ri at Tsetang. These early myths are no doubt Bön in origin, but have been appropriated by Buddhism, so that the monkey is seen as a manifestation of Avalokiteshvara (Tibetan: Chenresig), the Bodhisattva of Compassion. Upon descending to earth, the monkey sat in a cave on Gangpo Ri and meditated. Sinmo, the ogress, no doubt miserable that her only companion in Tibet was a meditating monkey, sat outside the cave and wept until she aroused his compassion and lured him out. The two had six children, who are seen as the ancestors of the six main tribes of Tibet.

Another origin myth concerns the first Tibetan king. Again, it takes place near Tsetang, in the Yarlung Valley region. King Nyentri Tsenpo is alleged to have descended from the heavens via a 'sky-cord', whereupon he was recognised as a king by 12 local chieftains. King Nyentri Tsenpo and his suc- cessors returned to the heavens via this sky-cord until the time of the 6th Tibetan king, Drigum – a particularly inauspicious name, which means 'slain by pollution'. The king was indeed slain – by a mortal rival – and from this time the remains of Tibetan kings were earth-bound and buried in the funerary mounds which can be seen at Chongye, near Tsetang.

Yarlung Valley Dynasty (?-842)

As early myths of the origin of the Tibetan people suggest, the Yarlung Valley was the cradle of the civilisation of central Tibet. The early Yarlung kings, though glorified in legend, were probably no more than chief- tains whose domains extended not much further than the Yarlung Valley area itself. A reconstruction of Tibet's first fortress, Yumbulagang, can still be seen in the Yarlung Valley, and it is here that the 28th King of Tibet is said to have received Tibet's first Buddhist scriptures in the mid-3rd century. According to legend, they fell on the roof of Yumbulagang.

Credible historical records regarding the Yarlung Valley dynasty do not emerge until the fledgling kingdom entered the interna- tional arena from the 6th century. By this time the Yarlung kings had made significant headway, through conquest and alliances, in unifying much of central Tibet. Namri Songtsen (circa 570-619), the 32nd Tibetan king, continued this trend and extended Tibetan influence into Inner Asia, defeating Qiang tribes on China's borders. But the true flowering of Tibet as an important regional power came about with the accession to rule of Namri Songtsen's son, Songtsen Gampo (circa 618-649).

Under Songtsen Gampo, central Tibet entered a new era. Tibetan expansion contin- ued unabated. The armies of Tibet ranged as far afield as northern India and emerged as a threat to the Tang dynasty in China. Both Nepal and China reacted to the Tibetan incursions by reluctantly agreeing to alliances through marriage. Princess Wencheng, Songtsen Gampo's Chinese bride, and Princess Bhrikuti, his Nepalese bride, became important historical figures for the Tibetans, as it was through their influence that Buddhism first gained royal patronage and a foothold on the Tibetan plateau.

King Songtsen Gampo's reign saw the establishment of the Jokhang and Ramoche temples and the construction of a fort on the site of what much later was to become the Potala Palace in Lhasa. Contact with the Chinese led to the introduction of the sciences of astronomy and medicine, and a Tibetan script was developed from Indian sources. It was used in the first translations of Buddhist scriptures, in drafting a code of law and in writing the first histories of Tibet.

For two centuries after the reign of Songtsen Gampo, Tibet continued to grow in power and influence. By the time of King Trisong Detsen (755-797), Tibetan influence extended across Turkestan and northern Pakistan, into Nepal and India, and in China Tibetan armies conquered Gansu and Sichuan. In 783 Tibetan armies overran Chang'an (present day Xi'an), the Chinese capital, forcing the Chinese to conclude a treaty that recognised new borders incorporating most of the Tibetan conquests.

A further Sino-Tibetan treaty was signed during the reign of King Tritsug Detsen Ralpachen (817-836). It was immortalised in stone on three pillars: one in Lhasa, outside the Jokhang; one in the Chinese capital of Chang'an; and one on the border of Tibet and China. Only the Lhasa pillar still stands (see the Lhasa chapter). Signatories of the treaty swore that '...the whole region to the east...being the country of Great China and the whole region to the west being assuredly that of the country of Great Tibet, from either side of that frontier there shall be no warfare, no hostile invasions, and no seizure of territory...'. The treaty went on to herald a new era in which 'Tibetans shall be happy in Tibet and Chinese shall be happy in China'.

Introduction of Buddhism

By the time Buddhism first arrived in Tibet during the reign of Songtsen Gampo, it had already flourished for some 1100 years and had become the principal faith of all Tibet's neighbouring countries. Buddhism was initially slow to take hold in Tibet.

The influence of Songtsen Gampo's Chinese and Nepalese wives was almost certainly limited to the royal court, and priests of the time were probably Indian and Chinese, not Tibetan.

It was not until King Trisong Detsen's reign that Buddhism began to make any real progress. Trisong Detsen was responsible for founding Samye Monastery, the first institution to carry out the systematic translation of Buddhist scriptures and training of Tibetan monks.

Still, the introduction of Buddhism to Tibet was no simple matter of adopting a proscribed body of precepts. By the 9th century many schools of Buddhism had evolved from the original teachings of Sakyamuni, and Tibetans were in no way confronted with a coherent unified body of beliefs. On a purely superficial level, Bud-

Songtsen Gampo

dhism encompassed the moral precepts and devotional practices of lay followers, the scholastic tradition of the Indian Buddhist universities and a body of mystic Tantric teachings that had a particular appeal to followers of the shamanistic Bön faith.

Contention over the path that Buddhism was to take in Tibet culminated in the Great Debate of Samye, in which King Trisong Detsen is said to have adjudicated in favour of Indian teachers who advocated a gradual approach to enlightenment founded in scholastic study and moral precepts. There was, however, much opposition to this institutionalised, clerical Buddhism, largely from supporters of the Bön faith. The next Tibetan king, Tritsug Detsen Ralpachen, fell victim to this opposition and was assassinated by his brother, Langdharma, who launched an attack on Buddhism. In 842 Langdharma was himself assassinated – by a Buddhist monk – and the Tibetan state quickly collapsed into a number of warring principalities. In the confusion that followed, support for Buddhism dwindled and clerical monastic Buddhism experienced a 150-year hiatus.

Second Diffusion of Buddhism (950-1200)

The collapse of the Tibetan state in 842 put a stop to Tibetan expansion in Asia; Tibet was never again to rise to arms. Overwhelmed initially with local power struggles, Buddhism gradually began to again exert its influence, giving the Tibetan mind a spiritual bent and turning it inward on itself. As the tide of Buddhist faith receded in India, Nepal and China, Tibet slowly emerged as the most devoutly Buddhist nation in the world.

While Tibetan Buddhist tradition holds that the collapse of the Tibetan state corresponds with the systematic persecution of Buddhism, many Western scholars hold that this was probably not the case. It is more likely that Buddhist institutions, such as Samye Monastery, brought into being by the state fell into neglect with the collapse of central power. There is evidence that Bud-dhism survived in pockets and received the patronage of some noble families in the 150 years that passed before the resurgence of monastic Buddhism.

The so-called Second Diffusion of the Dharma (sometimes translated as 'Law'), corresponds with two developments. Firstly, Tibetan teachers who had taken refuge in Kham, to the east, returned to central Tibet and established new monasteries in the late-10th century. Not long after, the kingdom of Guge in Western Tibet invited the Indian scholar Atisha (982-1054) to Tibet in the mid-11th century. Disciples of Atisha, chiefly Dromtönpa, were instrumental in establishing the Kadampa order and monasteries such as Reting in Ü.

This resurgence of Buddhist influence in the 11th century led to many Tibetans travelling to India to study. The new ideas that they brought back with them had a revitalising effect on Tibetan thought and produced other new schools of Tibetan Buddhism. Among them was the Kagyupa order, established by Marpa (1012-1093) the translator, and his disciple Milarepa (1040-1123). Meanwhile, in Sakya, the Kön family established a monastery in 1073 that was to emerge as the seat of the Sakyapa order.

Sakyapa Order Ascendancy & Mongol Overlordship

With the collapse of a central Tibetan state, Tibet's contacts with China dwindled. By the time the Tang dynasty reached the end of its days in 907, China had already recovered almost all the territory it had previously lost to the Tibetans. Through the Song dynasty (960-1276) the two nations had virtually no contact with each other, and Tibet's sole foreign contacts were with its southern Buddhist neighbours.

This was all set to change when Genghis Khan launched a series of conquests in 1206 that led to Mongol supremacy in the form of a vast empire that straddled Central Asia and China. China was not to fall to the Mongols until 1279, but in the meantime the Mongols made short work of Central Asia. Preoccupied with other matters, the Mongols did not give Tibet serious attention until 1239, when they sent a number of raiding parties into the county. Numerous monasteries were razed and the Mongols almost reached Lhasa before turning back.

Tibetan accounts have it that returning Mongol troops related the spiritual eminence of Tibetan lamas to Godan Khan, grandson of Genghis and ruler of the Kokonor region, and in response Godan summoned Sakya Pandita, the head of Sakya Monastery, to his court. The outcome of this meeting was the beginning of a priest-patron relationship between the deeply religious Tibetans and the militarily adventurous Mongols. Tibetan Buddhism became the state religion of the Mongol empire in east Asia and the head Sakya lama its spiritual leader, a position that also entailed temporal authority over Tibet.

The Sakyapa ascendancy lasted less than 100 years. It was strife-torn from the start. The Sakyapa relationship with the Mongol court and its rule of Tibet aroused the jealousy of other religious orders. Political intrigue, power struggles and violence were the order of the day. By 1350 Changchub Gyaltsen, a monk who had first trained in Sakya and then returned to his home district in the Yarlung Valley as a local official, contrived, through alliances and outright confrontation, to overturn the Sakya hegemony. Just 18 years later, the Mongol Yuan dynasty in China, lost its grip on power and the Chinese Ming dynasty was established.

Tibetan Independence

Certain Chinese claims on Tibet have looked to the Mongol Yuan dynasty overlordship of the high plateau, according to the priest-patron relationship that existed at the time, as setting a precedent for Chinese sovereignty of Tibet. In fact, Tibetan submission was offered to the Mongols before they conquered China and it ended when the Mongols fell from power in that country. When the Mongol empire disintegrated, both China and Tibet regained their independence. Sino-Tibetan relations took on the form of regular exchanges of diplomatic courtesies by two independent governments.

After defeating the Sakyapas, Changchub Gyaltsen undertook to remove all traces of the Mongol administration. In this he drew largely on the tradition of the former Yarlung kings: officials were required to dress in the manner of the former royal court; a revised version of King Songtsen Gampo's code of law was enacted; a new taxation system was enforced; and scrolls depicting the glories of the Yarlung dynasty were commissioned (though Changchub Gyaltsen claimed they were 'discovered'). The movement was nothing short of a declaration of Tibet's independence from foreign interference and a search for national identity.

Changchub Gyaltsen and his successors ruled Tibet until 1435 from Neudong, near the Yarlung Valley. Their rule was succeeded by the princes of Rinpung, an area southwest of Lhasa. In 1565, the kings of Tsang became secular rulers of Tibet from Shigatse. Spiritual authority at this time was vested in the Karmapa, head of a Kagyupa sub-order at Tsurphu Monastery.

Rise of the Gelugpa & the Dalai Lamas

In 1374, a young man named Tsongkhapa set out from his home near Kokonor in eastern Tibet to central Tibet, where he undertook training with all the major schools of Tibetan Buddhism. By the time he was 25 years old, he had already gained a reputation as a teacher and a writer, though he continued to study under eminent lamas of the day.

Tsongkhapa established a monastery at Ganden near Lhasa, and it was here that he had a vision of Atisha, the 11th-century Indian scholar who had been instrumental in the second diffusion of Buddhism in Tibet. At Ganden, Tsongkhapa maintained a course of expounding his thinking, steering clear of political intrigue, and espousing doctrinal purity and monastic discipline. Though it seems unlikely that Tsongkhapa intended to found another school of Buddhism, his teachings attracted many disciples, who found his return to the original teachings of Atisha an exciting alternative to the politically tainted Sakyapa and Kagyupa orders.

Disciples of Tsongkhapa, determined to

Reincarnation Lineages

It is not unusual for an important Tibetan lama to be a *trulku*, or 'incarnate lama'. There are thought to be several thousand of them in contemporary Tibet. The abbots of many monasteries are trulku, and thus abbotship can be traced back through a lineage of rebirths to the original founder of the monastery, or at least to an important figure associated with the founding of the monastery. Strictly speaking, however, this investiture of power through rebirth is known as *yangsid*, and properly a trulku is a manifestation of a tantric deity that repeatedly expresses itself through a series of rebirths. The honorific title *rinpoche*, meaning 'very precious', is a mark of respect and does not necessarily imply that the holder is a trulku. The most famous manifestation of a deity is of course the Dalai Lama lineage. The Dalai Lamas are manifestations of Avalokiteshvara, the Bodhisattva of Compassion. The Panchen Lama, on the other hand, is a manifestation of Manjushri, the Bodhisattva of Insight. There is no exclusivity in such a manifestation: Tsongkhapa, founder of the Gelugpa order, was also a manifestation of Manjushri, as traditionally were the abbots of Sakya Monastery.

As a general rule, the reincarnations of high-status lamas tend to be found in aristocratic families (as in the early Dalai Lamas) or in families where trulku have already been identified. The present Dalai Lama's family, for example, was by no means aristocratic, but his elder brother had already been identified as a trulku and his younger brother was also later recognised as a trulku. Disputes over trulku status are not uncommon. The discovery of an incarnate lama amongst their children is likely to mark the beginning of a major improvement in a family's fortunes, creating an incentive for fraud.

It is possible to see in the trulku system a substitute for hereditary power (as in Western royal lineages) in a society where many of the major players were celibate and unable to produce their own heirs. Not that celibacy was overwhelmingly the case. The abbots of Sakya took wives to produce their own trulku reincarnations, and it is not uncommon for rural trulkus to do the same. ∎

propagate their master's teachings, established monasteries at Dreprung (1416) and at Sera (1419). In 1445, yet another monastery (Tashilhunpo) was established at Shigatse, and the movement came to be known as the Gelugpa (Virtuous) order. The founder of Tashilhunpo, Genden Drup, was a nephew of Tsongkhapa, and shortly before his death he announced that he would be reincarnated in Tibet and gave his followers signs that would enable them to find him. His reincarnation, Genden Gyatso, served as the head of Dreprung Monastery, which was now the largest in Tibet, and further consolidated the prestige of the new Gelugpa order.

By the time of the third reincarnated head of the Gelugpa, Sonam Gyatso (1543-1588), the Mongols began to take an interest in Tibet's new and increasingly powerful order. In a move that mirrored the 13th-century Sakyapa entrance into the political arena, Sonam Gyatso accepted an invitation to meet with Altan Khan near Kokonor in 1578. At the meeting Sonam Gyatso received the title of *Ta-Le* (Dalai), meaning 'Ocean', and implying 'Ocean of Wisdom'. The title was retrospectively bestowed on his previous two reincarnations, and Sonam Gyatso became the 3rd Dalai Lama.

The Gelugpa-Mongol relationship marked the Gelupa's entry into turbulent waters of worldly affairs. Ties with the Mongols deepened when, at the 3rd Dalai Lama's death in 1588, his next reincarnation was found in a great grandson of Altan Khan. The boy was brought to Lhasa with great ceremony under the escort of armed Mongol troops.

It is no surprise that the Tsang kings and the Karmapa of Tsurphu Monastery saw this Gelugpa-Mongol alliance as a direct threat to their power. Bickering broke out, and in 1611 the Tsang king attacked Dreprung and Sera monasteries. The 4th Dalai Lama fled central Tibet and died at the age of 25 (probably poisoned) in 1616.

The Great 5th Dalai Lama

A successor to the 4th Dalai Lama was soon discovered, and the boy was brought to

Lhasa, again under Mongol escort. In the meantime, Mongol intervention in Tibetan affairs continued in the guise of support for the embattled Gelugpa order.

In 1621 a Mongolian invasion was turned back at the last minute through mediation by the Panchen Lama of Tashilhunpo Monastery, suggesting that there were probably elements of the Gelugpa order which preferred a truce with the kings of Tsang to outright conflict.

Whatever the case, it seems that proponents of Gelugpa domination had the upper hand, and in 1640 Mongol forces intervened on their behalf, defeating the Tsang forces. The Tsang king was taken captive and later executed, probably at the instigation of Tashilhunpo monks.

Unlike the Sakya-Mongol domination of Tibet, under which the head Sakya lama was required to reside in the Mongol court, the 5th Dalai Lama was able to carry out his rule from within Tibet. With Mongol backing, all of Tibet was pacified by 1656, and the Dalai Lama's control ranged from Kailash in the west to Kham in the east. The 5th Dalai Lama

The Great 5th Dalai Lama

had become both the spiritual and temporal sovereign of a unified Tibet.

The 5th Dalai Lama is remembered as having ushered in a great new age for Tibet. He made a tour of the monasteries of Tibet, and although he stripped most Kadampa monasteries – his chief rivals for power – of their riches, he allowed them to re-establish afterwards. A new flurry of monastic construction began, the major achievement being Labrang Monastery in Kham (Gansu Province, China). In Lhasa, work began on a fitting residence for the head of the Tibetan state: the Potala. He also invited Indian scholars to Tibet, and with Mongol financial support saw to the renovation and expansion of numerous temples and monasteries.

Manchu Intervention

Reincarnation lineages were probably first adopted as a means of maintaining the illusion of a continuous spiritual authority within the various monastic orders of Tibet. With the death of the 5th Dalai Lama, however, the weakness of such a system became apparent when it suddenly extended to the head of the Tibetan state. The great personal prestige and authority of the 5th Dalai Lama himself had played no small part in holding together a newly unified Tibet. When he died in 1682, the Tibetan government was confronted with the prospect of finding his reincarnation and then waiting some 18 years until the boy came of age. The Dalai Lama's regent decided to shroud the Dalai Lama's death in secrecy, announcing that the 5th had entered a long period of meditation.

In 1695 the secret leaked and the regent was forced to hastily enthrone the 6th Dalai Lama, a boy of his own choosing. The choice was an unfortunate one. The 6th soon proved himself to be more interested in poetry and sensual pleasures than in affairs of state. The enthronement of an inept head of state selected by the dubious means of auspicious tokens could not have come at a worse time.

In China the Ming dynasty had fallen in 1644 and the Manchus from the north swiftly moved in to fill the power vacuum, establishing the Manchu Qing dynasty (1644-1912). The events which followed are complicated. Basically, Tibet's ineffectual head of state, the Qing perception of the threat of Tibetan relations with the Mongols, disunity within the ranks of Tibet's Mongol allies and Qing ambitions to extend their power into Tibet, led to a Qing intervention that was to have lasting consequences for Tibet.

Tibet's dealings with the new Qing government went awry from the start. Kang Xi, the second Qing emperor, took offence that the death of the 5th Dalai Lama was concealed from him. At the same time, an ambitious Mongol prince named Lhabzang Khan came to the conclusion that earlier Mongol leaders had taken too much of a back-seat position in their relations with the Tibetans and appealed to Emperor Kang Xi for support. It was granted, and in 1705 Mongol forces descended on Lhasa, killed the Tibetan regent and took the 6th Dalai Lama with the intention of delivering him to Kang Xi in Beijing. The 6th died en route (probably murdered) and Lhabzang Khan installed a new Dalai Lama in Lhasa.

Lhabzang Khan's machinations backfired. The Mongol removal, possible murder, and replacement of the 6th Dalai Lama aroused intense hostility in Tibet. Worse still, it created enemies amongst other Mongol tribes, who saw the Dalai Lama as their spiritual leader. In 1717, the Dzungar Mongols attacked Lhasa, killed Lhabzang Khan and deposed the new Dalai Lama. Not that this solved anything in particular. The 7th Dalai Lama chosen by the Tibetans themselves, who had been discovered according to a prophesy by the 6th in Litang (present day Sichuan), was languishing in Kumbum Monastery under Chinese 'protection'.

The resulting confusion in Tibet was the perfect opportunity for which Emperor Kang Xi had been waiting. He responded by sending a military expedition to Lhasa in 1720. The Chinese troops drove out the Dzungar Mongols and were received as liberators by the Tibetans. It was unlikely they would be received any other way: with them they brought the 7th Dalai Lama.

Emperor Kang Xi wasted no time in declaring Tibet a protectorate of China. Two Chinese representatives, known as *Amban*s, were installed at Lhasa along with a garrison of Chinese troops. It was the thin end of the wedge, leading to two centuries of Manchu overlordship and serving as a convenient historical precedent for the Communist takeover nearly 250 years later.

Manchu Overlordship

The Manchu overlordship was characterised by repeated reactions to crises in the form of military interventions rather than a steady hand in governing Tibetan political affairs. Such interventions typically resulted in a reorganisation of the Tibetan government. After appointing a king at one stage, temporal rule reverted to the 7th Dalai Lama in 1750, following a Manchu intervention in response to the murder of the Ambans by a Tibetan mob.

The 7th Dalai Lama ruled successfully until his death in 1757. At this point it became clear, however, that another ruler would have to be appointed until the next Dalai Lama reached his majority. The post of regent was created, and it was decided that it should be held by a lama.

It is perhaps a poor reflection on the spiritual attainment of the lamas appointed as regents that few were willing to relinquish their hand on the helm once they had control of the ship. In the 120 years between the death of the 7th Dalai Lama and the majority of the 13th, actual power was wielded by the Dalai Lamas for only seven years. Three of them died very young and under suspicious circumstances. Only the 8th Dalai Lama survived his majority, living a quiet, contemplative life until the age of 45.

The last Chinese military intervention took place in reaction to a Gurkha invasion from Nepal in 1788. As usual there was an administrative reshuffle with short-lived consequences, and from this time Manchu influence in Tibet receded, though the post of Amban continued to be filled until the fall of the Qing dynasty in 1911. Perhaps the one significant outcome of the 1788 intervention was a ban on foreign contact, enacted due to fears of British collusion in the Gurkha invasion.

Barbarians at the Doorstep

The West's earliest contacts with Tibet were via Jesuit missionaries, some of whom were convinced it was the home of a lost Christian community known as the Kingdom of Prester John. In 1707 an early Jesuit mission was established in Lhasa (an earlier one still had been established in Tsaparang, Western Tibet). It survived until 1745, when it closed due to lack of funds and local opposition by monks. Just a year earlier, in 1706, another Jesuit, Ippolito Desideri, had arrived and in true Jesuit style set about mastering the language and customs of Tibet. He even managed to write a refutation of Buddhism in Tibetan – a piece that was much admired locally but failed to win any converts.

In fact, in these early days of Western contact with Tibet, there was little stopping travellers making their way to the Roof of the World but the hardships of the journey itself. This was to change with the expansion of British influence into the foothills of the Himalayas.

Early contacts between Britain and Tibet commenced with a mission to Shigatse headed by a Scotsman, George Bogle, in 1774. Bogle soon ingratiated himself with the Panchen Lama – to the extent of marrying one of his sisters. With the death of the 3rd Panchen Lama in 1780 and the Gurkha invasion of Tibet in 1788, however, Britain lost all official contact with Tibet.

In a parallel development to the north, Russia had long, like Britain, been seeking to extend its influence in Central Asia and was now making advances to Lhasa. By the late 19th century the British Raj was awash with rumours that China was willing to offer Russia its custodianship of Tibet in return for Russian recognition of Chinese sovereignty over its borders. The British knew that Lhasa had received Russian missions (while similar British advances had been refused), a Russian adviser was known to be present in Lhasa, and there was even wild conjecture

that the tsar of Russia was poised to convert to Buddhism.

It was against this background that Lord Curzon, viceroy of India, decided to nip Russian designs on the Roof of the World in the bud. In late 1903, an expedition led by Colonel Francis Younghusband entered Tibet via Sikkim. No senior representatives were sent by the Tibetan government to hear British requests for a diplomatic posting in Lhasa, and after wintering just 50 km inside the border the expedition continued to Gyantse. Tibetan soldiers, armed with antiquated weaponry and amulets designed to resist the bullets of British guns, suffered great losses and did little to slow the British advance.

The expedition hesitated at Gyantse and waited once again for the Tibetan government to send representatives. They never came. A month later the British expedition moved on to Lhasa, where it was discovered that the Dalai Lama had fled to Mongolia with his Russian adviser. However, an Anglo-Tibetan convention was signed via negotiations with Tri Rinpoche, a lama from Ganden whom the Dalai Lama had appointed as regent in his absence. British forces withdrew after spending just two months in Lhasa.

The missing link in the Anglo-Tibetan accord was a Manchu signature. In effect the accord implied that Tibet was a sovereign power with the right to make treaties of its own. The Manchus objected and in 1906 the British signed a second accord with the Manchus which recognised China's suzerainty over Tibet. In 1910, the Manchu Qing dynasty teetering on the verge of collapse, the Manchus made good on the accord and invaded Tibet, driving the Dalai Lama once again into flight – this time into the arms of the British in India.

Tibetan Independence Revisited

In 1911 a revolution finally toppled the decadent Qing dynasty in China. The spirit of revolt soon spread to Tibet, which was still under occupation by Manchu troops. In Lhasa, troops mutinied against their officers, and in other parts of Tibet fighting broke out between Tibetans and Manchu troops. By the end of 1912, the last of the occupying forces were escorted out of Tibet via India and sent back to China. In January 1913, the 13th Dalai Lama returned to Lhasa.

The new Chinese Republican government of Yuan Shikai, anxious to maintain control of former Qing territories, sent a telegram to the Dalai Lama expressing regret at the actions of the Manchu oppressors and announcing that the Dalai Lama was being formally restored to his former rank. The Dalai Lama replied that he was uninterested in ranks bestowed by the Chinese and that he was hereby assuming temporal and spiritual leadership of his country.

This reply has been read as a formal declaration of independence by Tibetans. It certainly was in spirit if not quite in the letter. As for the Chinese, they chose to ignore it, putting about that the Dalai Lama had responded with a letter expressing his great love for the Motherland. Whatever the case, Tibet was to enjoy 30 years free of interference from China. What is more, Tibet was suddenly presented with an opportunity to create a state that was ready to rise to the challenge of the modern world and if needs be protect itself from the territorial ambitions of China. Sadly, the opportunity foundered on Tibet's entrenched theocratic institutions, and Tibetan independence was a short-lived affair.

Attempts to Modernise

During the period of his flight to India, the 13th Dalai Lama had become intimate friends with Sir Charles Bell, a Tibetan scholar and political officer in Sikkim. The relationship was to initiate a warming in Anglo-Tibetan affairs and to see the British playing an increasingly important role as mediators in problems between Tibet and China.

In 1920 Bell was dispatched on a mission to Lhasa, where he renewed his friendship with the Dalai Lama. It was agreed that the British would supply the Tibetans with modern arms providing they agreed only to use them for self defence. The Dalai Lama readily agreed and a supply of arms and ammunition was set up. Tibetan military officers were trained in Gyantse and India, and a telegraph line was set up linking Lhasa and Shigatse. Other developments included the construction of a small hydroelectric station near Lhasa and the establishment of an English school at Gyantse. At the invitation of the Dalai Lama, British experts conducted geological surveys of parts of Tibet with a view to gauging mining potential.

It is highly likely that the 13th Dalai Lama's trips away from his country had made him realise that it was imperative that Tibet begin to modernise. At the same time he must also have been aware that the road to modernisation was fraught with difficulties. The biggest problem was the Tibetan social system itself.

Since the rise of the Gelugpa order, Tibet had been ruled as a theocracy. Monks, particularly those in the huge monastic complexes of Dreprung and Sera at Lhasa, were accustomed to a high degree of influence in the Tibetan government. And for the monks of Tibet, the principal focus of government was the maintenance of the religious state. Attempts to modernise were seen as inimical to this aim, and before too long began to meet with intense opposition.

Perhaps as much as anything else, the monastery complexes of central Tibet feared the increasing empowerment of lay elements in Tibetan society. The establishment of an army, for example, was seen as a direct threat to the monasteries rather than as a means of self defence against external threats to the nation. Most monasteries kept their own small armies of fighting monks, and the presence of a well-equipped state army posed the threat of state intervention in monastic disputes. In fact, such fears proved to be well founded when the Dalai Lama brought the newly established army into action to quell a threatened uprising at Dreprung Monastery.

Before too long, the 13th's innovations fell victim to a conservative backlash. Newly trained Tibetan officers were reassigned non-military jobs, causing a rapid deterioration of military discipline; a newly established police force was left to its own devices and soon became ineffective; the English school at Gyantse was closed down; and a motor mail service set up by the British was put to a stop.

Tibet's brief period of independence was troubled by more than just an inability to modernise, however. Conflict sprang up between the Panchen Lama and the Dalai Lama over the autonomy of Tashilhunpo Monastery and its estates. The Panchen Lama, after appealing to the British to mediate, fled to China, where he was kept for 14 years until his death. In 1933 the 13th Dalai Lama died, leaving the political arena open to intrigue and providing the Chinese Republican government with an opportunity to increase its influence in Lhasa. In 1947 an attempted coup d'état, known as the Reting Conspiracy, rocked Lhasa. And in 1949 the Chinese Nationalist government, against all odds, fell to Mao Zedong and his Communist 'bandits'.

Liberation

Unknown to the Tibetans, the Communist takeover of China was to open what is probably the saddest chapter in Tibetan history. The Chinese 'liberation' of Tibet was eventually to lead to 1.2 million Tibetan deaths, an assault on the Tibetan traditional way of life, the flight of the Dalai Lama to India and the large-scale destruction of almost every historical structure on the high plateau. The chief culprits were Chinese ethnic chauvinism and an epidemic of social madness known as the Cultural Revolution.

On 7 October 1950, just a year after the Communist takeover of China, 30,000 battle-hardened Chinese troops attacked central Tibet from six different directions. The Tibetan army, a poorly equipped force of some 4000 men, stood little chance of resisting the Chinese, and any attempt at defence soon collapsed before the onslaught. In Lhasa, the Tibetan government reacted by enthroning the 15-year-old 14th Dalai Lama,

an action that brought jubilation and dancing on the streets but did little to protect Tibet from advancing Chinese troops. An appeal to the United Nations was equally ineffective. To the shame of all involved, only El Salvador sponsored a motion to condemn Chinese aggression, and Britain and India, traditional friends of Tibet, actually managed to convince the UN not to debate the issue for fear of incurring Chinese disapproval.

Presented with this seemingly hopeless situation, the Dalai Lama dispatched a mission to Beijing with orders that they refer all decisions to Lhasa. As it turned out there were no decisions to be made. The Chinese had already drafted an agreement. The Tibetans had two choices: sign on the dotted line or face further Chinese aggression.

The 17-point *Agreement on Measures for the Peaceful Liberation of Tibet* promised a one-country two-systems structure much like that offered later to Hong Kong and Macau, but provided little in the way of guarantees that such a promise would be honoured. The Tibetan delegates protested that they were unauthorised to sign such an agreement and anyway lacked the seal of the Dalai Lama. Thoughtfully, the Chinese had already prepared a forged Dalai Lama seal, and the agreement was ratified.

Initially, the Chinese occupation of central Tibet was carried out in an orderly way, but tensions inevitably mounted. The presence of large numbers of Chinese troops in the Lhasa region soon depleted food stores and gave rise to massive inflation. Rumours of massacres and forced political indoctrination in Kham began to filter through to Lhasa. The Dalai Lama was invited to Beijing, where, amid cordial discussions with Mao Zedong, he was told that religion was 'poison'. And in 1956, the Preparatory Committee for the Autonomous Region of Tibet (PCART) was established. Although headed by the Dalai Lama, a majority of its seats were filled by Chinese puppets. In any case, real power lay in the hands of the Committee of the Communist Party in Tibet, which claimed no Tibetan representatives at all.

With armed revolt breaking out in Kham and Amdo (with covert CIA support) and protest emerging in central Tibet, the Dalai Lama returned to Lhasa from a trip to India to celebrate the 2500th anniversary of the birth of Buddha with a heavy heart. It seemed inevitable that Tibet would explode in revolt and equally inevitable that it would be ruthlessly suppressed by the Chinese.

1959 Uprising

The Tibetan New Year of 1959, like all the New Year celebrations before it, attracted huge crowds to Lhasa, doubling the usual population of the city. In addition to the usual festival activities, the Chinese had added a highlight of their own – a performance by a Chinese dance group at the Lhasa military base. The Dalai Lama's invitation to attend came in the form of a thinly veiled command. The Dalai Lama, wishing to avoid offence, accepted.

As preparations for the performance drew near, however, the Dalai Lama's security chief was surprised to hear that the Dalai Lama was expected to attend in secrecy and without his customary contingent of 25 bodyguards. Despite the Dalai Lama's agreement to these conditions, the news soon leaked, and in no time simmering frustrations at Chinese rule came to the boil amongst the crowds on the streets. It seemed obvious to them that the Chinese were about to kidnap the Dalai Lama. Large numbers of people gathered around the Norbulingka Summer Palace of the Dalai Lama and swore to protect him with their lives.

The Dalai Lama had no choice but to cancel his appointment at the military base. In the meantime the crowds on the streets were swollen by Tibetan soldiers, who changed out of their People's Liberation Army (PLA) uniforms and started to hand out weapons. A group of government ministers announced that the 17-Point Agreement was null and void, and that Tibet renounced the authority of China.

The Dalai Lama was powerless to intervene, managing only to pen some conciliatory letters to the Chinese as his people prepared for battle on the streets of Lhasa. In a last ditch effort to prevent bloodshed, the Dalai Lama even offered himself to the Chinese. His reply came in the sound of two mortar shells exploding in the gardens of the Norbulingka. The attack made it obvious that the only option remaining to the Dalai Lama was flight. On 17 March, the Dalai Lama left the Norbulingka disguised as a soldier. Fourteen days later he was in India.

Bloodshed in Lhasa

With both the Chinese and the Tibetans unaware of the Dalai Lama's departure, tensions continued to mount in Lhasa. Early in the morning of 20 March, the Chinese began to shell the Norbulingka and the crowds surrounding it, killing hundreds. Later, searching through the corpses, it became obvious that the Dalai Lama had escaped – 'abducted by a reactionary clique' went the Chinese reports.

The bloodshed continued. Artillery bombed the Potala, Sera Monastery and Medical College on Chagpo Ri hill. Tibetans armed with petrol bombs were picked off by Chinese snipers, and when a crowd of some 10,000 Tibetans retreated into the sacred precincts of the Jokhang that too was bombed. It is thought that after three days of violence around 10,000 to 15,000 Tibetans lay dead in the streets of Lhasa.

Socialist Paradise on the Roof of the World

The Chinese quickly consolidated on their quelling of the Lhasa uprising by taking control of all the high passes between Tibet and India. Freedom fighters were put out of action by Chinese troops and able-bodied young men rounded up, shot, incarcerated or put to work on Chinese work teams. As the Chinese themselves put it, they were liberating Tibet of reactionary forces and ushering in a new socialist society– naturally they did not bother to ask the Tibetans themselves whether they wanted a socialist paradise.

The Chinese abolished the Tibetan government and set about reordering Tibetan society in accordance with their Marxist principles. The educated and aristocratic were put to work on menial jobs and subject to struggle sessions, known as *thamzing*, which sometimes resulted in death. A ferment of class struggle was whipped up and former feudal exploiters – some of whom the poor of Tibet may have harboured genuine resentment for – were subject to punishments of awful cruelty.

The Chinese also turned their attention to Tibet's more than 6000 monasteries. Tibetans were refused permission to donate food to the monasteries, and monks were compelled to join struggle sessions, discard their robes and marry. Monasteries were stripped of their riches, Buddhist scriptures were burnt and used as toilet paper, and the vast wholesale destruction of Tibet's monastic heritage began in earnest.

Notable in this litany of errors was the Chinese decision to alter Tibetan farming practices. Instead of barley, the Tibetan staple, Tibetan farmers were instructed to grow wheat and rice. Tibetans protested that these crops were unsuited to Tibet's high-altitude conditions. They were right, and mass starvation resulted. By late 1961, it is calculated that 70,000 Tibetans had died or were dying of starvation.

By September 1961, even the Chinese-groomed Panchen Lama began to have a change of heart. He presented Mao Zedong with a 70,000-character report on the hardships his people were suffering and requested, among other things, religious freedom and an end to the sacking of Tibetan monasteries. Four years later he was to disappear into a high-security prison for a 10-year stay. His removal was for the Chinese the last obstacle to be cleared away in the lead-up to the establishment of the Tibetan Autonomous Region (TAR).

On 1 September 1965 the TAR was formally brought into being with much fanfare and talk of happy Tibetans fighting back tears of gratitude at becoming one with the great Motherland. The tears were set to keep on coming. In China trouble was brewing in the form of a social movement that came to be known as the Great Proletarian Cultural Revolution.

The Cultural Revolution

Amongst the writings of Mao is a piece entitled 'On Going too Far'. It was a subject on which he was particularly well qualified to write. What started as a power struggle between Mao and Liu Shaoqi in 1965 had become by August 1966 the Great Proletarian Revolution, a movement that was to shake China to its core, trample all its traditions underfoot, cause countless deaths and give over running of the country to mobs of Red Guards. All of China suffered in Mao's bold experiment to create a new socialist paradise, but it was Tibet that suffered most dearly.

The first Red Guards arrived in Lhasa in July 1966. Two months later, the first rally was organised and Chinese-educated Tibetan youths raided the Jokhang, desecrating whatever religious objects they could get their hands on. It was the beginning of the large-scale destruction of virtually every religious monument in Tibet, and was carried out in the spirit of destroying the 'Four Olds': namely, old thinking, old culture, old habits and old customs.

For more than three years the Cultural Revolution went about its destructive business of turning the Tibetan world on its head. Tibetan farmers were forced to collectivise into communes and told what to grow and when to grow it. Merry-making was declared illegal, women had their jewellery taken from them, and the traditional plaits of Tibetan men were cut off by Red Guards in the street. Anyone objecting was arrested and subject to thamzing. The Dalai Lama became Enemy of the People Number One and Tibetans were forced to denounce him as a parasite and traitor. The list goes on, a harrowing catalogue of crimes against a people whose only fault was to hold aspirations that differed from those of their Chinese masters.

By late 1969, the PLA had the Red Guards under control. Tibet, however, continued to be the site of outbreaks of violence. Tibetan uprisings were brief and subdued brutally. In

1972, restrictions on Tibetan's freedom of worship were lifted with much fanfare but little in the way of results. In 1975 a group of foreign journalists sympathetic to the Chinese cause were invited to Tibet. The reports they filed gave a sad picture of a land whose people had been battered to their knees by Chinese-imposed policies and atrocities that amounted to nothing less than cultural genocide.

The Post-Mao Years

By the time of Mao's death in 1976 even the Chinese themselves must have begun to realise that their rule in Tibet had taken a wrong turn. Rebellion was ever in the wings, and maintaining order on the high plateau was a constant drain on Beijing's coffers. Mao's chosen successor, Hua Guofeng, decided to soften the government's line on Tibet and called for a revival of Tibetan customs. In mid-1977 it was announced that China would welcome the return of the Dalai Lama and other Tibetan refugees, and shortly after the Panchen Lama was released from over 10 years of imprisonment.

The invitation to return to Tibet was taken cautiously by the Tibetan Government in Exile, and the Dalai Lama suggested that he be allowed to send a fact-finding mission to Tibet first. To the surprise of all involved, the Chinese agreed. As the Dalai Lama himself remarks in his autobiography, *Freedom in Exile*, it seemed that the Chinese were of the opinion that the mission would find such happiness in their homeland that 'they would see no point in remaining in exile'. In fact, the results of the mission were so damning that the Dalai Lama decided not to publish them.

Nevertheless, two more missions followed. Their conclusions were despairing. They catalogued 1.2 million deaths; the destruction of 6254 monasteries and nunneries; the absorption of two thirds of Tibet into China; 100,000 Tibetans in labour camps and extensive deforestation. In a mere 30 years, the Chinese had turned Tibet into a land of near unrecognisable desolation.

In China, Hua Guofeng's short-lived political ascendancy had been eclipsed by Deng Xiaoping's rise to power. In 1980, Deng sent Hu Yaobang on a Chinese fact-finding mission that coincided with the visits of those sent by the Tibetan Government in Exile.

Hu's conclusions, while not as damning as those of the Tibetans, painted a grim picture of life on the Roof of the World. A six-point plan to improve the living conditions and freedoms of the Tibetans was drawn up, taxes were dropped for two years and limited private enterprise was allowed. As was the case in the rest of China, the government embarked on a programme of extended personal freedoms in concert with authoritarian one-party rule.

The Deng Years

The early 1980s saw the return of limited religious freedoms. Monasteries that had not been reduced to piles of rubble began to reopen and some religious artefacts were returned to Tibet from China.

Importantly, there was also a relaxation of the Chinese proscription on pilgrimage. Pictures of the Dalai Lama began to reappear on the streets of Lhasa. Not that any of this pointed to a significant reversal in Chinese thinking on the question of religion which remained an opiate of the masses. Those who exercised their religious freedoms did so at considerable risk.

Talks aimed at bringing the Dalai Lama back into the ambit of Chinese influence continued, but with little in the way of results. A three-person team sent to Beijing from Dharamsala in 1982 heard lectures on how Tibet was part of China and were told in no uncertain terms that the Dalai Lama would be given a position in Beijing were he to return. By 1983 talks had broken down and the Chinese decided that they did not want the Dalai Lama to return after all.

Perhaps most dismaying for Tibetans, however, was the emergence of a Chinese policy of Han immigration to the high plateau. Sinicisation had already been successfully carried out in Xinjiang, Inner Mongolia and Qinghai, and now Tibet was targeted for mass immigration. Attractive salaries and interest-free loans were made available to Chinese willing to emigrate to Tibet, and in 1984 alone more than 100,000 Han Chinese took advantage of the incentives to 'modernise' the backward province of Tibet.

In 1986, a new influx of foreigners arrived in Tibet. The Chinese began to loosen restrictions on tourism, and a trickle of tour groups and individual travellers soon became a flood.

For the first time since the Chinese takeover, visitors from the West were given the opportunity to see first hand the results of Chinese rule in Tibet.

For the Chinese, the foreigners were a mixed blessing. The tourist dollars were appreciated, but foreigners had an annoying habit of sympathising with Tibetans. They also got to see things that the Chinese would rather they not see.

When in September 1987 a group of 30 monks from Sera Monastery began circumambulating the Jokhang and crying out 'Independence for Tibet' and 'Long live his Holiness the Dalai Lama', their ranks were swollen by bystanders and arrests followed. Four days later, another group of monks repeated their actions, this time brandishing Tibetan flags.

The monks were beaten and arrested. With Western tourists looking on, a crowd of some 2000 to 3000 angry Tibetans gathered. Police vehicles were overturned and Chinese police began firing on the crowd.

The Chinese response was swift. Communications were broken with the outside world and foreigners were evicted from Lhasa. It was still too late, however, to prevent eyewitness accounts of what had happened from reaching newspapers around the world. A crackdown followed in Lhasa, but it failed to prevent further protests in the following months.

The Mönlam festival of March 1988 saw shooting in the streets of Lhasa, and in December of the same year a Dutch traveller was shot in the shoulder; 18 Tibetans died and 150 were wounded.

The Dalai Lama & the Search for Settlement

By the mid-1970s, the Dalai Lama had become a prominent international figure, working tirelessly from his Government in Exile in Dharamsala, India, to make the world more aware of the plight of his people. His visits to the USA led to official condemnation of the Chinese occupation of Tibet. In 1987 he addressed the US Congress and outlined a five-point peace plan.

The plan called for Tibet to be established as a 'Zone of Peace'; for the policy of Han immigration to Tibet to be abandoned; for a return to basic human rights and democratic freedoms; for the protection of Tibet's natural heritage and an end to the dumping of nuclear waste on the high plateau; and for joint discussions between the Chinese and the Tibetans on the future of Tibet. The Chinese denounced the plan as an example of 'splittism'. They gave the same response, when, a year later, the Dalai Lama elaborated on the speech before the European Parliament at Strasbourg, conceding any demands for full independence and offering the Chinese the right to govern Tibet's foreign affairs.

The 14th Dalai Lama

Protests and crackdowns continued in Tibet through 1989, and despairing elements in the exiled Tibetan community began to talk of the need to take up arms. It was an option that the Dalai Lama had consistently opposed. If there was to be any improvements of the situation in Tibet, he reasoned, they could only be achieved through non-violent means. The Dalai Lama's efforts to achieve peace and freedom for his people were rewarded on 4 October 1989, when he was awarded the Nobel Peace Prize. It must have seemed small consolation for the civilised world's notable failure to put any real pressure on China regarding its activities in Tibet.

Tibet Today

Tibetans have won back many religious freedoms, but at great expense. Monks and nuns, who are often the focus of protests and Tibetan aspirations for independence, are regarded suspiciously by the authorities and are often subject to arrest and beatings. Nuns in particular, considering their small numbers, have been very active, accounting for 55 of 126 independence protests over the last six years according to recent reports. Once arrested and imprisoned, new rules make it impossible for nuns to return to their nunneries.

The Chinese officially deny any policy of Han immigration to Tibet, but for visitors who have made repeated trips to Tibet the increased numbers of Han Chinese are staggering. Chinese figures for the population of Lhasa, for example, indicate it is just over 87% Tibetan and just under 12% Han Chinese, a ratio that stretches the credulity of anyone who has visited the city in recent years. It is more likely that somewhere in the vicinity of 50% of Lhasa's population is Han Chinese.

At the same time that China denies a policy of Sinicisation in Tibet, recent Chinese media reports have trumpeted reforms aimed at attracting Chinese entrepreneurs to Tibet. In 1993, 5300 individual enterprises opened in Lhasa alone; most of them were undoubtedly Chinese. Figures released for Qinghai province (once Amdo) show the Han Chinese population at 59% and the Tibetan population at 20% (the rest is mainly Hui, or Muslim). Such figures bode badly for the TAR in the long term.

It must be said that great effort has been made to curb the worst excesses of the Chinese administration and that a comparatively softened line on minorities has improved conditions for many Tibetans. But the basic problems remain. Protests and government crackdowns have continued into the mid-'90s. The Chinese government has in no way relented in its basic position regarding Tibet as a province in China and is no closer to reaching an agreement of any kind with the Dalai Lama. And the issue of Han immigration to Tibet poses the grave danger that the Tibetans will become a minority in their own country.

GEOGRAPHY

The high plateau of Tibet is the result of a prodigious geological upheaval. The time scale is subject to much debate, but at some point in the last 100 million years the entire region lay beneath the sea. And that is where it would have stayed, had not the mass of land now known as India broken free from the proto-continent Gondwanaland and drifted off in a collision course with another proto-continent known as Laurasia. The impact of the two land masses drove up two vast parallel ridges, over 3000 km in length and in places almost nine km high.

In this way Tibet became one of the most isolated regions in the world, bounded to the south by the Himalayas, to the west by the Karakorum and to the north by the Kunlun ranges. In this remote but sprawling (nearly the size of western Europe) region the Tibetan people settled at altitudes that averaged between 3500 and 5000 metres.

There are really two Tibets. Greater Tibet can be identified with regions that were traditionally ethnic Tibetan. These include the Tibetan provinces of Kham and Amdo, which have been swallowed up by the Chinese provinces of Sichuan and Qinghai respectively. Both have been heavily

Sinicised. The area now known as the Tibetan Autonomous Region (TAR) corresponds approximately with what is sometimes referred to as 'political Tibet'. This region of central Tibet has a mild climate, supports agriculture and was the area that historically came under the control of successive Tibetan regimes. The last of these was the lamaist Gelugpa state.

The TAR covers an area of around 1.2 million sq km and encompasses the traditional Tibetan provinces of Ü (capital, Lhasa), Tsang (capital, Shigatse) and Ngari, or Western Tibet.

To the north of central Tibet are the harsh, high-altitude plains of the Chang Tang, both the highest and largest plateau in the world, occupying an area of over one million sq km. This area has no river systems, and supports little in the way of life. Dead lakes on the plateau are the brackish remnants of the Tethys Sea that found no run-off when the plateau started its ascent skyward.

The west of Tibet is similarly barren, though here river valleys provide grassy tracts that support nomads and their grazing animals. Indeed, the Kailash range in the far west of Tibet is the source of the subcontinent's four greatest rivers: the Ganges, Indus, Sutlej and Brahmaputra. The Ganges, Indus and Sutlej rivers all cascade out of Tibet in its far west, not far from

Kailash itself; but the Brahmaputra meanders the length of southern Tibet, sustaining the main population centres of Shigatse, Lhasa and Tsetang, before coiling back on itself and draining into India not far from the border of Burma.

The south-east of Tibet is not delineated by any major mountain ranges and is marked more by a gradual decline in elevations intercepted by smaller ranges that are the source of the Yangzi, Salween and Mekong rivers. Parts of this region are (or were – Chinese deforestation has made huge inroads into the region) heavily forested and support abundant wildlife.

CLIMATE

The high altitudes of the Tibetan plateau make for climatic extremes. At any time of the year, particularly in Western Tibet, it is a good idea to be prepared for sudden drops of temperature at night. But, basically, the Tibetan climate is not as harsh as many people imagine it to be.

The best time of year to be in Tibet is from May to the beginning of November, when temperatures start to plummet. Lhasa and Shigatse generally have very mild weather during these months, though July and August can be rainy – these two months usually see around half of Tibet's annual rainfall. In May and June there is a wind factor to consider,

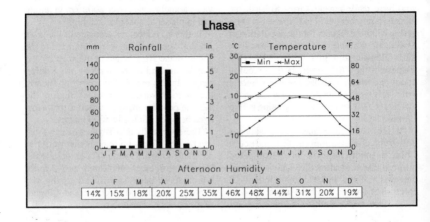

and dust storms are not unusual. These are not pleasant if you are hitching or trekking but usually come in squalls and can be seen coming.

October and November often bring dazzlingly clear weather and daytime temperatures can be quite comfortable at Tibet's lower altitudes. Trekkers will need suitably warm clothing through these two months, however.

The coldest months are from December to February. It is not impossible to visit Tibet in the winter, but high-altitude trekking becomes almost impossible. High passes sometimes become snowbound, which can make travel difficult. The low-altitude valleys of Tibet (around Lhasa, Shigatse and Tsetang) see very little snow.

Spring does not really get underway until April, though March can have warm sunny days and is not necessarily a bad month to be in Tibet. Again, though, sudden cold snaps can dump snow on passes at this time of the year.

FLORA

The vast differences in altitude on the Tibetan plateau give rise to various zones of flora. The high-altitude plains of the Chang Tang, for example, support little in the way of vegetation beside grasses such as spear grass. The river valleys of central Tibet have much more abundant vegetation. Juniper trees and willows are common and it is possible to come across wild flowers such as the pansy and oleander, as well as unique indigenous flowers like the *tsi-tog* (a light pink, high-altitude bloom). To the south, along the lower-altitude borders with Nepal are forests of pines, firs and spruces. The east of Tibet, which sees higher rainfalls than most of the rest of Tibet, has deciduous forests with oaks, elms and birches.

FAUNA

Early Western explorers who made their way to Tibet brought back tales of teeming wildlife on the high plateau. When, in the early 1980s, the Tibetan Government in Exile sent three investigative delegations to Tibet,

among the shocking news they returned with was that Tibet had been denuded of its wildlife. Stories of Chinese troops machine gunning herds of wild gazelles circulated with convincing frequency, and it had sadly become necessary to travel to extremely remote locations to see the wildlife that had once roamed freely on the plains of Tibet.

Some species have been designated as protected in recognition of their threat of extinction. These include the snow leopard, the white-lipped deer, the Tibetan antelope, the Tibetan wild ass, the black-necked crane and the wild yak. Although there are a lot of yaks about in Tibet, most of them are domesticated and many are a hybrid breed of yak and cattle. A curious omission from the list of protected species is the Tibetan brown bear, a big creature that stands nearly two metres tall. It is very rare and can only be found in the forests of southern Tibet.

If you are not trekking in Tibet and your travels are restricted to sights off the Friendship Highway you are unlikely to see anything much in the way of wildlife. On the road out to Kailash, however, it is not unusual to see herds of antelope *(chiru)* and wild asses *(kyang)*. Marmots are very common, and can often be seen perched up on their hind legs sniffing the air curiously outside their burrows – they make a strange bird-like sound when distressed. Himalayan mouse hares, a relative of the rabbit, are also very common.

A surprising number of migratory birds make their way up to the Tibetan plateau through spring and summer. They are most commonly found around the lakes of central Tibet. One of the best places to see them is Nam-tso lake, a section of which has been designated a bird preserve.

GOVERNMENT

Unfortunately it is necessary to make a distinction between how Tibet ran itself when it governed its own affairs, how it is run today by the Chinese and how it might govern itself should it ever have the chance to administer its own affairs.

The Lamaist State

From the ascendancy of the Gelugpas in 1642 until the Chinese takeover in 1951, Tibet was governed as a theocracy. At the very head of the governmental structure was the Dalai Lama. As this position was not earned according to merit, but 'inherited' through reincarnation, the quality of government was always something of an uncertainty. Another problem with government by reincarnated 'God King' was that it guaranteed long periods without a head of state between the death of a Dalai Lama and when the next one reached his majority. During these periods a regent, a position filled by a lama from one of the large Gelugpa monasteries around Lhasa, ruled in his place.

Beneath the Dalai Lama and the regent was the *lönchen*, which is sometimes translated as prime minister. It was not a fixed position and might be held by more than one person. Beneath the lönchen were various government offices, each of them comprising a determined ratio of monks and lay officials. The most important of these government offices was the *Kashag*. The Kashag was normally made up of four *Shapes*, or ministers. Shapes were selected by the Dalai Lama from a list of nominees drawn up by the Kashag itself.

In effect the Kashag was the last stop between the Dalai Lama or regent and all other organs of government. All issues of government reached the Dalai Lama by way of the Kashag, and outgoing policies and government decisions required the seal of the Kashag before they could be implemented. That is, providing the issues being dealt with were of a secular nature. All religious matters were dealt with by a parallel office known as the *Yigtsang*. The Yigtsang was responsible for the appointment of monks, for their training and for the administration of monastic affairs. It was headed by four monks.

Beneath these ministries were some 20 government offices with specific areas of interest. The most important of these was the *Tsigang*, an office that oversaw the collection of taxes and the settlement of tax disputes. A late development, in the 1860s, was the National Assembly, a body which grew in importance during the reign of the 13th Dalai Lama.

There were actually three different varieties of national assembly. The smallest was made up of members of the Yigtsang and the Tsigang, while the two larger bodies comprised abbots of the Gelugpa monasteries around Lhasa and various officials from other ministries. Meetings of the National Assembly were powerless to make decisions and were called by the Kashag on a consultative basis for important decisions.

The Communist State

Since 1965, Tibet has been administered as the Tibetan Autonomous Region (TAR). Not that there is anything particularly autonomous about its government. The Chinese make much of the fact that many high-ranking government positions are filled by Tibetans. One thing is certain, any Tibetan officials are out the minute they stop toeing the Chinese line.

The TAR is made up of the Municipality of Lhasa, five prefectures – Ali, Shigatse, Shannan, Nagqu and Chamdo – and 70 counties. The whole affair is presided over by the Communist Party of the Tibetan Autonomous Region, which basically calls all the shots. There are numerous other working committees and consultative bodies beneath the Communist Party right down to a local village level. Since October 1992, the Communist Party of the TAR has been headed by Chen Kaiyuan, a technocrat who backs economic reforms and is strongly opposed to pro-independence elements in Tibet.

Tibetan Government in Exile

The immediate result of the 1959 Lhasa uprising was the flight of the Dalai Lama and eventually 80,000 Tibetan refugees to India, Nepal, Bhutan and Sikkim. By 1970 there were some 100,000 Tibetan refugees in 45 settlements on the subcontinent, and they looked to the Dalai Lama's administration in Dharamsala as their government.

The Government in Exile initially established by the Dalai Lama consisted of the Dalai Lama's Cabinet, the Kashag and six portfolios: Home Affairs, Foreign Affairs, Religion & Culture, Education, Finance, and Security. Representative offices were opened in Delhi, Kathmandu, Gangtok, New York and later London and Tokyo.

Elections were called in 1960 for the establishment of a new body known as the Commission of People's Deputies. In 1963 a Constitution of Tibet was promulgated. This constitution, which combines the qualities of Buddhism with the needs of modern government is still in a draft form, awaiting the final approval of the people of Tibet, should they ever have the opportunity to vote for their own constitution. The constitution establishes executive power in the Dalai Lama and the Kashag, legislative authority in the Commission of People's Deputies and judicial authority in an independent Supreme Court. The government is supported by voluntary taxes from the exiled Tibetan community and by business interests.

In 1970 the Tibetan Youth Congress was established, a party which aims to increase the involvement of young Tibetans in government. It has some 10,000 members.

The Dalai Lama continues to be an active voice in the Tibetan struggle for independence. Foreign governments are careful, however, not to receive him in any way that recognises his political status as the head of an exiled government. The Chinese government continues to regularly protest the Dalai Lama's international activities.

ECONOMY

While perhaps not quite matching the juggernaut pace of economic reform elsewhere in China, the economy of Tibet is seeing rapid changes. Communications are being improved and local officials have been encouraging foreign investment. The successes of such reforms are inevitably exaggerated – as in a report which recently claimed that herders could now make direct-dial international calls with cellular phones – but the changes are obvious to anyone who

returns to Tibet after being away for a couple of years.

When the Chinese took over Tibet, the local economy had developed little in hundreds of years. It was largely agricultural and self-sufficient in its basic needs. Imports of such things as tea, porcelain, copper and iron from China were compensated by exports of wool and skins. Trading was carried out usually in combination with pilgrimage or by nomads. This movement provided a flow of goods to isolated farming communities that generally harvested barley for tsang, the Tibetan staple.

The Communist takeover changed all that. Tibet subsequently became part of the vast Communist effort to modernise China and has shared its disasters. Arguably, Tibet today is on the brink of sharing its more recent successes, though economic improvements foisted on a people by outsiders are unlikely to taste as sweet as those that are self-engineered.

Probably the most disastrous Communist economic policy in Tibet was collectivisation. The Tibetans had successfully eked a living out of the soil in Tibet for centuries, but in keeping with early Communist policy by 1966 virtually every village in Tibet had been collectivised into work units guided by instructions from above on what to plant and when to harvest it. Tibetans were instructed to plant the Chinese staples of rice and wheat, which were unsuited to the local conditions. Countless crops failed, causing mass starvation, something that was unheard of in old Tibet.

By the mid-1970s, the failure of collectivisation was widely recognised and Tibetans have been allowed to return to traditional methods of working the land. Chinese have since looked to other methods of developing the high plateau. One of these has been mining, which was traditionally inimical to the Tibetans, who thought it disturbed the sacred essence of the soil.

However, extensive surveys of Tibet's mining potential have been carried out in Tibet, bringing to light rich deposits of gold, zinc, copper, silver and other metals. Reports indicate that over 120 new mining sites have been opened up in recent years to exploit these resources and that mining accounts for one third of Tibet's industrial output.

Tibet, like other outlying regions of China rich in resources and blessed with cheap labour, is attracting considerable investment from the booming east coast regions of China. East coast investors are also attracted by favourable terms being offered by the local government to anyone with money to invest in 'opening up wasteland'. Over 30 joint ventures have also been set up with countries such as the USA, Malaysia, Nepal, Hong Kong and Taiwan.

Outside investment has also brought with it a surge in Han immigration to Tibet. Although no figures are available, it is plain that many Chinese people attracted by preferential loans and easy business opportunities are setting up shop in urban centres all over Tibet. In 1993 alone, over 2500 private enterprises were set up bringing the total figure to over 42,000. It is likely that many of these are being run by Han Chinese.

As the authorities trumpet rapid advances in industrial and agricultural output (the gross national product (GNP) of Tibet increased twofold from 1992 to 1993), there is a growing feeling among observers that China has switched from systematic persecution to a second far more sophisticated phase in assimilating Tibet into the Motherland. Foreign investment, Han immigration and an education system that exclusively uses the Chinese language at higher levels ensures that only Sinicised Tibetans will be able to actively participate in Tibet's economic advances. For Tibetans, apart from being crowded out of their home, Chinese economic control coupled with large numbers of Chinese settlers make the Tibetan dream of independence ever harder to realise.

POPULATION & PEOPLE

The TAR's population is thought to be 2.3 million. It is likely to be higher than this if Han immigrants and PLA troops stationed in Tibet were included, but the Chinese government is very coy about releasing figures that would make it clear just how many Chinese people there are in Tibet. A census conducted in 1990 indicated that there were 4,593,330 ethnic Tibetans in Tibet, Qinghai, Sichuan and Gansu. There are thought to be around 100,000 more Tibetans in exile, mainly in India but also in the USA and Europe.

Like the Han Chinese and almost all the other ethnic minorities of China, the Tibetans are classified as belonging to the Mongoloid family of peoples. They are probably descended from a variety of nomadic tribes who migrated from the north and settled to sedentary cultivation of Tibet's river valleys. About a quarter of Tibetans, however, are still nomadic.

ARTS

Almost all Tibetan art, with the exception of some folk crafts perhaps, is inspired by Buddhism. Wall hangings, paintings, architecture, literature, even dance, all in some way or another attest to the influence of the Indian religion that found its most secure nesting place in Tibet. At the same time, the arts of Tibet represent the synthesis of many influences. The Buddhist art and architecture of India and Nepal were an important early influence, as were the Central Asian Buddhist culture of Khotan and the 7th to 8th-century Buddhist culture of Kashmir. As China came to play an increasingly major role in Tibetan affairs, Chinese influences too were assimilated.

Dance & Drama

Anyone who is lucky enough to attend a Tibetan festival should have the opportunity to see performances of *cham*, a ritual dance performed by monks and lamas. Although every movement and gesture of cham has significance, the spectacle of the colourful masked dances no doubt also awed many simple Tibetans who attended the festivals.

Cham is a about the suppression of malevolent spirits. It is a solemn masked dance done to the accompaniment of long trumpets, drums and cymbals. The chief officiant is a black hat (unmasked) lama who is surrounded by a mandalic grouping of masked monks who represent manifestations of protective deities. The act of exorcism – it might be considered as such – is focussed on a *lingam*, a human effigy made of dough or perhaps wax or paper in which the evil spirits are thought to reside.

The proceedings of cham can be interpreted on any number of levels. Sometimes the black hat lama is identified with the monk who slew Langdharma, the anti-Buddhist king of the Yarlung era, and the dance is seen as echoing the suppression of malevolent forces inimical to the establishment of Buddhism in Tibet. Some anthropologists, on the other hand, have seen in cham, a metaphor for the gradual conquering of the ego, which is the aim of Buddhism. The ultimate destruction of the lingam that ends the dance might represent the ego itself. Whatever the case, cham is a splendid, dramatic performance and well worth going out of the way to see.

Performances of cham are usually accompanied by other, less significant performances that seem to have evolved as entertainment in festivals. These dances might depict the slaying of Langdharma or the arrival of the Indian teachers to Tibet at the time of the second diffusion of Buddhism.

Tibet also had a secular tradition of wandering minstrels. It is still possible to see them in Lhasa and Shigatse, where they play on the streets and occasionally (when they are not chased out by the proprietors) in restaurants.

Generally groups of two or three singers perform to the accompaniment of a Tibetan four-stringed guitar. In times past, groups of such performers travelled around Tibet, providing entertainment in villages which offered little distraction from the constant round of daily chores. These performers were sometimes accompanied by dancers and acrobats.

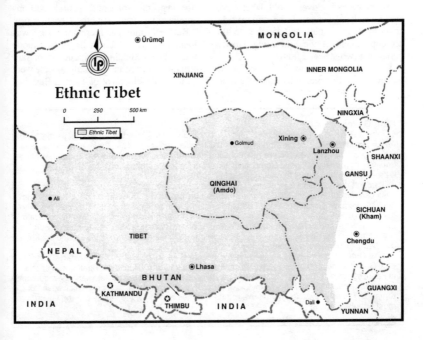

Music

Music is one aspect of Tibetan cultural life in which there is a strong secular tradition. In urban centres, songs were an important vent for social criticism; in his book *A History of Modern Tibet* Melvyn Goldstein translates many of the songs that were popular in the streets of Lhasa in the last years of the lamaist state. Some are overtly political, some ribald, as in the case of a song about a noblewoman who anoints her genitals daily with incense smoke in the hope of giving birth to the next incarnation of the Dalai Lama.

In Tibetan social life, both work and play are occasions for singing. Even today it is not uncommon to see monastery reconstruction squads pounding on the roofs of building and singing in unison. Where there are groups of men and women, the singing alternates between the two groups in the form of rhythmic refrains. Festivals and picnics are also occasions for singing.

As mentioned above, in old Tibet bards and musicians wandered the countryside, chanting heroic epics and singing to the accompaniment of the four-string Tibetan guitar or a two-stringed fiddle.

While the secular music of Tibet has an instant appeal for foreign listeners, the liturgical chants of Buddhist monks and the music that accompanies cham dances is a lot less accessible. Buddhist chanting creates an eerie haunting effect but soon becomes very monotonous. The music of cham is a discordant cacophony of trumpet blasts and boom-crash drums – atmospheric to the accompaniment of the dancing but not exactly the kind of thing you would want to slip into the CD player. The instruments used include long trumpets known as *dungchen*, human thigh-bone trumpets known as *kangling* and conch shells. Various kinds of cymbals and drums are also employed.

Literature

The development of a written script for Tibetan corresponds with the early introduction of Buddhism during the reign of Songtsen Gampo, and accordingly all that exists of a pre-Buddhist literary tradition in Tibet are oral traditions regarding the exploits of early kings and the origins of the Tibetan people. Some of these oral traditions were later recorded using the Tibetan script.

But for the most part literature in Tibet was dominated by Buddhism; firstly as a mode of translating Buddhist scriptures from Sanskrit into Tibetan; and secondly, as time went by, to the development of Tibetan Buddhist

King Gesar

Elizabeth Booz, in her book *Tibet* (Oddyssey 1994), compares King Gesar with England's King Arthur and his Knights of the Round Table. The comparison is apt. The stories of King Gesar of the kingdom of Ling, which have been passed down through generations as an oral narrative tradition, have many fairy-tale elements that are familiar to Westerners and, like King Arthur, King Gesar waits with his army to once again return to Tibet and liberate her from evil.

Through many hundreds of years of telling, the stories of King Gesar exist in many forms and have become interwoven with Bön and Buddhist qualities as well as drawing on folk stories from the Indian subcontinent. But at the heart of the King Gesar stories is the tale of a small boy who grew up in the clutches of a scheming, cruel uncle (Todong) who did all in his power to make sure that the boy never reached maturity and the throne. Naturally he fails and the boy, after sojourning with nomads in the desolate high hills of Tibet, returns to triumphantly win his throne and the heart of a beautiful princess in a horse-riding competition.

Like Guru Rinpoche, another semi-mythical figure close to the hearts of all ordinary Tibetans, King Gesar set out on a quest to liquidate the demons, spirits and evil kings of Tibet. And in another element common to Tibetan folklore King Gesar ended his days in quiet contemplation in mountain cave before passing away into the mythic world of Shambala. All these elements – high adventure, romance, fabulous exploits, hermit-like retreat – combine to make the stories of King Gesar the most popular of all. ∎

thought. There is nothing in the nature of a secular literary tradition – least of all novels – such as can be found in China or Japan.

Scholars working in the field point out that one of the great achievements of Tibetan culture was the development of a literary language which could, with remarkable faithfulness, reproduce the concepts of Sanskrit Buddhist texts. In the early 9th century, Tibetan-Sanskrit dictionaries were compiled that ensured a consistent conformity in all subsequent translations.

The alternative to Buddhist scriptures exists in an early tradition of fabulous tales, usually concerning the subjection of malevolent spirits and the taming of Tibet to allow the introduction of Buddhism. Many of these were passed from generation to generation orally, but some were recorded. Examples include the *Gesar* epic and the story of Guru Rinpoche, who is said to have been born in a lotus in the ancient kingdom of Swat before coming to Tibet and performing countless miracles to prepare the land for the diffusion of Buddhism.

Through the 12th and 13th centuries, Tibetan literary endeavour was almost entirely consumed by the monumental task of translating the complete Buddhist cannon into Tibetan. The result was the 108 volumes of canonical texts *(Kangyur)*, which record the words of the historical Buddha, and 208 volumes of commentary on the Kangyur by Indian masters *(Tengyur)* that make up the basic Buddhist scriptures shared by all Tibetan religious orders. What time was left from this was used in the compilation of biographies and the collection of songs of revered lamas. Perhaps most famous among these is the *Hundred Thousand Songs of Milarepa*, an ascetic who wrote many songs and poems around the theme of his quest for Buddhahood.

Very little of the Tibetan literary tradition has been translated into English. Translations that may be of interest include: *The Tibetan Book of the Dead* (Shambala 1975), a mysterious but fascinating account of the stages and visions that occur between death and rebirth; *The Jewel Ornament of Liberation* (Shambala 1986), which describes the path to enlightenment as seen by the chief disciple of Milarepa and founder of the Kagyupa order; and *The Life of Milarepa* (Shambala 1986), the autobiography of Tibet's most famous ascetic.

Architecture

Probably the most prominent Tibetan architectural motif is the stupa, or as it is known in Tibet the chörten. The construction of a chörten is an act of merit, and every element of the finished structure has some kind of religious significance. Its origins lie in the funerary cask of the historical Buddha, Sakyamuni. In time it came to be the foremost symbol of Buddhahood, and was used as a reliquary for high lamas and others of great spiritual attainment.

Like much other early Tibetan architecture, the chörten is an Indian borrowing. It is thought that Buddhist-inspired architecture during Tibet's first contact with the religion – the Jokhang in Lhasa for example – owed much to Indian and Nepalese influences. Still, a distinctively Tibetan style was soon to emerge and, with successive rebuildings and additions, early structures such as the Jokhang also began to take on the characteristics of that style.

Typical features of Tibetan design, which are repeated to a certain extent in the houses of nobility and even in villages throughout Tibet, are buildings with inward sloping walls made of large tightly fitting stones or sun-baked bricks. Roofs are flat, made from pounded earth and surrounded by walls. In larger structures, the roof is supported inside by wooden pillars. Early Indo-Nepalese influence, where it lingers on can be seen more in interior design than in the overall structure, and the same can be said of Chinese influence, which can be seen in later buildings.

A typical Tibetan home, like many monastic buildings, is usually a flat-roofed structure of one or two stories. The exteriors are generally white-washed brick, though in some areas, such as Sakya in Tsang, other colours may be used. The floors and roof are

Chörten at Horchu

made of pounded earth and supported by wooden beams. In rural Tibet, homes are often surrounded by walled compounds, and in some areas entrances are protected by painted scorpions.

Nomads, who take their homes with them, live in yak-hair tents which are normally roomy and can accommodate a whole family. An opening at the top of the tent lets out smoke from the fire.

Visual Arts

Much of Tibet's artistic heritage fell victim to the Cultural Revolution. What was not destroyed was in many cases ferreted away to China or onto the Hong Kong art market. Worse still, many of Tibet's traditional artisans were persecuted or fled Tibet. It is only in recent years that remaining artists have again been able to return to their work and start to train young Tibetans in skills that faced the threat of extinction. The vast amount of newly executed frescoes and statuary in reconstructed Tibetan monasteries and temples is testimony to the remarkable rebound these skills have made.

Tibetan painting is almost exclusively devotional in nature. With the exception of decorative design, the paintings found in shrines, monasteries and in *thangkas* (wall hangings) always depict Buddhist themes. Early Tibetan painting was heavily influenced by the Buddhist cultures to the south, and in keeping with Indian style generally depicted Buddhist deities.

These usually followed stereotyped forms with a central Buddhist deity surrounded by smaller, lesser deities. Poised above the central figure was often a supreme Buddha figure of which the one below was an emanation.

This Indian influence soon became subsumed under Tibetan developments, though the underlying forms changed little. The depiction of Buddhist deities, for example, gave way to the depiction of revered Tibetan lamas or Indian spiritual teachers.

In many thangkas and wall frescoes, the central image of a lama is surrounded by incidents from the lama's life. In the case of some mandalas, these surrounding scenes might be replaced by images from the lineage of the particular religious order the lama was associated with.

Chinese influence began to manifest itself more frequently in Tibetan painting from around the 15th century. The freer approach of Chinese landscape painting allowed some Tibetan artists to break free from some of the more formalised aspects of Tibetan religious art and employ landscape as a decorative motif in the context of a painting that celebrated a particular religious figure. This is not to say that Chinese art initiated a new movement in Tibetan art. The new, Chinese-influence forms coexisted with older forms, largely due to the fact that painting in Tibet was passed on from artisan to apprentice in much the same way that monastic communities maintained their lineages of teaching.

Like the painting of Tibet, Tibetan statuary is similarly religious in nature. Ranging from several cm to several metres in height, statues usually depict Buddhist deities, protective deities and revered lamas.

CULTURE

The Tibetans are such a deeply religious people that at least a basic understanding of Buddhism is essential to making any sense of their world. Buddhism permeates many facets of Tibetan daily life and shapes the aspirations of Tibetans in ways that are often quite alien to the Western frame of mind. The idea of accumulating merit, of sending sons to be monks, of undertaking pilgrimages, of devotion to the sanctity and power of natural places are all elements of the unique fusion between Buddhism and the older shamanistic Bön faith that took place on the Tibetan plateau and shaped its culture.

Although influenced by the cultures of its neighbours, Tibetan culture is markedly different to them. Unlike the subcontinental cultures to the south, Tibet never had a caste system, and the introduction of Buddhism provided a new element of social mobility. To be sure, the Tibetan nobility occupied a privileged position that was perpetuated through heredity; but with the rise of the great monasteries, religious leaders came to play an increasingly important role. Monks and incarnate lamas might come from any level of society, and once entering a monastery could through talent and hard work rise very high indeed.

The sheer religiosity of the Tibetan people makes for vast differences between the culture of Tibet and China. For the most part, religion in China was subsumed under the more socially pragmatic orientation of Confucianism. Although Tibetan lamas played a role in the pomp and ritual of the imperial Chinese court, the Chinese, with their deep-rooted family orientation and ideology of social obligations, were always far more rooted in the here and now than Tibetans – at least subsequent to the diffusion of Buddhism.

Traditional Lifestyle

Traditionally, Tibet encompasses many different lifestyles. The lifestyle of the Tibetan nobility for example was far removed from that of ordinary urban dwellers. But generally there are at least three distinctions that need to be made: those between the nomads, the farmers of the Tibetan valleys and the community of monks. Members of these groupings each led very different lives, though all share a deep faith in Buddhism. For more information on the lifestyle of the monastic community see the Religion section in this chapter.

Besides Buddhism, another feature that these Tibetan communities shared was a remarkable resistance to change. While religious orders rose and fell from power and the Mongolians and Chinese jostled for control of the high plateau, technological innovation of any kind was unheard of, and the fundamentals of the Tibetan lifestyle remained unchanged for centuries. Until the early 20th century, Tibet was a land in which virtually the only use for the wheel was as a device for activating mantras.

Farming Communities Farming communities in Tibet usually comprised a cluster of homes surrounded by the fields the people worked. The farming itself was carried out with the assistance of a *dzo*, a crossbreed between a bull and a female yak; or, if no cattle were available, by hand. Harvested grain was carried by donkeys to a threshing ground where it was trampled by cattle or threshed with poles. The grain was then cast into the air from a basket and the task of winnowing carried out by the breeze.

Such communities were effectively self-sufficient in their needs, and although it was a hard life it could not be described as grinding poverty. Village families pulled together in times of need, and plots of land were usually graded in terms of their quality and then distributed so that the land of any one family included both good and poorer quality land. Large families generally did their own farming, but in the case of families where the children were not old enough to help or had gone away to become monks or nuns, hired help was also used. On average, a family might have several plots of land (often in different areas), several cattle and perhaps some sheep. The sheep of a community grazed together and were often tended by children in nearby hills during the day, being brought back down to the village in the evening.

The homes in farming communities were, more often than not, one-storey buildings made of sun-baked bricks. There were usually three or four rooms and the buildings were surrounded by a walled compound. There might be a household shrine in the house or in a small building in the compound. There might also be several religious texts, held in a place of honour, but very few people in farming communities were literate, and the reading of the texts was reserved for occasions when a monk or holy man visited the village. Such visits were not necessarily so uncommon. Monasteries and nunneries were so widespread in old Tibet that most Tibetan villages were reasonably close to a religious institution. It was not unusual for monks to visit villages in their 'parish' and read from religious texts and say prayers for families before sprinkling them with water that dispelled evil. At the same time, one of the highlights of the year for rural Tibetans was visiting nearby monasteries at festival times.

Marriage was usually arranged by the families involved in consultation with a lama or shaman, and many Tibetan farming villages practiced polyandry. When a woman married the eldest son of a family she also married his younger brothers (providing they did not become monks). The children of such marriages referred to all the brothers as their father, and the practice was thought to make the question of inheritance of family property (mainly the farming land) less problematic. In any case, sons who thought they were getting a bad deal might always run away to become a monk.

Ordinary Tibetans did not bury their dead. The very poor were usually dumped in a river when they died. In settled farming communities it was the practice to take the dead to a high place, chop up the body and pound the bones together with *tsampa* (roasted barley flour) for the birds to eat, though as often as not the work might be done by wild dogs.

There was little in the way of entertainment for farming people. Lighting in the evenings was only available from yak-butter candles, but most people slept at nightfall and rose with the dawn. Occasionally a wandering band of musicians or a performing troupe might pass through the village and its surrounding area. Such performing troupes, usually comprising around eight members, but sometimes as many as 40, were required to perform free in Lhasa once a year as a kind of tax and then allowed to spend the rest of the year touring to generate their own profits.

Other than this, farming communities had to make their own entertainment. It was not unusual for villages to have one or two musical instruments and someone who could strike up a tune. In the summer months, picnics and singing were popular activities. When demands of work were at a minimum some villagers might elect to go on pilgrimage. It might be a short pilgrimage to a nearby sacred area or a long pilgrimage, a once-in-a-lifetime act of devotion to some particularly sacred area such as Lhasa or an important monastic institution.

Nomads The nomads of Tibet travel in

groups of several up to 20 or more families. They live in four-sided yak-hair tents, which are usually shared by one family, though a smaller subsidiary tent may be used when a son marries and has children of his own. The various families of a group pitch their tents at quite a distance from each other, however, usually because the poor quality of grazing land means that yaks have to cover a large area of land to feed. The decision to move from one area to another is made together by all the families in a particular group.

The interior of a nomad tent holds all the family's possessions. There will be a stove for cooking and boiling water. The principal diet of nomad people is tsampa and yak butter (mixed together with tea), dried yak cheese and sometimes yak meat. The tent will also house a family altar with Buddha images and yak-butter candles that are left burning night and day. Next to it is placed a box that contains the family's jewellery and other valuables. In the warm summer months it is not unusual for nomad people to sleep outside their tent on a sheepskin, covering themselves with rough yak-hair blankets.

Tending the herds of yaks and sheep is carried out by the men during the day. Women and children stay together in the camp where they are guarded by one of the men and the ferocious Tibetan mastiffs that are the constant companions of Tibet's nomads. The women and children usually work during the day doing daily chores around the camp and weaving blankets and tanning sheep skins.

Nomads graze their herds through the summer months and into late autumn. By this time the herds should be strong and healthy, and with the onset of winter it is time to go to the markets of some urban centre. The farmers of Tibet do the same, and trade between nomads and farmers provides the former with tsampa and the latter with meat and butter.

The nomads, like the farmers of Tibet, take their dead to high places and leave them for the birds. A ceremony is usually conducted first, however. The dead body is placed in a sitting position for a day and prayers are recited over it.

Nomad marriage customs, however, differ from those of farming communities in many ways. To a certain extent they are arranged by the families involved. When a child comes of a marriageable age, enquiries are made and when a suitable match is found the two people meet and exchange gifts. If they

Sky Burial

It is possible that the dead were disposed of by burial in the early history of Tibet. But at least since the first introduction of Buddhism the most common method has been sky burial. As even sky burial costs money, the dead of the very poor were traditionally dumped in a river. Lamas and senior monks were cremated, and in the case of important lamas their ashes interred in a funerary chörten.

As is famously known now, sky burial involves taking the body to a designated high place, dicing it up and leaving the resulting mess to birds of prey (usually vultures). It is an unusual custom and, as is the case with unusual customs, receives its fair share of interest from foreign visitors.

Naturally, Tibetans are very unhappy about camera-toting foreigners heading up to sky burial sites. The Chinese authorities do not like it either. If Tibetans find you at or near a sky burial ground, they usually respond by throwing rocks and, if you are really unlucky, chasing you away with the corpse knives. The Chinese approach is only slightly less unpleasant. Confiscation of your passport, lengthy scoldings and interrogations, followed by your signing an 'admission of guilt' are the order of the day.

Finally, even if Tibetans offer to take you up to a sky burial site, it is unlikely that other Tibetans present will be very happy about it. A group of Singaporean travellers were taken up to a sky burial site in Shigatse by a Tibetan and then stoned when they got there in mid-'94. And a Swedish traveller who followed in their footsteps alone the next day was arrested by the PSB. Sky burials are funeral services. Nobody invited you. Don't go. ■

like each other, these informal meetings and ritual exchanges of gifts may go on for some time. The date for a marriage is decided by an astrologer, and when the date arrives the family of the son ride to the camp of their prospective daughter-in-law to collect her. When they arrive there is custom of feigned mutual abuse that appears to verge on giving way to violence at any moment. This may continue for several days before the son's family finally carry off the daughter to their camp and she enters a new life.

Cultural Differences

The Tibetans are among the easiest people to get along with in Asia. The smiles are infectious and it is rare for major cultural differences to get in the way of communication. Problems do occur, however. Rumours abound of surly monks, of aggressive Tibetans at checkpoints (in particular in the Everest region) and of rip-offs. Some foreigners have a few bad experiences and come away disillusioned.

Nowhere is perfect. It is par for the course to encounter a few glitches wherever you are travelling. There is no reason for things to be different in Tibet. It is worth remembering that there is a lot of anger and long-harboured resentment under the surface in Tibet. Moreover, Tibetans in business and involved in the region's administration all have to cooperate in some way or another with the Chinese, and many have picked up habits that travellers in China will already have encountered all too often: rudeness, overcharging and obstructionism, for example.

In short, there are many situations in Tibet where you will be dealing with Chinese people or with Tibetans who operate within the Chinese scheme of things. There are few loose rules which can help to minimise problems in these situations.

Face Probably too much has been made of this concept, which is shared by many Asian peoples. It can loosely be described as 'status', 'ego' or 'self-respect' and is by no means alien to Westerners. It is about avoiding being made to look stupid or being forced to back down in front of others. Almost all Asian cultures prefer a friendly negotiated settlement of differences to confrontation, and will opt for compromises that many foreigners find unacceptable rather than have discussions degenerate into a dispute in which one party has to back down. Outright confrontation is a last resort, and it is best to first try and sort out problems with smiling persistence – when one tack fails, try another.

Gifts The giving of gifts is one cultural trait that the Tibetans share with the Chinese, though the motivations might differ. Rela-

Dalai Lama Pictures

The traveller's information network and some guidebooks (including earlier editions of this one) suggest bringing along Dalai Lama pictures to Tibet. It is actually a good idea (though they can be purchased in markets all over Tibet), and can sometimes bring the recipient great happiness. The question is when to give. Unfortunately, the indiscriminate handing out of Dalai Lama pics by travellers and tour groups has led to a situation (particularly in rural Tibet) where Westerners are seen as mobile Dalai Lama picture dispensing machines: say the magic words 'Dalai Lama picture', and out one pops. And if you reply that you don't have any, Tibetans will often point at your bulging backpack as if to say 'what's that full of then?'

I personally agree with advice given by Gary McCue, experienced Tibet traveller and author of *Trekking in Tibet – a traveler's guide*. Firstly, he suggests, never give out Dalai Lama photographs to those who ask for them – this only encourages Tibetans to hassle foreigners. Reserve them for Tibetans who tender some act of kindness. Secondly, be circumspect about handing out Dalai Lama pictures in public spaces. You can never be too sure who is watching, and it may have repercussions for the recipient. Lastly, bear in mind that pictures of the Dalai Lama with the Tibetan national flag are most definitely illegal. Handing these out will create problems for both the recipient and yourself. ■

tionships are highly valued in all Asian cultures and the giving of a gift helps to establish a relationship where there was not one before. If you are a smoker, walking up to someone with a smile and handing them a cigarette is a very effective way of getting business off to a good start. In rural Tibet, giving out gifts (Dalai Lama pictures, chocolates, whatever) is a particularly useful way of making sure you get a thermos of hot water when you stay overnight somewhere – your small act of friendliness will ensure that the recipient will take care of you.

Speaking Frankly It does not get you anywhere as a general rule. Nor are locals likely to reciprocate. Both Chinese and Tibetans are much more likely to tell you what they think you want to hear than what is actually the case. Read between the lines.

RELIGION

A basic understanding of Buddhism is essential to getting beneath the skin of things in Tibet. Buddhism's values and goals permeate almost everything Tibetan. To explore the monasteries and temples of Tibet, to mix with its people and know nothing of Buddhism is like visiting Rome and knowing nothing of Christianity. To be sure, it might still be an awe-inspiring experience, but much remains hidden and indecipherable.

For those who already do know something of Buddhism, who have read something of Zen, for example, Tibet can be baffling on another level. The grandeur of the temples, the worship of images and fierce protective deities that stand in doorways all seem to belie the basic tenets of an ascetic faith that is basically about the renunciation of the self.

Buddhism is perhaps the most tolerant of the world's religions, and wherever it went it adapted to local conditions. In effect, Buddhism became many things in many places, though in all cases its basic tenets remained very much the same. These basic tenets represent such a powerful statement that Buddhism, like all major religions, was able to continually renew itself through returning and reinterpreting the fundamentals of the faith. Christianity has renewed itself in this way, adapting to new historical circumstances and new cultural environments, and similarly Buddhism has grown like a dividing cell, creating countless new schools of thought which are nevertheless bound together like a single organism in their faith in the value of the original teachings of the historical Buddha, Sakyamuni.

In Tibet the establishment of Buddhism was marked by its interaction with the native religion, Bön. This shamanistic faith which encompassed gods and spirits who inhabited power places, exorcism and the cult of dead kings among other things, probably had a major influence on the direction Buddhism took in Tibet. But it was Bön that was transformed and tamed to the ends of Buddhism and not vice versa. The Bönpo order, as it survives today, is to all intents and purposes a school of Buddhism.

Historical Background of Buddhism

Buddhism originated in the north-east of India around the 5th century BC, at a time when the local religion was Brahmanism. The society had a simple, four-tiered caste system that was later to develop into the more complex caste system of Indian Hindu society. At the head of this caste system were the Brahmin, or priests. The Brahmin made offerings to *deva*, 33 gods who preserved the order of the cosmos. Some Brahmin, in preparation for presiding over offerings to the deva, partook of an asceticism that took them to remote places where they fasted, meditated and practiced yogic techniques.

The teachings of some of these ascetic Brahmin are thought to have given rise to the *Upanishads*, a collection of sacred Sanskrit texts that indicated an underlying principle in the cosmos known as *brahman*. This principle had its equivalent in the human mind, and was referred to as *atman*, the universal self. The yogic practitioner who achieved identity with atman achieved liberation from the cycle of death and rebirth and merged into brahman.

Many of the fundamental concepts of Buddhism, then, find their origin in the

Brahma

Brahman society of this time. The Buddha himself was one of many wandering ascetics whose teachings led to the establishment of rival religious schools. Jainism, a religion that found a basic life principle in all objects and aimed to attain identity with that principle through ascetic practices and even self-mutilation, was one of these schools. Buddhism was another.

The Life of the Buddha

The historical dates for the life of the Buddha are much debated, and recent scholarship has put previously long-held beliefs into question. A commonly accepted compromise is something like 480-400 BC, give or take half a century.

The Buddha was born Siddhattha Gotama in the small kingdom of Sakka on the border of contemporary Nepal. The name Sakyamuni, given to him in the Mahayana tradition, has its origin in the kingdom of Gotama's birth, meaning the 'Sage of Sakka'.

Little is known of the life of Sakyamuni.

It was probably not until some 200 years after his death that biographies were compiled, and by that time many of the circumstances of his life had merged with legend. It is known that he was born of a noble family and that he married and had a son before renouncing a life of comfort on a quest to make sense of the suffering in the world. Traditional Buddhist biographies, however, do not start with the birth of Sakyamuni, but with his early lives a '100,000 eons ago'. Thus his striving for Buddhahood passed through countless rebirths before he attained perfection.

Sakyamuni, at the age of 29, left his home, his wife and newly born son. This action is explained as being for the benefit of all sentient beings and set a precedent for the renunciation of domestic life by the members of later monastic communities. He studied with many of the great teachers of the day, passing up opportunities to become a teacher himself. Later he embarked on a course of intense asceticism, before concluding that such a path was too extreme.

At this point, rather than give up his quest, Sakyamuni recalled an earlier meditation state he had once achieved, a state of great bliss and peace. In the place now known as Bodh Gaya, he sat beneath a *bodhi* tree and meditated. Over the course of three moonlit nights he achieved knowledge of the final obstacles to his enlightenment, and at the break of dawn at the end of the third night he became a Buddha.

After achieving enlightenment, Sakyamuni sat for another three or four weeks contemplating his achievement. During this time Brahma Sahampata, the god of compassion, asked Sakyamuni to share his perfect knowledge with those who were ready to hear his teachings. Sakyamuni's compliance with this request is seen as evidence of his compassion, the ideal complement of perfected wisdom.

The Early Teachings of Buddhism

The early teachings of Buddhism are based on the original insights of Sakyamuni and form the basis of all further Buddhist thought. The later Mahayana school (to which Tibetan Buddhism belongs) diverged from these early teachings in some respects, but not in their fundamentals.

The Buddha began his teachings by explaining that there was a Middle Way that steered a course between sensual indulgence and ascetic self torment. This Middle Way could be followed by taking the Holy Eightfold Path. The philosophical underpinning of this path were the Four Holy Truths, which addressed the problems of *karma* and rebirth. These basic concepts are the kernel of early Buddhist thought.

Rebirth Life is a cycle of rebirths. The common assumption is that there are many rebirths, but in Buddhist thought they are innumerable. The word *samsara*, which means literally 'wandering on', is used to describe this cycle, and life is seen as wandering on limitlessly through vast eons of time, through the birth and extinction and rebirth of galaxies and worlds. There are six levels of rebirth, or realms of existence. It is important to accumulate enough merit to avoid the three lower realms, though in the long cycle of rebirth all beings pass through them at some point. The three lower realms comprise hells of torment, ghost worlds and the world of animals. The three higher realms are human beings, demigods and gods. These six levels are depicted on the Wheel of Life, which can often be seen at the entrance to monasteries. All beings are fated to tread this wheel continuously until they make a commitment to enlightenment.

Karma All beings pass through the same cycle of rebirths. Their enemy may once have been their mother, and like all beings they have lived as an insect, as a god and suffered in one of the hell realms. Movement within this cycle, though, is not haphazard. It is governed by karma.

Karma is a slippery concept. It is sometimes translated simply as 'action', but it also implies the consequences of action. Karma might be thought of as an over-arching condition of life. Every action in life leaves a

psychic trace that carries over into the next rebirth. It should not be thought of as a reward or punishment, simply a result. In Buddhist thought karma is frequently likened to a seed that ripens into a fruit: thus a human reborn as an insect is harvesting the fruits of a previous immoral existence.

Merit Given that karma is a kind of accumulated psychic baggage that we must lug through countless rebirths, it is the aim of all practicing Buddhists to try and accumulate as much 'good karma', or merit, as possible. Merit is best achieved through the act of rejoicing in giving, though merit can even be achieved through giving that is purely motivated by will for merit. The giving of alms to the needy and to monks, the relinquishing of a son to monkhood, acts of compassion and understanding are all meritorious and have a positive karmic outcome.

The Four Holy Truths If belief in rebirth, karma and merit are the basis of lay followers' faith in Buddhism, the Four Holy Truths might be thought of as the deep structure of the faith, its philosophical underpinning. The Buddha systematised the truths in the manner of medical practice of his time: (1) diagnose the illness, (2) identify its cause, (3) establish a cure, and (4) map a course for the cure. Their equivalents in Buddhism's diagnosis of the human condition are: (1) suffering *(dukkha)* caused by (2) desire *(tanha)*, which may be cured by (3) cessation of desire *(nibbana)*, which can be achieved by means of (4) the Holy Eightfold Path, or the Middle Way.

The first of the Four Holy Truths, then, is that life is suffering. This suffering extends through all the countless rebirths of beings, and finds its origin in the imperfection of life. Every rebirth brings with it the pain of birth, of ageing, of death, of association with unpleasant things, the loss of things we are attached to, and the failure to achieve the things we desire.

The reason for this suffering is the second Holy Truth, and lies in our dissatisfaction with imperfection, in our desire for things to

The Eight Auspicious Symbols

The Eight Auspicious Symbols are associated with gifts made to the Sakyamuni upon his enlightenment and appear as protective motifs throughout Tibet.

The **Precious Parasol** is usually placed over Buddha images to protect them from evil influences; it is a common Buddhist motif and can be seen as far away as Thailand and Japan.

The **Banner of Victory** heralds the triumph of Buddhist wisdom over ignorance.

The **White Conch Shell** is blown in celebration of Sakyamuni's enlightenment.

The **Two Golden Fishes** are shown leaping from the waters of their captivity; thus they represent liberation from the Wheel of Life.

be other than they are. What is more, this dissatisfaction leads to actions and karmic consequences that prolong the cycle of rebirths and may lead to even more suffering, much like a mouse running endlessly in a wheel.

. The third Holy Truth was indicated by the Buddha as nibbana, known in English as Nirvana. It is the cessation of desire, an end to attachment. With the cessation of desire comes an end to suffering, the achievement of complete non-attachment and an end to the cycle of rebirth – Nirvana, the ultimate goal of Buddhism. Nit-pickers might point out that the will to achieve Nirvana is a desire in itself. Buddhists answer that this desire is tolerated as a useful means to an end, but it is only when this desire too is extinguished that Nirvana is truly achieved.

The Holy Eightfold Path is the fourth of the Holy Truths, and prescribes a course that for the lay practitioner will lead to the accu-

mulation of merit and for the serious devotee may lead to Nirvana. The components of this path are: (1) right understanding, (2) right thought, (3) right speech, (4) right action, (5) right livelihood, (6) right effort, (7) right mindfulness, and (8) right concentration. Needless to say, each of these has a 'wrong' corollary.

The Schools of Buddhism

As is the case in all religious movements, not long after Sakyamuni's death, disagreements began to arise amongst his followers over whose interpretations best captured the true spirit of his teachings. The result was the development of numerous schools of thought and eventually a schism that saw the emergence of two principal schools: Hinayana and Mahayana.

Hinayana, also known as Theravada, might be seen as the more conservative of the two, a school that encouraged scholasticism

The **Vase of Great Treasures** is a repository of the jewels of enlightenment.

The **Eight-Spoked Golden Wheel** represents the Noble Eightfold Path, and is also referred to as the Wheel of Dharma.

The **Knot of Eternity** is a commonly seen Tibetan motif, representing the entwined, never ending passage of harmony and love.

The **Lotus Flower** stands for Sakyamuni's purity and his compassion.

and close attention to what was considered the original teachings of Sakyamuni. Mahayana, on the other hand, with its elevation of compassion to an all-important idea, took Buddhism in a new direction. It was the Mahayana school that made its way up to the high Tibetan plateau and took root there, at the same time travelling to China, Korea and Japan. Hinayana retreated into southern India and took root in Sri Lanka and Thailand.

Mahayana The claims that Mahayanists made for their faith were many, but the central issue was a change in orientation from individual pursuit of enlightenment to bodhisattvahood. The bodhisattva, rather than striving for complete non-attachment, aims, through compassion and self-sacrifice, to achieve enlightenment for the sake of all beings.

In another development, Sakyamuni began to take on another form altogether. Mahayanists maintained that Sakyamuni had already attained Buddhahood many eons ago and that he was a manifestation of a long-enlightened transcendent being who sent such manifestations to many world systems to assist all beings on the road to enlightenment. There were many such transcendent beings, the argument ran, living in heavens or 'Pure Lands' and all were able to project themselves into the innumerable worlds of the cosmos for the sake of sentient life there.

The philosophical reasoning behind the Mahayana transformation of Buddhism is extremely complex, but it had the effect of allowing Mahayanists to produce new revealed texts that recorded the words of Sakyamuni as they appeared in dreams and visions. It also had the effect of producing a pantheon of transcendent bodhisattvas, a feature that made Mahayana more palatable to cultures which already had gods of their own. In Tibet, China, Korea and Japan the Mahayana pantheon came to be identified with local gods. In Tibet, in particular, many stories of the taming of local gods by their Mahayana equivalents came into being.

Vajrayana (Tantrism) A further Mahayana development that is particularly relevant to Tibet is Tantrism, or Vajrayana. The words of Sakyamuni were recorded in sutras and studied by both students of Hinayana and Mahayana, but according to followers of Vajrayana, a school that emerged from around 600 AD, Sakyamuni left a corpus of esoteric instructions to a select few of his disciples. These were known as *tantra*.

Tantric adepts claimed that through using unconventional techniques they could jolt themselves towards enlightenment, shortening the long road to bodhisattvahood. The process involved identification with a tutelary deity invoked through deep meditation and recitation of the deity's mantra. The most famous of these mantra is the *om mani padme hum* mantra of Avalokiteshvara, the patron saint of Tibet. Tantric practice employs Indian yogic techniques to channel energy towards the transformation of enlightenment. Such yogic techniques might even include sexual practices.

Most of the images of deities in Tibetan monasteries and temples are Tantric in nature. Together they show the many facets of enlightenment – at times kindly, at times wrathful. Sometimes these deities are pictured at the centre of a mandala, which is a symbolic representation of the world they inhabit. The Tantric adept who identifies with a particular deity will visualise the mandala as a three-dimensional world, a feat of meditational concentration that takes many years of training to achieve.

Tibetan Buddhism & Its Schools
The introduction of Buddhism to Tibet is attended by legends of the taming of local gods and spirits and their conversion to Bud-

---

Sutra & Tantra
Lurking in the minefield of Buddhist terminology that makes even the briefest of excursions into Tibet so bewildering is the distinction between sutras and tantras. To understand the difference properly it is useful to go back to the schism in Buddhism that gave rise to the two major schools of Hinayana and Mahayana. The Hinayana school is the older, and is based on the teachings of Sakyamuni, the historical Buddha, which were recorded in the Sutras of the Pali Canon. These sutras can be translated as their Biblical equivalent 'scriptures'.

So far so good. The situation is complicated, however, with the rise of Mahayana. Mahayanists claimed to have discovered another body of sutras which were entrusted to supernatural beings until sufficiently spiritually advanced human beings appeared in the world to receive them. In this way a second, Mahayana, canon came into being. It also set the precedent that Buddhist practice could be informed not only by the teachings of a living Buddha, but through revelations that came from beyond this world.

As the name suggests tantras are associated with Tantric Buddhism, also known as Vajrayana. Just as sutra reveal the teachings of Sakyamuni, every tantra can be traced back to a revelation from a particular deity. Tantra have their origin in Indian devotional cults. They involve practices and rituals that were revealed to an adept by a particular deity and then transmitted by that adept to a disciple and so on through many hundreds of years. In this sense, tantra need not be written down, and may sometimes be orally transmitted.

The earliest Tibetan tantra are associated with the Nyingmapa order and came to Tibet via Guru Rinpoche in the 8th century. They are practiced by all Tibetan schools of Buddhism and are called the Old Tantra. The later schools of Tibetan Buddhism – Kagyupa and Sakyapa – supplemented these tantra with revelations of their own, and these came to be known as the New Tantra. The New Tantra are all associated with places in Tibet visited by Guru Rinpoche, and 'discovers' *(terton)* of these tantra are thought to be manifestations of Guru Rinpoche's students. ■

dhism as protective deities. This panoply of Buddhas, bodhisattvas and sages occupies a mythic world in the Tibetan imagination. Avalokiteshvara is perhaps chief among them, manifesting himself in early Tibetan kings and later in the Dalai Lamas. Guru Rinpoche, the Indian sage who bound the native spirits and gods of Tibet into the service of Buddhism, is another. And there are countless others worshipped in images throughout the land: Tara, Manjushri, Milarepa, Marpa, Tsongkhapa among others.

The anthropologist Geoffrey Samuel has referred to these figures as 'culture heroes' and 'trans-historical figures of power and authority'. They might be seen as belonging to a shamanistic stream of Tibetan Buddhism which has always coexisted with the monastic, clerical side of Tibetan Buddhism. While the clerical side of Buddhism concerns itself largely with textual study and analysis, the Tantric shamanistic side seeks revelation through identification with these deified beings and through their 'revealed' words or writings *(terma)*.

It is useful to consider the various schools of Tibetan Buddhism as revealing something of a struggle between these two orientations: shamanism and clericism. Each school finds its own resolution of the problem. In the case of the last major school to arise, the Gelugpa order, there was a search to return to the doctrinal purity of clerical Buddhism. But even here, the Tantric forms were not discarded altogether; it was merely felt that many years of scholarly work and preparation should precede the more esoteric Tantric practices.

The clerical and shamanistic orientations can also be explained as the difference between state-sponsored and popular Buddhism respectively. There was always a tendency for the state to emphasise monastic Buddhism, with its communities of rule-abiding monks. Popular Buddhism, on the other hand, with its long-haired, wild-eyed ascetic recluses capable of performing great feats of magic, had a great appeal to the ordinary people of Tibet, for whom ghosts and demons and sorcerers were a reality.

Nyingmapa Order The Nyingmapa Order is the 'Old School', and traces its origins back to the teachings and practices of Guru Rinpoche, who came to Tibet from India in the 8th to 9th centuries. As Buddhism fell into decline until the second diffusion of the faith in the 11th century, the Nyingmapa failed to develop as a powerful, centralised

The Mandala

The mandala is a fascinating concept, as well as often making for quite a beautiful artistic creation in itself. In a sense you might think of a mandala as being something like the 3D pictures that have become popular over the last few years. What on the surface appears a plain two-dimensional design, with the right visual approach, emerges as a three-dimensional picture.

In the case of the mandala the correct visual approach is achieved through meditation. The mandala is associated with Tantric Buddhism and is chiefly used in a ritual known as *sadhana*, or 'means for attainment'. According to this ritual, the adept meditates on, invokes and identifies with a specific deity, before dissolving into emptiness and reemerging as the deity itself. The process, insofar as it uses the mandala as an aid, involves a remarkable feat of imaginative concentration.

A typical mandala will figure a central deity surrounded by four or eight other deities who are aspects of the central figure. These surrounding deities are often accompanied by a consort. There may be several circles of these deities, totalling several hundred in all. These deities and all other elements of the mandala have to be visualised as the three-dimensional world of the central deity. One ritual calls for the adept to visualise 722 deities with sufficient clarity to be able to see the 'whites of their eyes' and hold this visualisation for four hours.

The ultimate aim of mandala visualisation, however, is to enter the three-dimensional world of the mandala and to merge with the deity at the centre of that world. ■

school, and for the most part prospered in villages throughout rural Tibet and was administered by local shaman-like figures.

With the second diffusion of Buddhism and the emergence of rival schools, the Nyingmapa order experienced something of a revival through the 'discovery' of hidden texts in the power places of Tibet visited by

Important Figures of Tibetan Buddhism

The following is a brief guide to some of the gods and goddesses of the Tibetan Buddhist pantheon. It is neither exhaustive nor scholarly, but it may help you to recognise a few of the statues you encounter in gompas during a trek.

Padmasambhava – the 'lotus-born' Buddha – assisted in establishing Buddhism in Tibet in the 8th century. He is regarded by followers of Nyingmapa Buddhism as the second Buddha. He is also known as Guru Rinpoche.

Avalokiteshvara – 'glorious gentle one' – one of the three great saviours or Bodhisattvas. He is the Bodhisattva of compassion and is often pictured with 11 heads and several pairs of arms. His Tibetan name is Chenresig.

Manjushri – the 'princely lord of wisdom' – is regarded as the first divine teacher of Buddhist doctrine. He is also known as Jampel.

Vajrapani – 'thunderbolt in hand' – is one of the three great saviours or Bodhisattvas. He is also known as Channadorje. The thunderbolt represents power and is a fundamental symbol of Tantric faith; it is called a *dorje* in Tibetan and *vajra* in Sanskrit.

Guru Rinpoche. In many cases these 'revealed' texts, known as terma, were discovered through yogic-inspired visions by spiritually advanced Nyingmapa practition-ers, rather than found under a pile of rocks or in a cave. But, however they came about, these terma gave the Nyingmapa a new lease of life.

Sakyamuni – the 'historical Buddha' – born in Lumbini in southern Nepal in the 5th century BCE, he attained enlightenment under a pipal (Bo) tree and his teachings set in motion the Buddhist faith. In Tibetan-style representations he is always pictured sitting cross-legged on a lotus flower throne.

Maitreya – the 'Buddha of the future'. He is passing the life of a Bodhisattva and will return to earth in human form 4000 years after the disappearance of Buddha (Sakyamuni).

Milarepa was a great Tibetan magician and poet who is believed to have attained the supreme enlightenment of Buddhahood in the course of one life. He lived in the 11th century and travelled extensively throughout the Himalayan border lands. Most images of Milarepa picture him smiling, holding his hand to his ear as he sings.

Tara – 'the saviouress' – has 21 different manifestations or aspects. She symbolises fertility and is believed to be able to fulfil wishes. Statues of Tara usually represent Green Tara, who is associated with night, or White Tara, who is associated with day.

They gave rise to the *dzogch'en*, or Great Perfection teachings. Much maligned by other Tibetan schools, dzogch'en postulates a primordial state of purity that pre-exists the duality of samsara and enlightenment, and offered a Tantric short cut to Nirvana. Such ideas were to influence other orders in the 19th century with the advent of the Rimed Movement.

The Nyingmapa never had the centralised power of other major Tibetan schools of Buddhism, and can be considered as representing an extreme of the shamanistic orientation.

Its fortunes improved somewhat with the accession of the 5th Dalai Lama, who was born into a Nyingmapa family. He personally saw to the expansion of Mindroling and Dorje Drak monasteries, which became the head Nyingmapa monasteries of Ü and all Tibet.

Kagyupa Order The Kagyupa ('Whispered Transmission') order traces its lineage back to early Indian teachers, but the impetus behind its establishment was Marpa (1012-1093), a married Tibetan yogin renowned for his translations and Tantric powers. He took on a disciple, Milarepa, who in turn became a renowned yogin, meditating in high moun-

tain caves and composing songs. Milarepa is a perfect example of the non-monastic ascetic for whom textual study is less important than Tantric experience, and legends accumulated around him: in particular, he is supposed to have overcome and taught mountain goddesses with the use of Tantric sexual techniques.

The influence of one of Milarepa's disciples, Gampopa, led to the establishment of numerous monasteries that became major teaching centres, eventually overshadowing the ascetic-yogin origins of the Kagyupa. The yogin tradition did not die out completely, however, and Kagyupa monasteries also became important centres for synthesising the clerical and shamanic orientations of Tibetan Buddhism.

Several sub-orders of the Kagyupa sprung up with time, the most prominent of which was the Karma Kagyupa, also known as the Karmapa. The practice of renowned lamas reincarnating after death probably originated with this sub-order, when the abbot of Tsurphu Monastery, Dusum Khenyapa (1110-1193) announced that he would be reincarnated as his own successor. The 16th Karmapa died in 1981, and his successor, the 17th, is resident at Tsurphu Monastery, near Lhasa.

Red Hats Versus Yellow Hat
The terms 'Red Hat' and 'Yellow Hat' have been avoided in this book, though they are widely used elsewhere. The main reason is that they represent a simplification that gives rise to confusion. The old adage, don't judge a Buddhist by his bowler, is a good one to follow in Tibet.

The distinction is actually Chinese. The Chinese differentiated between the yellow-hatted Gelugpa order and the red-hatted Kagyupa order – disputants for religious and political ascendancy until the 17th-century Mongol intervention – through their headgear. By extension, the distinction identified the Gelugpa as the Yellow Hats and all other Tibetan schools of Buddhism as Red Hats.

It is a distinction that makes little sense of the complexity of Tibet's religious orders. Confusion also arises due to the fact that the Karmapa, head of the Karma Kagyupa sub-order, is often referred to as the Black Hat lama. It makes a lot more sense to see the major orders of Tibetan Buddhism, not in terms of their dress sense, but in terms of their respective historical rise to power.

The Nyingmapa order, then, is the oldest of the Tibetan schools of Buddhism, tracing its origins back to the early establishment of Buddhism in the reign of King Songtsen Gampo. Tibetans sometimes refer to them as the Old School. The middle period of the second diffusion of Buddhism in the 11th century saw the rise of the New School Sakyapa and Kagyupa orders. The 15th-century search for doctrinal purity gave rise to the Gelugpa order, which by the 17th century had become dominant in Tibet. ∎

Sakyapa Order With the second diffusion of Buddhism in the 11th and 12th centuries, many Tibetan monasteries became centres for the textual study and translation of Indian Buddhist texts. One of the earliest major figures in this movement was Sakya Pandita (literally the 'Scholar from Sakya').

Sakya Pandita's renown as a scholar led to him being recognised as a manifestation of Manjushri, the Bodhisattva of Insight, as were subsequent abbots of Sakya. In the 13th and 14th centuries, the Sakyapa became embroiled in politics and implicated in the Mongol overlordship of Tibet. Nevertheless, at the same time Sakya emerged as a major centre for the scholastic study of Buddhism, and attracted students such as Tsongkhapa, who initiated the Gelugpa order.

Gelugpa Order It may not have been his intention, but Tsongkhapa (1357-1419), a monk who left his home in Kokonor at the age of 17 to study in central Tibet, is regarded as the founder of the Gelugpa order (Virtuous School), which came to dominate Tibetan political and religious affairs.

Tsongkhapa studied with all the major schools of his day, but was particularly influenced by the Sakyapa and the Kadampa orders. The Kadampa order had its head monastery at Netang, near Lhasa, and it was here that the 11th-century Indian sage Atisha spent the last of his days. The Kadampa had sustained the teachings of Atisha, which are a sophisticated synthesis of conventional Mahayana doctrine with the more arcane practices of Tantric Buddhism, and emerged as a major school, emphasising scholastic study. It may never have matched the eminence of the Kagyupa and Sakyapa orders, but in the hands of Tsongkhapa the teachings of the Kadampa order established a renewal in Tibetan Buddhism.

After having a vision of Atisha, Tsongkhapa elaborated on the Indian sage's clerical-Tantric synthesis in a doctrine known as *lamrim*, or the 'gradual path'. Tsongkhapa basically advocated a return to doctrinal purity and monastic discipline as prerequisites to advanced Tantric studies. He did not, as it is sometimes maintained, advocate a purely clerical approach to Buddhism, but he did reassert the monastic body as the basis of the Buddhist community and maintain that Tantric practices should be reserved for the advanced student.

Tsongkhapa established a monastery at Ganden, which was to become the head of the Gelugpa order. Other monasteries were also established at Dreprung, Sera (Lhasa) and at Shigatse. Although the abbot of Dreprung was titular head of the order (and

---

The World of a Monk

The Western term 'monk' is slightly misleading when it is used in Tibetan Buddhism. The Tibetan equivalent would probably be *trapa*, which means literally 'scholar' or 'student', and is an inclusive term that covers the three main categories of monastic inmates. These should be distinguished again from lamas, who as spiritual luminaries have a privileged position in the monastic hierarchy, may have considerable wealth and, outside the Gelugpa order, are not necessarily celibate.

The first step for a monk, usually after having completed some prior study, is one of two lesser vows: the *genyen* or *getsul* ordinations – renunciations of secular life that include a vow of celibacy. This marks the beginning of a long course of study which is expected to lead to the full *gelong* vows of ordination. While most major monasteries will have a number of gelong monks, it is by no means certain that all monks achieve gelong status.

These three divisions do not exhaust the categories of monks in a monastery. There are usually specific monastic posts associated with administrative duties, with ritual and with teaching. Gelong vows are also supplemented by higher courses of study, which are rewarded in the Gelugpa order by the title *geshe*. In pre-modern Tibet, the larger monasteries also had divisions of so-called 'fighting monks', or monastic militias. To a large extent they served as a kind of police force within a particular monastery; but there were also times when their services were used to hammer home a doctrinal dispute with a rival monastery. ■

is to this day), it was the Dalai Lamas who came to be increasingly identified with the order's growing political and spiritual prestige.

LANGUAGE

The two principal languages of Tibet are Tibetan and Chinese. The importance of Chinese is an unfortunate reality in Tibet, and all Tibetans undertaking higher studies do so in Chinese. In fact, in urban Tibet – the countryside is another matter – almost all Tibetans speak Chinese. Nevertheless, even if you have studied or picked up some Chinese in China, it is worth trying to get a few phrases of Tibetan together. It will be much appreciated by Tibetans you encounter on your travels.

Chinese and Tibetan have little in common linguistically. They use different sentence structures, and the tonal element in Tibetan is far less crucial to conveying meaning than it is in Chinese. Also, unlike the dialects of China (and Japanese, Korean and Vietnamese), Tibetan does not and never has used Chinese characters as its written language.

Tibetan

Tibetan is classed as belonging to the Tibeto-Burman family of languages. It differs in many ways from Chinese, having a different written language, a different grammar and being non-tonal. Lhasa dialect, which is the standard form of Tibetan, does employ a system of rising and falling tones, but the differences are subtle and meaning is made clear by context. Beginners need not worry about it.

Grammar Like Chinese, Tibetan has no articles (the, a) and does not use plurals. Here the similarity ends, however. Tibetan differs from European and Chinese languages in employing a subject-object-verb sentence structure. Thus, where in English we would say I (subject) see (verb) John (object), in Tibetan the sentence is rendered *nga* (subject) John (object) *thong gi duk* (verb). In another marked difference with Chinese, Tibetan also has tenses and 'conjugates' its verbs with particles. There is also a fairly complicated system of prepositions (in, on, at etc) in Tibetan.

If all this makes Tibetan sound extremely difficult to pick up on the road, do not worry. Providing you relax a little, it is fairly easy to get together a basic repertoire of phrases that will win you friends and help to get things done.

Written Language The Tibetan script was developed during the reign of Songtsen Gampo in the 7th century. It was developed on Indian models and comprises 30 basic letters (each of which may be written in three different styles depending on the context in which a text is to be used), including the

Tibetan Alphabet – 30 consonants, plus four vowels (at right), written from left to right in four vowel 'a', and four extra vowel signs for 'e', 'i', 'o' and 'u'. This 7th-century Tibetan script was based on the language that was spoken in Tibet at the time, and spellings have never been revised since. This means that, due to significant changes in spoken Tibetan over the last 12 centuries, written Tibetan and spoken Tibetan are very different, making the development of a transliteration system for speakers of European languages a formidable task.

Romanisation There is no commonly accepted romanisation system for Tibetan. Some academic texts use a romanisation system that is based on written Tibetan, but for those who have not studied the written language of Tibet the results are usually unintelligible. Some examples of this system include: Dreprung (Monastery), which is rendered as *'bras spungs*; Gyantse, which is rendered as *rgyal rtse*; and Shigatse, which is rendered as *gzhis ka rtse*. It is the kind of system that works best in the cloistered halls of academia and simply will not do in the real world.

The alternative, then, to basing romanised Tibetan on the written language is to base it on contemporary Lhasa dialect as it is spoken. This is what most writers on the subject of Tibet generally do, and already certain standards have begun to emerge. Most guides and histories, for example, use the same spellings for towns (Lhasa,

Shigatse, Gyantse, etc) and for major geographical features. In the case of less well known Tibetan names, however, there is a lot of disagreement in English sources.

In this book I have tried not to introduce new complexities to the various spellings available and have generally chosen the most widely used term. In cases where there is wide disagreement, I have chosen the spelling that is easiest to pronounce.

Pronunciation

Like all foreign languages Tibetan has its fair share of tricky pronunciations. There are quite a few consonant clusters, and Tibetan is a language (like Korean and Thai) that makes an important distinction between aspirated and non-aspirated consonants. Naturally, the best way to approach these difficulties is to work through a phrasebook with a native speaker or with a tape. The *Tibetan Phrasebook* (Snow Lion 1987) comes with a tape and is an excellent phrasebook to travel with in Tibet. Lonely Planet also publishes a *Tibetan Phrasebook*.

Vowels

The following pronunciation guide is based on standard British pronunciation – North Americans beware.

a as the 'a' in 'father'
ay as the 'ay' in 'play'
e as the 'e' in 'met'

different kinds of script.

ee as the 'ee' in 'meet'
i as the 'i' in 'begin'
o as the 'o' in 'slow'
oo as the 'oo' in 'soon'
ö as in German, like the 'u' in 'put'
u as the 'oo' in 'woo'
ü as in German, like the 'u' in 'flute'

Consonants

With the exception of the consonants listed below, Tibetan consonants should be pronounced as in English. Where consonants are followed by an 'h', it means that the consonant is aspirated (accompanied by a puff of air). An English example might be 'kettle', where the 'k' is aspirated and the 'tt' is non-aspirated. The distinction is fairly important, but in simple Tibetan the context should make it clear what you are talking about even if you get the sounds muddled up a bit.

ky as the 'kie' in 'Kiev'
ng as the 'ng' in 'sing'
r produced with a slight trill, as in Spanish
ts as the 'ts' in 'bits'

Pronouns

I
nga
ང་
you
kerang
ཁྱེད་རང་
he, she
khong
ཁོང་
we
nga-tso
ང་ཚོ་
you all
kerang-tso
ཁྱེད་རང་ཚོ་
they
khong-tso
ཁོང་ཚོ་

Useful Phrases

hello
tashi dele
བཀྲ་ཤིས་བདེ་ལེགས་
goodbye (when staying)
kale phe
ག་ལེ་ཕེབས་
goodbye (when leaving)
kale shoo
ག་ལེ་བཞུགས་
thank you
thoo jaychay
ཐུགས་རྗེ་ཆེ་
yes, OK
la ong,
ལགས་འོང་
sorry
gonda
དགོངས་དག་
I want...
nga la...go
ང་ལ་······དགོས་
I don't understand.
ha ko ma song.
ཧ་གོ་མ་སོང་
Do you understand?
ha ko song-ngey?
ཧ་གོ་སོང་ངས་
I understand.
ha ko song.
ཧ་གོ་སོང་
How much?
ka tsö ray?
ག་ཚོད་རེད་
It's expensive.
gong chenpo ray.
གོང་ཆེན་པོ་རེད་
What's your name?
kerang gi ming la karey zer gi yö?
ཁྱེད་རང་གི་མིང་ལ་ག་རེ་ཟེར་གི་ཡོད་
My name is...and you?
ngai...ming la, a ni kerang zer gi yö?
ངའི་མིང་ལ་······ཟེར་གི་ཡོད་ཨ་ནི་ཁྱེད་རང་
Where are you from?
kerang ka-ne ray?
ཁྱེད་རང་ག་ནས་རེད་
Do you speak English?
injeeke shing gi yö pe?
དབྱིན་ཇི་སྐད་ཤེས་ཀྱི་ཡོད་པས་

Time

What's the time?
chutsö katsö ray?
ཆུ་ཚོད་ག་ཚོད་རེད་

...hour...minute
...chutsö...karma
ཆུ་ཚོད་ ་་་ སྐར་མ་

When?
kadü?
ག་དུས་

now
thanda
ད་ལྟ་

today
thiring
དེ་རིང་

tomorrow
sangnyi
སང་ཉིན་

yesterday
kesa
ཁ་སང་

morning
shogay
ཞོགས་གས་

afternoon
nying gung gyab la
ཉི་ན་གུང་རྒྱབ་ལ་

evening/night
gonta
དགོང་དག་

Accommodation

hotel
dhönkhang
མགྲོན་ཁང་

Do you have a room?
kang mi yöpe?
ཁང་མི་ག་ཡོད་པས་

How much is it for one night?
tsen chik la katsö ray?
མཚན་གཅིག་ལ་ག་ཚོད་རེད་

I'd like to stay with a Tibetan family.
nga phöbe mitsang nyemdo dendö yö.
ང་བོད་པའི་མི་ཚང་མཉམ་དུ་བསྡད་འདོད་ཡོད་

I need some hot water.
nga la chu tsapo go.
ང་ལ་ཆུ་ཚ་པོ་དགོས་

Getting Around

I want to go to...
nga...la drondö yö
ང་ ་་་་ ལ་འགྲོ་འདོད་ཡོད་

I am getting off.
nga phap gi yin.
ང་བབས་ཀྱི་ཡིན་

What time do we leave?
ngatso chutsö katsö la dro gi yin?
ང་ཚོ་ཆུ་ཚོད་ག་ཚོད་ལ་འགྲོ་གི་ཡིན་

What time do we arrive?
ngatso chutsö katsö la lep gi yin?
ང་ཚོ་ ཆུ་ཚོད་ག་ཚོད་ལ་སླེབ་ཀྱི་ཡིན་

airport
namdrutang
རྣམ་གྲུ་ཐང་

bus
lamkhor
ལྡངས་འཁོར་

bicycle
kanggari
ཀང་སྐྱ་རི་ལ་

Where can I get a bicycle?
kanggari kaba ragi ray?
ཀང་སྐྱ་རི་ལ་ག་པར་རག་གི་རེད་

How much per day?
nyima chik la katsö ray?
ཉི་མ་གཅིག་ལ་ག་ཚོད་རེད་

I'm lost.
nga lam khag lag song.
ང་ལམ་ཁག་ལག་སོང་

Where is the...?
...kaba yo ray?
ག་པར་ཡོད་རེད་

right
yeba
གཡས་པ་

left
yönba
གཡོན་པ་

straight ahead
shar gya
ཤར་རྒྱག་

north/south/east/west
chang/lo/shar/noop
བྱང་ལྷོ་ཤར་ནུབ་

porter
dopo khur khen
དོ་པོ་ཁུར་མཁན་

pack animals
kel semchen
ཁལ་སེམས་ཅན་
yak
ya
གཡག་

Geographical Terms
road/trail
lam
ལམ་
mountain
ree
རི་
cave
trapoo
བྲག་ཕུག་
river
tsangpo
ཚངས་པོ་
valley
loong shon
ལུང་གཤོང་
lake
tso
མཚོ་
waterfall
papchu
བབས་ཆུ་
hot spring
chuzay
ཆུ་ཚན་

Medical
I'm sick.
nga bedo mindu.
ང་བདེ་པོ་མི་འདུག
Please call a doctor.
amjee ke tangronang.
ཨེམ་ཆི་སྐྱེད་བཏང་རོགས་གནང་
hospital
menkang
སྨན་ཁང་
diarrhoea
troko she
གྲོད་ཁོག་བཤལ་
fever
tsawa
ཚ་བ་

Countries
I'm from...
nga....ne yin
ང་་་ནས་རེད་
Australia
otalee
ཨོ་ཊ་ལི་ཡ་
Canada
janada
ཅ་ན་ད་
France
farensi
ཕ་རན་སི་
Germany
jarman
འཇར་མན་
New Zealand
shinshilen
ཤིན་ཤི་ལེན་
UK
injee lungpa
དབྱིན་ཇི་འི་ལུང་པ་
USA
amerika
ཨ་མི་རི་ཀ་

Numbers
Note: the word in brackets is added before one *chik* etc to make the compound numbers.

1	*chik*	གཅིག་
2	*nyi*	གཉིས་
3	*sum*	གསུམ་
4	*shi*	བཞི་
5	*nga*	ལྔ་
6	*troo*	དྲུག་
7	*dün*	བདུན་
8	*gye*	བརྒྱད་
9	*gu*	དགུ་
10	*chu*	བཅུ་
11	*chu chik*	བཅུ་གཅིག་
15	*cho nga*	བཅོ་ལྔ་

18	chob gye	བཅོ་བརྒྱད་
20	nyi shu (tsa)	ཉི་ཤུ་
21	nyi shu tsa chik	ཉི་ཤུ་རྩ་གཅིག་
30	sum shu (so)	སུམ་བཅུ་(སོ)་
40	shi chu (zhe) chig	བཞི་བཅུ་(ཞེ)་
50	nga chu (nga)	ལྔ་བཅུ་(ང)་
60	troo chu ray	དྲུག་བཅུ་(རེ)་
70	dun chu don	བདུན་བཅུ་(དོན)་
80	gye chu gya	བརྒྱད་བཅུ་(གྱ)་
90	gu chu go	དགུ་བཅུ་(གོ)་
100	chik gya	གཅིག་བརྒྱ་
200	ngi gya	གཉིས་བརྒྱ་
1000	chik tong	ཆིག་སྟོང་

Chinese

The official language of China is Mandarin, which in Chinese is usually referred to as *pŭtōnghuà*. This term means literally 'common speech' and is taught throughout China as a linguistic standard for the many dialect and minority-language speakers of China. It is based on, though by no means the same as, the dialect spoken in Beijing and much of northern China.

Dialect speakers of Chinese have a huge head start in learning Mandarin over speakers of non-Chinese languages such as Tibetans. For a start, all Chinese dialects (and some are as different as Dutch and German) share the same written language. Many Westerners understandably find this puzzling. It has to do with the simplicity of Chinese grammar and the fact that all Chinese words are represented not by a phonetic script but by ideographs, or characters. While a character contains a single idea it might be read in various ways: thus the characters for American in Mandarin read *meiguoren*, in Cantonese *meigwokyan*, and in Hokkienese *bigoklang*. In terms that make more sense to Westerners, think of the numbers from one to 10; now think of them again in French or German. The Arabic numerals we use operate in much the same way for us as that characters do for the Chinese.

Dialect speakers have other advantages in learning Mandarin of course. All Chinese dialects are tonal and share many grammatical characteristics. Speakers of non-Chinese languages who choose (or in the case of Tibetans are forced) to learn Chinese are confronted with a language in which they have to master a difficult tonal system and get several thousand characters under their belt if they want to be literate.

Grammar This is the easy bit. If Chinese were non-tonal it would be as easy to get a traveller's vocabulary together in China as it is in Indonesia. There are no articles (a, the), no tenses and no plurals. In fact, once you cotton on to the idea that constructing a Chinese sentence is simply a matter of stringing words together, you can make a lot of progress very quickly.

The important thing to bear in mind is that Chinese, like English, follows a subject-verb-object structure. Thus Chinese constructs the sentence I (subject) go (verb) to the shop (object) the same way as English without the preposition (to) and the article (the): *wǒ* (subject) *qù* (verb) *shāngdiàn* (object).

Those travelling from China into Tibet or from Tibet onwards into China are well advised to pick up a Chinese phrasebook such as Lonely Planet's *Mandarin Chinese Phrasebook*. It should help you through most of your travel needs, both in Tibet and China.

Tones As already mentioned, the dialects of China are tonal. In other words, every Chinese morpheme (the basic building blocks of meaning) has a tonal value. In Mandarin there are four of these tones. Other dialects generally have more; Cantonese, for example, has six or nine depending on how you count.

Tones are a real mental block for many students of Chinese. Yet all of the tones of Mandarin are used in English as an emotive overlay to our daily speech – for emphasis or for querying. The difference in Chinese is that the tones make a difference to meaning.

The standard example given for learning Chinese tones is *ma*, which can variously mean 'mother', 'hemp' (yeah, as in 'dope'), 'horse' or 'scold'.

| high tone | | mā | mother |

rising tone	má	hemp
falling-rising tone	mǎ	horse
falling tone	mà	scold

Note in the phrases following no tone marks are indicated for some words. This is because certain Mandarin words comprise two characters in which the second has a 'neutral' tone. Don't worry about it overly.

Pinyin The standard form of romanisation for Mandarin adopted by the PRC is known as *pinyin*. It means literally 'spell the sounds', and once you get used to the idiosyncracies of its spellings it is a very accurate way of representing the sounds of Mandarin. The pronunciation of pinyin spellings are by no means obvious to speakers of European languages, however, and need to be memorised. There is no way of knowing, for example, that a pinyin 'x' is pronounced like an English 's' or that 'zh' is pronounced like a 'j'. See the following Pronunciation section for guidelines.

Pronunciation If you are going to really use a Mandarin phrasebook effectively, you need to internalise the pronunciation of pinyin. The best way is naturally to learn pinyin with a native speaker or with a tape. Failing this, the following guidelines should be of some assistance.

The pronunciation given in this section is for standard Mandarin as spoken in northern China. Unfortunately you are unlikely to meet many northern Chinese in Tibet. Most of the Han Chinese settlers, businesspeople and officials in Tibet are from Sichuan province, where a southern form of Mandarin is spoken. Even for students of Chinese who have studied for many years, the Sichuan accent can be baffling. Deng Xiaoping is from Sichuan, and many northern Chinese complain that his speeches, delivered in thick Sichuanese, are incomprehensible. You will just have to persevere with this obstacle to communication.

Vowels

Mandarin vowel sounds can be fairly tricky for English speakers. In some cases they change depending on the consonant that precedes them, and in other cases they are sounds that are not used in English.

The following vowel sounds follow standard British pronunciation – North Americans beware.

a	as the 'a' in 'father'
ai	as the 'y' in 'fly'
ao	as the 'ow' in 'cow'
e	as the 'ur' in 'blur'
ei	as the 'ay' in 'way'
i	as the 'ee' in 'meet' when preceded by **j**, **q**, **x** or **y**
i	as the 'e' in 'her' when preceded by other consonants
ian	as in 'yen'
iao	as in exclamation of pain 'yow!'
ie	as the 'ere' in 'here'
o	as the 'o' in 'or'
ou	as the 'oa' in 'boat'
u	as the 'u' in 'flute' when preceded by **j**, **q**, **x** or **y**
u	as the 'oo' in 'woo' when preceded by other consonants
ü	as in German or as the 'u' in 'flute'
ui	as in 'way'
uo	as in 'war'

Consonants

Pinyin consonants present certain difficulties for students of Chinese. Do not assume that consonants are pronounced as you would pronounce them in English or in other European languages.

One point worth noting briefly is that some consonants have the same pronunciation. This is not a redundancy. While q and c, for example, have the same pronunciation, the value of the following vowel changes depending on which is used. Thus ci is pronounced 'tser', while qi is pronounced 'tsee'. There are three such pairs of consonants: c and q, j and z, and s and x.

c	as the 'ts' in 'bits'
ch	as the 'ch' in 'church'
j	as the 'ds' in 'suds'
h	as the gutteral Scottish 'loch'

q	as the 'ts' in 'bits'
r	somewhere between an English 'r' and the 's' in 'pleasure'
s	as the 's' in 'sock'
sh	as the 'sh' in 'shack'
x	as the 's' in 'sock'
z	as the 'ds' in 'suds'
zh	as the 'j' in 'judge'

Pronouns

I
wǒ
我
you
nǐ
你
he, she, it
tā
他
we, us
wǒmen
我们
they, them
tāmen
他们
you all
nǐmen
你们

Useful Phrases

hello
nǐ hǎo
你好
goodbye
zàijiàn
再见
thank you
xièxie
谢谢
you're welcome
búkèqi
不客气
sorry
duìbuqǐ
对不起
It doesn't matter.
méishì.
没事

no, not available, none, etc
méiyǒu
没有
no, not so
búshì
不是
I'm a foreign student.
wǒ shì liúxuéshēng.
我是留学生
What's to be done?
zěnme bàn?
怎么办?
I want...
wǒ yào...
我要...
I don't want...
wǒ búyào...
我不要...
I don't understand.
wǒ bùdǒng.
我不懂
Do you understand?
nǐ tīngdedǒng ma?
你听不懂吗?
I understand.
wǒ tīngdedǒng.
我听得懂

Money

How much?
duōshǎo qián?
多少钱?
That's too expensive.
tài guìle.
太贵了
Bank of China
zhōngguó yínháng
中国银行
RMB (currency of China)
rénmínbì
人民币
change money
huànqián
换钱
travellers' cheque
lǚxíng zhīpiào
旅行支票

Post & Telecommunications

post office
yóujú
邮局

letter
xìn
信

envelope
xìnfēng
信封

parcel
bāoguǒ
包裹

air mail
hángkōng
航空

stamps
yóupiào
邮票

postcard
míngxìnpiàn
明信片

poste restante
cúnjú hòulínglán
存局後领栏

telephone
diànhuà
电话

telephone card
diànhuàkǎ
电话卡

international call
guójì diànhuà
国际电话

collect call
duìfāng fùkuǎn diànhuà
对方付款电话

direct-dial call
zhíbō diànhuà
直拨电话

fax
chuánzhēn
传真

Time

What's the time?
jǐdiǎnle?
几点了?

..hour...minute
...diǎn...fēn
…点…分

When?
shénme shíhou?
什么时侯

now
xiànzài
现在

today
jīntiān
今天

tomorrow
míngtiān
明天

yesterday
zuótiān
昨天

(in the) morning
zǎoshang
早上

(in the) afternoon
xiàwǔ
下午

(in the) evening/night
wǎnshang
晚上

Wait a moment.
děng yīxià/yīhuǎr.
等一下

Places to Stay

hotel (generic)
lǚguǎn
旅馆

hostel
zhāodàisuǒ/lǚshè
招待所/旅社

tourist hotel
bīnguǎn/fàndiàn/jiǔdiàn
宾馆/饭店/酒店

dormitory
duōrénfáng
多人房

single
dānrénfáng
单人房

double
shuāngrénfáng
双人房

bed
chuángwèi
床位
laundry
xǐ yīfu
洗衣服

Getting Around
I want to go to...
wǒ yào qù...
我要去…
I want to get off.
wǒ yào xià chē.
我要下车
luggage
xíngli
行李
I want to depart at...
wǒ yào...diǎn zǒu
我要…点走
Could you buy a ticket for me?
nǐ kěyǐ bāng wǒ mǎi piào ma?
你可以帮我买票吗?
buy (a) ticket(s)
mǎi piào
买票
What time does it go?
jǐdiǎn zǒu?
几点走?
What time does it arrive?
jǐdiǎn dào?
几点到?
airport
jīchǎng
机厂
bus station
qìchēzhàn
汽车站
bus
gōnggòng qìchē
公共汽车
minibus
xiǎoxíngchē/miànbāochē
小行车/面包车
bicycle
zìxíngchē
自行车
Can I hire a bicycle?
kěyǐ zū zìxíngchē ma?
可以租自行车吗?

How much per hour/day?
yītiān/yīgezhōngtou duōshǎo qián?
一天/一个钟头多少钱?
I'm lost.
wǒ mílùle.
我迷路了
Where is the...?
...zài nǎr?
…在哪儿?
right
yòu
右
left
zuǒ
左
straight ahead
yīzhí zǒu
一直走
north/south/east/west
běi/nán/dōng/xī
北/南/东/西

Geographical Terms
road/trail
lù
路
mountain path
shānlù
山路
mountain
shān
山
river
hé
河
valley
shāngǔ
山谷
lake
hú
湖
waterfall
pùbù
瀑布
hot spring
wēnquán
温泉

Emergency

police
jǐngchá
警察
Fire!
huǒzāi!
火灾!
Help!
jiùmìng a!
救命啊!
Thief!
xiǎotōu!
小偷!

Public Security

Public Security Bureau (PSB)
gōngānjú
公安局
Foreign Affairs Branch
wàishìkē
外事科
I'd like to extend my visa.
wǒ xiǎng yáncháng wǒde qiānzhèng.
我想延长我的签证
I'd like to apply for a travel permit to...
wǒ xiǎng shēnqǐng yīge tōngxíngzhèng dào...
我想申请一个通行证到...
Travel Permit
wàibīn tōngxíngzhèng
外宾通行证

Medical

I'm sick.
wǒ shēngbìngle.
我生病了
I'm injured.
wǒ shòushāngle.
我受伤了
hospital
yīyuàn
医院
pharmacy
yàodiàn
药店
diarrhoea
lādùzi
拉肚子

fever
fāshāo
发烧
giardia
āmǐbā fùxiè
阿米巴腹泻
hepatitis
gānyán
肝炎
rabies
kuǎngquǎnbìng
狂犬病
tetanus
pòshāngfēng
破伤风
flu
gǎnmào
感冒

Countries

I'm from...
wǒ cóng....lai
我从...来
Australia
àodàlìyà
澳大利亚
Canada
jiānádà
加拿大
Denmark
dānmài
丹麦
France
fàguó
法国
Germany
déguó
德国
Netherlands
hélán
荷兰
New Zealand
xīnxīlán
新西兰
Spain
xībānyá
西班牙
Sweden
ruìdiǎn
瑞典

Switzerland
ruìshì
瑞士
UK
yīngguó
英国
USA
měiguó
美国

Numbers

0	*líng*	零
1	*yī*	一
2	*èr/liǎng*	二/两
3	*sān*	三
4	*sì*	四

5	*wǔ*	五
6	*liù*	六
7	*qī*	七
8	*bā*	八
9	*jiǔ*	九
10	*shí*	十
11	*shiyī*	十一
12	*shíèr*	十二
20	*èrshí*	二十
30	*sānshí*	三十
100	*yībǎi*	一百
200	*liǎngbǎi*	两百
300	*sānbǎi*	三百
1000	*yīqiān*	一千
10,000	*yīwàn*	一万
100,000	*sshíwàn*	十万

Facts for the Visitor

VISAS & EMBASSIES

Visas for individual travel in China are easy to get. China will even issue visas to individuals from countries which do not have diplomatic relations with the People's Republic of China (PRC).

Visas are readily available in Hong Kong and from Chinese embassies in most Western and many other countries. If you cannot wait until you get to Hong Kong or if you want to fly direct to China, then enquire first at the nearest Chinese embassy.

Bear in mind, however, that if you want more than 30 days in China, it is always better to obtain a visa via a travel agency than to apply directly at a Chinese embassy. Most agencies should be able to arrange a 60 or 90-day visa. The only catch with these visas is that they start ticking away from the moment they are issued, *not* from the day you enter the country. Standard 30-day visas are valid from the date of entry you indicate on your application.

Visa applications require two passport-sized photos. Your application must be written in English, and you are advised to have one entire blank page in your passport for the visa.

The visa application form asks you a number of questions – your travel itinerary, means of transport, how long you will stay etc – but you can deviate from this as much as you want. You *do not* have to leave from the place you specify on your visa application form. Whatever you do, however, do not let on that you plan to visit Tibet when you fill in this section. When listing your travel itinerary, pick the obvious contenders: Beijing, Shanghai, Guilin and so on.

If you want more flexibility to enter and leave China several times, multiple-entry visas are available through some travel agencies. This is particularly useful if you intend to follow complicated routes in and out of China via Hong Kong, Macau, Korea, Nepal, Pakistan, Thailand, Mongolia, Russia etc.

Multiple-entry visas cost approximately HK\$750 and are valid for six months, allowing an unlimited number of border crossings during this time. But there is a catch – you can only stay in China for 30 days at a time and getting this extended is close to impossible. Another minor catch is that these are in fact business visas, and normally will only be issued if you've been to China at least once before and have a stamp in your passport to prove it.

One-month single-entry visas are valid from the date of entry that you specify on the visa application. But all other visas are valid from the date of issue, *not* from the date of entry, so there is no point in getting such a visa far in advance of your planned entry date.

In Hong Kong

In Hong Kong, the cheapest visas (HK\$90 for 2½-day service, HK\$240 for same day) can be obtained from the Visa Office (☎ 5851794, 5851700) of the Ministry of Foreign Affairs of the PRC, 5th floor, Low Block, China Resources Building, 26 Harbour Rd, Wanchai. You'll have to queue and do not expect so much as a smile, but you'll save a few dollars. It is open Monday to Friday, from 9 am to 12.30 pm and 2 to 5 pm, and on Saturday from 9 am to 12.30 pm. From Tsimshatsui, Kowloon (Hong Kong), the cheapest and easiest way to get there is to take the Star Ferry to Wanchai Pier (not to Central!) – Wanchai Pier is one block away from the China Resources Building. Otherwise, it is a rather long hike from either the Wanchai or Causeway Bay MTR (Mass Transit Railway) stations.

There are numerous travel agencies in Hong Kong that issue Chinese visas. Besides saving you the hassle of visiting the visa office and queuing, a few travel agents can get you more time than the usual 30 days. For a standard single-entry tourist visa valid for one or two months, issued in two working days, expect to pay around HK$120 to HK$140. For a visa issued in 24 hours, HK$180; issued the same day, HK$280. Dual-entry visas cost double.

In Kathmandu

Do not even consider trying to obtain a Chinese visa in Kathmandu unless you are planning to visit Tibet on an expensive group tour. Even if you are planning to whizz through Tibet as quickly as possible and head into China, the Chinese assume that all travellers in Kathmandu are primarily interested in getting into Tibet and for this reason will not issue visas to independent travellers. The best course of action is to obtain a visa before you get to Kathmandu, at home, in Delhi or in Bangkok. Once you have a visa there should be no problem crossing over into Tibet from Nepal – it would be wise to verify this with other travellers beforehand if possible.

Chinese Embassies

Some of the addresses of Chinese embassies and consulates in major cities overseas include:

Australia
15 Coronation Drive, Yarralumla, ACT 2600 (☎ (06) 273 4780, 273 4781)
Consulate: 77 Irving Rd, Toorak, Melbourne, Victoria 3142 (☎ (03) 8220604)

Austria
Metternichgasse 4, 1030 Vienna (☎ (06) 75 31 49, 713 67 06)

Belgium
443-445, Avenue de Tervueren, 1150 Brussels (☎ (02) 771 33 09, 771 26 81)

Canada
515 St Patrick St, Ottawa, Ontario KIN 5H3 (☎ (613) 2342706, 2342682)

Denmark
25 Oregards alle, DK 2900 Hellerup, Copenhagen 2900 (☎ (1) 62 58 06, 61 10 13)

France
11 Ave George V, 75008 Paris (☎ 01.47.23.36.77, 01.47.36.77.90)

Germany
Kurfürstenallee 12, 5300 Bonn 2 (Bad Godesberg) (☎ (0228) 36 10 95, 36 23 50)

Italy
56 via Bruxelles, 56-00198 Rome (☎ (06) 841 34 58, 841 34 67)

Japan
3-4-33, Moto-Azabu, Minato-ku, Tokyo 106 (☎ (03) 34033380, 34033065)

Nepal
Baluwatar, Kathmandu (☎ (01) 412332, 415383)

Netherlands
Adriaan Goekooplaan 7, 2517 JX, The Hague (☎ (070) 355 15 15, 355 92 09)

New Zealand
2-6 Glenmore St, Wellington (☎ 4721382, 4721384)

Spain
C/Arturo Soria 113, 28043 Madrid (☎ (01) 519 4242, 519 3651)

Sweden
Lidovagen 8 115 25, Stockholm (☎ (08) 783 67 39, 783 01 79)

Switzerland
Kalecheggweg 10, 3006 Bern (☎ (031) 44 73 33, 43 45 93)

UK
49-51 Portland Place, London WIN 3AH (☎ (0171) 636 2580, 636 1835)

USA
2300 Connecticut Ave NW, Washington, DC 20008 (☎ 3282500, 3282517)
Consulates: 3417 Montrose Blvd, Houston, Texas 77006; 104 South Michigan Ave, Suite 1200, Chicago, Illinois 60603; 1450 Laguna St, San Francisco, California 94115; 520 12th Ave, New York, New York 10036

Visa Extensions

Visa extensions are handled by the Foreign Affairs Section of the local Public Security Bureau (PSB) – the police force. Government travel organisations – like CITS – have nothing to do with extensions so do not bother asking. Extensions cost Y25 and are available in Lhasa, Shigatse and Tsetang. Visa-extension regulations changed in mid-'94, and at present 30-day visas can only be extended once for 15 days. It is very unusual for a second extension to be granted no matter what the circumstances are – you will simply be directed to the CAAC office in Lhasa and told to get out of the country quick.

Foreign Embassies in China

The Nepalese consulate is the nearest thing Tibet has to an embassy. For details see the Lhasa chapter. If you need to contact your embassy you will need to ring or write to

Beijing, where all of China's foreign embassies are. It is not a good idea to send your passport to any of the addresses listed below to obtain a visa for the next stop of your travels. China's postal service is simply not reliable enough, and some travellers have been left stranded in Lhasa with no passport for weeks on end. Go in person.

In Beijing there are two embassy compounds – Jianguomenwai and Sanlitun. Thus the address would be the one listed below followed by, for example, Jianguomenwai, Beijing.

The following embassies are in Jianguomenwai:

Austria
    5 Xiushui Nanjie (☎ 5322061; fax 5321505)
Bangladesh
    42 Guanghua Lu (☎ 5322521)
Bulgaria
    4 Xiushui Beijie (☎ 5322232)
Czech Republic
    Ritan Lu (☎ 5321531; fax 5324814)
India
    1 Ritan Donglu (☎ 5321908; fax 5324684)
Ireland
    3 Ritan Donglu (☎ 5322691)
Israel
    Room 405, West Wing, China World Trade Centre, 1 Jianguomenwai Dajie (☎ 5050328)
Japan
    7 Ritan Lu (☎ 5322361)
Mongolia
    2 Xiushui Beijie (☎ 5321203)
New Zealand
    1 Ritan Dong 2-Jie (☎ 5322731; fax 5324317)
North Korea
    Ritan Beilu (☎ 5321186)
Philippines
    23 Xiushui Beijie (☎ 5322794)
Poland
    1 Ritan Lu (☎ 5321235; fax 5325364)
Romania
    corner of Ritan Dong 2-Jie and Ritan Donglu (☎ 5323315)
Singapore
    1 Xiushui Beijie (☎ 5323926; fax 5322215)
Slovakia
    Ritan Lu (☎ 5321531; fax 5324814)
Sri Lanka
    3 Jianhua Lu (☎ 5321861; fax 5325426)
Thailand
    40 Guanghua Lu (☎ 5321903; fax 5323986)
UK
    11 Guanghua Lu (☎ 5321961)

USA
    Embassy: 3 Xiushui Beijie (☎ 5323831 ext 274)
    Consulate: Bruce Building, 2 Xiushui Dongjie (☎ 5323431 ext 225)
Vietnam
    32 Guanghua Lu (☎ 5321125)

The Sanlitun Compound in Beijing is home to the following embassies:

Australia
    21 Dongzhimenwai Dajie (☎ 5322331; fax 5324605)
Belgium
    6 Sanlitun Lu (☎ 5321736; fax 5325097)
Cambodia
    9 Dongzhimenwai Dajie (☎ 5321889; fax 5323507)
Canada
    19 Dongzhimenwai Dajie (☎ 5323536; fax 5324072)
Denmark
    1 Sanlitun Dong 5-Jie (☎ 5322431)
Finland
    Tayuan Diplomatic Building, 14 Liangmahe Nanlu (☎ 5321817; fax 5321884)
France
    3 Sanlitun Dong 3-Jie (☎ 5321331)
Germany
    5 Dongzhimenwai Dajie (☎ 5322161; fax 5325336)
Hungary
    10 Dongzhimenwai Dajie (☎ 5321431)
Italy
    2 Sanlitun Dong 2-Jie (☎ 5322131; fax 5324676)
Malaysia
    13 Dongzhimenwai Dajie (☎ 5322531; fax 5325032)
Myanmar (Burma)
    6 Dongzhimenwai Dajie (☎ 5321584; fax 5321344)
Nepal
    1 Sanlitun Xi 6-Jie (☎ 5321795)
Netherlands
    1-15-2 Tayuan Building, 14 Liangmahe Nanlu (☎ 5321131; fax 5324689)
Norway
    1 Sanlitun Dong 1-Jie (☎ 5322261; fax 5322392)
Pakistan
    1 Dongzhimenwai Dajie (☎ 5322504)
Portugal
    Bangonglou 2-72 (☎ 5323497; fax 5324637)
Russia
    4 Dongzhimen Beizhongjie, west of the Sanlitun Compound in a separate compound (☎ 5322051; fax 5324853)
Spain
    9 Sanlitun Lu (☎ 5321986; fax 5323401)

Sweden
    3 Dongzhimenwai Dajie (☎ 5323331; fax 5323803)
Switzerland
    3 Sanlitun Dong 5-Jie (☎ 5322736; fax 5324353)

DOCUMENTS

Given the Chinese preoccupation with impressive bits of paper, it is worth carrying around a few business cards, student cards and anything else that is printed and laminated in plastic.

These additional IDs are useful for leaving with bicycle-renters, who often want a deposit or other security for their bikes – sometimes they ask you to leave your passport, but you should insist on leaving another piece of ID or a deposit. Some hotels also require you to hand over your passport as security, even if you've paid in advance – an old expired passport is useful for these situations.

If you are travelling with your spouse, a photocopy of your marriage certificate just might come in handy should you become involved with the law, hospitals or other bureaucratic authorities. Useful, though not essential, is an International Health Certificate to record your vaccinations.

Chinese student cards, bona fide or otherwise, remain useful despite the fact that the authorities are aware that China is flooded with fakes. Generally, it will help if you can muster together a few phrases of Chinese – at least saying 'I am a student' in Chinese as you hand over the card will give you a bit more credibility.

Passport

A passport is essential, and if yours is within a few months of expiry, get a new one now – many countries will not issue a visa if your passport has less than six months of validity remaining. Be sure that your passport has at least a few blank pages for visas and entry and exit stamps. It could be embarrassing to run out of blank pages when you are too far away from an embassy to get a new passport issued or extra pages added.

Losing your passport is very bad news

indeed. Getting a new one takes time and money, particularly if you are in Tibet. If you lose your passport, you will need to travel to Beijing to apply for a new one. You will definitely need some ID including your photo – many embassies require this before issuing a new passport. Some embassies will accept a driver's license but others will not – again, an expired passport will often save the day.

Chinese Documents

Foreigners who live, work or study in China will be issued with a number of documents, and some of these can be used to obtain substantial discounts on trains, flights, hotels, museums and tourist sites. The most frequently faked document is the so-called 'white card', a simple student ID card with pasted-on photo and usually kept in a red plastic holder (some call it a 'red card' for this reason).

In Tibet it will give you discounts on official bus tickets (not private minibuses), international phone calls and entry tickets for monasteries and other sights. The main saving is likely to be on bus tickets.

Travel Permit

In the early 1980s only 130 places in China were officially open to foreign tourists. Then the number swept to 244, and nowadays most of the country is open except for certain remote border areas, especially those inhabited by ethnic minorities.

Tibet is slightly more complicated than anywhere else in China when it comes to travel permits. The official line in the two provinces that border Tibet and are most used by travellers as points of entry – Sichuan and Qinghai – is that a permit is required to visit Tibet full stop. This is not true. Even if you fork out whatever local authorities are charging for the 'permit', you will never see anything that looks remotely like a travel permit. You are basically paying a bribe that will allow you to travel to Tibet independently.

A real Alien Travel Permit (usually just called Travel Permit) is granted by the PSB for travel (independent or group) to an area that is officially closed. In Tibet itself there are very few areas that fit this category, but applying for travel permits has become something of an institution, and most Lhasa travel agencies, for example, will insist that you obtain one just to visit Sakya or Tsetang. It is very unlikely that such a permit will be checked by anyone once it has been issued.

Another point worth bearing in mind in Tibet is that, if you do stray into some remote area armed with a travel permit and it is checked by local authorities, there is a good chance that you will still be fined because the permit was issued outside the area in question. This is pure corruption and there is little you will be able to do about it.

A travel permit lists the modes of transport you are allowed to take: plane, train, ship or car – and if a particular mode is crossed out then you cannot use it. In Tibet the only mode you will be able to use is car, a wide-ranging category that includes buses, landcruisers, trucks and, at a pinch, tractors.

If you manage to get a permit for an unusual destination, the best strategy is to get to that destination as fast as you can. Other PSBs do not have to honour the permit and can cancel it and send you back. Take your time getting back – you are less likely to be hassled if you are returning to civilisation. Transit points usually do not require a permit, and you can stay the night.

CUSTOMS

Chinese border crossings have gone from being severely traumatic to exceedingly easy for travellers. Although there seem to be lots of uniformed police around, the third degree at Customs seems to be reserved for pornography-smuggling Hong Kongers rather than the stray backpacker.

Note that there are clearly marked 'green channels' and 'red channels', the latter reserved for those with such everyday travel items like refrigerators and colour TV sets.

You are allowed to import 600 cigarettes or the equivalent in tobacco products, two litres of alcoholic drink and one *pint* of perfume. You are allowed to import only 3000 *feet* of movie film, and a maximum of 72 rolls of still film. Importation of fresh fruit is prohibited.

It is illegal to import any printed material, film, tapes, etc 'detrimental to China's politics, economy, culture and ethics'. This is naturally a particularly sensitive area in Tibet, but even here it is highly unusual to have Chinese Customs officials grilling travellers about their reading matter. Some travellers have reported being asked whether they have a Tibet guidebook with them when crossing the border from Nepal to Tibet. The appropriate answer is 'no' – again, this is the exception rather than the rule, however.

MONEY
Currency

The Chinese currency is known as Renminbi (RMB) or the 'People's Money'. The basic unit of this currency is the *yuan* – designated in this book by a capital 'Y'. In spoken Chinese, the word *kuai* is almost always substituted for yuan – in spoken Chinese, it is pronounced *mao*. Ten *fen* make up one jiao, but these days fen are becoming rare because they are worth so little – some people will not accept them.

RMB comes in paper notes issued in denominations of one, two, five, 10, 50 and 100 yuan; one, two and five jiao; and one, two and five fen. Coins are in denominations of one yuan; five jiao; and one, two and five fen. The one-fen note is small and yellow, the two-fen note is blue, and the five-fen note is small and green – all are next to worthless.

Former visitors to China will no doubt cherish fond memories of the Foreign Exchange Certificate (FEC). Well, it is gone, and with it has gone a whole dimension of travel in China. To listen to many travellers in the past, the whole point of their trip was to thwart the authorities' attempts to have them spend their special foreigners' money. But whatever nostalgic memories you might have for the FEC, life is a lot simpler in China without it.

Exchange Rates

At the time of writing, exchange rates were:

Australia	A$1	=	Y6.38
Canada	C$1	=	Y6.02
France	Ffr1	=	Y1.57
Germany	DM1	=	Y5.45
Hong Kong	HK$1	=	Y1.08
Japan	Y100	=	Y8.36
Netherlands	g1	=	Y4.90
New Zealand	NZ$1	=	Y5.36
Switzerland	Sfr1	=	Y6.44
UK	UK£1	=	Y13.29
USA	US$1	=	Y8.39

Changing Money In Tibet, the only place to change foreign currency and travellers' cheques is the Bank of China. The Holiday Inn Lhasa has an exchange service but it is only available for guests. The sensible thing to do is to change as much money as you think you need in Lhasa. There will not be many other opportunities to change money – particularly travellers' cheques – elsewhere in Tibet. Along with Lhasa, Shigatse and Zhangmu have branches of the Bank of China. If you are travelling upcountry, try and get your cash in small denominations: Y100 and Y50 bills are sometimes difficult to get rid of in rural Tibet.

Australian, Canadian, US, UK, Hong Kong, Japanese and most West European currencies are acceptable at the Bank of China. For cash transactions outside the bank, you will need to have US dollars.

Since the floating of the RMB, there is no problem taking the currency out of the country. It would be sensible to change it back into a more useful currency, however. Keep a couple of exchange receipts just in case, though you should not need them.

Black Market There is really not much of a black market in Tibet anymore. Money-changers still work the streets of Lhasa, but as they offer the same rates as the bank (usually slightly less) and there is a *huge* problem with counterfeit notes in China, you would be foolish to use their services.

Change a small amount with them if you get caught cashless after hours.

Counterfeit Notes Chinese authorities have recently been confronted with a deluge of counterfeit notes. The main culprit is the colour photocopier. Very few Tibetans or Chinese will accept a Y100 or Y50 note without first subjecting it to intense scrutiny, and many will not accept old, tattered notes. If you are having trouble spending older notes, they can be exchanged for small change at the Bank of China – counterfeits, however, will simply be confiscated.

How do you recognise a counterfeit? Locals all seem to have their own methods – some reliable, some not. The Chinese government recommends that you first do the obvious (which many Tibetans and Chinese do not), and look for a water mark. If it does not have one, it is obviously a fake. Colours of a note are also an important sign: reds and yellows are much more pronounced in a counterfeit. Drawn lines tend to be less distinct in a fake note. Finally, a popular method on the street is simply to feel the texture of the note between one's fingers. A real note will feel slightly rougher than a counterfeit, which is generally smooth.

Travellers' Cheques Besides the advantage of safety, travellers' cheques are useful to carry in Tibet and China because the exchange rate is actually more favourable than what you get for cash. Cheques from most of the world's leading banks and issuing agencies are now acceptable at the Bank of China – stick to the major companies such as Thomas Cook, American Express and Bank of America, and you'll be OK.

Credit Cards You'll get very few opportunities to splurge on the plastic in Tibet unless you spend a few nights in the Holiday Inn Lhasa. The Lhasa branch of the Bank of China provides credit card advances. It is the only place in Tibet that does.

Telegraphic Transfers Getting money sent to you while you are in China is a real drag, and it is even worse if you happen to be in Lhasa – try to avoid it. On the average, it takes about five weeks for your money to arrive. If you have high-placed connections in the banking system it can take considerably less time, but most travellers are not so fortunate.

Costs

How much will it cost to travel in Tibet? This really depends on how much of Tibet you want to see and how quickly you want to see it. Accommodation is still very economical in Tibet, food is a little more expensive than elsewhere in China, but the major expense – unless you have oodles of time and enjoy rough travelling – is getting around. There is very little in the way of public transport in Tibet, hitching is very time-consuming and if you really want to get around you will probably have to consider hiring a vehicle at rates of approximately US 50 cents per km.

Of course travel costs can be reduced by sharing transport with other travellers, but even so you are probably going to find yourself spending more money on getting around than you would in other parts of China. The per-person cost for a group of six travelling from Lhasa to the Nepalese border, for example, is around US$120. Getting into Tibet also costs. Even the bus fare from Golmud has risen to around US$120 and will probably continue to rise as locals get greedier and travellers willing to pay continue to turn up.

Basic costs, however, are still very reasonable. If you are staying in Lhasa and visiting the surrounding sights you can do it comfortably on around US$10 to US$15 per day – US$4 for accommodation, US$3 on food and the rest on transport and entry fees. You'll be looking at similar costs in other parts of Tibet that you use as a base.

Price Gouging Foreigners are usually charged more for most things in China, and Tibet is no exception. This situation certainly exists in many other developing countries, but the big difference is that in China it is official policy. Every business from the air-

lines and railways to museums and parks are told *by the government* to charge foreigners more. With such official support, many Chinese (and unfortunately Tibetans too) view ripping off foreigners as their patriotic duty. Sometimes the charge is just a little bit more than a local would pay, but at other times it is 20 times more than the local price.

There is very little that you can do about this situation. A student card sometimes serves to waive these foreigners' surcharges, and in some situations determined haggling can bring prices down; but in the case of things like air and bus tickets you just have to pay up and shut up.

Bargaining

Basic bargaining skills are essential for travel in Tibet. You can bargain in shops, hotels, street stalls, travel agents, with rickshaw drivers, with most people – but not everywhere. In large stores where prices are clearly marked, there is usually no latitude for bargaining. In small shops and street stalls, bargaining is expected, but there is one important rule to follow – be polite.

Tibetans are no less adept at driving a hard deal than the Chinese, and like the Chinese aggressive bargaining will usually only serve to firm their conviction that the original asking price is the one they want. Try to keep smiling and firmly whittle away at the price. If this does not work, try walking away. They might call you back, and if they do not there is always somewhere else.

WHEN TO GO

Climate is not such a major consideration as many people might imagine when visiting Tibet. To be sure, winter is very cold and snowfalls can sometimes make travel difficult; but some travellers swear by the winter months. At this time there are few travellers about and Lhasa, for example, is at its most colourful, crowded with nomads.

Spring, early summer and late autumn are probably the best times to be in Tibet. From mid-July through to the end of September, the monsoon starts to effect parts of Tibet. Travel to Western Tibet becomes more difficult and the Friendship Highway sometimes becomes impassable on the Nepal side or on the border itself.

WHAT TO BRING

Bring as little as possible to Tibet. It is much better to buy things as you need them than to throw things away because you've got too much to carry. Lightweight and compact are two words that should be etched in your mind when you are deciding what to bring. Drill holes in the handle of your toothbrush if you have to – anything to keep the weight down!

That advice having been given, there are some things you will want to bring from home.

Carrying Bags

The first thing to consider is what kind of bag you will use to carry all your goods.

Backpacks are the easiest type of bag to carry and a frameless or internal-frame pack is the easiest to manage on buses and trains. The 'expandable' type are most convenient – a clever arrangement of straps cause these packs to shrink or expand according to how much is inside. Packs that close with a zipper can be secured with a padlock. Any pack can be slit open with a razor blade, but a lock will usually prevent pilfering by hotel staff and baggage handlers at airports.

Chinese-made luggage looks good but is generally of poor quality. Zippers are the biggest problem; the stitching also has a tendency to disintegrate. The only good things we can say about Chinese backpacks is that they are cheap and will not attract as much attention as Western models.

Whatever you bring, make it small. A day pack is useful; you can dump your main luggage in a hotel or the left-luggage room at the railway station and head off. A day pack is good for hiking and for carrying extra food on long train rides. A beltpack is OK for maps, extra film and other miscellanea, but do not use it for valuables such as your travellers' cheques and passport – it is an easy target for pickpockets.

If you do not want to use a backpack, a shoulder bag is much easier to carry than a suitcase. Some cleverly designed shoulder bags can also double as backpacks by rearranging a few straps. Forget suitcases.

Clothes

In theory, you only need two sets of clothes – one to wear and one to wash. In Tibet, no matter what time of year you are travelling, you should come prepared with some warm clothing. In the summer months, a couple of inner T-shirts and a good sweater will do the trick unless you are planning to be trekking at high altitudes or heading out to Western Tibet. At other times of the year, ideally you should have thermal underwear, a down jacket, gloves and even a balaclava to protect your ears. Such items can be purchased in Kathmandu or in Chengdu.

Some clothing items can be bought in Lhasa or Shigatse, but the selection is limited and the quality poor. It is much better to come prepared. Good walking boots and heavy socks are essential. Items such as a wide-brimmed hat or a cap to keep off the sun can be bought in Lhasa very cheaply. It is unusual to get rained on in Tibet, but rain pants and a rain poncho can be useful and help to retain body heat.

The question of whether you need a sleeping bag or not depends entirely on where you plan to go and how you plan to travel. Those who aim to spend some time in Lhasa and then head down to Nepal via the sights of Tsang will not need one. Anyone planning on trekking or heading out to Western Tibet should definitely bring one along.

Necessities

A good pair of sunglasses is absolutely essential. Bollés and Ray Bans will block out the UV light and protect your eyes. Also essential is sunscreen (UV) lotion. Hong Kong is a good place to pick up sunscreen with high-protection factors – Tibet is not a good place to work on a tan.

Some pharmaceutical items are hard to find, examples being shaving cream, decent razor blades, mosquito repellent, deodorant, dental floss, tampons and contact lens cleaning solution. Chinese nail clippers are poor quality. If possible, bring a supply of lip salve. Most travellers' lips start to crack within a few days of arriving in Tibet, and if untreated can become *very* painful – you know you are in trouble when your lips start bleeding every time you smile.

An alarm clock is essential for getting up on time to catch flights and buses – make sure yours is lightweight and bring extra batteries. Size AA rechargeable batteries can be bought in China but the rechargers are bulky – bring a portable one and plug adaptors if you cannot live without your Walkman. A gluestick is convenient for sealing envelopes and pasting on stamps.

Following is a checklist of things to consider packing:

Passport, visa, documents (vaccination certificate, diplomas, photocopy of marriage certificate, student ID card), money, money belt or vest, air ticket, address book, reading matter, pen, notepad, gluestick, namecards, visa photos (about 20), Swiss army knife, camera and accessories, extra camera battery, colour slide film, radio, a Walkman and rechargeable batteries, small battery recharger (220 V), padlock, cable lock (to secure luggage on trains), sunglasses, contact lens solution, alarm clock, sweater (only in winter), torch (flashlight) with batteries and bulbs, comb, compass, day pack, long pants, short pants, long shirt, T-shirt, nylon jacket, sweater (only in winter), raincover for backpack, umbrella or rain poncho, razor, razor blades, shaving cream, sewing kit, spoon, sun hat, sunscreen (UV lotion), toilet paper, tampons, toothbrush, toothpaste, dental floss, deodorant, shampoo, laundry detergent, underwear, socks, flip flops, nail clipper, tweezers, vitamins, laxative, Lomotil, condoms, contraceptives, special medications you use and medical kit (see Health section)

Gifts

It is nice to be able to cement friendships or reward favours with a gift. The obvious gift in Tibet is a photograph of the Dalai Lama. Bring some along by all means, but be discriminate in handing them out. Do not give them to people who wander up and ask for a Dalai Lama picture; reserve these photos for people who you feel deserve a gift of some kind. The same applies to other items such as pens – often requested by small children.

TOURIST OFFICES

Tibet is a province of China and does not have tourist offices as such. There are a number of Chinese state-sponsored organisations that provide information on travel in Tibet, but as you might expect they are not particularly forthcoming on information that is useful to individual travellers. Similarly the Tibetan Government in Exile does not provide information specifically related to travel in Tibet. As yet the government has not set up a Tourism Department – understandably not a high priority.

There are numerous Tibet information services scattered around the world and for some travellers these may be worth contacting for background information and information on the latest developments in Tibet. Some of these offices are as follows:

Australia
  Tibet Information Centre: 3 Weld St, Yarralumla, ACT 2600 (☎ 03-616-285-4046)
  Australian Tibetan Society: PO Box 39, Gordon, New South Wales, 2072 (☎ 02-371-4239)
Canada
  Canada-Tibet Friendship Society: PO Box 6588, Postal Section A, Toronto, Ontario, M5W 1X4 (☎ 0416-531-3810)
Denmark
  Danish-Tibetan Cultural Society: St Sohoj, Horsholm Kongevej 40, Horsholm, 2970 (☎ 042-865-715)
France
  Foundation Alexandra David-Neel: Samten Dzong, 27 Avenue du Marachel Juin, Digne, 04000 (☎ 092-31-32-38)
Germany
  Deutsch-Tibetische Kulturgesellshaft: Fritz-Pullig Str 28, Sankt Augustin 2, D-5205 (☎ 02241-20-36-10)
  Tibet Information Service: Florastrasse 22, Langenfeld, D4018 (☎ 02173-75151)
Holland
  Stichting Ontmoeting Met Tibetaanse: Postbus 340, Tilburg, 5000 AH (☎ 013-421-7201)
India
  Library of Tibetan Works & Archives: Gangchen Kyishong, Dharamsala, HP, 176215 (☎ 01892-2467)
  Tibet House: 1 Institutional Area, Lodhi Rd, New Delhi, 110003 (☎ 611-515)
  Tibetan Government in Exile, Office of Information: Gangchen Kyishong, Dharamsala, 176215 (☎ 892-4357)

Japan
  Tibetan Cultural Centre in Japan: 2-31-22,
  Nerima, Nerima-ku, Tokyo (☎ 03-3991-5411)
Nepal
  Office of Tibet (Nepal): PO Box 310, Lazimpat,
  Kathmandu (☎ 97-714-19240, fax 97-7141-
  1660)
Sweden
  Svenska Tibetkommitten: Bondegaten 9 A, 5TR,
  Stockholm, S-116 23 (☎ 08-714-9102)
UK
  Office of Tibet, Tibet House, 1 Culworth St
  London NW87AF UK (☎ 4471-722-5378, fax
  4471-722-0362)
  Orient Foundation: Queen Anne House, 11 Char-
  lotte St, Bath, Avon, BA1 2NE
  (☎ 0225-336-010)
  Tibet Foundation: 10 Bloomsbury Way, London,
  WC1A 2SH (☎ 0171-404-2889, fax 0171-404-
  2366)
  Tibet Information Network: 7 Beck Rd, London,
  E8 4RE (☎ 0181-533-5458)
USA
  Orient Foundation: 261 Madison Avenue, South
  Suite 103, Bainbridge Island, Washington, 98110
  (☎ 0206-842-1114)
  Seattle Tibetan Cultural Centre: 5042 18th
  Avenue NE, Seattle, Washington, 98105
  (☎ 0206-522-6967)
  Tibet House, New York: 3rd Floor, 241 East 32nd
  St, New York, New York, 10016
  (☎ 1212-213-5010, fax 1212-779-9245)
  Tibetan Cultural Centre: 3655 South Snoddy Rd,
  Bloomington, Indiana, 47401
  (☎ 0812-855-8222)

Tourist Offices in China & Tibet

Tibet Tourism Office The main function of
this state-sponsored organisation is to direct
travellers onto group tours in Tibet. In some
cases, if you are flying from Beijing or
Chengdu, it may not be possible to buy an air
ticket without having organised a Tibet Entry
Confirmation Letter through this organisation. Try organising a ticket on your own
first. Otherwise, phone numbers for this
organisation are as follows: Beijing (☎ 01-
401-8822) and Chengdu (028-333-3988).

The equivalent of the Tibet Tourism
Office also has offices in Hong Kong, where
it is known as China Tibet Qomolangma
Tourism (☎ 838-3391) and in Kathmandu,
where it is known as Tibet Tourism Office in
Kathmandu (☎ 01-419-778).

CITS The China International Travel Service
(CITS) deals with China's foreign tourist
hordes, and mainly concerns itself with
organising and making travel arrangements
for group tours.

CTS The China Travel Service (CTS) was
originally set up to handle tourists from
Hong Kong, Macau and Taiwan, and foreign
nationals of Chinese descent (Overseas
Chinese). In recent years, it has become a
keen competitor with CITS. CITS is trying
to cash in on the lucrative Taiwan and Hong
Kong markets, while CTS is targeting the
Western market which was previously the
exclusive domain of CITS.

While few travellers use CTS for travel in
Tibet, many use the CTS offices in Hong
Kong and Macau to obtain visas and book
trains, planes, hovercraft and other transport
to China. CTS can sometimes get you a
better deal on hotels booked through its
office than you could obtain on your own (of
course, this does not apply to backpackers'
dormitories). CTS has 19 branch offices in
Hong Kong, and the Kowloon, Mongkok and
Wanchai offices are open on Sunday and public
holidays. These offices can be crowded – avoid
this by arriving at 9 am when the doors open.

CYTS The name China Youth Travel Service
(CYTS) implies that this is some sort of
student organisation, but these days CYTS
performs essentially the same services as
CITS and CTS. Being a smaller organisation,
CYTS seems to try harder to compete against
the big league. This could result in better
service, but not necessarily lower prices.
CYTS is mostly interested in tour groups, but
individual travellers could find it useful for
booking air tickets or sleepers on the trains.

Other Agencies in Tibet There are a host of
smaller agencies operating in Tibet, mainly
out of Lhasa. Most of them are geared to the
needs of individual travellers and can help
with the hire of vehicles and so on. See the
Lhasa chapter for more details.

Foreign Reps

CITS The main office of CITS in Hong Kong (Tsimshatsui East) can book air tickets to China and has a good collection of English-language pamphlets. The main office and Central branch office are open Monday to Friday from 9 am to 5 pm and Saturday from 9 am to 1 pm; the Mongkok branch office keeps longer hours (Saturday from 9 am to 6.30 pm and half a day on Sunday).

Outside China and Hong Kong, CITS is usually known as the China National Tourist Office. Overseas CITS representatives include:

Australia
China National Tourist Office, 11th floor, 55 Clarence St, Sydney NSW 2000
(☎ (02) 299 4057; fax 290 1958)
France
China National Tourist Office, 51 Rue Saint-Anne, 75002 Paris (☎ (1) 42.96.95.48; fax 42.61.54.68)
Germany
China National Tourist Office, Eschenheimer Anlage 28, D-6000 Frankfurt (☎ (069) 55 52 92; fax 597 34 12)
Hong Kong
Main Office, 6th floor, Tower Two, South Seas Centre, 75 Mody Rd, Tsimshatsui East, Kowloon (☎ 7325888; fax 7217154)
Central Branch, Room 1018, Swire House, 11 Chater Rd, Central (☎ 8104282; fax 8681657)
Mongkok Branch, Room 1102-1104, Bank Centre, 636 Nathan Rd, Mongkok, Kowloon (☎ 3881619; fax 3856157)
Causeway Bay Branch, Room 1104, Causeway Bay Plaza, 489 Hennessy Rd, Causeway Bay (☎ 8363485; fax 5910849)
Japan
China National Tourist Office, 6F Hachidal Hamamatsu-cho Building, 1-27-13 Hamamatsu-cho Minato-ku, Tokyo (☎ (03) 34331461; fax 34338653)
UK
China National Tourist Office, 4 Glentworth St, London NW1 (☎ (0171) 935 9427; fax 487 5842)
USA
China National Tourist Office, Los Angeles Branch, 333 West Broadway, Suite 201, Glendale, California 91204 (☎ (818) 545 7505; fax 545 7506)
New York Branch, Lincoln Building, 60E, 42nd St, Suite 3126, New York, New York 10165 (☎ (212) 867 0271; fax 599 2892)

CTS China Travel Service has overseas representatives which include the following offices:

Australia
Ground floor, 757-759 George St, Sydney, NSW 2000 (☎ (02) 2112633; fax 2813595)
Canada
556 West Broadway, Vancouver, BC V5Z 1E9 (☎ (604) 8728787; fax 8732823)
France
10 Rue de Rome, 75008, Paris (☎ (1) 45.22.92.72; fax 45.22.92.79)
Germany
Düsseldorfer Strasse 14 6000, Frankfurt 1 (☎ (069) 25 05 15; fax 23 23 24)
Hong Kong
Central Branch, 2nd floor, China Travel Building, 77 Queen's Rd, Central (☎ 5217163; fax 5255525)
Kowloon Branch, 1st floor, Alpha House, 27-33 Nathan Rd, Tsimshatsui (☎ 7214481; fax 7216251)
Mongkok Branch, 62-72 Sai Yee St, Mongkok (☎ 7895970; fax 3905001)
Wanchai Branch, ground floor, Southern Centre, 138 Hennessy Rd, Wanchai (☎ 8323888)
China Hong Kong City Branch, 10-12 China Hong Kong City, 33 Canton Rd, Tsimshatsui (☎ 7361863)
Indonesia
PT Cempaka Travelindo, Jalan Hayam Wuruk 97, Jakarta-Barat (☎ (21) 6294256; fax 6294836)
Japan
Nihombashi-Settsu Building, 2-2-4, Nihombashi, Chuo-Ku, Tokyo (☎ (03) 3273-5512; fax 3273-2667)
Macau
Edificio Xinhua, Rua de Nagasaki (☎ 700888, fax 706611)
Malaysia
Yuyi Travel Sdn Bhd, 1st floor, Sun Complex, Jalan Bukit Bintang 55100, Kuala Lumpur (☎ (03) 2427077; fax 2412478)
Philippines
489 San Fernando St, Binondo, Manila (☎ (2) 47-41-87; fax 40-78-34)
Singapore
Ground floor, SIA Building, 77 Robinson Rd, 0106 (☎ 2240550; fax 2245009)
Thailand
559 Yaowaraj Rd, Bangkok 10500 (☎ (2) 2260041; fax 2264712)
UK
24 Cambridge Circus, London WC2H 8HD (☎ (0171) 836 9911; fax 836 3121)

USA

> 2nd floor, 212 Sutter St, San Francisco, California 94108 (☎ (800) 332 2831, (415) 398 6627; fax 398 6669)
>
> Los Angeles Branch, Suite 138, 223 East Garvey Ave, Monterey Park, California 91754 (☎ (818) 288 8222; fax 288 3464)

PUBLIC SECURITY BUREAU (PSB)

The Public Security Bureau (PSB) is the name given to China's police, both uniformed and plain-clothes. Its responsibilities include suppression of political dissidence, crime detection, preventing foreigners and Chinese or Tibetans from having sex with each other (no joke), mediating family quarrels and directing traffic. A related force is the Chinese People's Armed Police Force (CPAPF), which was formed several years ago to absorb cuts in the People's Liberation Army (PLA). The Foreign Affairs Branch of the PSB deals with foreigners. This branch (also known as the 'entry-exit' branch) is responsible for issuing visa extensions and Alien Travel Permits.

The PSB is responsible for introducing and enforcing regulations concerning foreigners. So, for example, they bear responsibility for exclusion of foreigners from certain hotels. If this means you get stuck for a place to stay, they can offer advice. Do not pester them with trivia or try to 'use' them to bully a point with a local street vendor. Do turn to them for mediation in serious disputes with hotels, restaurants, taxi drivers etc. This often works since the PSB wields god-like power – especially in remote areas.

In Tibet it is fairly unusual for foreigners to have problems with the PSB. It does of course depend on what you get up to when you are there. Making an obvious display of your political sympathies (assuming they are pro-Tibetan) is guaranteed to lead to problems. Photographing Tibetan protests will lead to confiscation of your film and possibly a brief detention. Attempting to travel into or out of Tibet on any of the closed routes (mainly to Sichuan or Yunnan) is likely to end in an unpleasant encounter somewhere en route.

If you do have a run-in with the PSB, you may have to write a confession of your guilt and pay a fine. In more serious cases, you can be expelled from China (at your own expense). But in general, if you are not doing anything particularly nasty like smuggling suitcases of dope through Customs, the PSB will probably not throw you in prison.

BUSINESS HOURS & HOLIDAYS

Banks, offices, government departments and the PSB are open from Monday to Saturday. As a rough guide only, they open around 8 to 9 am, close for two hours in the middle of the day (often one hour in winter or three during a heat wave in summer), then reopen until 5 or 6 pm. Sunday is a public holiday, but some businesses are open Sunday morning and make up for this by closing on Wednesday afternoon. CITS offices, Friendship Stores and the foreign-exchange counters in the tourist hotels and some of the local branches of the Bank of China have similar opening hours, and are generally open on Sunday as well, at least in the morning.

Many parks, zoos and monuments have similar opening hours, and are also open on Sunday and often at night. Shows at cinemas and theatres end around 9.30 to 10 pm.

The PRC has nine national holidays during the year:

New Year's Day
> 1 January

Spring Festival
> Usually in February. This is otherwise known as Chinese New Year and starts on the first day of the old lunar calendar. Although officially lasting only three days, many people take a week off from work. Be warned: this is China's only three-day holiday and, unless you have booked a month or two in advance, this is definitely not the time to cross borders (especially the Hong Kong one) or to look for transport or accommodation. Although the demand for accommodation skyrockets, many hotels close down at this time. Book your room in advance and sit tight until the chaos is over!

International Working Women's Day
> 8 March

International Labour Day
> 1 May

Youth Day

4 May – commemorates the student demonstrations in Beijing on 4 May 1919, when the Versailles Conference decided to give Germany's 'rights' in the city of Tianjin to Japan

Children's Day

1 June

Anniversary of the founding of the Communist Party of China

1 July

Anniversary of the founding of the Chinese PLA

1 August

National Day

1 October – celebrates the founding of the PRC on 1 October 1949

CULTURAL EVENTS

The Tibetan cultural heritage took such a hammering during the Cultural Revolution that traditional festivals, once important highlights of the Tibetan year, are only now starting to revive. Tibetan festivals are held according to the lunar calendar, which usually lags at least a month behind our Gregorian calendar. You will need to ask around for the exact dates of festivals.

The following are some of the more important festivals your trip might coincide with:

New Year Festival (Losar)

Taking place in the first week of the first lunar month, Losar is a colourful week of activities; Lhasa is probably the best place to be. There are performances of Tibetan drama, pilgrims make incense offerings and the streets are thronged with Tibetans dressed in their finest.

Lantern Festival

Held on the 15th of the first lunar month, huge yak-butter sculptures are placed around Lhasa's Barkhor circuit.

Mönlam

Known also as the Great Prayer Festival, this is held mid-way through the first lunar month (officially the 25th). An image of Maitreya from Lhasa's Jokhang is borne around the Barkhor, attracting enthusiastic crowds of locals and pilgrims.

Birth of Sakyamuni

This is not exactly a festival, but the seventh day of the fourth lunar month is an important pilgrimage date and sees large numbers of pilgrims in the Holy City of Lhasa and other sacred areas in Tibet.

Sakayamuni's Enlightenment

The 15th day of the fourth lunar month is an occasion for outdoor operas and also sees large numbers of pilgrims at Lhasa's Jokhang and on the Barkhor circuit.

Tashilhunpo Festival

During the second week of the fifth lunar month, Shigatse's Tashilhunpo Monastery becomes the scene of a festival, and a huge thangka is hung.

Worship of the Buddha

During the second week of the fifth lunar month, the parks of Lhasa, in particular the Norbulingka, are crowded with picnickers.

Dreprung Festival

The 30th day of the sixth lunar month is celebrated with the hanging of a huge thangka at Dreprung Monastery. Lamas and monks do masked dances.

Shötun

The Yoghurt Festival is held in the first week of the seventh lunar month. It starts at Dreprung Monastery and moves down to the Norbulingka. Operas and masked dances are held, and locals take the occasion as another excuse for more picnics.

Bathing Festival

The end of the seventh and beginning of the eighth lunar months sees locals washing away the grime of the previous year in rivers.

Gyantse Festival

In the first week of the eight lunar week a festival with horse racing is held in Gyantse.

Harvest Festival

In the first week of the eighth lunar month Tibetans get together and party in celebration of this traditional festival.

Labab Düchen

Commemorating Buddha's descent from heaven, the 22nd day of the ninth lunar month sees large numbers of pilgrims in Lhasa.

Paldren Lhamo

The 15th day of the 10th lunar month has a procession around the Barkhor bearing Paldren Lhamo, protective deity of the Jokhang.

Tsongkhapa Festival

Respect is shown to Tsongkhapa, the founder of Gelugpa order, on the anniversary of his death on the 25th of the 10th lunar month; monasteries light fires and carry images of Tsongkhapa in procession.

Shigatse New Year Festival

The Shigatse New Year Festival is held in the first week of the 12th lunar month.

Year End Festival

Dancing monks can be seen on the 29th of the 12th lunar month in this festival held to dispel the evil of the old year and auspiciously usher in the new one.

POST & TELECOMMUNICATIONS

Tibet is poorly developed when it comes to post and telecommunications. Get all your postcards sent and make all your telephone calls in Lhasa. It is possible to send postcards and letters from Shigatse and Tsetang, but phone calls are near impossible. Lhasa is also the only place in Tibet from where it is possible to send international parcels.

Postal Rates

Letters Rates for international surface mail are shown in the table. For air mail add Y0.50 to the figures.

Postcards International postcards cost Y1.10 by surface mail and Y1.60 by air mail to anywhere in the world.

Aerogrammes These are Y1.90 to anywhere in the world.

Letters

Weight	Rate
0-20 grams	Y1.50
20-50 grams	Y2.90
50-100 grams	Y4.50
100-250 grams	Y8.80
250-500 grams	Y17.90
500-1000 grams	Y34.90
1000-2000 grams	Y49.40

Printed Matter

Weight	Rate
0-20 grams	Y1
20-50 grams	Y1.50
50-100 grams	Y2.80
100-250 grams	Y5.30
250-500 grams	Y9.90
500-1000 grams	Y15.80
1000-2000 grams	Y26.10

Small Packets

Weight	Rate
0-100 grams	Y3.50
100-250 grams	Y7
250-500 grams	Y12.60
500-1000 grams	Y20.90
1000-2000 grams	Y39

Printed Matter Rates for international surface mail are shown in the table. Each additional kg above 2000 grams costs Y11. For air mail add Y0.40 to the figures.

Small Packets Rates for international surface mail are shown in the table. For air mail add Y0.40 to the figures.

Parcels Rates vary depending on the country of destination. The charge for a one-kg parcel sent by surface mail from China to the UK is Y52, to the USA Y30.60, and to Germany Y35.60. The charge for a one-kg parcel sent by air mail to the UK is Y82, to the USA Y77, and to Germany Y70.60.

Post offices are very picky about how you pack things; do not finalise your packing until the thing has got its last Customs clearance. Most countries impose a maximum weight limit (10 kg is typical) on packages received – this rate varies from country to country but the Chinese post office should be able to tell you what the limit is. If you have a receipt for the goods, then put it in the box when you are mailing it, since it may be opened again by Customs further down the line.

Sending Mail

The international postal service seems efficient, and air-mail letters and postcards will probably take around seven to 10 days to reach their destinations. If possible, write the country of destination in Chinese, as this should speed up the delivery.

Receiving Mail

There is a poste restante service care of the Lhasa GPO, but it would be foolhardy to risk sending poste restante letters anywhere else in Tibet. All incoming mail is recorded in a book which is held in the poste restante section of the Lhasa Main Post Office. There is a charge of Y1 for each item of mail you receive.

Telephone

China's creaky phone system is being overhauled, at least in major cities. Whereas just a few years ago calling from Beijing to Shanghai could be an all-day project, now you can just pick up a phone and dial direct. Making international calls has also become much easier.

The improvements in China's telecommunications network has even been extended to Lhasa (elsewhere in Tibet, forget it). Both the Main Post Office and the telecommunications building in Lhasa have international direct-dial telephones.

Domestic long-distance rates from Lhasa vary according to distance, but are cheap. International calls are expensive. Rates for station-to-station calls to most countries in the world are Y18 per minute. Hong Kong is slightly cheaper at Y12 per minute. There is a minimum charge of one minute. Calls are placed by paying a deposit and then calling direct from a phone booth. Time the call yourself if you want to limit your call to certain time. After you make the call, the cost is deducted from your deposit and the balance returned to you. The time is computer controlled and you are not going to be cheated. Telephone cards are also available at a cost of Y150 for Y100 worth of calls.

If you are expecting a call – either international or domestic – try to advise the caller beforehand of your hotel room number. The operators frequently have difficulty understanding Western names, and the hotel receptionist may not be able to locate you. If this cannot be done, then try to inform the operator that you are expecting the call and write down your name and room number – this will increase your chances of success.

Fax, Telex & Telegraph

The Holiday Inn and Tibet Hotel in Lhasa operate business centres complete with fax and telex services, and these are the best places to go if you are serious about getting through to the outside world. Telex services may work at the Lhasa Main Post Office and telecommunications building, but sending a fax is a very hit-and-miss affair. No confirmation note is provided and users are forced to pay for a fax they have no certainty even went through.

TIME

Time throughout China – including Tibet – is set to Beijing time, which is eight hours ahead of GMT/UTC. When it is noon in Beijing it is also noon in far-off Lhasa, even if the sun only indicates around 9 or 10 am.

When it is noon in Lhasa the time in other cities around the world is as follows:

Frankfurt	5 am
Hong Kong	noon
London	4 am
Los Angeles	8 pm
Melbourne	2 pm
Montreal	11 pm
New York	11 pm
Paris	5 am
Rome	5 am
Wellington	4 pm

ELECTRICITY

Electricity is 220 V, 50 cycles AC. Plugs come in at least four designs – three-pronged angled pins (like in Australia), three-pronged round pins (like in Hong Kong), two flat pins (US-style but without the ground wire) or two narrow round pins (European-style). Conversion plugs are easily purchased in Hong Kong but are damn near impossible to find in China.

Considering the remoteness of Tibet, it is surprising just how many towns and villages are supplied with electricity. Nevertheless, most monasteries are very poorly lit and in Western Tibet there is very little in the way of electricity. Bring a good torch or flashlight. Chinese flashlights are awful – 50% of the time they do not work and the bulbs seldom last as long as the batteries. Bring a small but good-quality torch from abroad.

LAUNDRY

Most of the Tibetan-style hotels in the major towns of Tibet will do your laundry for a small fee. It is not unusual for them to get it all muddled up, however, and things often go missing. Chinese hotels and up-market options in Lhasa will also do laundry but are usually more expensive.

WEIGHTS & MEASURES

The metric system is widely used in China. However, the traditional Chinese measures are often used for domestic transactions and you may come across them. The following equations will help.

Metric		Chinese		Imperial
1 metre	=	3 chi	=	3.28 feet
1 km	=	2 li	=	0.62 miles
1 hectare	=	15 mu	=	2.47 acres
1 litre	=	1 gongsheng	=	0.22 gallons
1 kg	=	2 jin	=	2.2 pounds

BOOKS

Literature on Tibet is abundant. Quite a bit of it is of the woolly, how to find enlightenment in the mysterious Land of Snows variety, but there is still a lot of very good stuff about.

People & Society

Probably the best wide-ranging introduction to Tibet can be found in *Tibet – its history, religion and people* (Penguin 1972) by Thubten Jigme Norbu and Colin Turnbull. As the principal author is Tibetan, it is an account from within Tibet and is perhaps not as objective as it might have been. The book does, however, offer a great deal of insight into how Tibetans perceive and organise their world.

Another illuminating glimpse of the Tibetan experience is provided by *Freedom in Exile – the autobiography of the Dalai Lama* (Penguin 1990). With great humility the Dalai Lama outlines his personal philosophy, his hope to be reunited with his homeland and the story of his life.

Also highly recommended is John Avedon's *In Exile from the Land of Snows* (Vintage 1986). This is largely an account of the Tibetan community in Dharamsala, but is an excellent and informative read. For those with an academic bent, look out for *Civilised Shamans – Buddhism in Tibetan Societies* (Smithsonian Institution Press 1993) by Geoffrey Samuel, a fascinating anthropological investigation into the nature of Tibetan Buddhism and its relationship with the indigenous Bön faith – heavy but rewarding reading.

History

It is difficult to find a general history of Tibet that is worth recommending. The standard text is *Tibet & its History* (Shambhala 1984) by Hugh Richardson, a book which is weak on the early history of Tibet and concentrates mainly on the years from the Gelugpa ascendancy to the Chinese takeover. *A Cultural History of Tibet* (Shambhala 1968) by David Snellgrove and Hugh Richardson is perhaps a better introduction to the history and culture of Tibet, but is marred for the general reader by the use of a scholarly and at times indecipherable transliteration system of Tibetan – Samye Monastery for example is rendered *bSam-yas*.

The most accessible history of modern Tibet is *Tears of Blood – a cry for Tibet* (HarperCollins 1992) by Mary Craig. This riveting and distressing account of the Tibetan experience since the Chinese takeover is a catalogue of misery, but should be read by every visitor to Tibet.

An excellent scholarly account of modern Tibet is available in Melvyn Goldstein's *A History of Modern Tibet 1913-1959 – the demise of the lamaist state* (University of California Press 1989). It gives a blow by blow account of the critical years that saw Tibet lose what independence it had to its powerful northern neighbour. Interestingly, it pulls no punches in showing the intrigues, superstitions and governmental ineptitude that led to the demise of the Lhasa government. For anyone with a serious interest in modern Tibetan history this is the definitive account.

Travel Guides

The market has been flooded with guides to Tibet in recent years, and this is one of them. Interestingly, however, general guides aimed at the first-time visitor to Tibet are sparse on the ground.

The Odyssey Illustrated Guide to Tibet (The Guidebook Co 1994) is an exception to this rule, and provides good background reading on Tibet and its attractions with an attractive format. Unlike some of the other books around it is also fairly portable. That said, very few travellers take it with them to Tibet.

Books which assume a reasonably deep interest in Tibet and possibly some prior study of the culture include Stephen Batchelor's classic *The Tibet Guide* (Wisdom 1987), the pick of the pack for serious travellers. Consider getting a copy to read before or after your trip – it is a hefty book to lug around with you. It has been out of print for over a year, but a new edition is due in 1995.

The much-anticipated new arrival on the Tibet guidebook scene is Victor Chan's *Tibet Handbook – a pilgrimage guide* (Moon 1994). This voluminous guide (1099 pages) is difficult to assess. It is without a doubt the most comprehensive guide ever written on Tibet and any serious student of the culture should get hold of a copy. Unfortunately, for the average traveller the book is simply too bulky, too baffling in its organisation and simply too comprehensive to be a useful guide. Travellers using the pilgrimage guide complain that there is so much in the book that it is almost impossible to choose an itinerary – a remarkable, fascinating achievement but probably better off on the bookshelf than in your backpack.

A less bulky companion for the serious traveller is Keith Dowman's *The Power Places of Central Tibet – the pilgrim's guide* (Routlege & Kegan Paul 1988). This interesting (though often obscure to the uninitiated) guide is based on a Tibetan pilgrimage guide by Kyentse Rinpoche (1820-92). It provides background information on sites, both artificial and natural, that are sacred to Tibetans and the object of devotional pilgrimage.

Finally, the best companion to the book you are holding in your hands is *Trekking in Tibet – a traveler's guide* (Cordee 1991) by Gary McCue. This well-researched guide has detailed information on treks around Lhasa, Ü, Tsang and Western Tibet, and is indispensable for anyone whose primary

interest in Tibet is to explore the country on foot.

Travel in Tibet

There are a number of books around documenting the exploits of visitors to Tibet. A classic is Heinrich Harrer's *Seven Years in Tibet* (HarperCollins 1992), translated from German in 1952. It is an account of Harrer's sojourn in Tibet in the final years before the Chinese takeover. He wrote a less worthy sequel in *Return to Tibet*. For starry-eyed dreamers of the Land of Snows *Magic & Mystery in Tibet* (Unwin 1965) by Alexandra David-Neel has the lot – flying nuns, enchanted daggers, ghosts and demons, and also some interesting background information on the mystic side of Tibet.

Anyone heading out to Western Tibet simply has to get hold of a copy of a *A Mountain in Tibet* (Futura 1983) by Charles Allen. This superbly crafted book takes a look at the holy mountain of Kailash and the attempts of early European explorers to reach it and to determine its geographical significance. Peter Hopkirk's *Trespassers on the Roof of the World – the race for Lhasa* is another book that is primarily interested in the European assault on Tibet, but again it is a superb read.

An interesting, little known book worth looking out for is *Captured in Tibet* (Oxford 1990) by Robert Ford. This account by a radio operator employed by the Tibetan government and his subsequent incarceration by the Chinese after their takeover deserves more readers. Ford, as a technician is not blind to the inefficiencies that characterised the former lamaist government but at the same time has a great sympathy for the Tibetan people.

Vikram Seth writes of his epic journey to Tibet across China back in the pioneering days of Tibet independent travel in *From Heaven Lake* (Vintage 1987). It is a straight travel book, and not particularly illuminating on the subject of Tibet, but it is one of the best around all the same.

There are a couple of early travel books around that make for good reads. One of the

A: Roof of the Jokhang, Lhasa (CT)
B: Inside the Jokhang, Lhasa (CT)
C: Front of the Jokhang, Lhasa (CT)

A: Prayer flags in the snow (CT)
B: Barkhor Square (CT)
C: Prostrators, the Jokhang, Lhasa (CT)
D: Prostrators, the Jokhang, Lhasa (CT
E: Prostrators, the Jokhang, Lhasa (CT

classics is Robert Byron's *First Russia, then Tibet* (Penguin 1985). Peter Flemming has written an exciting blow-by-blow account of the British 1904 invasion of Tibet led by Francis Younghusband: *Bayonet's to Lhasa* (Oxford 1961).

Finally, Walt Unsworth has written a 700-page book simply called *Everest* (Grafton 1991). This is the perfect companion for a trip to base camp and further, even if it is a bit hefty to lug around with you. It has fascinating accounts of all the early attempts on the peak and some of the key successful later attempts.

Buddhism

A good, lucid exposition of Tibetan Buddhism? Well, they are not that easy to come by. A lot of them seem to assume that you want to do it rather than just know about it, which of course is a tricky theoretical distinction. But assuming you just want some background to the Buddhist culture of Tibet, the best starting point is a primer on Buddhism in general. The classic for many years now is *Buddhism* by Christmas Humphries – available in Penguin. Another good primer is *A Short History of Buddhism* (Allen & Unwin 1982) by Edward Conze.

Slightly more academic and not that easy to get hold of is an *Introduction to Buddhism – teachings, history & practices* (Cambridge University Press 1990) by Peter Harvey. The fact that Harvey's analysis is rooted both in the theory and practice of Buddhism makes his book particularly interesting, though he spends little time on Tibetan Buddhism. For reading on Mahayana Buddhism in particular *Mahayana Buddhism* (Unwin 1981) by Beatrice Lane Suzuki is a good reference, though slightly tendentious.

The classic introduction to Tibetan Buddhism – though many of its conclusions and observations are disputed by contemporary Tibetologists – is Charles Bell's *The Religion of Tibet* (Oxford University Press 1931). *Civilised Shamans*, probably the best recent book on Tibetan Buddhism, is included in the People & Society entry above.

Bookshops

Bookshops in Tibet? Forget it. Bring your own reading material because the only way you will find anything in Tibet is to swap with other travellers. Bookshops are bad enough in the big cities of China, but in Tibet you'll be lucky to even stumble across a musty copy of *Pride and Prejudice*.

If you are coming in from either Kathmandu or Hong Kong, however, both of these cities are excellent places to stock up on reading material. Kathmandu, with its dozens of cheap second-hand bookshops simply brimming with novels and books about India, Nepal and Tibet, is the best place to stock up. Hong Kong has the disadvantage of being expensive. Still a few good books are essential for travel and are worth splashing out on.

MAPS

It should not come as any surprise that good mapping for Tibet is not particularly easy to come by. Most importantly, if good mapping is crucial to you, do not leave it until you get to Tibet. Stock up on maps at home, in Kathmandu or in Hong Kong.

In Lhasa two maps are available: one in Chinese (and possibly also Tibetan) and one in English. The Chinese map, *Xizang Zizhiqu Ditu* is reasonably detailed, shows major roads and towns and has a scale of 1:2,200,000. It is of very limited use, however, if you do not read Chinese. The English-language map, *China Tibet Tour Map* by the Mapping Bureau of the Tibet Autonomous Region (1993) is a serviceable alternative if you are just travelling around Tibet by road – it would not be very reliable for hiking with. Place names sport some very unconventional spellings and some features seem to be inaccurately placed.

Maps to look out for in Kathmandu include *Tibet – South-Central* by Nepa Maps – 'for extreme and soft trekking' as the mapmakers point out. It is better than the Chinese produced maps, including some topographic features and altitudes but you probably would not want to strike off into the middle of nowhere armed only with it and a compass. Look out also for *Latest Map of Kathmandu to Tibet* by Mandala Maps. It has a scale of 1:000,000, the mapmakers claim, by which they probably mean 1:1,000,000. It is not a bad map but it will almost definitely fall apart after you have opened it up a couple of times.

Back at home, see if you can get hold of the *Map of the People's Republic of China*, produced jointly by the Cartographic Publishing House of China and Esselte of Sweden. Although this huge fold-out map covers all of China, the section on Tibet and the surrounding provinces of Sichuan and Qinghai is very useful. Along with pinyin, Chinese characters are also included, which is very helpful for organising transport. Also worth looking out for is the Nelles Verlag *Himalaya* map, which has excellent detail for central Tibet.

Some of the most detailed maps of China and Tibet available in the West are the aerial survey 'Operational Navigation Charts' (Series ONC). These are prepared and published by the Defense Mapping Agency Aerospace Center, St Louis Air Force Station, Missouri 63118, USA. Cyclists and mountaineers have recommended these highly because of their extraordinary detail. In the UK you can obtain these maps from Stanfords Map Centre, 12-14 Long Acre, London WC2E 9LP (☎ 0171-8361321) or from The Map Shop (☎ 016-8463146), A T Atkinson & Partner, 15 High St, Upton-on-Severn, Worcestershire, WR8 OHJ.

The best maps available for Tibet, published by the US Department of Defense, are the Joint Operations Graphic (JOG) Series 1501 at a scale of 1:250,000. These maps are very difficult to obtain and are semi-classified, but remarkably have been reprinted in Victor Chan's *Tibet Handbook – a pilgrimage guide*, with key additions of religious sites and trekking routes added. For anyone really serious about mapping, this alone should make the book worth buying.

MEDIA
Newspapers
Unless you have fluent Chinese or Tibetan,

you can forget about browsing through newspapers while you are in Tibet. The Beijing English-language publication *The China Daily* occasionally turns up a couple of weeks late, but is a boring read anyway. No foreign newspapers or magazines are available in Lhasa, even at the Holiday Inn.

Radio & TV
There is unlikely to be anything that you would want to watch or listen to on the television or the radio while you are in Tibet. Broadcasts are made in both Mandarin and Tibetan.

FILM & PHOTOGRAPHY
Tibet is one of the most photogenic countries in the world. Bring as much film as you dare (see Customs). There are always notices at the Yak Hotel in Lhasa posted by travellers who have unexpectedly run out and are seeking more slide film – a rare commodity in Lhasa.

Bear in mind, when taking photographs in Tibet, that special conditions prevail. For one, the dust gets into everything – make a point of carefully cleaning your lenses as often as possible. The high altitudes in Tibet also mean that you are dealing with very unusual light conditions. The best time to take photographs is when the sun is low in the sky: early in the morning and late in the afternoon. This does not mean that you should not take photographs at other times, but simply that getting a good exposure becomes more difficult – you are likely to end up with a shot full of dark shadows and bright points of light.

One useful accessory to cope with Tibet's harsh light conditions is a polarising filter. When using it, turn the filter until the contrasts improve; if there are any clouds in the sky, they will become whiter as the sky itself becomes a deeper shade of blue.

Tibet is a great place for portraits. Generally, Tibetans do not mind their photographs being taken. Naturally, it is best to ask first. Tibetans, like other Asian people, do not like having their photographs being taken while they are working (as in monastery restoration crews) and cannot understand why anyone would want to take such a photograph anyway. Be discrete in taking such photographs and try not to upset anyone.

It is not uncommon for Tibetans to ask you to take their photograph. Usually this is because they assume that you have a polaroid camera and can hand them the results immediately. You should try and explain, with sign language if necessary, that you cannot give them a photograph on the spot before shooting.

Buying Film
If you use print film, it is fairly easy to pick up new supplies in Lhasa and Shigatse – Fuji and Konika film are available, almost always in 100 ASA. If, on the other hand, you are using slide film, you should bring as much as you think you need; stock up in Hong Kong or Kathmandu. China is not a good place to buy slide film.

Processing
Believe it or not, it is actually possible to process print film in Lhasa, and with fairly good results. Down in the area of the Potala are a number of shops with the latest Japanese photoprocessing machines. Photos can be processed in a few hours at a reasonable cost.

Do not even think about processing slide film in Tibet, even if someone in Lhasa claims it is possible. Leave your film for home, Bangkok or Hong Kong. Even Kathmandu, with the exception of a couple of professional outfits, is a very risky proposition.

Prohibited Subjects
Photography from planes and photographs of airports and military installations are prohibited; bridges may even be a touchy subject, but it is unlikely.

Restrictions on photography are also imposed at most monasteries, museums and archaeological sites. This has absolutely nothing to do with religious sensitivity and everything to do with China protecting its inept postcard industry; in the case of flash photography such restrictions do protect wall murals from damage. Inside monasteries, a fee is often imposed for taking a photograph. Generally this is Y50 per shot. You are free to take photographs of the exteriors of monasteries, however.

Be aware that these rules are generally enforced. If you want to snap a few photos where you should not, then start with a new roll of film – if it is ripped out of your camera at least you do not lose 20 other photos as well.

HEALTH
Tibet poses particular risks to your health, though for the large part these are associated with the average high altitude of the plateau. There is no need to be overly worried: very few travellers are adversely affected by the altitude for very long, and greater risks present in the form of road accidents and dog bites.

Sensible travellers will be as prepared as possible when travelling to Tibet. It is a very isolated place, and outside Lhasa there is very little in the way of expert medical care available. Read the following section carefully for information on how to make your trip a safer one.

Travel Health Guides
There are a number of books available on travel health. Probably the best around is *Staying Healthy in Asia, Africa & Latin America* (Volunteers in Asia). Another good, comprehensive guide is Dr Richard Dawood's *Travellers' Health* (Oxford University Press).

Those considering taking their children to Tibet should consider travelling with a copy of *Travel with Children* (Lonely Planet Publications) by Maureen Wheeler.

Predeparture Preparations
Get your teeth checked and have any necessary dental work done before you leave home. Always carry a spare pair of glasses, contact lenses or your prescription in case of loss or breakage.

Health Insurance Although you may have medical insurance in your own country, it is probably not valid in China. But ask your insurance company anyway – you *might* already be covered.

A travel insurance policy is a very good idea and investment – the best policies protect you against cancellation penalties on advance-purchase flights, against medical costs through illness or injury, against theft or loss of possessions, and against the cost of additional air tickets if you get really sick and have to fly home.

Obviously, the more extensive the coverage, the higher the premiums, but at a minimum you should at least be covered for medical costs due to injuries. Read the small print carefully since it is easy to be caught out by exclusions – injuries due to 'dangerous activities' like skiing or bicycling might be excluded, for example.

If you undergo medical treatment, be sure to collect all receipts and copies of your medical report, in English if possible, for your insurance company.

If you purchase an International Student Identity Card (ISIC) or Teacher Card (ISTC), you may be automatically covered depending on which country you purchased the card in. Check with the student travel office to be sure.

If you are neither a student nor a teacher, but you are aged between 15 and 25 years, you can purchase an International Youth Identity Card (YIEE) which entitles you to the same benefits. Some student travel offices also sell insurance to others who do not hold these cards.

Medical Kit You should assemble some sort of basic first-aid kit. You will not want it to be too large and cumbersome for travelling,

---

Tibetan Medicine

The basic underpinnings of Tibetan medicine share much with other Asian medical traditions, which according to some scholars made their way to the East via India from ancient Greece. While the Western medical tradition treats symptoms that indicate a known medical condition (measles or mumps, say), the Eastern medical tradition looks to symptoms as indications of an imbalance in the body and seeks to restore that balance.

It is wrong to assume, however, that Tibetan medicine was practiced by trained doctors in clinics scattered across the land. The Tibetan medical tradition is largely textual, derives from Indian sources and was studied in some monasteries in much the same way that Buddhist scriptures were studied. When Tibetans needed medical help they usually went to a local 'apothecary' who sold concoctions of herbs; equally, help was sought in prayers and good luck charms.

The theory of Tibetan medicine is based on an extremely complex system of checks and balances between what can be broadly described as three 'humours' (related to state of mind), seven 'bodily sustainers' (related to the digestive track) and three 'eliminators' (related to the elimination of bodily wastes). And if the relationship of the three humours of desire, egoism and ignorance with bodily functions were not complex enough, there is the influence of harmful spirits to consider. There are 360 harmful female influences, 360 harmful male influences, 360 malevolent Naga (water spirits) influences and finally 360 influences stemming from past karma. All these combine to produce 404 basic disorders and 84,000 illnesses!

How does a Tibetan doctor go about assessing the condition of a patient? The most important skill is pulse diagnosis. A Tibetan doctor is attuned to 360 'subtle channels' of energy that run through the body's skin and muscle, internal organs, and bone and marrow. The condition of these channels can be ascertained through six of the doctor's fingers (the first three fingers of each hand). Tibetan medicine also relies on urine analysis as an important diagnostic tool.

If Tibetan diagnostic theory is mainly Indian in influence, treatment owes as much to Chinese medicine as to Indian. Herbal concoctions, moxibustion (a treatment that involves burning mugwort) and acupuncture are all drawn on to restore balance to the body. Surgery was used in the early days of Tibetan medicine, but was outlawed in the 9th century when a king's mother died during an operation. ■

but some items which could be included in your medical kit are:

Band-Aids or gauze bandage with plaster (adhesive tape); a thermometer; tweezers; scissors; UV lotion; multi-vitamins; water-sterilisation tablets; chapstick (lip salve); antibiotic ointment; an antiseptic agent (Dettol or Betadine); any medication you are already taking; diarrhoea medication (Lomotil or Imodium); rehydration mixture for treatment of severe diarrhoea; paracetamol (Panadol), ibuprofen or aspirin for pain and fever; antihistamine (such as Benadryl) useful as a decongestant for colds, allergies, to ease reactions to insect bites or stings; a course of antibiotics (probably 30 tablets of 250 mg tetracycline, but check with your doctor); Flagyl (for giardia) and contraceptives, if necessary.

Some of these medications are available in Lhasa at low cost, but finding them when you urgently need them can often prove problematic.

Ideally, antibiotics should be administered only under medical supervision and should never be taken indiscriminately. Overuse of antibiotics can weaken your body's ability to deal with infections naturally and can reduce the drug's efficacy on a future occasion. Take only the recommended dose as prescribed. It is important that once you start a course of antibiotics, you finish it even if the illness seems to be cured earlier. If you stop taking the antibiotics after one or two days, complete relapse is likely. If you think you are experiencing a reaction to any antibiotic, stop taking it immediately and consult a doctor. Antibiotics can be bought cheaply across the counter in many countries in South-East Asia (Taiwan and Thailand are good places to stock up).

Vaccinations The single vaccination requirement for entering China applies only for those who arrive within six days of leaving or transiting a yellow fever infected area.

This is not to say that you can forget about vaccinations altogether; you should give them particular thought if you are travelling on to Nepal. Gamma Globulin (for hepatitus A), typhoid and tetanus are all worthwhile vaccinations for Tibet. Other vaccinations recommended by various health authorities include: cholera (not necessary for Tibet, but a possible risk elsewhere in the region), meningitis (necessary for Nepal but not Tibet), rabies (it is uncertain whether there is rabies in Tibet; note that vaccination does not make you immune and any bites should be followed by further treatment), hepatitis B, BCG (tuberculosis), polio, diphtheria and TABT (protects against typhoid, paratyphoid A and B, and tetanus).

You should have your vaccinations recorded in an International Health Certificate. If you are travelling with children, it is especially important to be sure that they've had all necessary vaccinations.

Basic Rules

Almost everyone gets sick at least once while they are in Tibet. The good news is that it is very rarely anything more than a dose of the runs that generally clears up in a day or so. Paying attention to what and where you eat and drink will help to minimise the risks of being laid up for a few days.

Water If possible, try to avoid drinking unboiled or untreated water in Tibet. In urban centres this is no problem as Tibetans, like the Chinese, boil their drinking water. In the country you should boil your own water or treat it with water purification tablets. Soft drinks and beer are always available wherever there is a shop, and these are always safe to drink. Locally brewed beer, *chang*, however, is another matter. It is often made with contaminated well water – add a purification tablet to it if possible.

Water Purification Even though water boils at a lower temperature at high altitudes, providing you are below 6000 metres, boiling water should be enough to kill the organisms that cause intestinal problems. You can boil your own water if you carry an electric immersion coil and a large metal cup (plastic will melt).

Bringing water to a boil is sufficient to kill most bacteria, but 20 minutes of boiling is required to kill amoebic cysts. While these nasty things are relatively rare, they are not unknown in Tibet.

In situations where it is not possible to boil water, water purification tablets should be used. Water is more effectively sterilised by iodine than by chlorine tablets; the former kills amoebic cysts. However, iodine is not safe for prolonged use, and also tastes horrible.

Food Sad to say, Chinese restaurants are almost always more hygienic than their Tibetan counterparts. Tibetan restaurants in Lhasa generally seem to be OK, but outside Lhasa it is almost always better to eat Chinese food if it is available. Basically it is a matter of using common sense – a grotty, dirty little restaurant is likely to be serving grotty, dirty food.

Those travelling upcountry are advised to bring a supply of instant noodles. *Tsampa*, a mixture of barley flour mixed with whatever fluid is available (even beer), quickly becomes very boring if you are not Tibetan.

Nutrition It is very difficult to have a balanced diet in Tibet. Outside Lhasa and Shigatse, there is very little in the way of fruit or vegetables. You might consider taking a supply of dried fruit with you, though there is only so much of this stuff you can lug around. If you are planning to travel for an extended period in Tibet, it would be wise to bring a supply of multi-vitamins along.

Toilets Chinese toilets might be fairly dismal, but Tibetan toilets make them look like little bowers of heaven. The standard model is a deep hole in the ground that bubbles and gives off noxious vapours. On the plus side, Tibetans seem to like doing their business in high places, and there are some fabulous 'toilets with a view' in Tibet. Honours go to the Samye Monastery guesthouse and the small village of Passum en route to Everest Base Camp.

With the exception of the odd hotel here and there, toilets in Tibet are of the squat variety – as the clichés go, good for the digestion and character building too. Stock up on toilet paper in Lhasa and Shigatse. And finally, a tip for the boys: if there's nobody about, the women's toilets are always cleaner than the men's – strange, that...

Other Precautions Good sunglasses are an essential protection against harmful UV rays up on the high plateau. Do not even consider buying Chinese-made sunglasses; they are useless. You should also use zinc cream or some other barrier cream for your nose and lips.

If you are sweating profusely, you are going to lose a lot of salt and that can lead to fatigue and muscle cramps for some people. If necessary you can make it up by putting extra salt or soy sauce in your food (a teaspoon a day is plenty), but do not increase your salt intake unless you also increase your water intake.

Everyday Health The normal body temperature is 98.6°F or 37°C; more than 2°C higher is a 'high' fever. A normal adult pulse rate is from 60 to 80 per minute (children from 80 to 100, babies from 100 to 140). You should know how to take a temperature and a pulse rate. As a general rule the pulse increases about 20 beats per minute for each 1°C rise in fever.

Respiration (breathing) rate is also an indicator of illness. Count the number of breaths per minute: between 12 and 20 is normal for adults and older children (up to 30 for younger children, 40 for babies). People with a high fever or serious respiratory illness (like pneumonia) breathe more quickly than normal. More than 40 shallow breaths a minute in an adult usually means pneumonia.

Altitude Sickness

Acute Mountain Sickness (AMS) is associated with a rapid ascent to high altitudes, something you are very likely to do when you visit Tibet. AMS is a notoriously fickle affliction and can visit even the most seasoned high-altitude trekker or walker. But for the average person, AMS, or at least some of its symptoms, is likely to be experienced upon first reaching altitudes of between 3600 and 4200 metres.

The major risk factor in AMS is the speed with which you make your ascent. Travellers who fly or bus into Lhasa, which is at just over 3600 metres, are much more likely to experience symptoms of AMS than someone who (if it were possible) hiked there. As almost all travellers arrive in Tibet by way of a very rapid ascent, you can expect to experience some symptoms of AMS. In most cases they are mild, belonging to the benign variety of AMS, and recede within a few days or, at the most, a week.

Causes AMS is linked to low atmospheric pressure. Those who travel up to Everest Base Camp, for instance, have reached an altitude where atmospheric pressure is about half that of sea level. The problem at these kinds of altitudes is a lack of pressure to drive the oxygen into the blood supply.

Fortunately the body automatically starts to compensate for reduced levels of oxygen in the blood by rapid breathing and increased heart beat. With time the blood's oxygen-carrying capabilities will also improve. In cases where the ascent is too high and too fast, however, these compensatory reactions may not kick into gear fast enough and the result will be hypoxia, a condition resulting from a shortage of oxygen.

Benign AMS Some of the symptoms of benign AMS are likely to be experienced by all visitors to Tibet. A typical symptom is sleeplessness: many travellers have trouble sleeping for the first few days after arriving in Lhasa, a problem which in rare cases persists as long as a week. Other typical symptoms are loss of appetite, weariness, headache and nausea. In some cases (though this is rare), the nausea may result in vomiting. If all these symptoms are combined and persist, they should be taken as an important warning that you are at risk of experiencing the next, and more dangerous, stage of AMS.

Malignant AMS Malignant AMS can be life threatening and any signs of its onset should

be taken very seriously indeed. Those experiencing malignant AMS may not themselves be in a position to recognise the symptoms, and trekkers should keep an eye on each other and be prepared to make a decision to take someone lower if they are displaying any of the typical symptoms of the illness.

Malignant AMS takes two forms, though it is not unusual for them to occur together: pulmonary AMS and cerebral AMS. The pulmonary form is characterised by a build-up of fluid in the lungs. The victim will be constantly breathless, even while resting; characteristically there will be a cough that produces white sputum and the victim's lips turn blue. Cerebral AMS is characterised by headaches, abnormal behaviour and a condition referred to as the 'drunken walk'. These signs should be taken very seriously; if victims are not taken to lower altitudes it is usual for them to fall into a coma which usually results in death.

One thing to note is that, while the symptoms of benign AMS often precede those of malignant AMS, this is not necessarily the case. Malignant AMS sometimes strikes with little or no warning.

Treatment The most effective treatment for malignant AMS is to get down to a lower altitude as quickly as possible. In less severe cases the victim will be able to stagger down with some support. It is often the case, however, that victims will need to be carried. Whatever the case, do not delay. Instant action may save the victim's life. Delay may be *fatal*.

In the case of pulmonary AMS, a descent of 700 to 1000 metres generally sees immediate improvement in the condition. Victims of cerebral AMS, however, particularly if they have fallen into a coma, should be flown out of Tibet as quickly as possible. Even after the descent, it is not uncommon for coma to persist.

With the exception of Lhasa, it is highly unlikely that oxygen will be available. If it is available, it is a poor substitute for rapid descent and should be administered in combination with the latter. A high oxygen concentration and high flow rate is required.

Doctors are divided about the use of medication for treating AMS. Again, it is only effective in combination with a descent to lower altitudes. Diamox (acetazolamide) is thought to be effective for treating benign AMS, but generally is unnecessary – consult your physician.

Prevention As already noted, the best prevention for AMS is to avoid rapid ascents to high altitudes. If you fly or bus to Lhasa, take it easy for at least three days – for most travellers this is enough to get over any initial ill-effects. At this point you might step up your programme by visiting a few sights around town. Within a week you should be ready for something a bit more adventurous, but do not push yourself to do anything that you are not comfortable with.

On arriving in Tibet, smokers should try and cut back on smoking as much as possible – ideally stop altogether. Tobacco smoke reduces the lungs' ability to absorb oxygen. Alcohol should also be avoided, as it will dehydrate you, and in dry Tibet it is necessary to keep your fluid intake up.

Trekkers should bear in mind the climber's adage: 'climb high, sleep low'. High day climbs followed by a descent back to lower altitudes for the night are good preparation for high-altitude trekking.

Finally, the symptoms of AMS, however mild, are a warning. Take them seriously and do not overexert yourself when your body is telling you to take it easy.

Other Medical Problems & Treatment
Self-diagnosis and treatment can be risky, so wherever possible seek qualified help. Although we give treatment dosages in this section, they are for emergency use only. Medical advice should be sought before administering any drugs.

Sunburn It is very easy to get sunburnt at high elevations. Sunburn can be more than just uncomfortable. Among the undesirable effects are premature skin ageing and possible skin cancer in later years. Sunscreen (UV lotion), sunglasses and a wide-brimmed hat are good means of protection.

Sunscreens are rated by a sun protection factor (SPF). The number on a sunscreen indicates the protection factor the sunscreen provides: thus an SPF of 12 means that you can spend 12 hours in the sun and receive the same amount of sun that you would receive in one hour without the sunscreen. In Tibet, the higher the protection factor the better. Lotions with SPFs of 40 or higher are available.

Those with fair complexions should bring reflective sunscreen (containing zinc oxide or titanium oxide) with them. Apply the sunscreen to the nose and lips (and possibly the tops of your ears if you are not wearing a hat), it is effective for protecting particularly sensitive areas.

Cold Winter in Tibet is not to be taken lightly. Too much cold is probably more dangerous than too much heat, and can lead to the fatal condition known as hypothermia. If you are trekking at high altitudes or simply taking a long bus trip over mountains, particularly at night, be prepared.

Hypothermia occurs when the body loses heat faster than it can produce it and the core temperature of the body falls. It is surprisingly easy to progress from very cold to dangerously cold due to a combination of wind, wet clothing, fatigue and hunger, even if the air temperature is above freezing. It is best to dress in layers; silk, wool and some high-tech artificial fibres are all good insulating materials. A hat is important as a lot of heat is lost through the head. A strong, waterproof outer layer is essential, as keeping dry is vital. Carry basic supplies, including food containing simple sugars to generate heat quickly and lots of fluid to drink.

Symptoms of hypothermia are exhaustion, numb skin (particularly toes and fingers), shivering, slurred speech, irrational or violent behaviour, lethargy, stumbling, dizzy spells, muscle cramps and violent bursts of energy. Irrationality may take the form of sufferers claiming they are warm and trying to take off their clothes.

To treat hypothermia, first get the patient out of the wind and/or rain, remove their clothing if it is wet and replace it with dry, warm clothing. Give them hot liquids – not alcohol – and some high-energy, easily digestible food. This should be enough for the early stages of hypothermia, but if it has gone further it may be necessary to place the victim in a warm sleeping bag and get in with them. Do not rub them. Hypothermia dulls sensitivity to pain, and putting someone too near a fire or stove can easily cause burns without anyone realising it. The same goes for putting someone in too hot a bath.

Motion Sickness Motion sickness is a normal reaction to unpredictable movement and is something that experienced travellers rarely suffer from. Your Chinese and Tibetan neighbours on buses and trucks are far more likely to succumb – if they start looking green, be ready to jump out of the way.

The usual symptoms are familiar to anyone who has suffered from motion sickness: discomfort in the stomach, sweating and increased salivation followed by nausea and vomiting. Interestingly, a desire to sleep is also classified as a symptom of motion sickness, and it may be the only symptom experienced – something most bus travellers should be familiar with.

Most preventives to motion sickness are based on common sense. Eat lightly before travelling; try and sit towards the front or centre of a bus (not the back, where movement is greatest); if you start to feel the onset of motion sickness, open a window – fresh air helps. It is thought that most preventive medications are fairly ineffective in minimising the effects of motion sickness, though they may have a placebo effect.

Diarrhoea Travellers' diarrhoea has been around a long time – even Marco Polo had it. Diarrhoea is often due simply to a change of diet or bacteria or minerals in the local water which your system is not used to. If

you do get diarrhoea, the first thing to do is wait – it rarely lasts more than a few days.

Diarrhoea will cause you to dehydrate, which will make you feel much worse. The solution is not simply to drink water, since it will run right through you. You'll get much better results by mixing your water with oral rehydration salt, a combination of salts (both sodium and potassium chloride) and glucose. Dissolve the powder in *cool* water (never hot!) and drink, but do not use it if the powder is wet. The quantity of water is specified on the packet. Oralit is also useful for treating heat exhaustion caused by excessive sweating.

If the diarrhoea persists then the usual treatment is Lomotil or Imodium tablets. The maximum dose for Lomotil is two tablets three times a day. Both Lomotil and Imodium are prescription drugs in the West, but are available over the counter in most Asian countries. However, neither is available in China – a good Chinese equivalent is berberine hydrochloride *(huang lian su)*. Anti-diarrhoeal drugs do not cure anything, but slow down the digestive system so that the cramps go away and you do not have to go to the toilet all the time. Excessive use of these drugs is not advised, as they can cause dependency and other side effects. Furthermore, the diarrhoea serves one useful purpose – it helps the body expel unwanted bacteria.

Fruit juice, tea and coffee can aggravate diarrhoea – again, water with oral rehydration salts is the best drink. It will help tremendously if you eat a light, fibre-free diet. Yoghurt or boiled eggs with salt are basic staples for diarrhoea patients. Later you may be able to tolerate rice porridge or plain white rice. Keep away from vegetables, fruits and greasy foods for a while. If the diarrhoea persists for a week or more, it is probably not simple travellers' diarrhoea – it could be dysentery and it might be wise to see a doctor.

Giardiasis Commonly known as giardia, this is an infection with *Giardia lamblia* another type of amoeba which causes severe diarrhoea, nausea and weakness, but does not produce blood in the stool or cause fever. Unlike amoebic dysentery, which is most common in the tropics, giardiasis is found in mountainous and cold regions. Epidemics have been reported in Zermatt, Switzerland; Aspen, Colorado (USA); St Petersburg (Leningrad) in Russia; and Tibet. Mountaineers often suffer from this problem. Just brushing your teeth using contaminated water is sufficient to make you get giardiasis. Many kinds of mammals harbour this parasite, so you can get it easily from drinking 'pure mountain water' unless the area is devoid of animals.

Although the symptoms are similar to amoebic dysentery, giardia will not migrate to the liver and other organs – it stays in the intestine and therefore is much less likely to cause long-term health problems.

Giardiasis can only be cured with an anti-amoebic drug like metronidazole (Flagyl) – again, never drink alcohol while taking Flagyl. Without treatment, the symptoms may subside and you might feel fine for a while, but the illness will return again and again, making your life miserable.

To treat giardia, the proper dosage of Flagyl is different than for amoebic dysentery. Take one 250-mg tablet three times daily for 10 days. It can sometimes be difficult to rid yourself of giardia, so you might need laboratory tests to be certain you are cured.

Flagyl is not easily obtained in Tibet, though equivalent drugs are available in Lhasa. If you are going to be travelling in high mountain areas, it might be prudent to keep your own stock of Flagyl with you.

Bacillary Dysentery Diarrhoea with blood or pus and fever is usually bacillary dysentery. Since it is caused by bacteria infecting the gut, it can be treated with antibiotics like tetracycline, or a sulphur drug, but before you roll out the heavy artillery, be sure you've really got this disease. If you do take tetracycline, the usual dose is 250-mg tablets, taken four times daily for about a week. In most cases, bacillary dysentery will

eventually clear up without treatment – the exception might be for children, who seem to be more vulnerable to this type of infection. Be sure to use water with rehydration salts to prevent dehydration.

Amoebic Dysentery Diarrhoea with blood or pus but without fever is usually amoebic dysentery. This is a disease you should not neglect because it will not go away by itself. In addition, if you do not wipe out the amoeba while they are still in your intestine, they will eventually migrate to the liver and other organs, causing abscesses which could require surgery. It is not common in Tibet, but is easily mistaken for giardiasis (which *is* common in Tibet – see the above section).

The most sure-fire cure for amoebic dysentery is metronidazole (Flagyl), an anti-amoebic drug. It will wipe out amoeba no matter where they reside in the body, even if in the liver and other organs. The dosage is three 250-mg tablets (750 mg) three times daily for seven to 10 days. Flagyl is also available in 500-mg tablets, so in that case you take 1½ tablets per dose. If you take Flagyl, *do not* under any circumstances consume alcohol at the same time – not a drop! Flagyl and alcohol together can cause a severe reaction.

Hepatitis Hepatitis is a disease which affects the liver. There are several varieties, most commonly hepatitis A and B.

Hepatitis A This occurs in countries with poor sanitation – this definitely includes Tibet. It is spread from person to person via infected food or water, or contaminated cooking and eating utensils.

Hepatitis is often spread in China and Tibet due to the custom of sharing food from a single dish rather than using separate plates and a serving spoon. It is a wise decision to use the disposable chopsticks now freely available in most restaurants in Tibet, or else buy your own chopsticks and spoon.

Symptoms appear from 15 to 50 days after infection (generally after around 25 days) and consist of fever, loss of appetite, nausea, depression, complete lack of energy, and pains around the bottom of your rib cage (the location of the liver). Your skin turns progressively yellow and the whites of your eyes change from white to yellow to orange.

The best way to detect hepatitis is to watch the colour of your urine, which will turn a deep orange no matter how much liquid you drink. If you have not drunk much liquid and/or you are sweating a lot, do not jump to conclusions since you may just be dehydrated.

The severity of hepatitis A varies; it may last less than two weeks and give you only a few bad days, or it may last for several months and give you a few bad weeks. You could feel depleted of energy for several months afterwards. If you get hepatitis, rest and good food is the only cure; do not use alcohol or tobacco since that only gives your liver more work to do. It is important to keep up your food intake to assist recovery.

A vaccine for hepatitis A came on the market in 1992. At the time of writing it was available in Hong Kong (two shots, two weeks apart). Check with your doctor.

Hepatitis B This is transmitted in similar ways to the AIDS (HIV) virus for example, by sexual intercourse; by contaminated needles; or, in the case of infants, by being inherited from an infected mother. Some Chinese 'health clinics' re-use needles without proper sterilisation – no one knows how many people have been infected this way. Acupuncture can also spread the disease.

There is a vaccine for hepatitis B, but it must be given before you've been exposed to the virus. Once you've got the virus, you are a carrier for life and the vaccine is useless. Therefore, you need a blood test before the vaccine is administered to determine if you are a carrier. The vaccine requires three injections each given a month apart, and it is wise to get a booster every few years thereafter. Unfortunately, the vaccine is expensive.

Other Recent research has found other varieties of hepatitis of which little is yet known. Hepatitis C and other strains are considered serious. These are usually spread by blood transfusions and therefore are not diseases that you are going to pick up through casual contact.

Typhoid Typhoid fever is another gut infection transmitted in contaminated water and food. As with cholera, epidemics can occur after floods because of sewage backing up into drinking water supplies. Vaccination against typhoid is useful but not totally effective. Typhoid is one of the most dangerous infections, so medical help must be sought for it.

In the early stages of infection, typhoid victims may feel like they have a bad cold or flu on the way, as early symptoms are a headache, a sore throat, and a fever which rises a little each day until it is around 40°C or more. Without treatment, the illness will either kill you or begin to subside by the third week.

Chloramphenicol is the recommended antibiotic but there are fewer side effects with ampicillin. The adult dosage is two 250-mg capsules, four times a day. Children aged between eight and 12 years should have half the adult dose; younger children should have one-third the adult dose.

Patients who are allergic to penicillin should not be given ampicillin.

Polio Polio is also a disease spread by insanitation and is found more frequently in hot climates. The effects on children can be especially devastating – they can be crippled from an early age. An excellent vaccination is available, and having a booster every five years is recommended.

Diseases Spread by People & Animals
Respiratory Infection The China Syndrome, one of the greatest hazards to your health in China and Tibet, is a host of respiratory infections which we normally call 'the flu' or just 'the common cold'. You may have heard of the 'Shanghai flu', or various other influenza strains named after Chinese cities.

The fact is that China is one vast reservoir of respiratory viruses and practically the entire population is stricken during the winter, but even during the summer it is easy to get ill.

What distinguishes the Chinese flu from the Western variety is the severity and the fact that the condition persists for months rather than days. Like any bad cold, the flu starts with a fever, chills, weakness, sore throat and a feeling of malaise normally lasting a few days. After that, a prolonged case of coughing and bronchitis sets in, characterised by coughing up large quantities of thick green phlegm, occasionally with little red streaks (blood). It is the bronchitis that really gets you – it makes sleep almost impossible, and this exhausting state of affairs can continue for as long as you stay in the country. Sometimes it even leads to pneumonia.

Why is it such a serious problem in China? Respiratory infections are aggravated by cold weather, air pollution, chain-smoking and overcrowded conditions which increase the opportunity for infection. But the main reason is that Chinese people spit a lot, thereby spreading the disease. It is a vicious circle: they are sick because they spit and they spit because they are sick.

During the initial phase of influenza, bed rest, drinking warm liquids and keeping warm are helpful. The Chinese treat bronchitis with a powder made from the gall bladder of snakes – a treatment of questionable value, but there is probably no harm in trying it.

If you continue to cough up green phlegm, run a fever and cannot seem to get well, it is time to roll out the heavy artillery – you can nuke it with antibiotics. Tetracycline (250 mg) taken orally four times daily for a minimum of five days is usually highly effective, but note the previously mentioned warnings about using antibiotics.

Finally, if you cannot get well in China, leave the country and take a nice holiday on a warm beach in Thailand.

No vaccine offers complete protection, but there are vaccines against influenza and pneumococcal pneumonia which might help. The influenza vaccine is good for no more than a year.

Tetanus It would be prudent to get a tetanus vaccination before your arrival in Tibet. If you've already been vaccinated once, you still need a booster every five years to maintain immunity.

Rabies Officially there is no rabies in Tibet. All the same, there are an awful lot of rabid-looking dogs about. If you are bitten, it would be foolish not to get treatment. Recent surveys by the Chinese indicate that incidents of rabies may have been found in Qinghai Province, which borders Tibet. Some travellers have also written in and told us about an outbreak of rabies in the area of Tsurphu Monastery north of Lhasa. Take care.

If you are bitten by an animal (or are even licked on a break in the skin), try to get the wound flushed out immediately with soapy water. It would be prudent to seek professional treatment since rabies carries a nearly 100% fatality rate if it reaches the brain. How long you have from the time of being bitten until it is too late varies – anywhere from 10 days to a year depending on where you were bitten. Those bitten around the face and upper part of the body are in the most immediate danger. Do not wait for symptoms to occur – if you think there is good chance that you've been bitten by a rabid animal, get medical attention promptly. At the time of writing, treatment for rabies was not available anywhere in Tibet and it was necessary to fly to Kathmandu or Chengdu.

A pre-exposure vaccine for rabies exists, though few people bother to get it because the risk of infection is so low. The vaccine will not give you 100% immunity, but will greatly extend the time you have for seeking treatment, and the treatment will not need to be nearly so extensive. Given the very real risks of being bitten in Tibet, this is a vaccine well worth considering.

Tuberculosis It is very unlikely that as a traveller you are going to contract tuberculosis (TB), although the disease is on the increase in the developing world. Children under the age of 12 are at more risk and should be vaccinated at least six weeks before travelling (it takes this long for immunity to develop). Travellers who are HIV positive are particularly at risk from this opportunistic infection.

Eye Infection Trachoma is a common eye infection which is easily spread by contaminated towels (the kind handed out by restaurants and airlines). The best advice about wiping your face is to use disposable tissue paper. If you think you have trachoma, you need to see a doctor – the disease can damage your vision if untreated. Trachoma is normally treated with antibiotic eye ointments for about four to six weeks. Be careful about diagnosing yourself – simple allergies can produce symptoms similar to eye infections, and in this case antibiotics can do more harm than good.

Sexually Transmitted Disease (STD) Sex is not one of the big attractions of the Land of Snows but, just in case, the altitude offers no protection against the usual run of risks associated with unprotected sexual activity.

The most common sexually transmitted diseases (STDs) are gonorrhoea and syphilis. Sores, blisters or rashes around the genitals, discharges or pain when urinating are common symptoms. Symptoms may be less marked or not observed at all in women. Syphilis symptoms eventually disappear completely but the disease continues and can cause severe problems in later years, and if untreated can be fatal. The treatment of gonorrhoea and syphilis is by antibiotics.

There are numerous other STDs, for most of which effective treatment is available. However, there is neither a cure nor a vaccine for herpes and AIDS. Apart from sexual abstinence, using condoms is the most effective preventative. Condoms are available in China – the word is *bǎoxiǎn tào* which literally translates as 'insurance glove'.

The Chinese government announced in early 1993 that foreigners with more than 12 Chinese entry stamps in their passports would have to undergo 'five-minute AIDS tests' right at the border crossing! Exactly how crossing the border 12 times could cause AIDS has not been explained. It seems that Hong Kongers, Taiwanese and others of 'Chinese descent' do not need to undergo the tests – apparently they are immune to AIDS. There is much suspicion that the real intention was to rake in a little more cash – foreigners must pay for the tests. Whether or not a five-minute AIDS test is accurate has been hotly debated, and at the time of writing it was far from clear whether the rule would actually be enforced or quietly discarded.

The HIV (AIDS) virus can also be spread through infected blood transfusions; most developing countries cannot afford to screen blood for transfusions. It can also be spread by dirty needles – vaccinations, acupuncture, ear piercing and tattooing can potentially be as dangerous as intravenous drug use if the equipment is not clean.

Malaria You are not at risk from malaria in Tibet. Those travelling on to Nepal or the south-west of China should consult with a physician on possible prophylactics or see the Health sections of Lonely Planet's guides to these countries.

Cuts & Bites Treat any cut with care; wash it out with sterilised water, preferably with an antiseptic (Betadine) keep it dry and keep an eye on it. It would be worth bringing an antibiotic cream with you. Cuts on your feet and ankles are particularly troublesome – a new pair of sandals can quickly give you a nasty abrasion which can be difficult to heal. For the same reason, try not to scratch mosquito bites. See the Rabies sections above for information on animal bites.

Bedbugs & Lice Bedbugs live in various places, but particularly in dirty mattresses and bedding. Spots of blood on bedclothes or on the wall around the bed can be read as a suggestion to find another hotel. Bedbugs leave itchy bites in neat rows that swell up, but they generally heal quickly if you do not scratch.

All lice cause itching and discomfort. They make themselves at home in your hair (head lice), your clothing (body lice) or in your pubic hair (crabs). You catch lice through direct contact with infected people or by sharing combs, clothing and the like. Powder or shampoo treatment will kill the lice and infected clothing should then be washed in very hot water.

Women's Health

Gynaecological Problems Poor diet, lowered resistance due to the use of antibiotics for stomach upsets and even contraceptive pills can lead to vaginal infections when travelling in hot climates. Keeping the genital area clean, and wearing skirts or loose-fitting trousers and cotton underwear will help to prevent infections.

Yeast infections, characterised by a rash, itch and discharge, can be treated with a vinegar or even lemon-juice douche or with yoghurt. Nystatin suppositories are the usual medical prescription. Trichomonas is a more serious infection; symptoms are a discharge and a burning sensation when urinating. If a vinegar-water douche is not effective, medical attention should be sought. Flagyl is the prescribed drug and male sexual partners must also be treated

Pregnancy The first four months of pregnancy can be a risky time to travel in remote areas as far as your own health is concerned, as most miscarriages happen during this time and they can occasionally be dangerous.

The last three months should be spent within reasonable distance of good medical care. A premature baby (as early as 24 weeks into the pregnancy) will stand a chance of survival if it is born in a well-equipped hospital.

Pregnant women should avoid all unnecessary medication, but vaccinations and malarial prophylactics should still be taken where possible. Check with your physician before embarking on your trip. Additional care should be taken to prevent illness and particular attention should be paid to diet and nutrition. Alcohol, nicotine and other drugs are to be avoided, particularly during the first four months of pregnancy.

WOMEN TRAVELLERS

Sexual harassment is extremely rare in Tibet and foreign women seem to be able to travel with no risks. Naturally, it is worth noticing what local women are wearing and how they are behaving, and making a bit of an effort to fit in, as you would in any other foreign country. Tibetan women dress (probably because of the harsh climate) in bulky layers of clothing that mask their femininity. It would be wise to follow their example and dress modestly.

DANGERS & ANNOYANCES
Theft

Tibet is very poor and it is to be expected that there will be a risk of theft when travelling through it. That said, Tibet is much safer than many other provinces of China and other countries in the region (like Nepal and Thailand). Travellers trekking in the Everest region have reported problems with petty theft, and pickpockets work some parts of Lhasa.

Pickpocketing is the most common form of theft. The best protection is attentiveness to your surroundings and avoiding situations where you are caught up in crowds. Some thieves may even try to grab your bag and run away, but more common is razoring of bags and pockets in crowded places like buses. The big cities of China are far more dangerous in this respect than Lhasa and the rest of Tibet.

Be careful in public toilets – quite a few foreigners have laid aside their valuables, squatted down to business, and then straightened up again to discover that someone had absconded with the lot.

Do not leave anything valuable in hotel rooms, particularly dormitories. There are at least a few people who subsidise their journey by ripping off their fellow travellers.

Money belts are best worn inside your clothing. The bulging money belts that travellers wear around their waists are an invitation to theft, particularly if you drift off to sleep on a crowded bus. Keeping all your eggs in one basket is not advised – to guard against possible loss you could leave a small stash of money (say US$100) in your hotel room or buried in your backpack, with a record of the travellers' cheque serial numbers and your passport number. Other things of little or no apparent value to the thief – things like film – should be safeguarded, since to lose them would be a real heartbreak to you. Make a copy of your address book before you leave home.

Small padlocks are useful for backpacks and some dodgy hotel rooms. Bicycle chain locks come in handy not only for hired bikes but for attaching backpacks to railings or luggage racks.

Loss Reports If something of yours is stolen, you should report it immediately to the nearest Foreign Affairs Branch of the PSB. They will ask you to fill in a loss report before investigating the case and sometimes even recovering the stolen goods.

If you have travel insurance (recommended), it is essential to obtain a loss report so you can claim compensation. For theft of major items, a few countries even permit a tax deduction.

Staring Squads

It is very unusual to be surrounded by staring Tibetans and Chinese in Lhasa, but upcountry is another affair. Trekkers will soon discover that it is not a good idea to camp beside Tibetan villages. The spectacle of a few foreigners putting up tents is probably the closest such people will ever come to TV and the whole village will come out in force to watch. It is not unusual to get up in the morning and find half the village still sitting and watching.

Everybody reacts to this kind of thing differently, but it soon becomes extremely difficult to nonchalantly ignore. There is no antidote to it.

Beggars

Being a devout Buddhist region, Tibet has a long tradition of begging. It is unusual to sit down in a restaurant in Tibet without being pestered by women with babies in their arms,

---

Undercover Monks

Frequent travellers to Tibet will tell you that some of the monks in Tibet's larger monasteries are not what they seem. There is no reason to believe that someone in a monk's or nun's habit is actually a monk or a nun. They may in fact be working for the Chinese government undercover. And if this reeks ever so slightly of paranoia, give some thought for a US couple who brought three taped speeches of the Dalai Lama with them to Tibet and handed one to a monk at Tashilhunpo Monastery in Shigatse.

After being tailed by two plainclothes Chinese police, they were stopped at a checkpoint and a boy in civilian clothes, whom they recognised as one of the 'monks' from Tashilhunpo, identified them. At the Shigatse police station they were interrogated and then taken back to their hotel room, which was searched; the two remaining cassette tapes and some Dalai Lama pictures were confiscated. They were detained in Shigatse for four days and subject to further interrogations and threats before signing statements to the effect that they were guilty of 'distributing propaganda'. Finally they were escorted to Gonggar Airport and deported to Kathmandu.

There are several issues at stake in this story. Firstly, it is unreasonable to trust anyone, including monks, when it comes to sensitive issues that might be construed as political. Secondly, even if you get away with it, any incriminating material that you hand a Tibetan could have serious consequences for the recipient (torture, jail) if it is discovered. And thirdly, never forget that Tibet is a highly politicised issue, and even the simple act of handing out a Dalai Lama picture is significant to the Chinese authorities.

The safest path is to avoid handing out anything 'political' at all times. But in particular be wary of monks who speak English and act as guides at monasteries; even more, do not hand out pictures of the Dalai Lama to those who request them. ∎

wizened old men, urchins dressed in rags, boy monks and even itinerant musicians. Generally, they approach with thumbs up and mumble *guchi guchi* – 'please, please', not an Italian designer label. Tibetans with money are generally very generous with beggars and usually hand out a couple of *mao* to anyone who requests it. If you do give (and the choice is entirely yours), give the same amount Tibetans do; do not encourage beggars to make foreigners a special target by handing out large denominations. The giving of pens and Dalai Lama pictures to whomever asks for them is not advised.

Dogs

Tibet is infested with dogs. Many of them are barely alive and drag themselves along trailing half-chewed-off legs. They are not a pleasant sight. Unfortunately they also roam monasteries and urban streets in vicious packs, and care should be taken to keep them at a distance. Hurling a few rocks in their direction will let them know you are not in the mood for company, while a hefty stick is good for action at close quarters. Do not underestimate the ones asleep in the shadows; they can spring into action at any moment and give you a nasty bite. See the Rabies entry of the Health section above for more information on what to do if you are bitten.

ACTIVITIES
Adventure Sports

Tibet offers the type of topography to entice mountaineers, whitewater rafters, hang gliding enthusiasts, and others who want to pursue their adventurous hobbies in the world's highest mountains.

The problem, as always, are those faceless, sombre figures known collectively as 'the authorities'. High-ranking cadres, the PSB, the military, CITS and others in China with the power to extort money know a good business opportunity when they see it. Foreigners have been asked for as much as US$1 million for mountaineering and rafting permits. The amount demanded varies con-

siderably depending on who you are dealing with, and the price is always negotiable.

In many cases, it is doubtful that the law really requires a permit. A Chinese person may climb the same mountain as you without having any authorisation at all, and it may be perfectly legal. But many local governments simply make up the law as they go along. In general, when foreigners do something which is deemed unusual – and hang gliding, bungy jumping, kayaking etc, are unusual in China – a permit will be required and a fee will be charged. The more unusual the activity, the higher the fee demanded.

Trekking

One of the remarkable things about Tibet, considering the difficulties placed in the way of those heading up there by Chinese authorities, is that once you are up on the high plateau there is considerable freedom to strike off on foot and explore the Tibetan valleys and ranges. Of course no one at CITS or any other Chinese organisation will tell you this; but nevertheless it is the case. Experienced and hardy trekkers have the opportunity to visit places that are almost impossible to get to any other way, and are unlikely to find any official obstacles placed in their way.

Individual Trekking Several popular treks are included in this book, but those with a particular interest in individual trekking should buy a copy of Gary McCue's *Trekking in Tibet*. This book has comprehensive details on numerous treks around Lhasa, Ü, Tsang and Western Tibet, and is essential for first-time trekkers in Tibet.

The trick of individual trekking is to get to a village close to where you want to start your trek. It is often possible to hire pack animals in such places. Of course, you might want to carry your own gear, but in the high elevations of Tibet every kg of baggage you have to lug with you quickly becomes a heavy burden.

If you are on your own and plan to trek, you should perhaps put up notices at the Yak

A: The Potala (CT)
B: Rickshaw on the streets of Lhasa (CT)
C: Tibetan headdress and the Jokhang, Lhasa (CT)

Barkhor Square stalls with the Jokhang, Lhasa (CT)

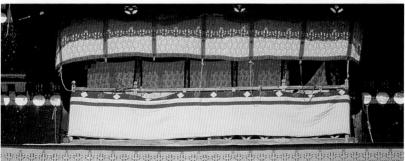

A: Inner courtyard of the Jokhang, Lhasa (CT)
B: Detail from the Potala, Lhasa (CT)

A: Pilgrims, the Barkhor, Lhasa (CT)
B: Crowds at the Barkhor, Lhasa (CT)
C: Prayer wheels, the Barkhor, Lhasa (CT)
D: Tibetans watching a performance, the Barkhor, Lhasa (CT)

or Banak Shol hotels in Lhasa for trekking companions. Once you get off the beaten track in Tibet, you are really off the beaten track. Solitary trekkers in Tibet are travelling at great risk to their personal safety, and in the case of an accident might have to wait a long time before they are found – if at all. Do not do it.

Naturally, those planning on trekking in Tibet need to be self-sufficient. Sometimes food and accommodation is available in Tibetan villages, but this cannot be counted on. You will need to bring your own food, camping equipment and a good sleeping bag. See the Health section above for information on medical supplies you should bring with you. Most of all, do not attempt difficult treks without first having spent sufficient time acclimatising to Tibet's high elevations. Start with a series of low intensity walks, building up to hikes of a couple of days; make sure you are fit enough to get there *and* back.

Group Trekking The alternative to individual trekking is of course to explore Tibet with an experienced commercial trekking company. For those with the money to spare (usually no less than US$200 per day), there is a lot to be said to taking this course of action.

A standard organised trek organised at home will include a Western leader, a local leader, porters, a cook and so on. All your practical needs will be taken care of and you will be free to enjoy the trekking itself.

Some companies that can organise treks in Tibet are as follows:

Australia
    Everest Trekking, Suite 108, 822 High St, Kew East, Vic 3102 (☎ 810 9504)
    Peregrine Adventures, 258 Lonsdale St, Melbourne, Vic 3000; (☎ 663 8611)
    5th Floor, 38 York St, Sydney NSW 2000, (☎ 290 2770)
    Australian Agencies Adventure Holidays, 860 Military Rd, Mosman, NSW 2088 (☎ 960 1677 3588)
    World Expeditions, 441 Kent St, Sydney, NSW 2000 (☎ 264 3366)

UK
    Bales Tours, Bales House, Barrington Rd, Dorking, RH4 3EJ (☎ 01306 885991)
    Naturetrek 40, The Dean Alresford Hampshire, SO24 9AZ (☎ 01962 733051) Regent Holidays, 15 John St, Bristol BS1 2HR (☎)0117 921 1711
USA
    InnerAsia Expeditions, 2627 Lombard St, San Francisco,CA 94123, (☎ (415) 922 0448
    Wilderness Travel, 801 Allston Way, Berkeley, CA 94710 ☎ (510) 548 0420
    Mountain Travel-Sobek, 6420 Fairmount Ave, El Cerrito, CA 94530, (☎ (510) 527 8100)
    Adventure Center, Adventure Department, 1311 63rd St, STE 200, Emeryville, CA 94608 (☎ (510) 654 1879)

HIGHLIGHTS

The highlights of Tibet will depend largely on your interests. For trekkers, for example, Tibet offers the opportunity to tread paths in some of the world's highest places. For the average traveller and first-time visitor to Tibet, however, there are a few well-trodden trails that take in Tibet's main attractions.

The chief goal of travellers to Tibet is Lhasa itself. Naturally, *everyone* goes there. But the traveller population is still far from reaching the plague proportions of cities like Kathmandu and Bangkok, and there is enough to see in and around the city to keep you busy for at least a week. The monastic institutions of Dreprung and Sera are close by, and Ganden Monastery, which is rapidly being rebuilt, is an easy day trip away.

The road between Lhasa and Kathmandu is the chief travellers' route through Tibet. This route, which basically follows the Friendship Highway from Lhasa to Kathmandu, allows a number of detours to the highlights of Tsang province. These include Yamdrok-tso lake, Gyantse and Shigatse. Both Gyantse and Shigatse are worth a stop for a day or two to see the sights and get a glimpse of urban life in Tibet. They are more laid-back than Lhasa. Also en route and a popular destination is Sakya, a small monastery town just 20 km off the Friendship Highway. Closer to the border, and emerging as the most popular trekking destination in Tibet is the Everest region.

From Lhasa, less travellers head east

towards the Yarlung Valley. The most popular destination in this part of Tibet (Ü) is Samye Monastery. This secluded monastery in the middle of a sandy plain next to the Brahmaputra River (Tsang-po) is the perfect place to kick back for a few days and enjoy some day hikes. Further east is the Yarlung Valley with major sights such as Tibet's first castle, Yumbulugang and the ancient burial mounds of the early Tibetan kings at Chongye. While, for the average traveller, the burial mounds themselves might be something of an anticlimax, the Yarlung and Chongye valleys are superb areas to hike around undisturbed by other travellers.

Much talked about, little visited, is of course Mt Kailash out in Western Tibet. Those travelling out there are looking at a journey of around 15 to 20 days. It has become easier to get permission to travel out into this region in recent years. The main attraction is the area's remoteness. There may not be much of cultural interest en route to and around Kailash, but the trip provides the opportunity to see some of the most rugged and breathtaking scenery in the world.

Trekking

As already mentioned, those planning on trekking extensively in Tibet should get hold of a copy of Gary McCue's *Trekking in Tibet – a traveler's guide*.

Several mini-treks are detailed in this book, but there are countless other possibilities for keen walkers. Some popular areas for trekking include Nam-tso and Yamdrok-tso lakes. Hiking around either of these lakes could take over two weeks. Lhamo La-tso lake, north-east of Tsetang in Ü is another challenging trekking destination, though not as popular as Nam-tso and Yamdrok-tso.

Pilgrimage

Pilgrimage is practiced throughout the Buddhist world, though as a devotional exercise it has been raised to a level of particular importance in Tibet. This may be because of the nomadic element in Tibetan society; it may also be that in a mountainous country with no roads and no wheeled vehicles, walking long distances became a fact of life, and by visiting sacred places en route could be combined with accumulating merit. But there is also the Tantric orientation of Tibetan Buddhism to consider, and the fact that many 'power places' of Tibet have been sanctified by yogins who have used them as meditational retreats.

The immediate motivations of pilgrimage are many, but for the ordinary Tibetan amount to a means of accumulating merit, and for the more spiritually advanced a route to enlightenment. The lay practitioner might go on pilgrimage in the hope of winning a better rebirth, or simply because of a vow to take a pilgrimage if a bodhisattva granted a wish. In India, the bodhi tree under which Sakyamuni achieved enlightenment is an important pilgrimage destination. In Tibet, there are countless pilgrimages, ranging from sacred lakes and mountains to caves that have served as meditational retreats for important yogin to monasteries and temples and, in the case of Lhasa, an entire city.

According to Victor Chan, in his *Tibet Handbook – a pilgrimage guide*, the three foremost pilgrimages of Tibet are all mountains: Mt Kailash, in Western Tibet; Mt Tapka Shelri and the Tsari Valley, in south-east Tibet; and Mt Lapchi, east of Nyalam. There are many others. Lakes that attract pilgrims include Yamdrok-tso, Nam-tso and Lhama La-tso. There are also sites of 'geomantic perfection', as Keith Dowman in *The Power Places of Central Tibet* refers to them: they are usually associated with Guru Rinpoche and attract large numbers of Tibetan pilgrims. Either of the above books are useful guides for Western pilgrims.

Pilgrimage is naturally not just a matter of walking to a sacred place and then going home. There are a number of activities that focus the concentration of the pilgrim. The act of *kora*, of circumambulating the object of devotion is chief among these. Others include prostrating, reciting mantras, meditating and making offerings. And while circumambulating a pilgrim site, there are usually stops of spiritual significance. The Kailash kora, for example is a treasure trove of these, encompassing sky burial sites, stones that have 'flown' from India, monasteries, bodhisattva footprints, and even at one point a *lingam*, or penis-print. ■

The Everest region has emerged as the most popular area for trekking in recent years. For less experienced trekkers the advantage of trekking in this region is that locals are used to the needs of foreign walkers and it is fairly easy to hire pack animals and guides, particularly from Tingri. See the Everest Region entry in the Tsang chapter for more details.

Second to Everest in popularity are the Kailash and Manasarovar regions in Western Tibet. Both the Kailash and Manasarovar circuits are sacred pilgrimages for Tibetans and are beautiful areas to trek in. The Kailash circuit is the easier of the two, but with some perseverance Lake Manasarovar can be trekked around in about four days.

Finally, see the Ganden-Samye trek entry in the Ü chapter. This trek takes around three or four days and connects two of central Tibet's most important monasteries.

Monasteries

Tibet is a land of monasteries. Although many of them were badly damaged or destroyed in the Cultural Revolution, most of them are now beginning to bounce back. Lhasa and its environs is the best place to visit Tibetan monasteries. The sprawling Gelugpa institutions of Dreprung, Sera and Ganden were once the largest monastic institutions in the world, and nowadays the monks are starting to come back. Ganden, for example, is the scene of almost frantic renovation and rebuilding.

Samye Monastery is the most ancient of Tibet's monasteries, and is around a day's travel from Lhasa. There is accommodation at the monastery and some travellers end up spending a few days there, relaxing and using the monastery as a base for walks to meditation retreats in the nearby hills.

The major monastery complexes of Tsang are Tashilhunpo (Shigatse) and Sakya. Tashilhunpo is not the friendliest of monasteries, but the monastery itself is magnificent. It is one of the few monasteries of Tibet that was spared in the Cultural Revolution. Sakya, on the other hand, is an eerie, fortress-like monastery and well worth an overnight stop.

There are other, smaller monasteries scattered all over Tibet. Sometimes these are the best places to visit. The monks are often very happy to have a foreign visitor and will sit down to share some tea with you and show you around. If you see a monastery while you are trekking in Tibet, always make a point of calling in.

ACCOMMODATION

Outside Lhasa, Shigatse and Tsetang, the Tibet traveller is not going to be overwhelmed with accommodation options. The standard hotel in rural Tibet is a truck stop with a row of rooms each containing four or five beds. Hot water is provided in thermoses and usually a basin is provided for washing in. Electricity and running water are luxuries that cannot be expected. At least such places are cheap – from around Y8 to Y15 on average – and bedding is provided.

It is sometimes possible for trekkers to stay with Tibetan families. Some families living on popular trekking routes have a room that they hire out to foreign trekkers. Food is sometimes available, but if not they can usually offer you hot water. Sometimes a charge of Y1 is asked for hot water – it is not a lot of money considering the effort involved in producing the stuff.

In Tibetan urban centres like Lhasa, Shigatse, Gyantse and Tsetang, there is more choice and conditions are better. Most travellers opt to stay in Tibetan-run hotels, which are always friendlier and more atmospheric than their Chinese counterparts. Due to demand, hot showers are becoming more common in such hotels.

Camping

A large proportion of the Tibetan population are nomads, and there is a strong tradition of making your home wherever you can hammer in a tent peg. You probably run the risk of an unpleasant run-in with the PSB if you attempt to set up a tent in Lhasa, but get 20 km or so out of town and the nearest patch of turf is yours for the picking.

Guesthouses & Hotels

Most of the accommodation used by foreigners in Tibet could be classed as guesthouse accommodation. In Lhasa there are a few clean, well-run Tibetan-style guesthouses and similar set-ups can be found in Gyantse, Shigatse and Sakya. Some monasteries, such as Samye in Ü also have guesthouses, though monastery guesthouses are always a lot more basic than those in the towns.

Tibetan-style guesthouses tend to be much more friendly and homey than Chinese guesthouses; prices are also lower. In Lhasa Tibetan guesthouses have dorms, triples and doubles for an average of around Y25 per person.

Accommodation elsewhere in Tibet is cheaper – around Y15 – but standards are not as high as those in Lhasa. Outside Lhasa and Shigatse, you cannot expect to find budget guesthouses with running water, though all guesthouses will provide hot water for drinking – if there is enough, you can use it for a quick wash.

There is hotel-style accommodation in Lhasa, Shigatse and Tsetang. Naturally, Lhasa has the best selection. There is even a branch of the Holiday Inn group in Lhasa, and this offers the best accommodation standards in all of Tibet – at a price of course. With the exception of the Holiday Inn, all hotel accommodation in Tibet is Chinese run. Average standards prevail.

Truck Stops

Travellers making their way out to Mt Kailash will probably get to sample quite a few truck stops. They are basically just places to crash out after a long day of travelling. The bedding is usually filthy (it is good to have a sleeping bag or an inner sheet) and you may have to pay to get your thermos of hot water. If you value your privacy it is a good idea to pay for a whole room (usually four or five beds), because the staff at truck stops like to fill rooms up before they open up another room. Some truck stops will have an attached restaurant, but in remote parts of Western Tibet this is less the case.

Army Camps

An increased number of privately-run guesthouses and truck stops in Tibet means that travellers rarely have to stay in army camps anymore – a frequent occurrence, even on the road between Lhasa and the Nepal border, back in the early days of individual travel. Rates are usually around Y10 per bed and there is usually food available.

FOOD

The food situation can get a bit depressing if you are in Tibet for an extended stay. Nevertheless, the situation has improved vastly over the last five or six years. Fresh vegetables are more widely available than they once were, and there are now a lot more (mainly Chinese) restaurants around.

Tibetan

Tellingly, the basic Tibetan meal is *tsampa*, a kind of dough made with roasted barley flour, yak butter (if available) and water, tea or beer – something wet. It has a certain novelty value the first time you try it, but only a Tibetan can eat it every day and still look forward to the next meal.

No, Tibetan cuisine is not going to win any prizes. In Lhasa there are a few restaurants about that have elevated a subsistence diet into the beginnings of a cuisine, notably the Tashi restaurants. But outside Lhasa, Tibetan food is limited mainly to *momo*s and *thukpa*.

Momos are small dumplings filled with meat and or vegetables. They are actually pretty good, but it's rare to come across them outside Lhasa and Shigatse.

More common is thukpa, a noodle soup with meat and or vegetables. Thukpa is often served at restaurants associated with monasteries. In more remote towns, if there is a restaurant, it is likely to be thukpa that they are serving.

Also popular amongst nomads is dried yak or lamb meat. It is pretty chewy stuff. Sometimes you will see bowls of little white lumps drying in the sun – even the flies leave this stuff alone. It is dried yak cheese and is eaten as a sweet.

For the first half-hour it is like having a

small rock in your mouth, but eventually it starts to soften up and taste like old, dried yak cheese.

Chinese

Han immigration into Tibet has done wonders for the restaurant scene. Even most Tibetans have to admit that Chinese food is better than tsampa, momos and thukpa. All of the Tibetan urban centres have Chinese restaurants these days, and they can also be found on major roads, even on the road out to Kailash.

Chinese food in Tibet is almost exclusively Sichuanese. This is the hottest of the Chinese regional cuisines, but it is rarely made with as many spices in Tibet as it is in Sichuan itself.

Very few Chinese restaurants have English menus. Usually the dishes on offer are written on a board, and if you do not read Chinese the only thing you'll gather from it are the range of prices. This is rarely a problem, as in most restaurants you can wander out into the kitchen and point to the vegetables and meats that you want fried up.

Some common dishes follow:

plain white rice
  mǐfàn
  米饭
steamed buns
  mántou
  馒头
steamed meat buns
  bāozi
  包子
boiled dumplings
  jiǎozi
  饺子
fried rice with vegetables
  shūcài chǎofàn
  蔬菜炒饭
fried noodles with vegetables
  shūcài chǎomiàn
  蔬菜炒面
noodle soup
  tāngmiàn
  汤面

spicy hot bean curd
  mápó dòufǔ
  麻婆豆腐
fried chicken with peanuts
  gōngbǎojīdīng
  宫宝鸡丁
fish-tasting eggplant
  yúxiāng qiézi
  鱼香茄子
red-cooked eggplant
  hóngshāo qiézi
  红烧茄子
fried beansprouts
  qìngchǎo dòuyá
  炒豆芽
fried green vegetables
  chǎo qīngcài
  炒青菜
fried green beans
  chǎo biǎndòu
  炒扁豆
fried rice with egg
  jīdàn chǎofàn
  鸡蛋炒饭
fried tomatoes and eggs
  fānqié chǎodàn
  番茄炒蛋
fried rice with beef
  niúròusī chǎofàn
  牛肉丝炒饭
double-cooked pork
  huíguō ròu
  回锅肉
egg soup
  dànhuā tāng
  蛋花汤
meat and vegetable soup
  zhàcài ròusì tāng
  榨菜肉丝汤

DRINKS

The local beverage that every traveller ends up trying at least once is yak-butter tea. It is unusual to meet a foreigner who is really sold on the stuff – do not drink it cold; the butter congeals into little lumps of grease.

The more palatable alternative to yak-butter tea is sweet milk tea. It is similar to the tea drunk by the British. Chinese tea is also widely available. Tibetans do not drink coffee and you will not find any outside Lhasa. Soft drinks, mineral water and beer are all widely available throughout Tibet. In many remote areas, even if there is nothing else available to drink, there will at least be beer on sale.

The Tibetan brew is known as *chang* a fermented barley beer. It has a rich, fruity taste, and ranges from disgusting to pretty good. Those trekking in the Everest region should try the local variety, which is served in a big pot full of fermented barley; hot water is poured into it and the liquid is drunk through a wooden straw – it is very good.

The main brand of beer available in Tibet is Wuquan, a Sichuan brew that is pretty good. Blue Ribbon is a US beer brewed in China under franchise; it is pretty good. Out in Western Tibet, Xinjiang beer is available. Some travellers swear by Chinese brandy *(bailandi)*, which at around Y8 per bottle is remarkably cheap.

ENTERTAINMENT
Hopefully entertainment is not high on your list of priorities. If it is, go somewhere else. The Tibetan idea of fun is having a picnic and getting sloshed on chang. In general, foreigners make their own entertainment in Tibet, and evenings in the hotels of Lhasa and Shigatse often see groups of travellers knocking back a couple of beers and swapping tall stories while someone strums *Tears from Heaven* or *Knocking on Heaven's Door* (not *again*!) in the background.

Lhasa has a burgeoning nightlife scene, but very little in the way of cultural entertainment. Like the rest of China, karaoke bars have taken off in a big way in urban centres. Lhasa is the karaoke capital of Tibet, but you will also find bars in Shigatse, Gyantse, Tsetang and even far-away Ali. It is worth dropping into one of them once, but you would have to be decidedly odd to make a habit of it.

A karaoke bar will have drinks available at slightly inflated prices (from Y10 to Y15 or more for a beer) and customers have to pay to sing a song – the price depends on the bar. Some bars in Lhasa alternate between karaoke sessions and dancing, and can be innocent, good fun. Rumours abound that Lhasa karaoke bars are fronts for prostitution; it is very likely, but as a foreigner you will be insulated from such activities.

The PSB does not look too kindly on foreigners seeking out night time entertainment in venues frequented by locals. Some travellers have been warned off from dancing and chatting with locals. Proceed with caution.

Those seeking out cultural entertainment will probably have to wait for a festival. Festivals often include performances of *cham* (monks dancing) and Tibetan opera, but unfortunately such times represent your only opportunity to see them.

THINGS TO BUY
Tibet is not a particularly good place for souvenir hunting. To be sure, there are purchases to be made, but much of the stuff you see in markets and so on has been humped over the high passes from Nepal and can probably be bought cheaper in Kathmandu, where you will have a better selection of quality goods.

Some travellers buy a Tibetan carpet and send it home. There are carpet factories in Lhasa and in Shigatse producing new carpets of average quality. Good quality traditional carpets, on the other hand, are harder to come by. A small contingent of frequent travellers to Tibet have made carpets their business and if you fall in with some of them they may give you some tips for finding one for yourself.

For an overview of possible purchases in Tibet, the best place to look is the Barkhor in Lhasa. The entire Barkhor circuit is lined with stalls selling all kinds of oddities. Prayer flags and shawls, prayer wheels and daggers are all popular buys. Be prepared to bargain for any purchase. You can probably reckon at least halving the price, but there are no hard and fast rules. If you look like a sucker, you might be quoted a price that is 10 times the real value of what you want to buy. Shop around for a while and get a feel for prices; asking other travellers what they paid for their souvenirs is also a good approach.

Other possible buys are Tibetan ceiling drapes and thangkas. Some of the ceiling drapes and door curtains are very tasteful and can be bought in Lhasa and Shigatse. Most of the thangkas for sale are gaudy – good ones do not come cheap.

Getting There & Away

Tibet is not the most accessible of destinations, but then that is half the fun. The only flights to Tibet are to Lhasa from either Kathmandu in Nepal or Chengdu in China. The Kathmandu flights basically grind to a halt during the winter months and there are frequent cancellations of Chengdu flights at this time also. Overland routes into Tibet involve days of gruelling travel either from Nepal or from China. The only officially sanctioned overland route from China into Tibet is via the Qinghai-Tibet Highway, which runs between Lhasa and Golmud.

At the time of writing bureaucratic obstacles to entering Tibet – a potentially more insurmountable barrier than the Himalayas – had loosened considerably. All present indications suggest that this will remain the case, with the Chinese government announcing recently that it hopes tourist figures to quadruple in Tibet over the next decade. Such hopes, however, rest squarely on the assumption that Chinese development of the high plateau will proceed unmarred by Tibetan resentment and protest.

It is to be expected that if major protests emerge, there will be – probably temporary – restrictions on access to Tibet by foreign travellers and tourists. It would be wise to check on the latest developments in Tibet before setting out – see the list of Tibetan associations in the Facts for the Visitor chapter.

AIR

Air access to Tibet is limited to either Kathmandu in Nepal or Chengdu in China. Individual travellers planning on flying from Kathmandu should arrive in Kathmandu with their Chinese visa already organised. You will stand a much better chance of getting on a flight this way.

There are no discounted tickets available for flights into Tibet. For flights to China or Nepal, however, it is worth shopping around.

Buying a Plane Ticket

For budget travellers buying a plane ticket is a major outlay and can eat into savings that might otherwise be spent on the road. It is worth spending some time looking into the various airlines that fly into the region you are visiting and their comparative costs. Also bear in mind that it is worth starting early – often the cheaper airlines need to be booked months in advance, and this can usually be done with a deposit. Talk to friends who have travelled recently and check newspapers for bargains. At this point you can start ringing around travel agencies (while airlines can provide flight timetables, they rarely have the cheapest prices). Find out the fare, the route and duration of the flight, and importantly, check for any restrictions on the ticket (see Restrictions in the Air Travel Glossary in this chapter).

Be wary of impossibly cheap flights advertised in newspapers. It is often the case that they are booked out...'but a slightly more expensive ticket is available'; before you know it you are booked on an inconvenient routing and paying more than you want to. Another common ploy is to tell you that just a couple of seats are still available and you will have to pay up before 5 pm. Do not fall into these traps. Take your time. It always pays off to be a bit cautious.

In the UK and the USA many of the cheapest flights are offered by small 'bucket' agencies whose names have not reached the phone directory yet. There is no need to assume that such agencies are in the business of ripping travellers off, but again they should be approached with caution. Standard procedure in buying plane tickets is to pay a deposit of around 20% and the balance upon issue of the ticket. Avoid agencies which demand you pay the full ticket price in advance. Always demand a receipt for any money you fork out.

An alternative to these risks is to pay a little more and make your bookings with a reputable well-established agency. Firms such as STA, who have offices worldwide, Council Travel in the USA or Travel CUTS in Canada are all good options.

Once you have bought your ticket, copy out its ticket and flight numbers and keep this information somewhere separate from the ticket. If the ticket is lost or stolen, this information will help you to get a replacement.

Try and buy travel insurance as early as possible. Buying it too late might mean, for example, that you are not covered for delays to your flight due to industrial action.

Round-the-World Fares

Although you will not find a round-the-world (RTW) fare that includes Lhasa, it should not be so difficult to find one that includes Hong Kong or Kathmandu. The only drawback is that you will probably have to return to your point of origin after visiting Tibet to pick up your onward flight.

There are basically two types of RTW ticket: airline tickets and agent tickets. Airline tickets are usually put together by two or more airlines, which combine their routes to provide a round-the-world flight. Agent tickets are usually cheaper, representing a collection of cheap fares strung together by a travel agency. The latter probably will not offer as many route options as the former, and there will be various ticket limitations to bear in mind – check to see if you get a refund if you miss a flight for example.

To/From China

The flight options from China to Lhasa are daily from Chengdu in Sichuan or once weekly from Beijing. Plans are also afoot to establish a flight from Chongqing, also in Sichuan, but this is unlikely to be particularly convenient for many travellers if it does eventuate. Rumours of a Canton-Lhasa flight have circulated for some years now without ever coming to anything.

Flights between Chengdu and Lhasa cost Y1490, while flights between Beijing and Lhasa (with a change of planes in Chengdu) cost Y2700. You will be very lucky, however, if this is all you end up paying for the flight. Both in Beijing and Chengdu, local authorities will often require that you pay for a permit to visit Tibet before the ticket can be issued. As of yet there is no fixed price for this 'permit' (you will never see this document, if it in fact exists), and travellers in mid-1994 were being charged between US$50 and US$300 on top of the flight cost.

This is one situation that is worth some forethought. If it is at all possible to predict when you are going to visit Tibet, try buying your air ticket to Lhasa before you get to China. Hong Kong is worth a try, but even better is to buy it at home before you set off on your trip. It might tie up your travel itinerary somewhat, but it may save you up to US$300 in extortionate 'permit' fees.

To/From Nepal

Flights between Kathmandu and Lhasa operate twice weekly and cost Y1680. These flights may be cancelled at the slightest whiff of trouble in Lhasa and shut down during the winter months. You will also need a valid Chinese visa in order to buy a ticket in

Winter Flights

Flights to and from Lhasa are frequently cancelled or delayed in the winter months. This can present particular problems to those leaving Tibet with a connecting flight to somewhere else. Numerous travellers have missed flights out of Chengdu because of cancellations in Lhasa. If you miss a CNAC flight out of Chengdu, you will be hard pressed to get a refund of any kind and will probably have to buy a new ticket. The only way around this really is to give yourself some leeway in Chengdu. As inconvenient as it may sound, it may be a good idea to give yourself a couple of days in Chengdu between flights. ∎

Kathmandu, and the Chinese embassy in Kathmandu is not in the habit of giving Chinese visas to individual travellers. Ideally you should arrive in Kathmandu armed both with a Chinese visa and a Kathmandu-Lhasa flight ticket if you want to be sure of using this method of entry to Tibet.

Getting To/From the Region

Travel to Tibet is complicated by the fact that there are no direct flights. You will have to stop over in Kathmandu or in China if you are making a beeline direct for Tibet. Very few Tibet travellers, however, make their way directly to Tibet. Most individual travellers make their way to Tibet as part of a grand overland trip through China, Nepal, India and onwards.

Those travelling first to either China and Hong Kong or to India and Nepal, should consult Lonely Planet's respective travel survival kits for these countries. Below is some basic information on getting into the region of Tibet.

To/From Australia & New Zealand Check major newspapers and the Travel Agents section of the Yellow Pages for information

---

Air Travel Glossary

Apex Apex, or 'advance purchase excursion' is a discounted ticket which must be paid for in advance. There are penalties if you wish to change it.

Baggage Allowance This will be written on your ticket: usually one 20 kg item to go in the hold, plus one item of hand luggage.

Bucket Shop This is an unbonded travel agency specialising in discounted airline tickets.

Bumped Just because you have a confirmed seat doesn't mean you're going to get on the plane – see Overbooking.

Cancellation Penalties If you have to cancel or change an Apex ticket there are often heavy penalties involved, insurance can sometimes be taken out against these penalties. Some airlines impose penalties on regular tickets as well, particularly against 'no show' passengers.

Check In Airlines ask you to check in a certain time ahead of the flight departure (usually 1½ hours on international flights). If you fail to check in on time and the flight is overbooked the airline can cancel your booking and give your seat to somebody else.

Confirmation Having a ticket written out with the flight and date you want doesn't mean you have a seat until the agent has checked with the airline that your status is 'OK' or confirmed. Meanwhile you could just be 'on request'.

Discounted Tickets There are two types of discounted fares – officially discounted (see Promotional Fares) and unofficially discounted. The lowest prices often impose drawbacks like flying with unpopular airlines, inconvenient schedules, or unpleasant routes and connections. A discounted ticket can save you other things than money – you may be able to pay Apex prices without the associated Apex advance booking and other requirements. Discounted tickets only exist where there is fierce competition.

Full Fares Airlines traditionally offer first class (coded F), business class (coded J) and economy class (coded Y) tickets. These days there are so many promotional and discounted fares available from the regular economy class that few passengers pay full economy fare.

Lost Tickets If you lose your airline ticket an airline will usually treat it like a travellers' cheque and, after enquiries, issue you with another one. Legally, however, an airline is entitled to treat it like cash and if you lose it then it's gone forever. Take good care of your tickets.

No Shows No shows are passengers who fail to show up for their flight, sometimes due to unexpected delays or disasters, sometimes due to simply forgetting, sometimes because they made more than one booking and didn't bother to cancel the one they didn't want. Full fare passengers who fail to turn up are sometimes entitled to travel on a later flight. The rest of us are penalised (see Cancellation Penalties).

On Request This is an unconfirmed booking for a flight, see Confirmation.

Open Jaws A return ticket where you fly out to one place but return from another. If available this can save you backtracking to your arrival point.

on agencies dealing with tickets to China, India and Nepal. Both STA and Flight Centres International are reliable agents that are represented in most Australian and New Zealand cities.

Those flying to China from this region should bear in mind that it is much cheaper to fly to Hong Kong than direct to China. The cheapest fares will be advance purchase fares, which vary in cost seasonally, and will probably be with airlines that stop in another South-East Asian capital en route. The cheapest one-way (low season) tickets to Hong Kong from Australia cost around

A$750; return tickets will cost at least A$1100.

Return advance purchase fares to the sub-continent from Australia range from around A$1275 to A$1575 depending on the season and the destination. Prices for flights to New Zealand range from around NZ$1820 to NZ$2170.

To/From Europe Those flying from Europe have the option of flying to Beijing with CAAC and bypassing Hong Kong. This would be the best option for travellers looking at getting to Tibet as quickly as

Overbooking Airlines hate to fly empty seats and since every flight has some passengers who fail to show up (see No Shows) airlines often book more passengers than they have seats. Usually the excess passengers balance those who fail to show up but occasionally somebody gets bumped. If this happens guess who it is most likely to be? The passengers who check in late.

Promotional Fares Officially discounted fares like Apex fares which are available from travel agents or direct from the airline.

Reconfirmation At least 72 hours prior to departure time of an onward or return flight you must contact the airline and 'reconfirm' that you intend to be on the flight. If you don't do this the airline can delete your name from the passenger list and you could lose your seat. You don't have to reconfirm the first flight on your itinerary or if your stopover is less than 72 hours. It doesn't hurt to reconfirm more than once.

Restrictions Discounted tickets often have various restrictions on them – advance purchase is the most usual one (Apex). Others are restrictions on the minimum and maximum period you must be away, such as a minimum of 14 days or a maximum of one year. See Cancellation Penalties.

Standby A discounted ticket where you only fly if there is a seat free at the last moment. Standby fares are usually only available on domestic routes.

Tickets Out An entry requirement for many countries is that you have an onward or return ticket, in other words, a ticket out of the country. If you're not sure what you intend to do next, the easiest solution is to buy the cheapest onward ticket to a neighbouring country or a ticket from a reliable airline which can later be refunded if you do not use it.

Transferred Tickets Airline tickets cannot be transferred from one person to another. Travellers sometimes try to sell the return half of their ticket, but officials can ask you to prove that you are the person named on the ticket. This is unlikely to happen on domestic flights, on an international flight tickets may be compared with passports.

Travel Agencies Travel agencies vary widely and you should ensure you use one that suits your needs. Some simply handle tours while full-service agencies handle everything from tours and tickets to car rental and hotel bookings. A good one will do all these things and can save you a lot of money but if all you want is a ticket at the lowest possible price, then you really need an agency specialising in discounted tickets. A discounted ticket agency, however, may not be useful for other things, like hotel bookings.

Travel Periods Some officially discounted fares, Apex fares in particular, vary with the time of year. There is often a low (off-peak) season and a high (peak) season. Sometimes there's an intermediate or shoulder season as well. At peak times, when everyone wants to fly, not only will the officially discounted fares be higher but so will unofficially discounted fares or there may simply be no discounted tickets available. Usually the fare depends on your outward flight – if you depart in the high season and return in the low season, you pay the high-season fare. ■

possible. Numerous other airlines fly to Hong Kong, which should work out around the same price as flying to Beijing.

Airfares to the subcontinent are much cheaper in the UK than they are in the rest of Europe – about half-price if you shop around.

To/From Hong Kong Hong Kong is the main entry point for China, although you might avoid the latter by flying to Kathmandu, which costs around US$320. Most travellers make their way into the PRC by train or ferry, but for those with limited time there are direct flights from Hong Kong to Chengdu or Beijing – Chengdu would be the logical destination unless you have business in Beijing.

Hong Kong once had a reputation as being a great place to pick up cheap tickets. This is no longer true, and in the case of flights to China is particularly untrue. There is no discounting on China flights, making them very expensive. Hong Kong agents do not deal with CAAC flights and you will need to go to one of Hong Kong's CAAC offices. The Central office is on the ground floor, 17 Queen's Rd (☎ 840-1199), while the Kowloon office is on the ground floor, Mirador Mansion, 54-64B, Nathan Rd, Tsimshatsui (☎ 739-0022).

The alternative to CAAC is Dragonair, a Hong Kong based outfit that offers better service (and higher safety standards) than CAAC at around the same flight prices. Dragonair tickets can be booked through travel agencies. From Hong Kong to Chengdu costs around US$300 with either airline.

A final point worth making with regard to Hong Kong is that it is worth considering flying from Shenzhen or Canton to Chengdu or Beijing. Shenzhen in particular is just a hop skip and a jump from Hong Kong, and tickets from Shenzhen to other parts of China are half the price of tickets from Hong Kong. Tickets from Shenzhen and Canton can be booked in Hong Kong at CAAC offices.

To/From Thailand Bangkok is a popular place to pick up air tickets, and prices are generally very competitive. The best place to shop around is Kao San Rd, the Bangkok Backpacker town. Flights to Kathmandu can be picked up for around US$250 (don't forget to organise your Chinese visa in Bangkok too), while flights to Calcutta via Myanmar cost around US$220. Flights to Hong Kong cost around US$150 one way, but flights direct to China are expensive. An exception to the latter are flights with Thai and CAAC from Bangkok and Chiang Mai to Kunming. From Bangkok to Kunming costs around 4000 baht one way, around 5100 baht return.

To/From the UK There are some very good deals available in London's bucket shops for flights to Beijing, Hong Kong and major Indian cities, mainly New Delhi. Those looking at travelling via the subcontinent and shaving costs wherever possible will undoubtedly find it cheapest to fly to New Delhi and then travel overland to Nepal (the trip can be done for less than US$10). Fares to India generally range from around UK£220 one way or UK£325 to UK£440 return. It pays to shop around. Check the travel sections of newspapers and 'what's on' magazines like *Time Out*.

The above applies equally to flights to Hong Kong and China. If you shop around it should be possible to get reasonably cheap prices on flights to Beijing with CAAC or perhaps with Aeroflot. Flights with more economical airlines to Hong Kong will work out a little more expensive but not much more.

To/From the USA & Canada It is far cheaper to fly to Hong Kong from the USA or Canada than it is to fly to India. This might work out quite well if your ultimate destination is India. Overland travel from Hong Kong to Nepal and India via Tibet is reasonably time consuming – but what a trip!

The cheapest prices on tickets to Hong Kong are offered by bucket shops run by ethnic Chinese. The highest concentration of these is in San Francisco, though Los

Angeles and New York are also good places to check out these agencies. Good deals are also available at more reliable long-running agencies: try Council Travel, Overseas Tours and Gateway Travel. Fares of around US$350 one way and US$650 return should be available if you shop around. Tickets to New Delhi or Bombay cost around US$1100 return. Canadian prices are very similar to those in the USA. Try Travel CUTS for good deals on tickets to Asia.

LAND

In theory there are a number of land routes into Tibet. In practice, however, most travellers only use one of two officially sanctioned routes: Kathmandu-Lhasa via the Friendship Highway or Golmud-Lhasa via the Qinghai-Tibet Highway. Other possible routes (as yet officially closed) are the Sichuan-Tibet Highway, the Yunnan-Tibet Highway and the Xinjiang-Tibet Highway. Of these the Yunnan-Tibet Highway is the 'most closed' (very few travellers, if any, are getting through to Tibet this way); the 'least closed' is the Xinjiang-Tibet Highway.

Nepal-Tibet (Friendship Highway)

The 920 km stretch of road between Kathmandu and Lhasa is known as the Friendship Highway. See the Tsang chapter for details of sights and landmarks en route. This highway is very well travelled nowadays and presents little in the way of problems.

From Kathmandu to the border town of Kodari transport is readily available in the form of buses and taxis. At the time of writing, there was nothing stopping travellers (providing they had a valid Chinese visa) heading up to the border and crossing over into Tibet. If you have arrived in Kathmandu without a Chinese visa you will be directed onto a tour. Some agencies in Kathmandu have found a loophole in this system and can put together 'disorganised' tours and organise visas for a price.

Travellers making their way from Kathmandu need not worry about onward transport once they have crossed the border

into Tibet. The Tibetan border town of Zhangmu is awash with vehicles looking for paying passengers to Shigatse or Lhasa. The going price for the two to three-day trip is Y300 to Y400 (even in a landrover), which is a lot less than you would pay if you were coming from Lhasa.

The journey between Kathmandu and Lhasa is without a doubt one of the most spectacular in the world. From Kathmandu the road travels gently up to Kodari (1873 metres), before leaving Nepal to make a steep switch-back ascent to Zhangmu (2300 metres), the Tibetan border town. From here the road climbs and climbs, past Nyalam (3750 metres) to the top of the La Lung-la pass (5200 metres), where travellers from Kathmandu are likely to feel decidedly weak and wobbly with the altitude. Tingri (4342 metres) provides fabulous views of Mt Everest and the Himalayas and is where many travellers spend the night or travel on to Everest Base Camp. Further attractions en route are the monastery town of Sakya, Shigatse and Gyantse.

Qinghai-Tibet Highway

The 1115-km journey between Golmud and Lhasa is actually the subject of an ancient Chinese curse: 'may you travel by Chinese bus from Golmud to Lhasa'. No, I made that one up – but it deserves to be.

Golmud (3200 metres), the drab little Chinese town where the journey begins, is approached by rail or bus from Xining (capital of Qinghai province). If Golmud were not one of the most utterly depressing places in China, it would probably serve as a good place to hang out for a few days and acclimatise to the altitude. But it *is* one of the most utterly depressing places in China and consequently most people jump on a Lhasa-bound bus quicker than a CITS official can say 'give us your cash'.

If Golmud did not exist CITS would have to invent it. It is a perfect bottleneck to capture Lhasa-bound individual travellers and screw them for every yuan possible. CITS officials make it their job to form welcoming parties for all incoming buses and

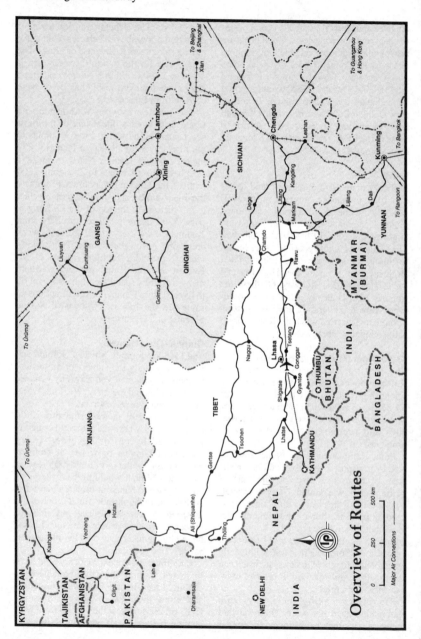

Overview of Routes

Major Air Connections ------

trains, and then start laying down the law: thou shalt only stay at the Golmud Guesthouse; thou shalt not hitchhike nor even stand on public thoroughfares with thine thumb extended; thou shalt pay extortionate sums to sit in a clapped-out Chinese bus for 30 hours, and so on, ad nauseam.

Buses for Lhasa leave from Golmud's Tibet bus station, and fares have been jumping so frequently over the last couple of years it is anyone's guess how much the journey will cost by the time you have this book in your hand. A recently published guidebook quoted the fare as Y70, when I was in Golmud in 1993 the fare was Y450, and when I returned in 1994 it had jumped to Y950. The justification for this price gouging (somebody – guess who – is getting very rich in Golmud) is the inclusion of a three-day tour of Lhasa on arrival. Most of the sights on this tour are within walking distance of the Yak Hotel, and your tour does not even include entry fees. Naturally, there are a lot of very pissed off travellers arriving in Lhasa from Golmud. Travellers making their way from Lhasa to Golmud by bus pay Y414.

The Qinghai-Tibet Highway is cold and bleak and almost devoid of interesting sights. Before setting off you should stock up on munchies and drinks and, if you have not already done so, buy some warm clothing. Xining is a better place to buy the latter than Golmud. Golmud has several markets and numerous shops where you can buy food and drinks.

The trip itself takes anywhere between 30 and 50 hours, longer if there is a serious breakdown. Even in summer it can get bitterly cold, especially up on the high passes, the highest of which is the Tangu-la pass (5180 metres). It is one of those once in a lifetime trips.

Sichuan-Tibet Highway

The road between Chengdu and Lhasa is either around 2400 km or around 2100 km, depending on whether you take the northern route or the southern route. It is currently closed to individual travellers, though the

occasional tour group passes along it. Like on the Yunnan and Xinjiang routes, all travellers should be prepared for a difficult trip that might end with a fine and an abrupt return to sender. The following brief description is not a recommendation that you try it.

While the occasional intrepid traveller still manages to make it through on this road, if your destination is Lhasa this is not the most sensible of routes to take. There is very little in the way of public transport; truck drivers face fines of up to Y2000 for carrying foreigners in their trucks; and it a dangerous trip – numerous accidents have occurred on it.

Food and accommodation is of a better standard and more widely available than on the Qinghai-Tibet Highway (where there is basically nothing) or in Western Tibet, however.

The early sections of the Sichuan-Tibet Highway have been open to foreigners for several years now. There are daily buses from Chengdu's Xinanmen bus station to Kangding, which is the last real town before the road divides into northern and southern routes. From Kangding onwards the risks of being caught, fined and sent back increase considerably. It is not a good idea to tell anyone that your destination is Lhasa. It may be possible to get a bus to the next town on the southern route, Litang (4700 metres), which is around 250 km west of Kangding. Onward travel to Markam, a farther 275 km west of Litang, is likely to be more difficult, and Markam itself is a town where the local PSB is particularly scrupulous about making sure that no travellers continue on to Lhasa.

The more than 780-km stretch of road between Markam and Bayi, a nondescript Chinese town that no one has a good word for, sees some amazing changes in scenery but is likely to be the biggest hurdle for travellers en route to Lhasa.

If you make it as far as Bayi, you will have to deal with the Bayi PSB. Many travellers have had problems with these people, and the best advice is to tell them you have come from Lhasa and let them have the pleasure of sending you back. From Bayi it is just 405 km to Lhasa. If you have made it this far, you will probably make it all the way.

The northern route involves a detour off the southern road just west of Kangding, travelling via Dege and Chamdo and rejoining the southern route around 300 km west of Markam. From Kangding there may be buses running the 305 km north-west to Ganzi, a monastery town. From here it is 207 km west to Dege, the next major town. From Dege to Chamdo is 339 km, and from Chamdo south to the southern route is a farther 171 km.

Yunnan-Tibet Highway

The Yunnan-Tibet Highway would be a wonderful way to approach Tibet were it ever to open. From Dali a road heads up to Zhongdian, a town which is now open, and from Zhongdian a road continues north 298 km to join with Markam on the Sichuan southern route. But unfortunately the Yunnan route is most definitely closed. There have been no reports of travellers successfully travelling on from Zhongdian, and those who have tried have been fined and sent back to Dali. Unconfirmed reports in mid-1994 claimed that two French travellers with bicycles had their bikes confiscated and were deported from China. Check the latest gossip in Dali if you are particularly interested in taking this route, but bear in mind that you may be given a nasty fine once you get out of Zhongdian.

Xinjiang-Tibet Highway

The Xinjiang-Tibet Highway is officially off limits, but interestingly quite a large number of travellers were managing to get through on the approximately 1350 km of road that separates Kashgar from Ali in Western Tibet (for information on travelling between Ali and Lhasa or Zhangmu see the Western Tibet chapter).

With at least two passes over 5400 metres, the Xinjiang-Tibet road is the highest in the world. It can be bitterly cold and closes down for the winter months from December through February. The whole trip takes around four days of travel, depending of course how lucky you are with lifts.

From Kashgar it is now possible to travel by bus to Yecheng, around 250 km and a day's travel to the south. There is no onward public transport from Yecheng to Ali but some travellers have successfully got lifts with trucks for around Y200. Be prepared for some serious haggling. From Yecheng to Ali is around three days of travel.

Overland Routes into China

Now that border crossings are possible between China and Nepal via Tibet, travellers from Europe can cover a great deal of distance without ever having to fasten their seat belts and put out their cigarettes. For more information on the Trans-Siberian Railway see Lonely Planet's *China – a travel survival kit* or more specialist publications such as *The Trans-Siberian Rail Guide* (Compass 1993) by Robert Strauss or the *Trans-Siberian Handbook* (Trailblazer) by Bryn Thomas.

The Karakorum Highway provides travellers with the opportunity to do a subcontinental circuit through Tibet, Nepal, India and Pakistan and back into China (in any order you like). For more information on the Karakorum Highway, see Lonely Planet's *Karakoram Highway – a travel survival kit*.

Hong Kong offers the easiest overland route into China, and travellers thinking of taking this route and travelling in China before making their way to Tibet should get hold of a copy of Lonely Planet's *China – a travel survival kit*. The same book has information on ferry access to China from Hong Kong, Japan and South Korea and also information on overland travel into China from Vietnam via Guangxi or Yunnan provinces.

Warning & Request

The information in this chapter is particularly vulnerable to change: prices for international travel are volatile, routes are introduced and cancelled, schedules change, special deals come and go, and rules and visa requirements are amended. Airlines and governments seem to take a perverse pleasure in making price structures and regulations as complicated as possible. You should check directly with the airline or a travel agent to make sure you understand how a fare (and ticket you may buy) works. In addition, the travel industry is highly competitive and there are many lurks and perks.

The upshot of this is that you should get opinions, quotes and advice from as many airlines and travel agents as possible before you part with your hard-earned cash. The details given in this chapter should be regarded as pointers and are not a substitute for your own careful, up-to-date research.

Getting Around

Tibet's transport infrastructure is poorly developed, and with the exception of the Friendship Highway and the Qinghai-Tibet Highway most of the roads are in very poor condition. Some work is being undertaken to improve this situation – a vital condition in Chinese plans to develop Tibet – but it is unlikely that travel in Tibet will become comfortable or easy in the near future.

The main problem for travellers who do not have oodles of time to trek across Tibet is that there is very little in the way of public transport in Tibet. There are no flights (excepting those to Kathmandu and Chengdu), no rail system and only a handful of buses and minibuses plying the roads between Lhasa and other major Tibetan towns such as Shigatse and Tsetang. So-called 'pilgrim buses' to monastery attractions have become more widespread in recent years, but are generally restricted to major monastic sights in the Lhasa region.

This situation leaves most travellers in the position of having to band together to hire 4WDs and minibuses to get around Tibet. The availability of such vehicles has rocketed recently, but in the peak summer months there can still be a squeeze and prices can rise. Travellers should bear in mind that, if they have limited time and want to see as much of Tibet as possible, they are probably going to end up spending quite a bit of money renting vehicles. Those with more time can, of course, trek or cycle their way around the high plateau.

BUS

Bus travel in Tibet is slow and gruelling. Most bus services originate in Lhasa and connect the capital with Shigatse, Tsetang and the border. Schedules tend to be slightly erratic. The Lhasa-Zhangmu service for example should run three times a month on the 2nd, 12th and 22nd but rarely does. A further annoyance is the fact that all public bus services exact a 100% surcharge on foreign travellers.

The usual rules concerning bus travel apply in Tibet. Try to avoid sitting in the back of the bus. The combination of bad suspension and shocking roads make for very bumpy bus journeys, and the back of the bus is the worst place to be. You will almost certainly be required to stow your baggage on the roof if you have a bulky backpack. If possible, check that it is tied down properly – bus drivers normally do a good job of checking such details – and lock your pack as a precaution against theft.

For long journeys it is a good idea to stock up on some snacks. Meal stops are usually infrequent and often yield fairly inedible fare.

Minibus

Private entrepreneurs are taking to the roads in increasing numbers, and minibus services are now available to many areas that are not served by buses. Minibuses are cheaper than public buses in that foreigners are only charged local prices. How long it will remain this way is anyone's guess. Local authorities were beginning to stop some minibus services between Lhasa and Shigatse in mid-1994 because foreign travellers were using them rather than the government buses. Given that the minibuses using this route were more comfortable, quicker and a third of the price of public buses, there is little surprise that foreigners were deserting the public services in droves.

Minibuses operate out of Lhasa to monastic sights such as Dreprung, Tsurphu, Ganden and Samye, and to Shigatse. From Shigatse, minibuses run to Gyantse. Ticket prices are very cheap.

VEHICLE RENTAL

Vehicle rental has become the most popular way of getting around in Tibet. There are numerous agencies dealing with the rental of landcruisers, jeeps and minibuses in Lhasa (see the Lhasa chapter) and a few also based in Shigatse. Costs are calculated on a per km basis, and if you are making a one-way trip (from Lhasa to the Nepal border for example) will include the cost of returning to Lhasa. The going price at the time of writing was between Y3.5 and Y4 per km. Cheaper rates are available for clapped out minibuses and Beijing jeeps.

Toyota Landcruisers are probably the most widely seen rented vehicles plying the high plateau loaded with backpackers. They have room for six or seven people and their luggage. Beijing jeeps are cheaper but can only hold around four people with their luggage, which ends up making them more expensive per person. Naturally, renting a minibus with 20 or more seats really spreads the costs around – but who can be bothered looking for 19 other travel companions?

The best place to hire vehicles is Lhasa. Before going ahead and organising a vehicle check the notice board at the Yak Hotel. There are usually dozens of notes here advertising seats on trips to all quarters of Tibet. The most popular options are to the Nepal border, lake Nam-tso and Mt Kailash. Day trips to places such as Ganden Monastery are also popular, and there are likely to be few notices advertising places on trips to more obscure destinations.

Actually hiring a vehicle is subject to all kinds of pitfalls. Drawing up a contract in English and Tibetan or Chinese is a good idea, but carries much less weight in Chinese-controlled Tibet than it would elsewhere in the world. It is not unusual for drivers to flaunt the conditions of a contract and in the end there is little that can be done about it. It is a good idea to reach an agreement that payment be delivered in two instalments: one before setting off and one on successful completion of the trip. The fact that you are holding back some of the payment gives you far more leverage in negotiating problems with drivers.

Finally, when hiring a vehicle it is important that you request to see your vehicle (and preferably meet the driver too) before you set off. There are some very dodgy vehicles bouncing along the roads of Tibet. Try to make sure that you don't get one of them.

TRUCKING

With the exception of travellers hitching out to Western Tibet or those making their way illegally from Chengdu to Lhasa, very few

---

Contracts

It has become standard practice amongst foreign travellers hiring vehicles to draw up a contract. The exact value of these contracts is somewhat dubious. They certainly do not mean a great deal to the average Tibetan or Chinese driver. And in the case of a one-way trip to the Nepal border, for example, how long are you prepared to hang around on the border waving the contract in the air and pouring over it with your driver and local PSB officials?

This is not to say that you shouldn't bother with a contract. Draw one up by all means. But try and keep it short and to the point. List your exact itinerary, the price and method of payment. Clauses that prevent the driver from picking up 'friends' and 'relatives' en route are useful if you do not want to be squeezed by freeloaders. But above all get together with the driver before the trip and go through the main points of the contract verbally. Both Chinese and Tibetans find the idea of a contract-based relationship cold and businesslike. You are likely to have much less problems on your trip if you can get on friendly terms with your driver –treat him with respect, give him some cigarettes or some kind of small gift – than by waving a contract in his face.

When I was last in town, a group of travellers heading out to the Nepal border were proudly showing around a contract of mind-numbing complexity they had put together. Loaded with draconian articles, it forbade the driver from picking up hitch-hikers or smoking, from seeking freebie meals from his passengers, and finally from playing his own music on the tape deck –the poor bastard. It was unlikely that they made any friends on that trip, and it is also an invitation to vengeful obstructionism. ■

foreigners travel by truck these days. The main reason is that the authorities impose heavy fines on truck drivers caught transporting foreign travellers. This is particularly the case on the Lhasa-Chengdu route, where fines of Y2000 prevail, plus whatever local officials demand in bribes.

There seems to be little stopping truck drivers picking up travellers making their way out to Western Tibet, however. There are no checkpoints on either the southern or northern routes, and providing you are prepared to pay your way it is usually possible to get a lift with a truck. At the time of writing, truckers were usually charging hitchers around Y400 for a lift from Ali to Lhasa. Some travellers were successfully getting lifts from Ali to Yecheng or Kashgar in Xinjiang province.

The most frequently seen truck in Tibet is the Dongfeng, a sturdy and basic Chinese-made vehicle with a carrying capacity of around 10 tonnes. It comes in a variety of models. The occasional Japanese-made truck also turns up.

If you hitch by truck in Tibet, be prepared to share the hardships of a trucker's life. You will probably end up helping to drag your vehicle out of rivers and sand drifts, and assisting in repairs. Particularly in Western Tibet the roads are atrocious and accidents, breakdowns and delays are par for the course.

Getting a Lift

Back in the early days of Tibet travel, truck depots were good places to organise lifts with trucks. Nowadays you will be drawing unwanted attention to yourself and your intentions by popping into depots in Tibet's urban centres. It is a far better course of action to get out on the road. Those planning on hitching along the Friendship Highway from Lhasa for example should at least get as far as Shigatse, preferably Lhatse. The Western Tibet chapter has information on hitching out to Mt Kailash.

One thing you do have to bear in mind is that it is very unusual nowadays to hear of people getting free lifts in Tibet. It does occur

occasionally, but more often than not you will be expected to pay for your lift. The amount is entirely negotiable, but in areas where traffic is minimal drivers will often demand quite large sums.

BICYCLE

Long-distance cyclists are once again appearing on the roads of Tibet. Some buy mountain bikes in China and bring them up to Lhasa; others cycle all the way up from Kathmandu. Some travellers even buy their bikes in Lhasa. Any of these options is currently feasible, and local authorities appear to be turning a blind eye to the phenomenon.

Rental

At present the only place in Tibet that you can easily rent bicycles is Lhasa. Rates of Y2 per hour prevail, and the bikes are usually clunky Flying Pigeons. Test the brakes and tyres before taking the bike out onto the streets of Lhasa. An extra padlock might be a good idea, as there is a problem with bicycle theft in Lhasa.

Touring

Restrictions on individual cycling in Tibet seem to have been lifted recently. This is not to say that it will necessarily stay that way, but in mid-1994 many travellers were undertaking their own cycle tours of Tibet, mainly between Lhasa and Kathmandu.

Despite the recent ease of access, Tibet still poses unique challenges to the individual cyclist. The roads are generally very bad even though there's not much traffic, wind squalls and dust storms can make the cyclist's work particularly arduous, the warm summer months can bring flash flooding, and then there is the question of your fitness. Tibet's high-altitude mountainous terrain is sure to test the determination of all cyclists who set out on its roads.

It is possible nowadays to buy mountain bikes in China and in Lhasa. Some cyclists have bought bikes in Lhasa and successfully cycled all the way to Kathmandu with them, where they have resold them for more than they paid for them. Not a bad deal. Do not expect the quality of such bikes to be equal to those you might buy at home, and they may not stand up to the rigours of extended touring.

Whether you bring a bike with you or buy one in China or Tibet, you will need to be prepared to do your own repairs. A full bicycle repair kit, two spare inner tubes, a spare tyre and chain, and preferably some spare spokes are essential. You will also need to be prepared with supplies and camping equipment as if you were trekking. Most long-distance cyclists will probably find accommodation and restaurants only available at intervals of two or three days of cycling.

Obviously you need to be in good physical condition to undertake road touring in Tibet. Experienced cyclists recommend a programme of training before heading off to Tibet. Spend some time acclimatising to the altitude and taking leisurely rides around Lhasa (for example) before setting off on a long trip.

On the plus side, while cycling in Tibet sees you on some of the highest altitude roads in the world, gradients are usually quite manageable. Tibetan roads are designed for low-geared Chinese trucks, and tackle the many high passes of the region via low-gradient switch-back roads. Most cyclists report that there are few occasions when it is necessary to get off their bikes and push.

Touring Routes The most popular touring route at present is Lhasa-Kathmandu. It is an ideal route in that it takes in most of Tibet's main sights, offers the cyclist superb scenery and features (for those travelling from Lhasa) a spectacular roller-coaster ride down from the high La Lung-la pass into the Kathmandu Valley. The trip takes a minimum of two weeks, though to do it justice and include stopovers at Gyantse, Shigatse and Sakya the trip will take more like 20 days. The entire trip is just over 940 km.

Very few travellers have been attempting this tour, but it is also possible to cycle to Everest Base Camp. Keen cyclists with good mountain bikes might want to consider this option as a side trip on the Lhasa-Kathmandu route. The trip would have to be tackled from the Shegar turn-off, and the trip would take around two days to Rongbuk Monastery.

Other possibilities are endless. Once the Lhasa-Tsetang Highway is completed (slated for late 1994) cycling in the Yarlung Valley region would be a wonderful option. Some cyclists even tackle the Qinghai-Tibet Highway between Lhasa and Golmud.

Hazards
Cycling in Tibet is not to be taken lightly. Traffic on Tibetan roads is relatively light, but cyclists do have to be prepared for some very erratic driving. Some cyclists have also complained of deliberate offensive driving by Chinese troop convoys, for whom driving a couple of foreign cyclists off the road is a brief escape from the tedium of soldiering up on the high plateau. It would be wise to pull off the road and wait for such convoys to pass.

Dirt roads prevail in Tibet, and these present particular problems. Cyclists who pick up too much speed on downhill stretches run the risk of slipping on gravel. Numerous cycling trips have been brought to an abrupt conclusion by such a misadventure. Be sensible. Wear a cycling helmet and lightweight leather gloves and, weather permitting, try to keep as much of your body covered with protective clothing as possible. A denim jacket, jeans, gloves and a helmet will protect you from the worst of gravel rash and head injuries if you take a tumble. It goes without saying that cyclists should also be prepared with a comprehensive first-aid kit. See the Health section in the Facts for the Visitor chapter for details.

TREKKING

As is the case in long-distance cycling, individual trekking is once again an option in Tibet. There is very little stopping those prepared for the rigours of high-altitude walking from exploring the Tibetan countryside on their own or in a small group.

Naturally you need to be in good physical condition to trek in Tibet. If you have an extended stay in Tibet, it is possible to get into condition during the course of your travels. It is better, however, to embark on a regime of exercise before you set out. It will make you no less susceptible to the effects of the altitude when you arrive, but it will help you to recover quicker and stand you in good stead on long days of walking.

All trekking in Tibet should be undertaken only after sufficient preparation. Once you get off the main roads of Tibet, there is nothing in the way of support services, little in the way of accommodation and food. Foolhardy sudden ascents run the risk of AMS (see the Health section of the Facts for the Visitor chapter) and you will have to deal with any medical emergencies yourself until you can get back onto a road and hitch somewhere for assistance. It is foolish to trek alone. Try and find at least one companion for any trekking expedition you make.

Wherever possible consider hiring local guides and pack animals. Prices are generally very reasonable in rural Tibet, and not having to labour under a heavy backpack will make an enormous difference to the quality of your trek.

There are several treks that have now emerged as popular options for travellers (Ganden-Samye, Everest Base Camp and the Kailash kora). Lake Nam-tso is also becoming a popular trekking destination. Most of these treks now follow fairly well-trodden trails, and locals are already used to the appearance of foreign backpackers. Burros and yaks are usually readily available for hire on such treks. Those attempting treks to more offbeat locations should get hold of Gary McCue's *Trekking in Tibet – a traveler's guide*. This book is full of useful

tips on trekking and also includes trekking routes in various regions of Tibet. Another useful book with extensive details of treks in Tibet is Victor Chan's *Tibet Handbook – a pilgrimage guide*.

LOCAL TRANSPORT

Local transport is only available in Lhasa and Shigatse. In some parts of Tibet it is possible to get short lifts with tractors, an extremely uncomfortable way to travel.

To/From the Airport

The only airport in Tibet serves Lhasa from the town of Gonggar. CAAC runs a bus service between the airport and Lhasa. See the Lhasa chapter for more details.

Bus

Minibuses ply the streets of Lhasa these days, and it is possible to get quickly from one end of town to the other for Y1. It is the only service of its kind in Tibet.

Rickshaw

Rickshaws are available in both Lhasa and Shigatse. They are a slow and expensive way to get around. In Lhasa for example it costs a minimum of Y7 to go from one end of town to the other and is much more time consuming than travelling by minibus. Serious haggling is required for hiring rickshaws.

Tractor

In Shigatse tractors serve as the town's public transport system and rides cost around Y2 or Y3. Elsewhere in Tibet the tractor can be a good option for short-distance trips. For a few yuan drivers are normally quite happy to have some passengers in the back. Rides of anything over 10 minutes quickly become excruciatingly painful.

Lhasa ལྷ་ས་

Lhasa, the heart and soul of Tibet, abode of the Dalai Lamas, an object of devout pilgrimage, is still, despite the large-scale encroachments of Chinese influence, a city of wonders. As you enter the Kyi Chu valley, either on the long haul from Golmud or from Gonggar airport, your first hint that Lhasa is close at hand is the sight of the Potala, a vast white and ochre fortress soaring head and shoulders over one of the world's highest cities. It is a sight that has heralded the marvels of the holy city to travellers for three centuries.

While the Potala dominates the Lhasa skyline and, as the residence of the Dalai Lamas, serves as a symbolic focus for Tibetan hopes of self-government, it is the Jokhang, some two km to the east of the Potala, that is the spiritual heart of the city. The Jokhang, a curious mix of sombre darkness, wafting incense and prostrating pilgrims, is the most sacred and active of Tibet's temples. Encircling it is the Barkhor, the holiest of Lhasa's devotional circumambulation circuits. And it is here that most visitors first fall in love with Tibet. The medieval push and shove of crowds from another time and place, the street performers, the stalls hawking everything from prayer flags to jewel-encrusted yak skulls, and the devout tapping their foreheads to the ground at every step is an exotic brew that few newcomers can resist.

The Potala and the Jokhang, though most prominent, are just two of the sights that Lhasa has to offer. Close to the Jokhang is a number of smaller active temples that are little visited by foreign travellers. The alleys running off the Barkhor circuit are cluttered with pool tables, market stalls and milling crowds from all over Tibet. The Norbulingka, summer palace of the Dalai Lamas, is a short distance away in the west part of town; and in Lhasa's low-lying surrounding hills are the important Gelugpa monasteries of Sera and Drepung.

Modern Lhasa divides clearly into a western, Chinese, section and an eastern, Tibetan, section. For travellers who have arrived from other parts of China, the Chinese part of town harbours few surprises. Nestled at the foot of the Potala and extending a couple of km eastward is an uninspired muddle of restaurants, karaoke bars, administrative blocks and department stores. The Tibetan part of town, which begins not far east of Ngangra Lam, is altogether more colourful and is the best area to be based in.

HISTORY

Lhasa rose to prominence as an important centre of administrative power in the 7th century AD, when Songtsen Gampo (618-649), a local ruler in the Yarlung Valley, continued the task initiated by his father of unifying Tibet in concert with other local chieftains. Songtsen Gampo moved his capital to Lhasa and built a palace on the site that is now occupied by the Potala. At this time the temples of Ramoche and the Jokhang were also established to house Buddha images brought as the dowries of Songtsen Gampo's Chinese and Nepalese wives. Both of the temples still stand in Lhasa, though little of their 7th-century origins remain.

The rule of the Yarlung kings from their new capital, Lhasa, lasted some 250 years. Despite the founding of the Jokhang, Buddhism seems initially to have been a courtly affair. Tibet's first monastic community, Samye, was not established until the rule of a later Lhasa king, Trisong Detsen (755-797). More energy was expended in waging war on Tibet's neighbours, China, Nepal and India, than in propagating the new faith. Eventually Buddhism came into increasing conflict with Bön, the native shamanistic faith of Tibet, and the two religions became the focus of courtly intrigues that led to a decline of royal power and the breakup of the

Lhasa regime into a number of competing fiefdoms in the early 10th century.

There is little to draw on in imagining the kind of capital Lhasa might have been in the time of the Lhasa kings. Chinese records from Dunhuang state that the capital of Lhasa was a walled city with flat-roofed houses and refer to the 'king and his nobles' as living 'in felt tents'. The same records refer to an aversion to washing, the eating of tsampa and the plaited hair of Tibetan women – customs that persist to the present day.

With the breakup of the early Lhasa state, Buddhism enjoyed a gradual resurgence at various monastic centres, notably Samye and Sakya. It was at the latter that the next large-scale Tibetan regime emerged with Mongol support in the 13th century. Subsequent Tibetan governments were located in Neudong (Ü) and Shigatse (Tsang). Lhasa languished in the back waters of Tibetan history until the 5th Dalai Lama (1617-1682) defeated the Shigatse Tsang kings with Mongol support.

The 5th Dalai Lama moved his capital to Lhasa. He built his palace, the Potala, on the site of the ruins of Songtsen Gampo's 7th-century palace. Lhasa has remained Tibet's capital since 1642, and most of the city's historical sights date from this second stage of the city's development. Very little remains of Lhasa's 7th-century origins.

Since the Chinese takeover, Lhasa has undergone a third stage of development that has undermined much of the city's original Tibetan qualities. Photographs of the city prior to 1951 reveal a small town nestled at the foot of the Potala and linked by an avenue to another cluster of residences in the area of the Jokhang. The population of the city prior to the Chinese takeover is thought to have been around 20,000 to 30,000. Today the city has a population of over 150,000, and it is likely that Chinese residents outnumber Tibetans. Shöl, the village at the foot of the Potala, is rapidly being crowded out by karaoke bars and hair salons, and the old West Gate has been torn down. The avenue linking the Potala with the area of the Jokhang is now basically one sprawling Chinatown, and the Tibetan quarter is now isolated to the eastern end of town.

Modern Lhasa in many ways provides the visitor with both the best and the worst of contemporary Tibet. After all, despite the city's rich historical associations and colourful Tibetan population, it is here that Chinese control is most trigger-happy, and much of the city's charm has fallen prey to Chinese 'modernisation'. The old Tibetan quarters of the Barkhor and Shöl (at the foot of the Potala) comprise only around 4% of the total area of contemporary Lhasa, but even these lingering enclaves of tradition are under threat. Visitors might want to take a look at the shopping mall that has been built on the eastern end of the Barkhor circuit itself. Reports in mid-'94 indicated that in March alone 18 Tibetan compounds had been demolished in order to clear land for new buildings.

ORIENTATION

While Lhasa has emerged as a surprisingly sprawling city in recent years, orientation is

Clay figurine at Nechung Branch Temple

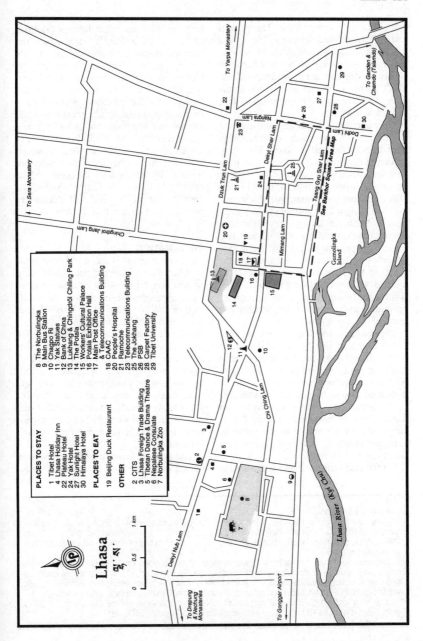

Lhasa

ལྷ་ས།

0   0.5   1 km

PLACES TO STAY

1 Tibet Hotel
4 Lhasa Holiday Inn
22 Plateau Hotel
24 Yak Hotel
27 Sunlight Hotel
30 Himalaya Hotel

PLACES TO EAT

19 Beijing Duck Restaurant

OTHER

2 CITS
5 Lhasa Foreign Trade Building
6 Tibetan Dance & Drama Theatre
7 Nepalese Consulate
8 Norbulingka Zoo
8 The Norbulingka
9 Main Bus Station
10 Chagpo Ri
11 Yak Statues
12 Bank of China
13 Lukhang & Chingdröi Chiling Park
14 The Potala
15 Workers' Cultural Palace
16 Potala Exhibition Hall
17 Main Post Office & Telecommunications Building
18 CAAC
20 People's Hospital
21 Ramoche
23 Telecommunications Building
25 The Jokhang
26 PSB
28 Carpet Factory
29 Tibet University

To Sera Monastery

Chingdröi Jang Lam

Dzuk Trun Lam

To Yerpa Monastery

Nangra Lam

Dekyi Shar Lam

To Ganden & Chamdo (Tsiamdo)

Dodhi Lam

Tsang Gyu Shar Lam

See Barkhor Square Area Map

Mimang Lam

Gumolingka Island

Chi Ching Lam

Dekyi Nub Lam

To Drepung & Nechung Monasteries

To Gongar Airport

Lhasa River (Kyi Chu)

still a relatively simple affair. The western end of the city is predominantly Chinese, and it is here that Lhasa's few up-market accommodation options can be found along with Chinese restaurants and government offices. The Tibetan eastern end of town has all the lower-end accommodation popular with individual travellers.

The principal thoroughfare for orientation is Dekyi Nub Lam, which becomes Dekyi Shar Lam in the east of town. This road, known as Beijing Lu in Chinese, runs from west to east past the Tibet Hotel, the Holiday Inn, the Yak statues, the Potala, the Main Post Office and into the Tibetan part of town not far after Nangra Lam (Jiefang Beilu) intersects it. Farther eastward Dekyi Shar Lam runs past the Yak and Banak Shol hotels, two of the most popular budget accommodation options. The Barkhor and the Jokhang, at the centre of the Tibetan quarter, are about 10 minutes' walk south of the Yak Hotel. There is a small Muslim quarter with a couple of operating mosques east of the Barkhor and south of the Banak Shol Hotel.

The Jokhang and Barkhor are between Dekyi Shar Lam and Tsang Gyu Shar Lam (Jinzhu Donglu) and are connected to these two main roads by a web of winding alleyways lined with the white-washed façades of traditional Tibetan homes. This Tibetan area is not particularly extensive. Rather than worry about orientation it is more fun to simply slip away from the Barkhor at some point and aimlessly wander the alleys. You won't stay lost for long.

For Tibetan pilgrims, who approach the holy city with somewhat different priorities to those of the average Western visitor, the principal points of orientation are Lhasa's three circumambulatory circuits: the Nangkhor, Barkhor and Lingkhor. The Nangkhor encircles the inner precincts of the Jokhang. The Barkhor traces the outskirts of the Jokhang in a circuit of approximately 800 metres – the most famous of Lhasa's pilgrimage circuits and probably the best introduction to the old town for newcomers. The Lingkhor is the devotional route that traditionally encompassed the entirety of the old city. Nowadays the Lingkhor includes a great deal of scenery that is of a decidedly secular and modern nature, but it is still used by pilgrims.

INFORMATION

Useful information is scarce in Lhasa. Most travellers find out more about what is going on and how things work by sitting around chatting amongst themselves in the courtyard of the Yak Hotel or at Tashi's I or II restaurants than they do by calling in to travel agents or government organisations like CITS. Bear in mind that all local travel agencies are self-serving and geared to misinforming individual travellers. Difficulties are always exaggerated and you will most likely be encouraged to apply for unnecessary permits and to join costly tours. Search out the advice of other more experienced travellers before committing yourself to anything.

This said, perhaps the best places to seek out the advice of locals are the Tashi restau-

Subversive Maps
The idea of a subversive map had never occurred to me until, while working on this book, I received a copy *On This Spot – an unconventional map & guide to Lhasa* (International Campaign for Tibet, 1994). If it is possible, try and pick up a copy before you go to Lhasa, though be discreet with it while you are there.

On This Spot has 131 entries, including most of the conventional sights of Lhasa. More interesting, however, is its inclusion of decidedly unconventional sights. This includes the locations and details of numerous uprisings, the sites of 'attractions' that have been torn down or blown up, the locations of PLA barracks and prisons, and lots more. It makes for fascinating reading.

The map costs US$5.95 and can be obtained from the International Campaign for Tibet (☎202-268-4123), 1518 K St, Suite 410, Washington, DC 20005, USA. ■

rants and the Yak Hotel, although the latter operates a travel agency (in the loosest sense of the word) which doesn't necessarily offer the cheapest prices and the best services in town. A final word on Lhasa-based travel agencies is that, while there is a profusion of operations all functioning under different monikers, many of them are in cohorts. Some travellers give up on one agency and move to another one only to find themselves dealing with the same people. Tread carefully – there are pitfalls at every step.

CITS

This outfit deserves a heading mainly by virtue of its stature as the giant of China tourism. You do not necessarily have to avoid its services, but you should expect to come up against the same problems that you encounter elsewhere – misinformation, price gouging and incompetence. Nevertheless, although CITS charges more than the smaller independent agencies around town, you can expect higher standards than at most places.

The CITS office (☎ 33787) is at 208 Dekyi Shar Lam and shares the same building as the Tibet Tourism Corporation (☎ 32980) and China Travel Service in Tibet (☎ 32980).

Holiday Inn Agencies

Very few individual travellers bother checking out the agencies based in the Holiday Inn on the assumption that they will be overpriced. This is a fair assumption, but on the whole prices are generally not that much more expensive than those being quoted in other parts of town. Service standards and spoken English are generally better, and some of the agencies here can be good sources of information and good places to organise vehicles.

Recommended agencies are China Tibet Travel & Tours (CTTT) (☎ 24305), 3rd Floor, North Block, Holiday Inn; China Tibet Qomolangma Travelways (CTQT) (☎ 36863), Room 1112, Holiday Inn; China Workers Travel Service (CWTS) (☎ 34472), Room 1104, Holiday Inn; and China Youth

Travel Service (CYTS) (☎ 35588/36699), Room 1106, Holiday Inn.

Private Outfits

Concentrated mainly in the old Tibetan part of town around the Yak and Banak Shol hotels are a number of smaller agencies that can provide limited information and offer reasonably cheap deals on vehicle rental. Most of them are fairly disorganised and are dedicated more to relieving you of the contents of your wallet than to providing reasonable levels of service.

Perhaps the pick of the bunch (and we're loathe to make any particular recommendations due to the inconsistency of service standards) is Shangrila Tours at the Sunlight Hotel. They tend to play by the book (no hiring trucks for Kailash and they'll probably tell you that you need a permit for Shigatse) and are slightly more expensive than some of the other agencies, but at least they seem to deliver the goods.

Other agencies are CITS (not the real thing) next to Tashi's 2 Restaurant, TGTS opposite Tashi's I Restaurant and Tibet Traffic Travel in the Banak Shol Hotel. The Yak Hotel also has an agency of sorts. All these places can provide information and vehicles with varying degrees of competence but complaints from travellers are frequent. None of them are recommended.

Public Security Bureau

The PSB is on Dodhi Lam and is open from 9 am to 1 pm and from 4 to 6.30 pm Monday to Saturday. It is not a good place for visa extensions, but then no PSB offices in Tibet are. From mid-'94, the PSB was adopting a policy of only offering 15-day visa extensions. There were no exceptions to this rule throughout Tibet, and in Chengdu the same rule applied. Make enquiries about the current situation before requesting a visa extension. The cost is Y25. Travel permits generally cost Y10 and are readily available.

Money

The Bank of China is just north of Dekyi Nub Lam – turn at the yak statues and look for it on the left. Opening hours are 9.30 am to 12.30 pm and 2 to 5.30 pm weekdays, 9.30 am to 12.30 pm Saturday, closed Sunday. Travellers' cheques and cash in most major currencies can be exchanged with a minimum of fuss. The sub-branch on Dekyi Shar Lam, between the Banak Shol and Kirey hotels, can also change cash and travellers' cheques and is a more convenient option for most travellers.

There is a black market for US dollars in Lhasa but, given that rates are slightly lower than those given at the bank, the risks involved (there are a lot of counterfeit Y100 notes floating about) make such transactions rather silly unless you are caught cashless after hours.

The Holiday Inn has an exchange service, but it is only available for hotel guests.

Credit Cards Credit card advances are available at the main branch of the Bank of China. Accepted cards are Visa, MasterCard, Diners Club and American Express.

Post

The Lhasa Main Post Office is on Dekyi Shar Lam about 15 minutes' walk west of the Yak Hotel. It is open from 9 am to 6.30 pm weekdays, 9 am to 12.30 pm Saturday, closed Sunday.

All poste restante is registered in a book and a charge of Y1 is levied on each collection. In practice, however, as there seldom seems to be any staff on duty, most travellers grab the bundle of letters and take what they want.

You will need to organise your own packaging for parcels. It is also a good idea to leave the parcel unsealed until you get to the post office. The staff will probably want to check the contents.

Telephone & Fax

There is a telecommunications building at the northern end of Dodhi Lam in the east of town and a more conveniently located centre in the Main Post Office building. Both follow the same opening hours as the Main Post Office, provide international direct-dial telephone services and can even send faxes for you. The latter is a bit touch and go; if you don't mind paying a little extra to make sure that your fax has got through, the service at the Holiday Inn is a more reliable option.

It is worth bearing in mind that there is a surcharge of 50% on international phone calls and faxes (introduced after the abolition of FEC) and that you are exempt from it if you have a student card – don't forget to bring it along if you have one.

International calls require a deposit of Y200. Change is provided after the cost of the call is deducted. It is refunded in total if you don't get through. Prepaid cards are also available (card phones can be used until 11.30 pm). They cost Y150 for Y100 in calls. The same deal is also available in the foyer of the Holiday Inn, where phones are available 24 hours a day.

Nepalese Consulate

The Nepalese Consulate (☎ 22880) is on a side street just south of the Holiday Inn and north of the Norbulingka. Visa-issuing hours are Monday to Saturday 9.30 am to 12.30 pm. Visa applications are issued the next day. At the time of writing the visa fee had changed three times in the previous year and was hovering precariously at US$15 for a 15-day visa and US$25 for a 30-day visa. It is possible to pay in RMB and you should remember to bring along one visa photo.

It is also possible to obtain visas for the same costs as above at Kodari, the Nepalese border town, though it would be sensible to check first that this has not been changed.

Books & Maps

Buying books and maps in Lhasa is almost a dead loss. There is very little in the way of decent mapping or reading material available in Lhasa. The Xinhua Bookstore on Mimang Lam (about 10 minutes' walk west of the Barkhor square) is a shambles and even the occasional Jane Austen or Charles Dickens title that once graced its shelves seem to have disappeared. Maps of Lhasa may or may not be available, but there should be Chinese maps of Tibet. The reception of the Yak Hotel has an excellent English map of Lhasa available.

China Tibet – Tour Map, produced by the Mapping Bureau of Tibet Autonomous Region, is a handy fold-out affair with very dubious place name spellings. At least it is in English. It is available at some of the travel agencies around town and in the gift shops at the Holiday Inn and the Tibet Hotel. Also available is *China's Tibet*, a horrible little monthly publication in which every article begins tellingly with the sentence: 'Since the peaceful liberation of Tibet...'. This one should be boycotted.

The only other English reading material available is a number of locally produced coffee-table publications with photographs and text on Tibet. None of them are of particularly good quality, but they are generally cheap and might be worth sending home as souvenirs. The gift shops at the Holiday Inn and Tibet Hotel have copies, as does the gift shop just inside the entrance to the Norbulingka.

Medical Services

Médecins sans Frontières is based in the Yak Hotel, but they shouldn't be bothered except in dire emergency. They are busy people and are in Tibet to help the locals – not travellers with colds.

In the case of an emergency you will probably be taken or directed to the People's Hospital on Dzuk Trun Lam. Expect minimal hygiene standards, but the staff are competent. Official policy, or so we were told, is to charge foreigners six times what the locals are charged. Don't be surprised when you get your bill, though there is some latitude for bargaining.

THE BARKHOR བར་འཁོར་

The first stop for most newcomers to Lhasa is the Jokhang in the heart of the old Tibetan part of town. But before even venturing into the Jokhang it is worth taking a stroll around the Barkhor, Lhasa's intermediate circumambulation route, a quadrangle of streets that surrounds the Jokhang and some of the old buildings adjoining it. It is an area unrivalled

in Tibet for its fascinating combination of deep religiosity and push-and-shove market economics. This is both the spiritual heart of the holy city and its main commercial district.

For your first visit, enter from the Barkhor square (at the eastern end of Mimang Lam), a large plaza that was cleared in 1985. The plaza comes in for a lot of criticism from Western commentators as being 'ill-conceived' and so on, but it is a popular meeting area for Tibetans. It certainly does have its moments of incongruity (note the gothic street lamps and the ill-kept, fenced-off garden at the western end of the plaza), but at least the Chinese gracefully resisted the temptation to plunk a Mao statue in the middle of it all. No doubt, for the Chinese, the clearing of a plaza in the centre of Lhasa makes it easier to keep an eye on the activities of locals, but the plaza has also become a focus for protest and has been the scene of pitched battles between Chinese and Tibetans on several occasions.

Protest is the exception rather than the norm, however, and visitors entering the Barkhor square are much more likely to be confronted with crowds of devout Tibetans filing past the magnificent frontage of the Jokhang than with monks dodging tear-gas canisters.

Close to the entrance to the Jokhang is a constant stream of Tibetans following the Barkhor circumambulation route in a clockwise direction. Look for the two pot-bellied, stone incense burners *(sangkang)* in front of the Jokhang. There are four altogether, the other two positioned at the rear of the Jokhang, comprising the four extremities of the Barkhor circuit. Behind the first two sangkang are two enclosures. The larger one harbours the stump of an ancient willow tree (allegedly planted by Princess Wencheng) and a stele inscribed with the terms of the Sino-Tibetan treaty of 822. The inscription guarantees mutual respect of the borders of the two nations – well, treaties were made to be broken. It is simply amazing that the stele was not hauled away in the Cultural Revolution.

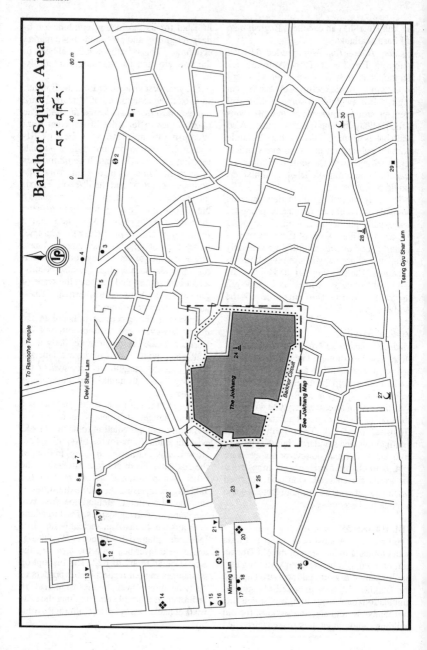

Barkhor Square Area

བར་འཁོར་

To Ramoche Temple

Dekyi Shar Lam

Mimang Lam

Tsang Gyu Shar Lam

The Jokhang

Barkhor Circuit

See Jokhang Map

PLACES TO STAY

1 Banak Shol Hotel
5 Kirey Hotel
8 Yak Hotel
22 Snowlands Hotel
29 Katag Hotel

PLACES TO EAT

7 Crazy Yak Saloon
10 Tashi Restaurant
12 Tashi II Restaurant
13 Lost Horizons
15 Alougang Restaurant (Pink Curtain)
21 Welcome Restaurant
25 Barkhor Cafe

OTHER

2 Bank of China (Branch Office)
3 Buy & Sell Antiques Shop
4 Gyume (Lower Tantric College)
6 Tromsik Khang Market
9 TGTS Travel Agency
11 CITS Travel Agent
14 People's Department Store
16 Minibus Stand
17 Xinhau Bookstore
18 Bus Booking Office
19 Tibetan Traditional Hospital
20 Tibet Travel Sales Centre
23 Barkhor Square
24 Meru Nyingba
26 Bus Station
27 Mosque
28 Ani Sangkhung
30 Main Mosque

Following the crowds into the Barkhor circuit, there is a curious sensation of having slipped through time into a medieval carnival. This is one part of Lhasa that has resisted any invasion of the modern world. Pilgrims from Kham, Amdo and farther afield, step blithely around a prostrating monk and stop briefly to finger a jewel-encrusted dagger at a street stall; children dressed like bit players in a stage production of *Oliver Twist* tug at the legs of a foreign visitor and beg for Dalai Lama pictures; a line of monks sit cross-legged on the paving stones before their alms bowls muttering mantras.

The whole circuit is lined with stalls selling everything a Tibetan or visiting tourist could possibly need. Some of the stalls sport a wide variety of souvenir items of dubious quality (be prepared to bargain hard), others specialise: some in hats, others in carpets, some in *kathak* (prayer shawls) and prayer flags, some in clothes – great browsing even if you are not in the mood for a purchase. One curiosity worth noting is that many of the stall keepers these days are Chinese. How times change. From razing monasteries and stripping monks of their vestments, the Chinese have moved to cashing in on the booming market for Tibetan religious items.

Running off the Barkhor circuit is a tangle of narrow alleys. Those running north up to Dekyi Shar Lam are also shopping streets that are worth exploring. Take the alley that leads up to Tromsik Khang Market past a myriad of stalls selling domestic goods (everyphing from thermoses to jerry cans) and pop into the market itself.

The yak-butter market on the ground floor is a remarkable, if pungent, experience. The alley that heads up to Dekyi Shar Lam just east of the Yak Hotel is notable for its outdoor pool tables where Khampas from the east of Tibet huddle over weathered felts and rarely pot a ball. Bring a camera.

THE JOKHANG ཇོ་ཁང་

Known in Tibetan as the Tsuglagkhang, the Jokhang is the most revered religious structure in Tibet. Although barely nothing remains of its 7th-century origins and most of the sculptures that adorn its interior post-date the assault of the Cultural Revolution, the Jokhang, bustling with worshippers and redolent with mystery, is an unrivalled Tibetan experience.

Entry to the Jokhang is free and it is effectively open daily from sunrise to sundown if you enter by the side door next to the main entrance.

History

Estimated dates for the Jokhang's founding range from 639 to 647. Construction was initiated by King Songtsen Gampo to house a Buddha image (Akshobhya) brought to Tibet as the dowry of his Nepalese wife Princess Bhrikuti. At the same time, Ramoche temple was also constructed to house another Buddha image (Jowo Sakyamuni) brought to Tibet by his Chinese wife Princess Wencheng. It is thought that after the death of Songtsen Gampo, Jowo Sakyamuni was moved from Ramoche and hidden in the Jokhang by Princess Wencheng, who feared a Chinese invasion. The image has remained in the Jokhang ever since, and is the most revered Buddha image in all of Tibet.

Princess Wencheng is said to have chosen the site of the Jokhang, and just to be difficult she chose Lake Wothang. The lake had to be filled in, but it is said that a well in the precincts of the Jokhang still draws its waters from those of the old lake. Over the years, many legends have coalesced around the task of filling in Lake Wothang. The most prominent of these is the story of how the lake was filled by a sacred goat (the Tibetan word for 'goat' *(ra)* is etymologically connected with the original name for Lhasa –

Rasa). A small statue of the goat can be seen in the Chapel of Maitreya on the south wall of the Jokhang's ground-floor inner sanctum.

Over the centuries, the Jokhang has undergone many renovations, but the basic layout is ancient and differs from many other Tibetan religious structures – one crucial difference is the east-west orientation of the building. Alterations were undoubtedly undertaken during the many centuries that Lhasa fell from prominence. During this time the Jokhang was probably administered by a succession of monks of various religious orientations. But the most drastic renovations took place during the reign of the 5th Dalai Lama in the 17th century. Lhasa returned to the centre stage of Tibetan affairs at this time and the Jokhang was enlarged accordingly.

In the early days of the Cultural Revolution, much of the interior of the Jokhang was desecrated by Red Guards and many objects are thought to have been removed. At one stage the monks' quarters were renamed Guesthouse No 5 and part of the Jokhang is claimed to have been utilised as a pigsty.

Demoness Subduing Temples

Buddhism's interaction with Bön – a shamanistic folk religion of ghosts and demons – and the inhospitable high places of the Tibetan plateau has led to many fables of Buddhism's taming and domestication of Tibet. Along with Guru Rinpoche's fabulous exploits, the early introduction of Buddhism to Tibet is attended by the story of a vast, supine demoness whose body straddled all the high plateau.

It was Princess Wencheng, the Chinese wife of King Songtsen Gampo, who divined the presence of this demoness. Through Chinese geomantic calculations she established that the heart of the demoness lay beneath a lake in the centre of Lhasa, while her torso and limbs lay far away in the outer dominions of the high plateau. As in all such fables, the demoness can be seen as symbolic of the inhospitability of Tibet and its need to be tamed before Buddhism could take root there. It was decided that the demoness would have to be pinned down.

The first task was to drain the lake in Lhasa of its water (read life-blood of the demoness) and build a central temple that would replace the heart of the demoness with a Buddhist heart. The temple built there was the Jokhang. A stake through the heart was not enough to put a demoness of this size out of action, however, and a series of lesser temples, in three concentric rings, were conceived to pin the extremities of the demoness.

There were four temples in each of these groups. The first are known as the *runo* temples and form a protective circle around Lhasa, pinning down the demoness's hips and shoulders. One of them is Tandruk Monastery in the Yarlung Valley. The second group, known as the *tandrul* temples, pin the knees and elbows of the demoness. And the final group, known as *yandrul* temples, pin the hands and feet. These last temples are found as far away as Bhutan and Kham (Sichuan), though the location of two of them is unknown. ∎

A: Monk, Shigatse (CT)
B: Children, Lhasa (CT)
C: Young Tibetan girl, Lhasa (CT)
D: Monk, Ramoche Temple, Lhasa (CT)
E: Monk with camera, Shigatse (CT)
F: Tibetan urchin, Sakya (CT)
G: Village children, Manasarovar (CT)

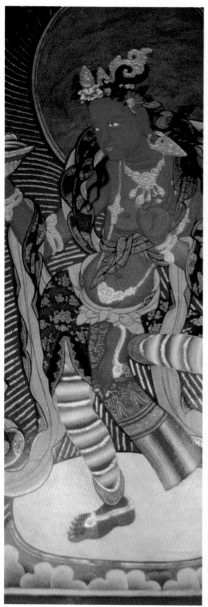

A: Images from Gyantse Kumbum (CT)
B: Detail of rug, Lhasa (RI)
C: Carpets, the Barkhor, Lhasa (CT)

Since 1980 the Jokhang has been restored and, without the aid of an expert eye, there is little sign of the misfortunes that have befallen the temple in recent years.

Inside the Jokhang

In front of the entrance to the Jokhang is a forecourt generally crowded with prostrating pilgrims. Take a look at the paving stones worn smooth by centuries of devotion.

Just inside the entrance to the Jokhang are the **Four Guardian Kings**, two on either side. Beyond this point is the **Main Assembly Hall**, a paved courtyard that is open to

the sky. There is not a lot to see here, except during festivals, when the Main Assembly Hall is often the focus of ceremonies. At the end of the courtyard and just before the entrance to the interior of the Jokhang itself is a long altar marked by a row of flickering butter lamps.

Entry to the Jokhang proper is via a short, dark corridor punctuated midway by a chapel on either side. The chapel to the left houses fierce, red-faced *nojin*, and the chapel to the right, *naga*, benign subterranean dragon-like creatures. Together they serve as protective deities.

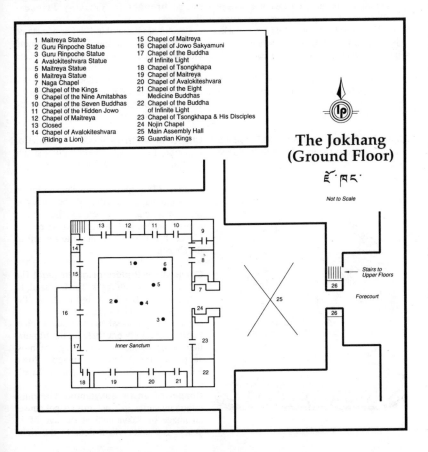

1 Maitreya Statue
2 Guru Rinpoche Statue
3 Guru Rinpoche Statue
4 Avalokiteshvara Statue
5 Maitreya Statue
6 Maitreya Statue
7 Naga Chapel
8 Chapel of the Kings
9 Chapel of the Nine Amitabhas
10 Chapel of the Seven Buddhas
11 Chapel of the Hidden Jowo
12 Chapel of Maitreya
13 Closed
14 Chapel of Avalokiteshvara
   (Riding a Lion)
15 Chapel of Maitreya
16 Chapel of Jowo Sakyamuni
17 Chapel of the Buddha
   of Infinite Light
18 Chapel of Tsongkhapa
19 Chapel of Maitreya
20 Chapel of Avalokiteshvara
21 Chapel of the Eight
   Medicine Buddhas
22 Chapel of the Buddha
   of Infinite Light
23 Chapel of Tsongkhapa & His Disciples
24 Nojin Chapel
25 Main Assembly Hall
26 Guardian Kings

**The Jokhang
(Ground Floor)**

ཇོ་ཁང་

Not to Scale

Inner Sanctum

Stairs to
Upper Floors

Forecourt

The inner sanctum of the Jokhang houses its most important images and chapels. Most prominent are six larger-than-life statues that dominate the central area. In the foreground and to the left is a six-metre statue of Guru Rinpoche.

The statue opposite it, to the right, is of Maitreya, the Future Buddha. At the centre of the hall, to the rear and between these two statues is a 1000-armed Avalokiteshvara. At the far right are two more Maitreya statues, one behind the other, and to the far rear, behind Avalokiteshvara, is another statue of Guru Rinpoche encased in a cabinet.

Encircling this enclosed area of statues is a collection of chapels. Tibetan pilgrims circle the central area of statuary in a clockwise direction visiting the chapels en route. There are generally queues for each of the chapels.

The chapels, following the clockwise route taken by pilgrims, are as follows (see the Jokhang map).

Chapel of Tsongkhapa and His Disciples
Tsongkhapa was the founder of the Gelugpa

Tsongkhapa

order, and you can see him seated centre, flanked by his disciples.

Chapel of the Buddha of Infinite Light The Panchen Lama is considered a reincarnation of this deity.

Chapel of the Eight Medicine Buddhas The Eight Medicine Buddhas are recent and not of great interest.

Chapel of Avalokiteshvara This chapel contains the Jokhang's most important image after Jowo Sakyamuni, the original image brought to Tibet by Princess Wencheng.

Legend has it that this 1000-armed statue of Avalokiteshvara spontaneously sprang into being and combines aspects of King Songtsen Gampo, his wives and two wrathful protective deities. The doors of the chapel are one of the few remnants of the Jokhang's 7th-century origins and were fashioned by Nepalese craftsmen.

Chapel of Maitreya Inside is a statue of Maitreya, four smaller bodhisattvas and a kneeling Maitreya of Wisdom.

Chapel of Tsongkhapa This chapel's image of Tsongkhapa, founder of the Gelugpa order, was commissioned by the subject himself and is said to be a precise resemblance. It is the central image to the left of the chapel.

Chapel of the Buddha of Infinite Light The second of the chapels consecrated to Amitabha, the Buddha of Infinite Light, the entrance to this chapel is protected by two fierce deities, as usual one red and one blue. Pilgrims generally pray here for the elimination of impediments to viewing the most sacred of the Jokhang's images, Jowo Sakyamuni, which waits in the next chapel.

Chapel of Jowo Sakyamuni The most important shrine in Tibet, this chapel houses an image of Sakyamuni at the age of 12 years. You enter via a door to the right.

Pilgrims circle the 1.5-metre statue of Sakyamuni, touch their forehead to his leg and exit by a door to the left. To the rear of Sakyamuni are other statues, including those of the 7th and 13th Dalai Lamas.

Chapel of Maitreya The Maitreya enshrined here is a replica of a statue that came to Tibet as part of the dowry of Princess Bhrikuti, King Songtsen Gampo's Nepalese wife. Surrounding the statue are eight images of Tara, a goddess who is seen as an embodiment of the enlightened mind of Buddhahood and who offers protection against the Eight Fears – hence the eight statues.

Chapel of Avalokiteshvara (Riding a Lion) Look to the left of the chapel for this – not the largest of the statues within – statue of Avalokiteshvara on the back of a lion. The other statues of the chapel are all aspects of Avalokiteshvara. At this point some pilgrims exit the chapel and take a flight of stairs to the next floor, while some complete the circuit on the first floor – if you're chapelled out (you've seen the important ones already), continue upstairs.

Guru Rinpoche Shrine Two statues of Guru Rinpoche and one of King Trisong Detsen can be found next to the stairs.

Chapel of Maitreya This, another Maitreya chapel, houses the Maitreya that is borne around the Barkhor on the 25th day of the first lunar month for the Mönlam festival. The Maitreya's yearly excursion is calculated to hasten the arrival of the Future Buddha. Look out also for the statue of the sacred goat mentioned in the Jokhang History section above.

Chapel of the Hidden Jowo This is the chapel where the Jowo Sakyamuni is said to have been hidden by Princess Wencheng. Inside is a statue of Amitabha and the Eight Medicine Buddhas

From this point are several chapels of limited interest to non-Tibetologists. The **Chapel of the Seven Buddhas** is followed by the **Chapel of Nine Amitabhas**. The last of the ground-floor chapels is the **Chapel of the Kings** which contains some original statues of Tibet's earliest kings. The central figure is Songtsen Gampo, and he is flanked by images of King Trisong Detsen (left) and King Ralpachen (right).

At this point (if you did not do so earlier) you should return to the rear of the inner chamber and climb the flight of stairs to the 2nd floor of the Jokhang. The 2nd floor of the Jokhang's inner sanctum is also ringed with chapels, though some of them are closed. Close to the stairway (just to the right as you exit) is the **Chapel of Guru Rinpoche**, the doorframes of which date back to the 7th century. Also worth a look is the **Chapel of Songtsen Gampo**, the principal Songtsen Gampo chapel in the Jokhang. It is positioned in the centre of the western wall (directly above the entrance to the ground-floor inner sanctum). The king is flanked by his two consorts, his Nepalese wife to the left and Chinese wife to the right. Also, importantly, his chang (barley beer) container is placed in front of him.

After exploring the interior of the Jokhang, the best part is arguably spending some time on the roof. There are various levels with stunning views of the sweeping, gilded roofs of the Jokhang, sometimes with the Potala in view as a breathtaking backdrop. It is also sometimes possible to find monks debating up here in the afternoon.

OTHER TEMPLES & MONASTERIES IN OLD LHASA

The old Tibetan quarter of Lhasa has a number of smaller active temples and shrines that are little visited by foreigners. It is worth spending a morning or an afternoon checking them out. Generally you will receive a friendly reception. Try and keep it that way by respecting local customs and asking politely for photographs.

Ramoche

Ramoche is the sister temple to the Jokhang. It was originally built to house the Jowo

Sakyamuni image that is now in the Jokhang. The principal image in Ramoche is Akshobhya, brought to Tibet in the 7th century as part of the dowry of King Songtsen Gampo's Nepalese wife. The image represents Sakyamuni at the age of eight years. It is said to have been badly damaged by Red Guards during the Cultural Revolution.

Built at the same time as the Jokhang, it is thought that, unlike the Jokhang, Ramoche was originally built in Chinese style. It was later rebuilt in Tibetan style and by the mid-15th century had become Lhasa's Upper Tantric College, Gyutö (see following for Lhasa's Lower Tantric College, Gyume). Today Ramoche is a little tired, and down at heel. It suffered extensive damage during the Cultural Revolution, and unlike at other Lhasa sights renovations seem to have been carried out with little zeal.

The Akshobhya image can be seen in the Tsangkhang, a small chapel at the far rear of the temple. There is a circumambulation circuit lined with prayer wheels around the perimeter of the temple. A Y15 entry fee is exacted on foreign visitors, and the zealous monk who collects the fee is not particularly interested in student cards.

Tsepak Lakhang

As you exit Ramoche look for an entrance just to the right. Pass a row of prayer wheels to a delightful newly opened chapel with three large statues. The central image is Amitayus, the Buddha associated with longevity. He is flanked by Maitreya and Sakyathupa (the Buddha of the Past). The young monks tending this place are very friendly, which comes as a relief after the sullenness of the residents next door at Ramoche.

Gyume

Gyume, or the Lower Tantric College, is just down the road from the Yak Hotel, opposite the Kirey Hotel. It is easy to miss – look for the No 20 scrawled on the door. This place gets very few foreign visitors.

Gyume was founded in the mid-15th

Amitayus

century and in its time was one of Tibet's foremost Tantric training colleges. In Lhasa, its importance was second only to the monasteries of Sera and Dreprung. Over 500 monks were once in residence, and students of the college underwent a physically and intellectually gruelling course of study. The college was thoroughly desecrated during the Cultural Revolution, and now only a handful of monks and novices are in residence here.

There is not a great deal to see nowadays at Gyume, but it is worth taking the flight of stairs up to the 2nd-floor chapel, where in an inner chapel there are some statues. The 3rd floor has a bronze image of Sakyamuni.

Gyume does not have regular opening hours and you may have to try several times before you find it open.

Meru Nyingba

This small monastery is a real treat. It is at the end of a small alley that runs from near the north-east corner of the Barkhor circuit. The main attraction is less the chapel than the courtyard area, which is invariably crowded with Tibetans thumbing prayer beads, lazily swinging prayer wheels and chanting under their breath. Sit quietly among them for a while with a camera in your hand and someone will invariably invite you to take their picture.

Meru Nyingba, like the Jokhang, originally dates back to the 7th century. Most of what you see today is of very recent construction, however.

Ani Sangkhung Nunnery

This small active nunnery is the only one within the precincts of the old Tibetan quarter. Again, there is not a great deal to see, but the nuns are friendly and seem genuinely pleased to have a foreign guest. Many visitors end up paying for their visit with a free English lesson. There is an official Y10 entry charge, but the nuns rarely seem to demand it.

The site of the nunnery probably dates back to the 7th century but it was a monastery at least until the 15th century. The main hall is up a flight of stairs on the 2nd floor. The principal image is a 1000-armed Avalokiteshvara.

The nunnery is a little difficult to find. It is on a narrow street south-east of the Barkhor. Look for the only yellow building on the street or ask for the ani gompa.

Mosques

There are a couple of mosques in the area around the Barkhor, serving Lhasa's 2000-strong Muslim population. It is dubious whether it is worth the effort of seeking them out. The main mosque, south-east of the Barkhor, is an uninspiring affair. It is possible to enter the inner courtyard, but there is a sign requesting that non-Muslims proceed no farther. There is another, newer mosque just west of the Ani Sangkhung nunnery. It is a bit more photogenic than the main mosque, but at the time of writing it was not possible to enter.

THE POTALA   རི་ཧྲ་ལ་

The Potala is Lhasa's cardinal landmark and a structure that deserves a place as one of the wonders of Eastern architecture. It looks best from a distance and it can be viewed and photographed from various places around town – notably from the top of Chagpo Ri and from the island in the Lhasa River.

As with many things Tibetan, there is some scholarly debate concerning the Potala's name. The most probable explanation is that it derives from the Tibetan name for Avalokiteshvara's Pure Land, also known as Potala. Given that Songtsen Gampo and the Dalai Lamas are maintained to be reincarnations of Avalokiteshvara, this connection is compelling.

Opening hours for the Potala are Monday and Thursday from 9 am to 12.30 pm. There is a shocking mark-up on the entry charge for 'foreign friends': Y45 as opposed to the Y1 paid by locals and pilgrims. A student card will get the price down to Y15. The high entry charge has come in for particular criticism from visitors due to the fact that, until recently, much of the interior of the Potala was closed to the public. Borrow a student card from someone if you find the entry fee unbearable.

Photographs of the interior of the Potala are only allowed after paying a fee of Y50. This is generally enforced, though if you find yourself alone in a room with a monk you can occasionally get away with handing out a Dalai Lama picture or just a polite request – don't count on it though.

On a final note, just after research for this book was completed, the Potala 're-opened' after five years of renovations. This means that there will be much more to see than the areas described in this section; opening hours are likely to have changed; and it is also possible that the entry charge will go up *again*.

History

Marpo Ri, the 130-metre 'Red Hill' that commands a view of all Lhasa, was the site of King Songtsen Gampo's palace in the 7th century, long before the construction of the present-day Potala. There is little to indicate what this palace looked like, but it is sure that royal precedent was a major factor in choosing the site of the Potala when the 5th Dalai Lama decided to move the seat of his Gelugpa government from Dreprung Monastery to more spacious quarters.

Work began first on the Potrang Karpo, or White Palace, in 1645. The nine-storey structure was completed three years later, and in 1649 the 5th Dalai Lama moved from Dreprung Monastery to his new residence. The circumstances surrounding the construction of the larger Potrang Marpi, or Red Palace, are subject to some dispute, however. In 1682 the 5th Dalai Lama died and his death was concealed until the completion of the Red Palace 12 years later in 1694. By some accounts, the work was initiated by the regent who governed Tibet from 1679 to 1703 and foundations were laid in 1690 (two years after the 5th's death). By other accounts, the Red Palace was conceived by the 5th Dalai Lama as a funerary chörten and work had already been going on for two years at the time of his death. In any event, the death of the 5th Dalai Lama was unannounced until he was put to rest in the newly completed Red Palace.

Since its construction, the Potala has been the home of each of the successive Dalai Lamas, although after the late 18th-century construction of the Norbulingka summer palace it served only as a winter residence. It was also the seat of the Tibetan government, and with chapels, cells, schools for religious training and even tombs for the Dalai Lamas it was virtually a self-contained world.

The 13th Dalai Lama undertook some renovation work in the early 20th century, demolishing sections of the White Palace to expand chapels. The Potala was also shelled briefly during the 1959 popular uprising against the Chinese. Fortunately, and miraculously, damage was not extensive. The Potala was also spared during the Cultural Revolution, reportedly at the insistence of Zhou Enlai, who is said to have deployed his own troops to protect it.

Inside the Potala

The Potala is a structure of massive proportions, an awe-inspiring place to explore, but still many visitors come away slightly disappointed. Unlike the Jokhang, which hums with activity, the Potala lies dormant like a huge museum, and the lifelessness of the building constantly reminds that the Dalai Lama has been forced to take his government elsewhere.

Entrance to the Potala is via Shöl village nestled at the southern foot of Marpo Ri. It was once Lhasa's red light district as well as housing a prison and some ancillary government buildings. Today it is an undistinguished cluster of Tibetan-style buildings and a couple of gift shops. Two access ramps snake up the southern side of the hill from Shöl (there is also a northern ramp which may offer access to the Potala on days that it is officially closed). Visitors to the Potala take the eastern entrance.

The entrance to the Potala takes you into **Deyang Shar**, the external courtyard of the Red Palace. From here a flight of steps leads into the **Red Palace**, the former living quarters of the Dalai Lamas. At this point, you continue climbing to the roof of the Potala and then make a gradual journey downwards, on the way taking in those parts of the Potala that are open.

Don't expect much to be open on the roof. The **Reception Hall** is an exception, and occasionally parts of the 13th and 14th Dalai Lamas' living quarters are open. Try slipping in behind a tour group if you have come unescorted by a guide.

Upper (4th) Floor The main attractions on the 4th floor are the **Chapel of Maitreya** and the **Tomb of the 13th Dalai Lama**. The Chapel of Maitreya contains an exquisite Maitreya image commissioned by the 8th Dalai Lama. The chapel was unfortunately damaged in a fire in 1984 (caused by an electrical fault) and many thangkas were lost. From here you visit three other chapels (**Chapel of Three-Dimensional Mandalas, Chapel of Victory Over Three Worlds** and **Chapel of Immortal Happiness**) before reaching the Tomb of the 13th Dalai Lama. Entrance is via a long corridor which leads to a gallery. You can look down on the tomb from above and then descend to look at it at ground level. Look for a famous three-dimensional mandala made of over 20,000 pearls on the altar.

Just before descending to the 3rd floor, there is a small chapel that is worthy of note: the **Chapel of Arya Lokeshvara**. Allegedly this is one of the few corners of the Potala that dates back to King Songtsen Gampo's 7th-century palace. It is the most sacred of the Potala's chapels and the image of Arya Lokeshvara inside is the most revered image housed in the Potala. There are many other highly revered statues in the chapel.

The 4th floor of the Potala is also home to the tombs of the 7th, 8th and 9th Dalai Lamas. They are usually closed to the public, though this may now have changed since the official re-opening of the Potala.

Third Floor The first of the chapels you come to on the 3rd floor is the **Chapel of Kalachakra**. It is noted for its three-dimensional mandala, which is over six metres in diameter and finely detailed. Next come the **Chapel of Sakyamuni** and the **Chapel of the Nine Buddhas of Longevity**.

The last of the chapels is, like the Chapel of Arya Lokeshvara on the floor above, said to date back to King Songtsen Gampo's original palace. It is thought to have once been the king's meditation cave. Today it is crowded with statues, the most important being one of King Songtsen Gampo himself.

Second Floor Closed to the public, there is virtually nothing to see on this floor. Again, it may now be open.

Lower Floor The lower floor, with its large **Assembly Hall**, the largest hall and centre of the Potala, is reached via a number of steep, dark staircases. The large throne that dominates one end of the hall was the throne of the 6th Dalai Lama. Four important chapels adjoin the hall.

The first chapel you come to is the **Chapel of Lamrim**. 'Lamrim' means literally the 'gradual path', and is used to refer to the graduated stages that mark the path to

enlightenment. The central figure in the chapel is Tsongkhapa, the founder of the Gelugpa order, with which lamrim texts are usually associated.

The next chapel, the **Chapel of the Eight Teachers**, is consecrated to eight Indian teachers who brought various Tantric practices and rituals to Tibet. The central figure is a silver statue of Guru Rinpoche.

In the west wing of the Assembly Hall is the awe-inspiring **Tomb of the 5th Dalai Lama**. His huge 14-metre chörten is gilded with some 3700 kg of gold. Flanking it are two smaller chörten containing the 10th (right) and 12th (left) Dalai Lamas.

The northern chapel of the Assembly hall contains statues of the first five Dalai Lamas and Sakyamuni. Also within the chapel is the tomb of the 11th Dalai Lama, who died at the age of 17 years.

At this point, you exit the Potala by a path that leads down to the site of Lhasa's erstwhile West Gate.

SIGHTS AROUND THE POTALA

A morning visit to the Potala can easily be combined with an afternoon excursion to some of the sights nearby.

Palha Lupuk

After you exit the Potala, a path takes you back down on to Dekyi Nub Lam at the site of Lhasa's old West Gate. On the other side of the road a path leads around Chagpo Ri, the hill that faces Marpo Ri, site of the Potala. Take this path and look for a flight of stairs several hundred metres on the right. The stairs lead up to Palha Lupuk, a cave temple that is said to have been the meditational retreat of King Songtsen Gampo.

The main attraction of the cave is its relief rock carvings. Some of them are thought to be over 1000 years old. Altogether there are over 70 carvings of bodhisattvas in the cave and on the cave's central column. Work on the carvings was probably undertaken at three different historical periods, but the oldest are generally the ones lowest on the cave walls. Many of the carvings were damaged in the Cultural Revolution and have since been repaired.

The yellow building next to Palha Lupuk is a chapel that gives access to the smaller meditation cave of King Songtsen Gampo's Chinese wife, Princess Wencheng. It is of less interest than Palha Lupuk, but worth a quick look if you are in the area.

Chagpo Ri

Apart from Palha Lupuk, there are a couple of other points of interest on Chagpo Ri, though the steel telecommunications mast that graces its summit is probably (for most visitors) not one of them. The hill was once the site of Lhasa's principal Tibetan medical college. Founded in 1413 by the 5th Dalai Lama, it was destroyed in the 1959 popular uprising.

Today, the hill's main point of interest is a series of rock carvings on cliff walls at three different places. Altogether there are over 5000 carvings, some of them dating back to the 7th century. The first carvings are thought to have been commissioned by King Songtsen Gampo and executed by Nepalese artists. A tradition of carving images on the cliffs of Chagpo Ri continued for another 1000 years. The best place to see the carvings is on the south-west end of the hill. There are more carvings on the north-east end of the hill.

Finally, for stunning views of the Potala, take the trail that begins opposite the exit for the Potala and walk 20 minutes to the summit of Chagpo Ri.

Bompo Ri

Several hundred metres to the west of Chagpo Ri, Bompo Ri is another hill with a couple of interesting sights. At the foot of the hill, close to Dekyi Nub Lam, is one of Lhasa's four former royal monasteries, **Kunde Ling**. The *ling*, or royal, monasteries were appointed by the 5th Dalai Lama, and it was from one of them that regents of Tibet were generally appointed. There is not much left of this one, but it is worth a quick look all the same.

At the top of the hill is **Gesar Temple**, a Chinese construction that dates back to the 18th century. It is the only Chinese temple in Lhasa and a quiet place for an afternoon walk.

Lukhang

Lukhang is a little-visited temple on a small lake island behind the Potala. The lake is in the Chingdröl Chiling Park, which is entered north of the CAAC building. It is open daily and entry is free.

The Lake of the Naga King in the park was created during the construction of the Potala. Earth used for mortar was excavated from here, leaving a depression that was later filled with water. Naga are a subterranean dragon-like species which were thought to inhabit the area, and the Lukhang, or Chapel of the Dragon King, was built to propitiate them by the 6th Dalai Lama. You can see Luyi Gyalpo, the Naga King, at the rear of the ground floor of the Lukhang. He is riding an elephant and protective snakes rise from behind his head.

The Lukhang is celebrated for its 2nd and 3rd-floor murals. They date from the 18th century. The 2nd-floor murals tell a story made famous by a Tibetan opera, while the murals on the 3rd floor depict different themes on each of the walls – monasteries, masters of Buddhism and the life cycle as perceived by Tibetan Buddhists.

Gumolingka Island

Gumolingka Island is south of the Potala and accessible from Tsang Gyu Nub Lam by way of a prayer-flag festooned bridge. The island, in the middle of the Lhasa River, is a classic position from which to view and photograph the Potala (get there early in the morning for the best light). It is also a popular picnic spot in the summer months and a favoured destination for outings during the September Washing Festival.

THE NORBULINGKA ནོར་བུ་གླིང་ཁ་

The Norbulingka, about 10 minutes' walk south of the Holiday Inn in the western part

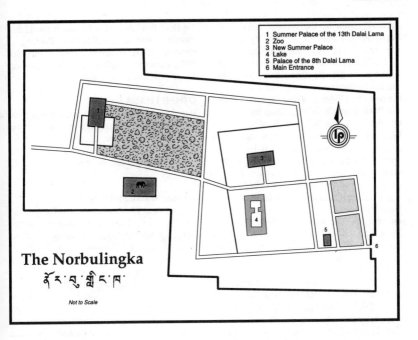

1 Summer Palace of the 13th Dalai Lama
2 Zoo
3 New Summer Palace
4 Lake
5 Palace of the 8th Dalai Lama
6 Main Entrance

The Norbulingka

ནོར་བུ་གླིང་ཁ་

Not to Scale

of town, is one of Lhasa's principal sights. Still, the Summer Palace of the Dalai Lamas rates a definite second to other points of interest in and around Lhasa, such as the Jokhang, the Potala, and Sera and Dreprung monasteries. The gardens are poorly tended and the palaces themselves are something of an anticlimax. Avoid the zoo at all costs – it is thoroughly depressing.

During the seventh lunar month of every year, the Norbulingka is crowded with picnickers for the Shötun (Yoghurt) Festival. Traditional Tibetan opera performances are also held at this time.

The Norbulingka is open daily and there is a Y17 entry charge.

History

The first summer palace to be constructed in the Norbulingka park area was founded by the 7th Dalai Lama in 1755. Rather than using the palace as a simple retreat, he decided to use the wooded environs as a base from which to administer the country, a practice that was to be followed by each of the Dalai Lamas who succeeded him. The 8th Dalai Lama (1758-1804) initiated further work on the Norbulingka, expanding the gardens and digging a lake which can be found just south of the New Summer Palace. The 13th Dalai Lama (1876-1933) was responsible for the three palaces in the northwest corner of the park. The 14th Dalai Lama built the New Summer Palace in 1956.

The 14th Dalai Lama made his escape disguised as a Tibetan soldier from the Norbulingka in 1959. Unfortunately all the palaces of the Norbulingka were damaged by Chinese artillery fire in the popular uprising that followed the Dalai Lama's flight. Repairs have been undertaken but they have failed to restore the palaces to their full former glory.

In the Grounds of the Norbulingka

The **New Summer Palace** (Takten Migyü

Potrang), built by the present Dalai Lama between 1954 and 1956 is probably the most interesting of the Norbulingka palaces.

The first of the rooms you visit is the **Dalai Lama's Audience Chamber**. Note the murals on the chamber's walls. They depict the history of Tibet in 301 scenes. Next come the **Dalai Lama's Private Quarters**, which consist of a meditation chamber and a bedroom. The rooms have been maintained exactly as the Dalai Lama left them, and apart from the usual Buddhist images they contain the occasional surprise: a Phillips radiogram and a stylish European bed among other things. Other rooms of interest in the New Palace include the library and a meditation room. The **Assembly Hall**, where the Dalai Lama would address heads of state, is home to a gold throne backed by murals of all 14 Dalai Lamas.

Behind the New Summer Palace, and perhaps of interest to automobile buffs, are three dilapidated vehicles slowly rusting away. The 1931 Dodge and two 1927 Austins were brought to Tibet in pieces on the backs of yaks and delivered to the 13th Dalai Lama as gifts. It was not until the 1950s that the present Dalai Lama got the vehicles going – they were then the only cars in Lhasa.

Palace of the 8th Dalai Lama The Kelsang Potrang, as it is known in Tibetan, is the first of the palaces from the entrance to the Norbulingka. It is of limited interest. Inside is a throne backed by statues of the Eight Medicine Buddhas. Several ferocious dogs scamper around the tops of the palace wall; they seem particularly incensed by the arrival of foreign visitors.

Palace of the 13th Dalai Lama The Chensek Potrang, as it is known in Tibetan, is in the western section of the Norbulingka, just on from the zoo (the shrieks of deranged monkeys should be warning enough to give the zoo a wide berth).

There is not a lot to see in the three-storey palace, but it is worth a visit all the same. The 2nd-floor living quarters remain as they were at the time of the 13th Dalai Lama and on the

1st floor is an assembly hall with the 13th's throne. Close to the Chensek Potrang is another, smaller palace also built by the 13th Dalai Lama. On the 2nd floor is a reception room with Buddhist statuary.

OTHER LHASA SIGHTS

Besides the monastic and temple sights of Lhasa, there are a number of lesser sights around town, some of which you may stumble across as you wander around and some you might like to make a special visit to.

Tibetan Traditional Hospital

The original Tibetan Traditional Hospital of Lhasa sat atop Chagpo Ri hill opposite the Potala. It was destroyed by artillery fire in the 1959 uprising. This one, on the north side of Mimang Lam, was set up by the 13th Dalai Lama in 1916.

Tibetan medical science is an arcane field whose theories are backed up by Tantric texts. Diagnosis is largely carried out by taking various pulses, and illnesses are thought to result from imbalances between 'humours'. It obviously owes something both to Indian medicine and to Chinese medicine. The influence of the latter can be seen in the use of moxibustion. Surgery is never used in Tibetan medicine, and patients requiring treatment of this kind have to visit one of Lhasa's Chinese hospitals.

Tibetan doctors still train at the Tibetan Medical Hospital, and on the top floor the traditional teaching thangkas are kept. If you are interested to see the clinic, you should make a polite request for one of the staff to show you around. It is a hospital. Do not go barging in.

Lhasa Carpet Factory

You do not necessarily have to be in the market for a carpet to call into the carpet factory. The weaving process is still carried out by hand on vertical looms, and the factory makes for an unexciting but interesting visit. It is in the south-east of town on Tsang Gar Shar Lam near the Tibet University.

Potala Exhibition Hall

On Dekyi Nub Lam, just below the Potala, this exhibition hall rarely shows any sign of life, though its opening hours are supposed to correspond with those of the Potala. This may all have changed with the new inauguration of the Potala. Check it out when you visit the Potala, but do not expect too much.

The Golden Yaks

These hardly rate as an attraction, but everybody passes them during their stay in Lhasa and, like me, probably wonders how on earth they came to be there. They are quite a recent addition, being unveiled on 26 May 1991 in celebration of the 40th anniversary of the 'liberation' of Tibet. It is difficult not to wonder whether the Chinese authorities were aware of the irony of having to call a temporary state of martial law, ban all foreign journalists and restrict all foreign tourists to their hotel rooms during the celebrations. At all events, the result is a depressingly uninspiring civic monument.

LHASA'S OUTLYING MONASTERIES

Within easy cycling distance of central Lhasa are the major Gelugpa monasteries of Sera and Dreprung. Both are worth visiting, even if you have only a brief stay in Lhasa.

Dreprung Monastery
འབྲས་སྤུངས་དགོན་པ་

About eight km to the west of central Lhasa, Dreprung was once the world's largest monastery, with a population of around 10,000 monks. It has suffered through the ages with assaults by the kings of Tsang and the Mongols, but it was left relatively unscathed during the Cultural Revolution and there is still much of interest left intact.

A brief word of warning should be given regarding Dreprung's dogs. Most Tibetan gompas are home to packs of dogs, who are thought to be reincarnations of monks who didn't get their lessons right and most definitely did not move up a rung on the karmic ladder. In Dreprung's case the dogs seem particularly savage. It is a good idea to bring a stick along. Several travellers have been bitten.

Dreprung is open from approximately 9 am to 4 pm. There may be breaks for lunch (any time from noon to 2 pm) and some or all chapels and colleges may be closed on Sunday. There is a Y10 entry charge.

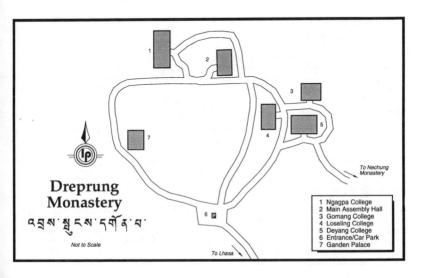

Dreprung
Monastery
འབྲས་སྤུངས་དགོན་པ་

Not to Scale

To Nechung Monastery

To Lhasa

1 Ngagpa College
2 Main Assembly Hall
3 Gomang College
4 Loseling College
5 Deyang College
6 Entrance/Car Park
7 Ganden Palace

History Dreprung was founded in 1416 by a charismatic monk and disciple of Tsong-khapa (founder of the Gelugpa order) called Jamyang Chöje. He was able to raise funds for the project quickly and within a year of completion the monastery already hosted a population of some 2000 monks.

In 1530 the 2nd Dalai Lama established the Ganden Palace, the palace that was home to the Dalai Lamas until the 5th built the Potala. It was from here that the early Dalai Lamas exercised their control over central Tibet, and the 2nd, 3rd and 4th Dalai Lamas are entombed here. Meanwhile the monastic population of Dreprung continued to grow. By the time of the 5th Dalai Lama in the early 17th century, the number of resident monks was somewhere between 7000 and 10,000. Today there are around 500 monks in residence.

Ganden Palace Following a clockwise circuit around Dreprung, the first of the buildings you come to is the Ganden Palace. Prior to the construction of the Potala, it was the residence of the Dalai Lamas. Although the palace building itself is impressive, there is little of note inside.

The Main Assembly Hall The Main Assembly Hall, or Tsomchen, is the principal structure in the Dreprung complex. The huge Assembly Hall itself is now only used on special occasions, but it is possible to imagine it crowded with monks in the monastery's heyday.

The interior of the hall is very atmospheric, draped with thangkas and marked by over 180 supporting columns. Sculptures of interest include those of Tsongkhapa, Jamyang Chöje and a series of Dalai Lamas – the 7th, 3rd, 4th, 5th (raised above the others), 9th and 8th. At either end of the altar is a group of eight arhats.

The 3rd floor of the Main Assembly Hall contains a chapel with the hall's most revered image, a massive statue of Maitreya, the Future Buddha, at the age of 12. The statue rises through three floors of the building from a ground-floor chapel that is usually closed. To the right of this chapel is a Tara Chapel. Tara is a protective deity, and in this case the three Tara images in the chapel are responsible for protecting Dreprung's drinking water, wealth and authority respectively.

There are three more chapels on the roof of the Main Assembly Hall. The Chapel of

---

The World of a Monk II

The great gelugpa monasteries of Dreprung, Sera and Ganden were like self-contained worlds. Dreprung, the largest of these monasteries, was home to around 10,000 monks at the time of the Chinese takeover in 1951. Dreprung, like the other major Gelugpa institutions, operated less as a single unit than as an assembly of colleges, each with its own interests, resources and administration.

The colleges, known as *tratsang*, were in turn made up of residences, or *khamtsen*. A monk joining a monastic college was assigned to a khamtsen according to the region he was born in. For example, Dreprung's Loseling college is thought to have been approximately 60% Kham. In total Loseling had 23 khamtsen, but the three most powerful khamtsen were all Kham controlled. This gave the monastic colleges a distinctive regional flavour, and meant that loyalties were generally grounded much deeper in the colleges than in the monastery itself.

At the head of a college was the abbot, a position that was filled by contenders who had completed the highest degrees of monastic studies. The successful applicant was chosen by the Dalai Lama. Beneath the abbot, was a group of religious heads who supervised prayer meetings and festivals and a group of economic managers who controlled the various khamtsens' estates and funds.

In the case of the larger colleges, estates and funds might be very extensive. Loseling college had over 180 estates and 20,000 serfs, among other holdings. For the most part, these holdings were not used to support monks – who were often forced to do private business to sustain themselves – but to maintain an endless cycle of prayer meetings and festivals that were deemed necessary for the spiritual good of the nation. ■

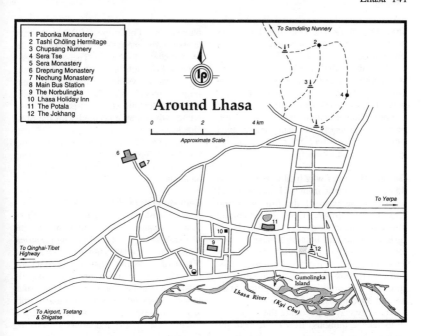

Around Lhasa

1 Pabonka Monastery
2 Tashi Chöling Hermitage
3 Chupsang Nunnery
4 Sera Tse
5 Sera Monastery
6 Dreprung Monastery
7 Nechung Monastery
8 Main Bus Station
9 The Norbulingka
10 Lhasa Holiday Inn
11 The Potala
12 The Jokhang

the Kings has statues of Tibet's early kings as well as the later Dalai Lamas. Also on the roof are chapels consecrated to Maitreya and Sakyamuni.

Ngagpa College Ngagpa is one of Dreprung's four colleges, and was devoted to Tantric study. It was originally built around a chapel founded by Tsongkhapa which can now be found at the rear of the Main Hall. The chapel is devoted to Yamantaka, a Tantric meditational deity who serves as an opponent to the forces of impermanence. The Yamantaka image still stands in the chapel.

Loseling College Loseling is the largest of Dreprung's colleges, and studies here were devoted to logic. The Main Hall houses a throne used by the Dalai Lamas, an extensive library and a long altar decorated with statues of various Dalai Lamas, Tsongkhapa and former Dreprung abbots. There are three

chapels to the rear of the hall. The one to the left houses 16 arhats, the central chapel a large Maitreya image, and the chapel to the right has a small Sakyamuni statue. On the 2nd floor is a chapel with a statue of Yamantaka (see the previous entry for Ngagpa College).

Gomang College Gomang is the second largest of Dreprung's colleges and follows the same layout as Loseling. The main hall has images of Tsongkhapa and a 1000-armed Avalokiteshvara. Again there are three chapels to the rear, the most important of which is the central chapel; it is chock-a-block with images. Like Loseling, there is a single protective chapel on the 2nd floor.

Deyang College The smallest of Dreprung's colleges, this one can safely be missed if you have had enough. The principal image in the Main Hall is Tsongkhapa, and in the chapel to the rear is a Maitreya image.

Dreprung Kora The Dreprung kora takes about 1½ hours at a leisurely pace (it is possible to do it quicker at hiking speed). Look for the path that leads from the north-west corner of the parking area in front of the Dreprung. There are good views along the way and also some rock carvings and murals of note. The kora climbs up to around 3900 metres and probably should not be attempted until you have had four or five days acclimatising in Lhasa.

Getting There & Away It takes around 40 to 45 minutes to cycle from the Barkhor area of Lhasa to Dreprung. Dreprung is situated (look for Dreprung above you and to the right). A dirt road heads up to Dreprung and, unless you have a mountain bike, you will be best off leaving your bike at the base of the hill. There should be someone to look after your bike just after the turn-off. The walk up to Dreprung takes around 30 minutes.

The easy way to get out to the monastery is to take a minibus. Buses run from the minibus area in front of the Barkhor square and cost Y3 to the base of the hill or Y5 to get up to the parking area in front of Dreprung. Not all the buses run up the hill.

Nechung Monastery
གནས་ཆུང་དགོན་པ་
Nechung is only five minutes' walk from Dreprung. Until 1959, it was the seat of the State Oracle. Oracles serve as mediums or mouthpieces of protective deities in Tibetan Buddhism and are thought to be possessed by the deity in question. The oracle at Nechung was the medium of Pehar, protector of the Buddhist state, and no important decision would be made by the Dalai Lamas without first consulting him. In 1959 the State Oracle fled with the Dalai Lama to India and Nechung is now cared for by a small number of resident monks.

Nechung is an eerie place associated with possession, exorcism and other pre-Buddhist rites. Note the blood-red doors at the entrance – the ivory-coloured paintings terminating in clawed feet are intended to be human skins. For images of Pehar, the protective spirit manifested in the State Oracle, see the chapel to the left. The statue shows Pehar in his wrathful aspect, while a thangka on the wall shows him in a more conciliatory frame of mind. On the 2nd floor is an audience chamber with a throne used by the Dalai Lamas when they consulted with the State Oracle.

Nechung has the same basic opening hours as Dreprung, and at the time of writing entry was free. See the Dreprung map for its location.

Sera Monastery སེ་ར་དགོན་པ་
Sera Monastery, around five km north of central Lhasa, was along with Dreprung one of Lhasa's two great Gelugpa monasteries. Its once huge monastic population of around 5000 monks has now been reduced to several hundred and the monastery has a slightly tired, down-at-heel atmosphere. Nevertheless it is still worth a visit; particularly from around 3.30 pm onwards, when debating is usually held in the monastery's Debating Courtyard.

Sera is frequently invaded by video-camera toting tour groups who toss money to the child beggars who infest the place. Try not to encourage the children, and if the tour groups annoy you sit down and wait them out – they very rarely linger long.

Like Dreprung, Sera has opening hours of around 9 am to 4.30 pm daily (a long lunch break is to be expected) and there is an entry charge of Y10, though this is not strictly enforced.

History Sera was founded by Sakya Yeshe, a disciple of Tsongkhapa, in 1419. In its heyday, Sera hosted a huge monastic population and five colleges of instruction, but at the time of the Chinese invasion in 1959 the colleges numbered three. Like Dreprung, the colleges of Sera specialised: Sera Me in the fundamental precepts of Buddhism; Sera Je in the instruction of itinerant monks from outside central Tibet; and Sera Ngagpa in Tantric studies.

Sera survived the ravages of the Cultural

Revolution with little damage, although many of the residential quarters were destroyed.

Sera Me College The first of the colleges you come across while following a clockwise route around Sera, this college dates back to the original founding of the monastery. The central image of the **Main Hall** is a copper Sakyamuni. To the rear of the hall are five chapels. To the far left is a chapel dedicated to Ta-og, Dharma Protector of the East. The next chapel is undistinguished, with a central statue of Tsongkhapa and a stupa. The central chapel contains statues of the Present, Future and Past Buddhas: Sakyamuni, Maitreya and Dipamkara, as well as 16 arhats for good measure.

The next chapel is home to Miwang Jowo, a Sakyamuni statue that dates from the 15th century and is the most sacred of the college's statues. The last chapel is dedicated to Tsongkhapa.

There are also two chapels on the 2nd floor. The first, after you mount the stairs is dedicated to Sakyamuni. The second is a Tara chapel and has 1000 statues of this protective deity.

Sera Ngagpa College A Tantric college, Ngagpa is also the oldest structure at Sera. The **Main Hall** is dominated by a statue of Sakya Yeshe, founder of Sera, and he is surrounded by other famous Sera lamas. There are two chapels to the rear of the hall, one with 16 arhats and one with a statue of the protective deity Yamantaka.

Sera Je College This is the largest of Sera's colleges. It has a breathtaking **Main Hall**, hung with thangkas and lit by shafts of light from high windows. There are also two thrones, one for the Dalai Lama and the smaller for the Panchen Lama.

To the left of the hall is a passage which leads, via a chapel dedicated to the Buddhas of the Three Ages (present, future and past), to the most sacred of Sera Monastery's chapels, the **Chapel of Hayagriva**. Hayagriva, or Tamdrin in Tibetan, is a wrathful meditational deity whose name means 'horse-headed'. He is the chief protective deity of Sera, and there is often a line of pilgrims waiting to touch their foreheads to his feet in respect. There is a second chapel for him on the 2nd floor, but here he is in another aspect with nine heads. The chapels

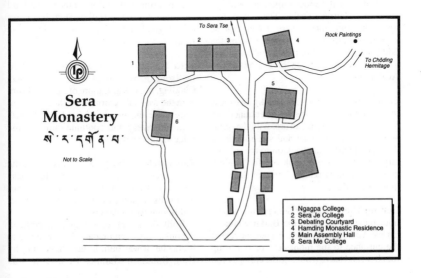

Sera Monastery

སེ་ར་དགོན་པ་

Not to Scale

To Sera Tse

To Chöding Hermitage

Rock Paintings

1 Ngagpa College
2 Sera Je College
3 Debating Courtyard
4 Hamding Monastic Residence
5 Main Assembly Hall
6 Sera Me College

to the rear of the hall are of less interest. There are three altogether and these are devoted to Maitreya, Tsongkhapa and Manjushri (a meditational deity embodying discriminative awareness). The latter is turning the Wheel of Dharma.

To the right of Sera Je is Sera's **Debating Courtyard**. There is usually debating practice here in the afternoons from around 3.30 to 4 pm. You will here it (much clapping of hands to emphasise points) as you approach Sera Je. It is well worth an hour of your time and provides a welcome relief from peering at Buddhist iconography.

Hamdong Monastic Residence Hamdong served as a residence for monks studying at Sera Je College. It is of fairly limited interest.

Main Assembly Hall The Main Assembly Hall is the largest of Sera's buildings and dates back to 1710. The Main Hall is particularly impressive and is noted for its wall-length thangkas. A statue of Sakya Yeshe, the founder of Sera, is the centrepiece and he is flanked by the 5th and 13th Dalai Lamas.

Of the three chapels to the rear of the hall, the central is the most important, with its six-metre Maitreya statue. The statue rises up to the 2nd floor, where it can also be viewed from the central chapel. Also on the 2nd floor (to the left of the central chapel) is a highly revered statue of a 1000-armed Avalokiteshvara.

Sera Kora The Sera kora (walk) takes less than an hour. It starts inside the entrance and heads west, describing an arc, with the occasional switch-back trail and steep sections, through the hills that back on to the monastery. On the descent, look out for brightly coloured rock paintings. Some of them are quite stunning.

Getting There & Away Sera is only a half-hour bicycle ride from the Barkhor area of Lhasa. You can either leave your bicycle at the entrance to the monastery or ride it up into Sera and leave it outside the colleges you

visit. It is possibly safest to leave it with the bicycle attendants at the entrance, but it is also difficult (but not impossible) to imagine anyone stealing it from inside the monastery.

Alternatively head down to the intersection of Ngangra Lam and Dekyi Shar Lam (the last turn before the Main Post Office as you head west) and look for the minibuses and jeeps that wait on the corner. They head up Sera every 10 minutes or so whenever they are full and cost Y1.

Around Sera Monastery
There are several walks in the area of Sera to rarely visited Buddhist sites. They should not really be attempted until you have had at least a few days in Lhasa acclimatising to the altitude. Another thing worth bearing in mind is that the white granite rock faces of the hills around Sera give off a lot of glare and can make for hot walking, particularly in the summer months. It is a good idea to get an early start.

Chöding Hermitage Chöding Hermitage was a retreat of Tsongkhapa, and predates Sera. There is not a great deal to see, but it is a short walk and the views from the hermitage are worthwhile. Look for the path behind the Main Assembly Hall of Sera. It follows the telegraph poles that climb up Sera Ütse ridge.

Sera Tse Sera Tse was another retreat used by Tsongkhapa. It is of more interest than Chöding, but it is also more of a climb. From Sera the walk takes around 1½ hours. To get there, take the tree-lined road that bisects Sera Monastery and continue climbing the ridge via a switch-back path.

Pabonka Monastery Pabonka is one of the most ancient Buddhist sites in the Lhasa region. It is little visited, but is only a one-hour walk from the Sera Monastery turn-off and is well worth the effort.

Built on a flat-topped granite boulder, Pabonka may even predate the Jokhang and Ramoche. It was built in the 7th century by King Songtsen Gampo. In 841 it was

Rock murals, Ganden Monastery (CT)

A: Detail of mandala (CT)
B: Avalokiteshvara (CT)
C: The Great 5th Dalai Lama (CT)

destroyed by King Langdharma and rebuilt in the 11th century. It was restored again by the 5th Dalai Lama, who added an extra floor to the two-storey building. It suffered more damage in the Cultural Revolution and has undergone repairs in recent years.

There is little to see on the 1st floor of Pabonka, but the 2nd floor has an assembly hall with a fine Sakyamuni statue. Other items of interest include some old thangkas and statues of the 5th Dalai Lama, Songtsen Gampo, Guru Rinpoche and Trisong Detsen. The throne is for the Panchen Lama.

To get to Pabonka, take a minibus or jeep to the Sera Monastery turn-off (see Sera Monastery, Getting There & Away, above). Rather than take the turn to Sera, keep to the left and look for a left turn a little up the road. The walk from here is fairly straightforward. You need to make a right turn at a T-junction, but you will see Pabonka up ahead perched on its granite boulder.

Walks Around Pabonka A few intrepid (and fit) travellers use Pabonka as a base for walks farther afield. These are serious day walks and should not be attempted until you are well adjusted to the altitude. Some travellers have also reported problems with dogs in this area – bring along a stick or keep some stones at the ready.

· For those who aren't so fit, an easy, short walk from Pabonka leads up to **Tashi Chöling Hermitage**. There is not a lot left to see at the hermitage, but again it affords good views. From Pabonka look for another granite boulder to the north-east (it is very close), and just before the boulder look for a path that leads up to a wider trail. The whole walk takes only around 20 minutes.

From Tashi Chöling, it is possible to take a slightly more arduous hike to **Chupsang Nunnery**. The trail drops down to the right from Tashi Chöling and follows a ravine. Ask for the ani gompa (nunnery) at the first village you reach. There are some 80 nuns resident at Chupsang. The entire walk takes from 30 to 40 minutes.

Samdeling Nunnery is a tough four-hour hike from Tashi Chöling (allow around two

hours for the descent). Take some water with you, though you will probably receive some butter tea from the nuns if you make it to the top. The trail heads to the left from Tashi Chöling and follows a steep ridge. The nunnery, home to more than 80 nuns, is at an altitude of over 4200 metres.

FESTIVALS

If it is at all possible, try and time your visit to Lhasa with one of the city's festivals. Pilgrims often flock to Lhasa at these times and the city takes on a colourful, party atmosphere.

The following Tibetan festivals are calculated according to the lunar calendar. Check beforehand for the precise dates.

New Year Festival (Losar) Taking place in the first week of the first lunar month, Losar probably sees Lhasa at its most colourful. There are performances of Tibetan drama, pilgrims make incense offerings and the streets are thronged with Tibetans dressed in their finest.

Mönlam Known also as the Great Prayer Festival, this is held midway through the first lunar month (officially the 25th). An image of Maitreya from the Jokhang is borne around the Barkhor, attracting enthusiastic crowds of locals and pilgrims.

Lantern Festival Held on the 15th of the first lunar month, huge yak-butter sculptures are placed around the Barkhor circuit.

Birth of Sakyamuni This is not exactly a festival, but the seventh day of the fourth lunar month is an important pilgrimage date and sees large numbers of pilgrims in the Holy City.

Sakyamuni's Enlightenment The 15th day of the fourth lunar month is an occasion for outdoor operas and also sees large numbers of pilgrims at
· the Jokhang and on the Barkhor circuit.

Worship of the Buddha During the second week of the fifth lunar month, the parks of Lhasa, in particular the Norbulingka, are crowded with picnickers.

Drepung Festival The 30th day of the sixth lunar month is celebrated with the hanging of a huge thangka at Drepung Monastery. Lamas and monks do masked dances.

Shötun The Yoghurt Festival is held in the first week of the seventh lunar month. It starts at Drepung Monastery and moves down to the Norbulingka. Operas and masked dances are held, and locals take the occasion as another excuse for picnics.

Bathing Festival The end of the seventh and beginning of the eighth lunar months sees locals washing away the grime of the previous year in the Lhasa River.

Labab Düchen Commemorating Buddha's descent from heaven, the 22nd day of the ninth lunar month sees large numbers of pilgrims in Lhasa.

Paldren Lhamo The 15th day of the 10th lunar month has a procession around the Barkhor bearing Paldren Lhamo, protective deity of the Jokhang.

PLACES TO STAY

As a general rule of thumb, accommodation in Lhasa divides into inexpensive Tibetan-style accommodation in the central Barkhor area and less conveniently located up-market digs on the outskirts of town. Almost all individual travellers head straight into the Barkhor area, where four Tibetan-style hotels dominate the backpacker market. The simple reason for this is that this is the best area of town to be based in, the service (while basic) is friendly in these hotels, and they are the best places to meet other travellers and get the current low-down on travel in Tibet.

At the time of writing there were 24 hotels in Lhasa that took foreign guests. Apart from the Tibetan-style hotels in the centre of town, and a handful of mid-range and up-market hotels on the outskirts of town, however, very few travellers were bothering with the largely Chinese-style alternatives. Most of them are not recommended, and in this accommodation section only the more popular options are listed.

Places to Stay – bottom end

Currently the most popular place with individual travellers is the *Yak Hotel* (☎ 23496). The hotel has two courtyards: one at the front (which tends to reverberate to the sound of landcruisers and buses backing in and out of it) and one to the rear. The rooms that front onto the rear courtyard are quietest, but at busy times of the year it will be difficult to find a vacant room. Sofas placed around the edges of the courtyards, and some tables and chairs sheltering under two Tibetan-style tarpaulins in the front courtyard are popular places to sit and chat. A shop next to reception sells soft drinks, beer and other essentials. This is also the place to organise bicycle hire, although it comes at the rather expensive rate of Y2 per hour.

The Yak has a wide range of rooms available, including some excellent mid-range options in the left-hand building of the front courtyard. Basic five-bed dorms cost Y25 per person. Ask to have a look at another dorm if you don't like the first one you see – some are much nicer than others. There are also some doubles and triples available at Y25 per bed; there are a couple of singles at Y25 to Y30, but they are seldom available. Better quality doubles range from Y95 to Y168. Doubles at Y135 include a toilet and a TV, while doubles at Y168 also include a shower (there is unlikely to be any water available in the winter months).

The availability of hot water has improved at the Yak over the last couple of years. Hot showers, in the far corner of the rear courtyard, are available most of the year from around 8 to 9 am and from around 5 to 7 pm.

The *Banak Shol* (☎ 23829), once *the* place to stay back in the early days of individual travel, is the second most popular hotel amongst individual travellers. It is not as clean or as efficiently run as the Yak, but it has a charm that the larger Yak doesn't. Guests can titillate themselves with the thought they have checked into a medieval monastic retreat (well, almost) as they enjoy the cosy Tibetan-style rooms fronted by verandas that face into the inner courtyard. In the evenings, guests sometimes retire to the roof for an impromptu party. The Kailash Restaurant on the 2nd-floor has also taken off as one of Lhasa's most popular places to eat.

Rates at the Banak Shol are basically a flat Y25 per bed, though there are some slightly more expensive options available. Extensions to the hotel were being carried out at the time of writing, and it remains to be seen what will come of them and what the rates will be. The new rooms may be worth checking out as an alternative to the mid-range rooms at the Yak.

On a final note, the Banak Shol may now be the best place for bicycle hire. Although they charge the same rates as the Yak, in mid-'94 the Banak Shol bought a whole fleet of new Flying Pigeons – most of the antiques at the Yak were falling apart.

Like the Banak Shol, *Snowlands* (☎ 23687) is another of Lhasa's long-stayers. It was a favourite back in the mid-'80s and has changed very little since then (they certainly haven't cleaned the high-altitude toilets). Many of Lhasa's repeat visitors, particularly those involved in carpet buying and doing business in the Barkhor area, seem to make this place their base. Rooms, mainly doubles and four-bed dorms, are in a quadrangle that faces onto an inner courtyard.

Nowadays, Snowlands is quieter than the Yak or the Banak Shol, though you pay for your solitude with lower service standards. Beds are Y25 and it is a good place to be based if you don't want to be in the thick of the travellers' scene. You will have to head down to the Yak or the Kirey hotels for a shower.

The fourth and least popular of the Barkhor area's Tibetan-run hotels is the *Kirey Hotel* (☎ 23462). This place deserves more custom than it gets. It is friendly, clean and has regular hot water. Like the other Tibetan-run hotels, it is built around a courtyard which, if the place ever became popular, might conceivably become a place for people to sit and swap the inevitable travellers' tales. Beds here come in at the same price as the other Tibetan-run hotels: Y25.

Inconveniently located in the north-east of town, by the telecommunications building, the *Plateau Hotel* (☎ 24916) also has inexpensive dorm beds at Y25, but no travellers seem to stay out here. There is really no reason to. It has little going for it, except perhaps as a stop-gap in the exceedingly rare event that everything else in the Barkhor area is booked out.

Places to Stay – middle

There is really very little to recommend in the way of mid-range accommodation in Lhasa. The Yak Hotel, mentioned above in the Accommodation – bottom end section, has a small number of doubles with mid-range standards at affordable rates, but other than this the only options are bureaucratically run Chinese establishments that attract very few foreign guests.

The *Sunlight Hotel*, near the south end of Dodhi Lam, is a lifeless kind of place with standard doubles at US$28. Hot water is available from 6.30 pm to 9.30 am and there is an international telephone service. It is quite a long trudge from here to the more interesting parts of town, and no bicycle hire is available.

The *Himalaya Hotel* (☎ 23775) is close to the Sunlight on the other side of the road. Like the more up-market Tibet Hotel, an attempt has been made to give this place something of a Tibetan character. The result is a slightly depressing fusion of Tibetan design and Chinese hotel management. Standard doubles are available from Y150.

A couple of other places with rates of between US$20 and US$30 for standard doubles can be found in the Chinese-run *Guesthouse of the Tibet Autonomous Region* (☎ 26091) at 196 Dekyi Nub Lam (Beijing Lu) and the *Yingbin Hotel* (☎ 22184) on Mimang Lam.

Places to Stay – top end

For those with money to spend on top-end accommodation, the best place to stay is the *Holiday Inn Lhasa* (☎ 32221). It is the only place in town that even approaches international standards. Originally opened as the Lhasa Hotel, the Holiday Inn group took over management of the hotel in 1986.

Whatever you might think about Lhasa sporting a Holiday Inn (some travellers even refuse to go up there for a banana sundae), the hotel is quite an achievement. It has a good selection of restaurants and bars, international direct-dial phones, satellite TV, in-house movies, a clinic with both Western and Tibetan doctors and over 480 air-con rooms. The hotel no longer has a travel department, but vehicles are available for hire at the front desk at rates that are quite competitive with the prices being quoted by private agencies in town. There are also a number of independent travel agencies based on the 1st floor of the hotel.

Rates for economy doubles are around US$70, while standard doubles come in at around US$110. Room prices fluctuate seasonally, which means that they may rise slightly higher than this in the peak summer months. Similarly, significant discounts are available in the low-season winter months, when occupancy rates plummet. Budget individual travellers who are looking for some comfort and a hot shower in the winter months (when hot water is generally not available at the other hotels around town) might want to ask about the economy triples. If you can get three people together and organise a discount, the result should be quite affordable.

A couple of hundred metres up the road from the Holiday Inn is the *Tibet Hotel* (☎ 34966). In keeping with its name, it strives to create a Tibetan ambience, but the results are somewhat surreal. Look for the wall frescoes of Tibetan landscapes set off by chandeliers and fairy lights. Service tends to dodder somewhere between apathy and incompetence, and there are sometimes water cuts. This said, the rooms are not bad and are considerably cheaper than those at the Holiday Inn. Standard doubles are US$40 in the high season (from early June to the end of September) and US$32 for the rest of the year.

Like the Holiday Inn, the Tibet Hotel has a host of guest services. International direct-dial phones, satellite TV, foreign exchange and so on are all available.

PLACES TO EAT

The restaurant scene in Lhasa has improved immensely over the last few years. For the most part this is due to Han Chinese immigration. The western end of town now has a huge selection of Chinese restaurants, mainly serving Sichuanese dishes, but other regional cuisines are also available. In the Tibetan quarter, Tibetans have also got in on the act and opened up a few restaurants that are very popular with the traveller set.

Most individual travellers stick to the Tibetan quarter around the Barkhor when it comes to meals. Tibetan cooking may not be one of the world's most exciting cuisines, but there are a few Tibetan restaurants in this area that serve up some very tasty dishes.

Tashi's Restaurant (Tashi I) deserves a special mention. This place has been running for a while now, and despite increased competition continues to be a favourite. The service is very friendly, the prices are cheap and everything on the menu is good. Special praise is reserved for the bobis (chepati-like unleavened bread), which most people order with seasoned cream cheese and fried vegetables or meat. Tashi's apple momos and cheesecakes are also a hit.

Tashi II offers the same dishes as the first Tashi restaurant and is only a few minutes' walk away. Service here is a little slower, but this place seems to have less of a problem with beggars and the interior is a bit roomier. It has also emerged as one of Lhasa's most popular travellers' eateries.

Newly opened in mid-'94, the *Kailash Restaurant* on the 2nd floor of the Banak Shol Hotel was doing excellent business at the time of writing. Prices are definitely higher than at the Tashi restaurants but, with dishes like vegetarian lasagne and yak burgers (as good as those at the Holiday Inn and much cheaper), the Kailash is the only place serving an alternative to Chinese and Tibetan fare in the old part of town. The restaurant's breakfasts (muesli brought in from Kathmandu, among other things) have also given it a devoted following. One caveat is that many travellers claim to have got sick after eating at the Kailash. Hopefully hygiene standards will improve as time goes by.

The *Alougang Restaurant*, popularly known as the Pink Curtain for the curtain that hangs at the entrance, is another place worth checking out. It is popular with locals and travellers alike, and is so busy in the evenings that you often have to wait for a table. Again, it is a bit more expensive than the Tashi restaurants but it is worth spending a bit extra for the interesting mix of Tibetan and Chinese food. There are some excellent stir-fried vegetable dishes available, but the most popular dishes are the curry potatoes, the 'lambs french fries' and the sweet and sour lamb (the latter is excellent).

The Pink Curtain is close to the minibus stand just down from the Barkhor. Walking west from the Yak Hotel, take the second left and look for the doorway with a pink curtain on the left just before the first intersection.

Next door to the Yak Hotel is the *Crazy Yak Saloon*. This place isn't as popular as it perhaps deserves to be. The food might be a little expensive and the menu a bit short on items, but what they have is very good. The Tibetan-style interior is also probably the best in this part of town. The food is mainly Chinese with a couple of Tibetan items thrown in.

Also close to the Yak Hotel is *Uncle Sam's*. There is a good chance that it will be closed by the time you have this book in your hands. The food was not very good and it was not getting much patronage from either locals or travellers.

Opposite Tashi II is *Lost Horizons*. Food standards are a bit dodgy but the lassis are a popular item. It is one of the few Lhasa restaurants that stays open late and it tends to fill up from around 10 pm, when travellers and locals call in for a couple of beers and a snack. If you are fed up with listening to Bob Marley as you travel around Asia, give the place a miss.

For not bad Chinese fare, check out *Followers* just down the road from the Kirey Hotel in the direction of the Banak Shol. Look out for the pool tables outside. It serves up basic Sichuanese cuisine – nothing exciting – but is a reliable option and the owner tries hard to please.

Down in the Barkhor square area there are also a couple of restaurants. Both the *Welcome Restaurant* and the *Barkhor Cafe* have roof-top dining areas which provide great views of the Jokhang and the Barkhor square. Unfortunately the food at neither place is worth recommending, though a late-afternoon beer enjoyed gazing over the Barkhor square is worth indulging in. The

only catch is that the beers are twice as expensive here than they are anywhere else in this part of town.

There are also many other restaurants in the Tibetan quarter. The ones listed here are restricted to restaurants that have caught on with individual travellers based in the nearby Tibetan hotels. Along Dekyi Shar Lam between the Kirey and Banak Shol hotels are a number of Muslim restaurants. Some travellers have had good meals in them and others claim to have had disappointing fare and then got sick. Check one of these places out if you are feeling a bit adventurous.

The best Chinese food in town is found in the west of town, which is predominantly Han Chinese. This area is such a long hike from the Tibetan quarter that very few travellers make the effort. Still, it is worth making at least one recommendation – the *Beijing Duck Restaurant*. This place has no English sign, but can be found on Ngangra Lam, the last street intersecting Dekyi Shar Lam before the post office. The restaurant is just up from a new fashion shop and is distinguished by its wood-panelled frontage.

The Beijing Duck Restaurant is expensive (Y98 for a whole duck) but is run by a couple of guys from Beijing and the fare is very authentic. It is well worth splashing out on with a couple of friends. On the corner of Ngangra Lam and Dekyi Shar Lam look out for the little outlet selling fried chicken – the Chinese sign announces it as 'American Fried Chicken'. It is excellent. Expect to pay between Y3 and Y4 for a chicken leg.

Up in the vicinity of the Holiday Inn are some up-market dining options, both Tibetan and Chinese. But the best up-market restaurants in town are actually in the Holiday Inn itself. Travellers who can't afford Holiday Inn prices (and they are fairly expensive) should call in to the snack bar just off the foyer: *One Minzu Lane*. This place has affordable coffee, sandwiches and sundaes. Afternoons often see this place crowded with refugees from the Tibetan quarter sipping on a coffee and wolfing down a peach melba – thoroughly decadent but irresistible to some.

Next door to One Minzu Lane is the *Hard*

Yak Cafe. Very good meals – including the famous yak burger with french fries – are available here for between Y40 and Y50. There is an outside patio next to a pond, which is a pleasant place to sit. You may see ducks having difficulty staying afloat – in other parts of the world ducks tend to float reasonably well on water, but Tibetan ducks seem to have a problem with buoyancy. It is possibly something to do with the altitude.

Gya Sey Kang is the Holiday Inn's Chinese restaurant, and probably the best in town. Prices are not as high as you might imagine, with main courses from around Y30. During the peak seasons the *Everest Restaurant* has an international buffet. The restaurant had not yet opened at the time of writing, but you can expect it to be fairly expensive. The *Himalaya Restaurant* serves Indian and Tibetan banquets. The Y200 price tag will put these out of reach of most travellers, but for those with some extra cash to spend on a splash-out meal this is some of the best food available in Lhasa. A small troupe of Tibetan musicians provides the background music and the restaurant's interior has been very tastefully executed.

ENTERTAINMENT

There is not a great deal in the way of entertainment options in Lhasa. Evenings see most travellers heading off to one of the restaurants in the Tibetan quarter and then retiring to the courtyard of the Yak Hotel, which is sometimes the scene of an impromptu party. For late night drinks, the most popular place is *Lost Horizons* (already mentioned in the Places to Eat section above). This place stays open until around 1 or 2 am and attracts an interesting mix of late-night foreigners and Tibetan low life – it is amazing that it has not been closed down by the PSB officials. The *Kailash Restaurant* in the Banak Shol Hotel also often stays open late if there are enough customers guzzling beer and swapping stories of Tibetan adventures.

Karaoke bars and discos are a recent addition to the Lhasa nightlife scene. Generally not many travellers venture into these places and some of those who have claim to have been harassed by plainclothes PSB. There is no need to be overly paranoid, providing you keep a relatively low profile. If there is PSB surveillance of Lhasa clubs, it is fairly unobtrusive. I popped into several karaoke bars and had interesting conversations with locals without any interference from the boys in blue.

Several of the discos around town, however, have uniformed PSB as door staff. If you venture into any of these places you can expect to have your movements monitored. Foreigners will be dissuaded from dancing with locals in no uncertain terms. It is best to avoid these places. Lost Horizons sometimes has dancing as do several of the smaller karaoke bars around town.

For straight drinking, *Altitudes* at the Holiday Inn has draft Lhasa beer (it is surprisingly good) in mock-English pub surroundings. This place is fairly dull, however, and would probably be more fun with a group.

Lhasa's cinemas are very unlikely to be showing anything you would want to watch. The Tibet Nyingghi Tourist Company, opposite the Snowlands Hotel, however, has a small video library. For Y3 per head they will play the movie of your choice while you relax on the comfortable sofas. Drinks are also available. Movie choices include the first two *Star Wars* pics, *Romancing the Stone* and *Big* with Tom Hanks. It is a fun place to fritter away an afternoon with some friends.

Unfortunately there is almost nothing in the way of cultural entertainment in Lhasa. For performances of Tibetan opera and dancing you will probably have to wait for one of Lhasa's festivals (see Festivals above). The Tibetan Dance & Drama Theatre opposite the Holiday Inn is for the most part a lost cause, though it might be worth enquiring at the Holiday Inn as to whether there will be any performances that coincide with your visit – it is unlikely.

THINGS TO BUY

Lhasa is no longer the backwater it once was,

and it is now a reasonably good place to stock up on basic supplies. There are numerous department stores around town selling both clothes and food. It is still a good idea to come supplied with your own photographic film, though Fuji and Kodak print film is readily available. Slide film is very hard to come by. Bring your own medical supplies. Items such as water-purifying tablets are not easy to find.

Food Supplies

Lhasa is the best place to stock up on food supplies for trips to Kailash and the Nepalese border. Instant noodles are readily available, and if you shop around there is a surprisingly wide variety. Other popular buys include the famous chocolate eggs (look out for them in the Barkhor market area and in the department stores) and biscuits.

One of the best places for food supplies is the People's Department Store just south of the Main Post Office. This place has an excellent selection of instant noodles, sweets and export-quality biscuits brought in from other parts of China. Canned fruits and Chinese desserts are also available. West of the Main Post Office, just before the Holiday Inn, the Lhasa Foreign Trade Building is also very well stocked. Not far from the Barkhor, the Tibet Travel Sales Centre is another department store that is worth checking out. The 3rd floor is a Friendship Store, and is slightly better stocked than the lower two floors. Close by, just before the department store as you walk down from the Barkhor square, is a small shop selling tea and three-in-one coffee sachets (it is about the only place in Tibet where you will find them).

In the Tibetan quarter, wander down to Tromsik Khang market for your food supplies. The lower floor is mainly given over to vendors of yak butter, but the 2nd floor has a wide range of other food supplies.

Clothes

For good-quality warm clothes it would be a good idea to think ahead and bring whatever you need with you. There are a couple of places around town selling down jackets and

so on, but the quality is not very good and you will have a poor selection to choose from.

West of the Yak Hotel on Dekyi Shar Lam are a couple of small operations selling jackets and so on. The best quality down jackets cost around Y200. There is a better selection up on the 2nd floor of the Lhasa Foreign Trade Building in the west of town just before the Holiday Inn.

Long-Distance Travel & Trekking Provisions

For basic supplies such as thermoses and water canisters, the best place to shop is the Barkhor area. The lanes that run from the Tromsik Khang market down to the Barkhor circuit have numerous stalls selling everything from ropes and twine to enamel mugs. Most of the stall holders are Uighurs from Xinjiang and enjoy some good-humoured bargaining.

Quality sleeping bags are almost impossible to get hold of in Lhasa. Look out for notices at the Yak and at the Banak Shol hotels advertising used sleeping bags for sale. They usually get snapped up very quickly. Surprisingly, there are sometimes tents for sale on the 2nd floor of the Lhasa Foreign Trade Building. The quality is better than you might expect.

Souvenirs

Most travellers do their souvenir shopping on the Barkhor circuit. Expect to be offered some outrageous prices for anything you are interested in and then settle in for some serious haggling. There is an awful lot of junk for sale in this part of town, but even some of the junky items have a certain charm.

Popular purchases include prayer wheels, rings, daggers and prayer flags, all of which are fairly portable. There are carpet stalls at a couple of points on the Barkhor circuit. Some travellers buy a carpet or two and send them home. Those with a particular interest in carpets might want to check out the carpet factory on Tsang Gyu Shar Lam, though it doesn't sport a particularly exciting selection.

For better quality souvenir items at marked-up prices, look out for the antique shops tucked away behind the stalls on the Barkhor circuit. The Buy & Sale Antique Shop opposite the Yak Hotel is another place worth checking out.

Also try the 1st floor of the Lhasa Foreign Trade Building, where items have very reasonable fixed prices – in particular check the Tibetan-style cloth bags.

The best place for T-shirts is the little place to the left of the entrance to the Potala. There are some excellent and quite unique T-shirts for sale here, as well as a selection of oil paintings by local artists on the 2nd floor. Opposite is Potala Arts & Crafts, which has thangkas, some souvenir books and postcards.

Another souvenir shop just inside the entrance to the Norbulingka has probably the best selection of colour coffee-table books about Tibet. They are hefty items but you could always send them home.

Finally, both the Tibet Hotel and the Lhasa Holiday Inn have souvenir shops. The Holiday Inn has the best postcards in town. Most of the items for sale in both these shops

Detail from a Tibetan rug

are fairly expensive, but at least the quality is good.

GETTING THERE & AWAY

While there are theoretically a number of ways to get to Lhasa, the main approach routes are by air from Chengdu (in Sichuan), by bus from Golmud (in Qinghai), and overland or by air from Kathmandu.

Air

At the time of writing Lhasa was connected only with Kathmandu and Chengdu by air – a once weekly flight to Beijing required a change of aircraft in Chengdu. There is much conjecture as to the reasons for Lhasa's isolation, particularly when China's air links are expanding so rapidly, but it is probably both a case of the authorities wanting to control tourist numbers in Tibet and of a shortage of the specially pressurised aircraft that are able to land at Gonggar airport.

Rumours of a Hong Kong or a Canton flight seem to be simply rumours, but there is a strong likelihood that a Chongqing flight will have been established by the time this book is in your hands. The reason for this is no doubt the increasing numbers of Sichuanese Han Chinese doing business in Tibet and Tibet's increasing economic reliance on its nearest developed Chinese province.

Flights between Chengdu and Lhasa (twice daily) are now Y1490, and will no doubt have risen again by the time this book goes to press. In Chengdu, it is anyone's guess whether the South-West China Airlines booking office will sell you a ticket. As of June 1994 foreigners were required to obtain a Tibet permit via an agency. Costs varied between US$50 and US$300. Prior to June of that year many travellers had been buying their own tickets over the counter without any permit problems. Try planning ahead and buying your ticket in Hong Kong or better still at home before you set off on your trip, though there are no guarantees that even this will work. Once you have a ticket in your hand, there should not be any problems. Officials at both Gonggar and

Chengdu airports are not in the habit of grilling foreigners about permits.

Flights between Beijing and Lhasa operate once a week on Sunday. A change of flights is required in Chengdu, and the total cost is Y2700. Kathmandu flights are twice a week on Tuesday and Thursday and the cost is Y1680. Those planning to fly Kathmandu-Lhasa should arrive in Nepal with a Chinese visa already prepared. Organising one in Kathmandu is an experience most people would sensibly choose to avoid.

Despite the fact that there is a huge CAAC booking office on Ngangra Lam, foreigners are now required to head up to the Tibet Hotel to make their flight bookings. The Tibet Air Travel Service office is on the ground floor of the hotel and is open from 9.30 am to 12.30 pm and 2 to 4 pm. There is a Y30 booking charge. Many travellers object to the latter charge, but everyone has to pay it.

Arrival The new Gonggar airport is now completed and is a vast improvement on the old one. Remember to hang on to the numbered stub for your luggage receipt. The staff here are very scrupulous about making sure that no one heads off with any one else's backpack. Other than this everything is fairly straightforward. If you have made it this far without a permit, there doesn't seem to be anyone concerned about it.

Airport buses loiter outside the main terminal long enough to collect everyone on the flight, and the two-hour trip into town costs Y30 or Y15 with a student card. If you are desperate to only pay Y15, try climbing into the bus and paying the conductor directly, although you may not get away with this and it is a rather naughty thing to do.

Departure Departing from Gonggar airport involves you in one of China's best state-sponsored scams. An idea of startling simplicity and breathtaking audacity, it involves the building of a big, expensive airport hotel and then only providing a bus service for the early morning flights in the

afternoon. Basically you have the option of missing your flight by about 10 hours or spending the night in the airport hotel.

Many travellers nowadays avoid the inconvenience of spending a night in boring Gonggar by banding together and hiring a jeep or landcruiser to go out to the airport early in the morning. Costs work out at around Y70 per head if there are five or six of you.

There is a Y40 departure tax for flights to Chengdu and Y90 for flights to Kathmandu.

Bus

The only bus service between Lhasa and the outside world is to Golmud in Qinghai province. It is tempting to ask readers considering travelling to Tibet to boycott this service, given that local authorities in Golmud have so greedily upped prices over the last year or so. The price for a one-way ticket at the time of writing was Y950, up from Y450 the year before. Theoretically this patent price gouging is justified by the fact that the ticket includes a three-day tour of Lhasa. In reality, however, most travellers complain that the tour is a complete waste of time and one group of travellers, fed up with being shepherded around sights they would have preferred to see themselves, simply commandeered the minibus to the Holiday Inn, where they told their driver to wait for them while they had lunch in the Hard Yak Cafe.

The Golmud-Lhasa journey takes anywhere between 30 and 50 hours. Mishaps of one sort or another are almost inevitable, and it is not unusual to arrive in Lhasa at an hour when the city is the domain of rabid dogs and all the hotels are closed – you will just have to hammer on the doors of one of them and get the staff out of bed.

Tickets for buses from Lhasa to Golmud can be bought at the main bus station south of the Holiday Inn. A couple of the travel agents around town will also organise tickets for you for a nominal fee. Prices are Y414 for a Japanese bus or Y391 for a Chinese bus, and should include transport from your hotel to the bus station – tell the staff where you are staying when you book your ticket. For more information on the Lhasa-Golmud route see the Qinghai-Tibet section of the Getting There & Away chapter.

Buses for the Nepalese border (Zhangmu) depart from the main bus station only three times a month: on the 2nd, 12th, and 22nd. In practice these services are sometimes cancelled or leave before they were scheduled to leave and are generally a very unreliable means of getting to the border. The price is Y334.

Other services operating from the main bus station include to Tsetang (daily, Y94), Nagqen (daily Y111) and Shigatse (daily, Y95). Very few foreigners use the bus station's Shigatse service as there are now minibuses departing from in front of the Kirey Hotel from 7 am. They do the trip quicker than the public buses and cost only Y30. Since the completion of the new Lhasa-Shigatse highway, there is no public transport direct to Gyantse. It is necessary to travel to Shigatse first and then change to a private minibus or a public bus.

Minibus

Minibus connections between Lhasa and Shigatse have already been mentioned in the bus section above. Besides this service, a host of other minibus routes have sprung up in recent years. The main area to look for minibuses is directly east of the Barkhor square on Mi Mang Lam (see the Lhasa map). From here there are minibuses from around 7 am to Tsurphu Monastery (only one or two services a day) and to Dreprung Monastery (frequent). There may also be a service to Samye Monastery (to the ferry area) and to Tsetang, though you should check on this the day before you leave. There should also be a minibus service to Damxung (for Namtso lake) from in front of the Kirey Hotel every one or two days – check at the Kirey Hotel for more information.

Hitching

There are relatively few people hitching out of Lhasa these days. One of the main reasons is that the authorities have come down very heavily on truck drivers giving lifts to foreign travellers, particularly on the Yunnan and Sichuan routes in or out of Tibet. On either of these routes, very few drivers would be willing to risk the very high fines exacted for carrying foreign cargo.

Most of the hitching that travellers do in Tibet is out to Ali (en route to Mt Kailash or Kashgar) or to the Nepalese border. The best starting points for either of these routes are Shigatse and Lhatse. See the Bus entry above for information on the inexpensive minibus service to Shigatse.

Rented Vehicles

Rented vehicles have emerged as the most popular way to get away from Lhasa in recent years. The most popular route is a leisurely and slightly circuitous journey down to Zhangmu on the Tibetan-Nepalese border, taking in Yamdrok-tso lake, Gyantse, Shigatse, Sakya, Everest Base Camp and Tingri on the way. A six to seven-day trip of this sort in a landcruiser cost around Y6000 at the time of writing. Other popular trips included Mt Kailash and Nam-tso lake. See the appropriate sections for more details.

Check the Information section at the start of this chapter for a listing of some of the travel agencies around town. Be careful to shop around, and remember that cheapest isn't necessarily best. It is often worth spending a few hundred yuan extra (it is not much spread over five or six people) to hire a vehicle from a bigger and more reliable agency.

Also important is to talk to other travellers and get the latest low down on which agencies (and there are always a few about) are ripping people off.

GETTING AROUND

For those travellers based in the Tibetan quarter of Lhasa, most of the major inner-Lhasa sights are within fairly easy walking distance. Sights such as the Norbulingka over in the west of town are quite a long trudge. It would be better to take a minibus or hire a bicycle.

To/From Gonggar Airport

Gonggar airport is an inconvenient 95 km away from Lhasa. Airport buses leave every half-hour or so between 3 and 5 pm from the courtyard behind the CAAC building. The price is Y15 from Lhasa to Gonggar and Y30 from Gonggar to Lhasa. Special foreigners' rates apply in Gonggar, but no one seems to worry about this in Lhasa.

Travellers leaving Lhasa who want to avoid a night in Gonggar usually band together and hire a landcruiser to do the trip to the airport. Check the notice boards at the Yak and Banak Shol hotels. Hiring a vehicle for this trip should cost around Y400, which is fairly reasonable if you can get six or seven people together. The road has been asphalted for its entire length and it is a relatively smooth drive.

Minibus

Privately run minibuses are frequent on Dekyi Shar Lam, and run from just east of the Main Post Office up past the Holiday Inn. There is a flat Y1 charge. If you need to get up to the Holiday Inn or the Tibet Hotel this is the quickest and cheapest way to do it.

From the intersection of Dekyi Shar Lam and Ngangra Lam there are also jeeps and minibuses running up to Sera Monastery.

Rickshaw

There is no shortage of rickshaws plying the streets of Lhasa, but as they are slow and relatively expensive there is little incentive to use them. A trip between the Yak Hotel and the Holiday Inn for example costs around Y5 (after much haggling) and takes around 25 minutes. You'd be better off hiring a bicycle and peddling yourself around.

Bicycle

By bicycle is without a doubt the best way to get around once you have acclimatised to the altitude. You can hire bicycles at the Yak and Banak Shol hotels and the Holiday Inn (look for the building on the left just inside the main gates).

Both the Yak and the Banak Shol charge an expensive Y2 an hour or Y20 per day. At least no deposit is required.

It is a different story at the Holiday Inn, however. There they were charging Y10 an hour – plus a US$100 deposit. Give this operation a miss.

Bicycle theft has been a bit of a problem in Lhasa for some time now. Make it a rule to park your bike in the designated areas patrolled by matronly bicycle attendants (there is a flat charge of Y0.1) and your bike will go unmolested.

Leaving it unattended (particularly at night) and wandering off for an hour is almost an invitation to theft. Naturally it goes without saying that expensive mountain bikes require more care than a rusty old Flying Pigeon.

Nowadays it is even possible to buy mountain bikes in Lhasa. Check the area in the vicinity of the Potala on Dekyi Nub Lam for bike shops.

Prices start from around Y800. Don't expect the quality to be up to international standards, but plenty of travellers still manage to do long trips on the bikes without having them fall apart.

Those who have ridden their bikes through to Kathmandu report that the bikes have a high resale value there – possibly more than the original price in Lhasa, though this will depend on the condition the bike is in when you arrive.

Ü དབུས་

The traditional province known in Tibetan as Ü is the more easterly of the two central provinces that have long been at the centre stage of Tibetan politics and history. The westerly central province is Tsang, and its capital is Shigatse.

The province of Ü is effectively the heartland of all greater Tibet. It was from here, in the Yarlung Valley, that the earliest Tibetan kings launched their conquest and unification of the Tibetan plateau and ruled from Lhasa for three centuries. Political power later shifted to Sakya and Shigatse in Tsang, but returned to Ü when the 5th Dalai Lama reunited the country with Mongol support in 1642 and again made Lhasa the capital.

For most individual travellers the principal attractions of Ü are Tsurphu, Ganden and Samye monasteries and Nam-tso lake. The ancient province is also host to a large

The Karmapa Connection

Anyone who thinks of the Tibetans as a lofty, spiritually absorbed people should think again. Tibetan history has been dogged by factional intrigue, and the intrigues continue into the late 20th century.

In 1981 the 16th Karmapa died in Chicago. Administration of the Karmapa sect in Sikkim was subsequently passed down to four regents. Two of them, Situ Rinpoche and Shamar Rinpoche, were to become embroiled in a dispute that has caused a painful rift in the exiled Tibetan community.

At the centre of the dispute is the boy with an angelic smile who dispenses blessings at Tsurphu Monastery – the 17th Karmapa. In early 1992, the four regents announced the discovery of a letter written by the 16th Karmapa that provided critical clues as to the whereabouts of his reincarnation. Curiously, just a month later one of the regents was killed in a car crash in Sikkim. The local press declared 'suspicious circumstances'. If there were, they were never investigated, apparently at the request of figures close to the regent.

Two weeks after the accident, Shamar Rinpoche announced that the mystery letter was a fraud. The announcement was tardy. A search team was already in eastern Tibet, with Chinese permission, on the trail of the Karmapa's 17th reincarnation. By early June the boy had been found and the Dalai Lama had made a formal announcement supporting the boy's candidature. This was against a background of a brief occupation of Sikkim's Rumtek Monastery (now the head Karmapa monastery) by Indian troops and brawling by monks divided over the issue.

Shamar Rinpoche initially opposed the Dalai Lama's support, but after talks with the Dalai Lama changed his mind. Several days later, he changed his mind again. Aided by Western supporters he began a letter writing campaign. Meanwhile, the Chinese authorities went about formally enthroning the 17th Karmapa at Tsurphu, taking the occasion to announce that they had a 'historical and legal right to appoint religious leaders in Tibet'.

The issue still refuses to go away. Death threats have been made to various lamas who support the young 17th Karmapa. And in March 1994, Shamar Rinpoche announced that he had discovered the rightful reincarnation, a boy from Lhasa who had been spirited out of China via Chengdu, Hong Kong and into India. The fact that the boy was able to obtain travel papers points to high-up official involvement. There is much conjecture that the Chinese authorities are revelling in a dispute that is dividing the exiled Tibetan community and may even have fanned the flames a little here and there.

The official Chinese position of course is that the 17th Karmapa installed at Tsurphu is the only rightful claimant. And here lies the rub – with the Tibetan community divided now between Chinese-administered Tibet and an exiled government in Dharamsala, the question of where incarnate lamas are to be found is likely to be an increasingly prickly issue. For the Chinese authorities, the more incarnate lamas found in Tibet the better. Ultimately, they would reckon, it will weaken the spiritual authority of the Government in Exile and lend credence to their own claims that there is only one Tibet – a Chinese-controlled Tibet. ■

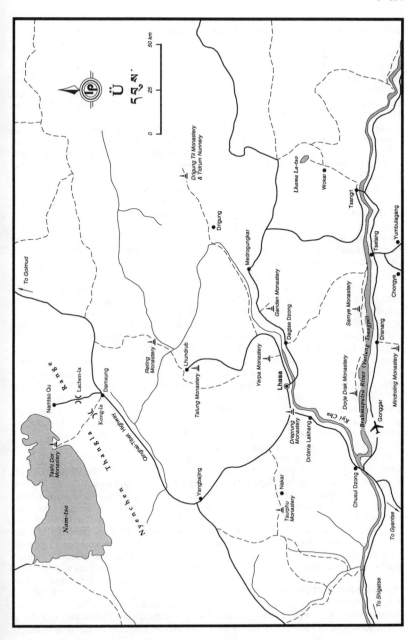

number of other sights that are little visited by foreign travellers, however. Messages on notice boards at the Yak and Banak Shol hotels seem to indicate that Lhamo La-tso lake, a lake of great spiritual importance for the Tibetan people, is growing in popularity. The Yarlung Valley, site of Yumbulagang and the nearby tombs of the Tibetan kings at Chongye, is well worth a visit, as are smaller monastery complexes such as Mindroling.

The entries in this chapter follow a clock-wise circumambulation of Lhasa starting at Tsurphu Monastery in the north-west and ending at Gonggar in the south-west.

GETTING AROUND

With the exception of a few of Ü's major attractions, public transport is a rarity. Tsurphu, Ganden and Samye monasteries are linked with Lhasa by public buses and minibuses, as is Tsetang – the nearest major town to the east of Lhasa and a good base for visits to the Yarlung Valley – but otherwise rented vehicles and hiking are the only ways to get around.

Those planning on renting vehicles should turn to the Information section of the Lhasa chapter for a listing of travel agencies. Some Ü sights, such as Nam-tso lake, are already popular destinations, and prices should be fairly competitive. In the case of less fre-quently travelled routes, travel agents tend to quote a little wildly. Calculate the distances involved and remember that there is a general charge of around Y4 per km.

There are a lot of hiking possibilities in Ü. Some of the more popular routes are described or hinted at in this chapter. Those with a keen interest in extended hikes, however, should get hold of a copy of Gary McCue's *Trekking in Tibet – a traveler's guide* or Victor Chan's *Tibet Handbook – a pilgrimage guide*. Victor Chan's opus, in particular, has exhaustive details on innu-merable treks and hikes in the Ü region.

TSURPHU MONASTERY

མཚུར་བུ་དགོན་པ་

Tsurphu Monastery (4480 metres), around 70 km north-west of Lhasa, is the seat of the Karmapa branch of the Kagyupa order of Tibetan Buddhism. The Karmapas are also known as the Black Hats, a title that dates back to 1256, when the 2nd Karmapa was invited to China by the emperor of the Yuan dynasty, Kublai Khan, and presented with a black hat embellished with gold. The hat is now kept at Rumtek Monastery in Sikkim.

It was the 1st Karmapa, Dusum Khyenpa, who instigated the Tibetan Buddhist tradi-tion of *trulku*, or the practice whereby a lama could choose his next reincarnation. The Karmapa lineage has been maintained until this day. Before his death, the 1st Karmapa indicated to followers certain signs that would enable them to find his reincarnation. It was a practice that was widely adopted by other sects, notably the Gelugpa in the Dalai Lama and Panchen Lama lineages.

Tsurphu Monastery fared badly in the Cul-tural Revolution and much of it is ruined today. Visiting it has become a popular day trip in recent years, however, mainly due to the presence of a recently installed boy Karmapa. There is some dispute as to the boy's incarnate authenticity, with a rival group in Delhi calling foul play and staging protests, but this has not stopped local Tibet-ans and visiting foreigners cruising up to the monastery in droves to receive a blessing from the boy Karmapa. Do not be surprised if he performs this service with a Coke in his hand – he did when I was there. The Karmapa makes a daily appearance at 1 pm.

History

Tsurphu was founded in the 1180s by Dusum Khenyapa, the 1st Karmapa, some 40 years after he founded the Karmapa sect in Kham, his birthplace. It was the third Karmapa mon-astery to be built, and after the 1st Karmapa's death it became the head monastery for the sect. The 2nd Karmapa was discovered nine years later. He visited China at the invitation of Kublai Khan and came back with the black hat after which the sect is also named. The 2nd Karmapa spent the latter part of his life supervising extensions to Tsurphu.

The Karmapa sect traditionally had strong ties with the kings and monasteries of Tsang, a legacy that proved a liability when conflict broke out between the kings of Tsang and the Gelugpa order. When the 5th Dalai Lama invited the Mongolian army of Gushri Khan to do away with his opponents in Tsang, the Karmapa's political clout effectively came to an end and Tsurphu Monastery was sacked. Shorn of its political influence, Tsurphu nevertheless bounced back as an important spiritual centre and is one of the few kagyupa institutions still functioning in the Ü region. When the Chinese forces invaded in 1951, there were some 1000 monks in residence.

The 16th Karmapa fled to Sikkim in 1959 after the popular uprising in Lhasa and founded a new Karmapa monastery in Rumtek. He died in 1981 and his reincarnation was announced by the Dalai Lama and other Tibetan religious leaders in June 1992 as an eight-year old Tibetan boy from Kham, Urgyen Thinle.

The Monastery
Extensive renovations have been undertaken at Tsurphu, and will probably continue now that the Karmapa is installed there. The main building is the **Zhiwa Dratsang**, which has an assembly hall and the Karmapa's throne on its 1st floor. The images to the left of the throne are the 1st, 2nd and 16th Karmapas. On the 2nd floor is a protector chapel.

Tsurphu Kora
The Tsurphu kora, a walk of two or three hours, is quite taxing if you are not acclimatised to the altitude. It winds its way up some 150 metres above the monastery, providing splendid views of Tsurphu below. Above the monastery are some meditation retreats and faint traces of rock paintings.

Take the road west of Tsurphu and bear left. Up ahead is a turn-off that snakes uphill eventually to the top of the ridge overlooking the monastery. From here the trail is fairly obvious, descending eastward down the ridge into a gully before returning to the entrance of Tsurphu.

Places to Stay & Eat
There is a monastery guesthouse at Tsurphu with basic accommodation for Y10, but little in the way of food.

Getting There & Away
Minibuses head out to Tsurphu from the Barkhor square in Lhasa from around 7 to 7.30 am. The cost is Y12.

NAM-TSO LAKE གནམ་མཚོ་
Nam-tso lake (4718 metres), approximately 190 km north of Lhasa, is the second largest salt-water lake in China, the first being Kokonor (Qinghai-hu) in Amdo (Qinghai). It is over 70 km long and reaches a width of 30 km. The Nyenchen Tanglha mountain range, with peaks of over 7000 metres, towers over the lake to the south. Getting to the lake requires crossing the range via the Kong-la pass (5150 metres).

Visits to Nam-tso lake have become increasingly popular with individual travellers over the last few years. The water is a miraculous shade of turquoise blue and there are magnificent views of the nearby mountains. The area where most visitors stay is also a bird sanctuary.

Whatever you do, however, do not sign up for a lift out here until you have been in Lhasa for at least a week. It is not unusual for visitors to get altitude sickness on an overnight stay out at the lake The sudden altitude gain of 1100 metres is not to be treated lightly.

Most travellers head out to Nam-tso as an overnight excursion from Lhasa in a small group. The popular place to stay is **Tashi Dor Monastery**, which is on an outcrop of land that juts into the south-east end of the lake. There is basic accommodation here for Y10 per person on an earthen floor room. It will not fit any more than around nine people, so if there happen to be two groups up there at once there can be problems. There is no food available.

Trekking at Lake Nam-tso
Some travellers make their way out to Namtso to trek. The high altitude of the area means that you need to be fairly fit and acclimatised to attempt this. You will also

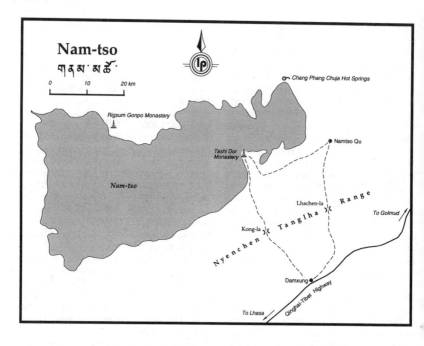

need to bring your own supplies, a tent and a good sleeping bag. Although Nam-tso is a salt-water lake, travellers who have trekked in the area report that the water is not particularly saline and can be drunk after it has been boiled or treated with water-purifying tablets.

A full circuit of the lake takes around 18 to 20 days – it is a pilgrimage route for some devout Tibetans. It is unlikely that many travellers will have time for a walk of this sort. Most people do a five or six-day hike from Tashi Dor Monastery or from the small town of Namtso Qu. An interesting three or four-day walk is to **Chang Phang Chuja**, which is on the north-eastern corner of the lake and has hot springs. It is a total of approximately 80 km for the round trip from Tashi Dor Monastery.

Getting There & Away

There is no public transport to Nam-tso lake. Most travellers band together in a group and hire a minibus or a landcruiser out to the lake. The average price for such a trip is around Y2000 return with an overnight stay at Tashi Dor Monastery. Look out for notices at the Yak and Banak Shol hotels in Lhasa if you are interested in joining such a group.

The nearest town to Nam-tso that is linked to Lhasa by public transport is Damxung on the Qinghai-Tibet highway. One option is to take a Golmud-bound bus as far as Damxung (Dangxiong), the other is to take a minibus from in front of the Kirey Hotel in Lhasa. The latter is cheaper and probably more convenient. Minibuses to Damxung cost Y15 and theoretically leave daily at around 7 am, but it would be best to check at the Kirey reception for the latest details – the service is a little erratic.

From Damxung, you have the option of hitching or hiking out to the village of Namtso Qu or to Tashi Dor Monastery. Both are around 40 km away. Some travellers have been lucky and got lifts, but it seems that

Festival scenes, Trandruk Monastery, Yarlung Valley (CT)

A: Guardian deity on roof of the Jokhang (CT)
B: The knot of eternity (CT)
C: Dharma Wheel with deer on roof of the Jokhang (CT)

Tashilhunpo Monastery, Shigatse (CT)

A: Tibetan trading woman (CT)
B: Tibetan man, Lake Manasarovar (CT)
C: Pilgrim, the Jokhang, Lhasa (CT)
D: Praying woman, the Barkhor, Lhasa (CT)
E: Woman, Tingri (RI)
F: Pilgrimage to Mt Kailash (CT
G: Nomad, La Lung-la (CT)
H: Monk, Chongye (CT)
I: Monk with trumpet (CT)

most end up walking. The main hurdle on the walk is the 5150 metre Kong-la pass around 15 km out of Damxung. It is a difficult walk.

YERPA ཡེ་ར་པ་

Yerpa, around 30 km to the north-east of Lhasa, is probably not of great interest for the average traveller but, for those with a particular interest in Tibetan Buddhism, Yerpa is one of the holiest cave retreats in Ü. Among the many ascetics who have sojourned here and contributed to the area's great sanctity are Guru Rinpoche and Atisha. King Songtsen Gampo also meditated in a cave here, after his Tibetan wife established the first of Yerpa's chapels.

At one time the hill at the base of the cave-dotted cliffs was home to Yerpa Monastery. The monastery, however, was effectively laid to waste in the Cultural Revolution and there is very little to see nowadays.

From the ruins of the monastery it is possible to see some of the cave retreats a couple of hundred metres off at the foot of the cliffs. There are others higher up. Many were desecrated by Red Guards, but some have survived. Monks have begun to return to Yerpa, so expect some of the caves to be occupied.

Getting There & Away

It is possible to hike from Lhasa to Yerpa in a single day. You should come prepared with a tent and sleeping bag, however, as there is no accommodation in the area.

To walk to Yerpa, head up to the intersection of Dzuk Tran Lam and Dodhi Lam and turn right opposite the telecommunications building. This road follows the northern bank of Kyi Chu river east out of Lhasa. About 2½ to three hours out of Lhasa, you will reach a hydroelectric power station. Shortly after this the road bears left up a mountainside to a pass. Yerpa village is visible from here, as is the side valley that leads from the village to Yerpa itself. Reckon on the entire walk taking between seven and eight hours.

TALUNG MONASTERY སྟག་ལུང་དགོན་པ་

Talung Monastery, around 65 km north of Lhasa, is one of a number of monasteries (see Yerpa above and Reting, and Ganden monasteries below) that can be visited in a circuit north and east of Lhasa with a rented vehicle. Public transport in this part of Ü is almost non-existent.

The sprawling monastic complex of Talung – it may at one time have had a population of some 7000 monks – was dynamited by Red Guards and now lies in ruins in the green fields of the Pak Valley. Rebuilding is being undertaken, but not on the scale of other more important monasteries in the area such as Ganden. Talung was the seat of the Talung school of the Kagyupa order.

The site's most important structure was its Tsuglagkhang, the Red Jokhang of Talung. The building is reduced to rubble but its walls still remain. It once housed a two-storey statue of Sakyamuni.

RETING MONASTERY རི་སྒྲེང་དགོན་པ་

Pre-1950 photographs show Reting Monastery sprawling gracefully across the flank of a juniper-clad hill in the Rong Chu valley. Like Ganden Monastery, it was devastated by Red Guards and its present remains hammer home the tragic waste caused by the ideological zeal of the Cultural Revolution.

The monastery dates back to 1056. It was initially associated with Atisha, the Indian scholar who first came to Tibet via the Guge kingdom of Western Tibet and then travelled to Ü, where he emerged as a principal catalyst in the revival of the near moribund Buddhist faith. In its later years, the monastery had an important connection with the Gelugpa order and the Dalai Lamas. Two regents – the de facto rulers of Tibet for the interregnum between the death of a Dalai Lama and the majority of his next reincarnation – were chosen from Reting abbots.

As is happening with other destroyed monasteries in Tibet, monks here have begun the slow and arduous process of rebuilding the work of centuries which was reduced to a pile of rocks with a few well-placed sticks of dynamite. The **Main Assembly Hall** has been reconstructed and contains murals of Tsongkhapa, other prominent lamas and Tantric deities associated with the Gelugpa order. The chapel to the rear of the hall contains Reting's most important image, a gold statue of Guhyasumaja – said to be the personal Tantric deity of Atisha.

Getting There & Away
Yerpa, Talung and Reting monasteries are probably best visited together in a rented vehicle. You might find it difficult to find companions to share the costs with, but this is not necessarily the case. There is usually a reasonable number of travellers in Lhasa with an interest in Tibetan Buddhism and a will to escape the madding crowds.

A trip of this sort is not so common so it would probably be worth shopping around for quotes on vehicles. The costs for a two-day trip should probably be between Y1000 and Y1300 for a landcruiser. It may be possible to do it cheaper.

DRIGUNG TIL MONASTERY & TIDRUM NUNNERY
འབྲི་གུང་མཐིལ་དགོན་པ་
གཏེར་སྒྲོམ་ཇ་ནེ་དགོན་པ་
Neither Drigung Til nor Tidrum (Drigung village is around 100 km north-east of Lhasa) have become popular destinations for individual travellers. They can only be reached by rented transport or by extensive walking. This area has long been a centre for meditative retreat and is dotted with meditation caves. Travellers who make it out here claim that it is well worth the effort.

Drigung Til is the head monastery of the Drigung school of the Kagyupa order. Although it suffered some damage in the Cultural Revolution, the monastery is in better shape than most of the other monastic centres in this part of Ü. It was first established in the mid-12th century. By 1250 it was already vying with Sakya for political power – as it happened, not a particularly good move. The Sakya forces joined with the Mongol army to sack Drigung Til in 1290.

The monastery is thought to have been completely destroyed. Thus chastened, the monastery subsequently devoted itself to the instruction of contemplative meditation.

Drigung Til sprouts from a high, steep ridge overlooking the Drigung Valley. A meandering thread of a path makes its way up into the monastic complex, although there is also vehicle access from the eastern end of the valley.

The **Main Assembly Hall** is probably the most impressive of the buildings at the monastery. The central figure inside is the founder of the monastery. You can see his footprint on a slab of rock at the foot of the statue.

About three hours' walk to the north of Drigung Til is Tidrum Nunnery, with its medicinal hot springs. The nunnery is set in a narrow gorge, and there is a guesthouse nearby set up apparently to accommodate visitors to the hot springs. Both Keith Dowman's *Power Places of Central Tibet* and Victor Chan's *Tibet Handbook – a pilgrimage guide* provide information on the Nangkhor (inner pilgrimage circuit) of Tidrum, which leads up to a Guru Rinpoche cave. It is by all accounts an arduous but splendid walk

Getting There & Away
The best way to get to Drigung Til and Tidrum is again by rented vehicle. The trip should take three or four hours and is feasible as a day trip if you set off early. Most visitors, however, spend at least one night in Tidrum. A two-day trip should cost around Y1200, but as usual it pays to shop around. The last section of road between Drigung Til and Tidrum is difficult for many vehicles, but can be walked in around 15 to 20 minutes. If you have a landcruiser there should not be any problems.

GANDEN MONASTERY
དགའ་ལྡན་དགོན་པ་
Ganden (4500 metres) was the first Gelugpa monastery and has remained the main seat of the order ever since. It was founded by Tsongkhapa, after many years of travel,

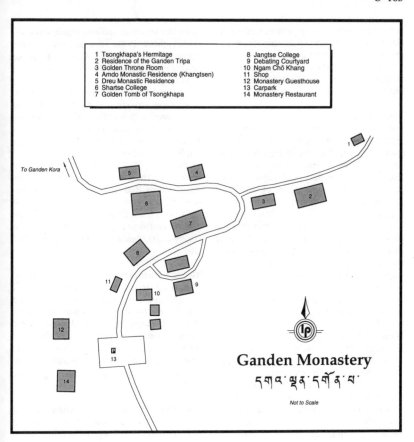

1 Tsongkhapa's Hermitage
2 Residence of the Ganden Tripa
3 Golden Throne Room
4 Amdo Monastic Residence (Khangtsen)
5 Dreu Monastic Residence
6 Shartse College
7 Golden Tomb of Tsongkhapa
8 Jangtse College
9 Debating Courtyard
10 Ngam Chö Khang
11 Shop
12 Monastery Guesthouse
13 Carpark
14 Monastery Restaurant

To Ganden Kora

Ganden Monastery

ངན་ལ་སྤུན་དགོན་པ་

Not to Scale

study, teaching and writing, in 1417. He died two years later and abbotship of the monastery passed on to one of his disciples, Gyeltsab Je. The post came to be known as the Ganden Tripa and was earned through scholarly merit. It is the Ganden Tripa, not, as one might expect, the Dalai Lama who is the head of the Gelugpa sect.

Of all the great monasteries of Tibet, it is Ganden that suffered most at the hands of the Red Guards. Today it is the scene of frenetic rebuilding, but this does not disguise the ruin that surrounds the new. The destruction was caused by artillery fire in 1966, and the

debris sprawls across a high ridge overlooking the Kyi Chu valley. Ganden might be a depressing experience were it not for the obvious zeal with which work teams are carrying out the large-scale reconstruction of the monastic buildings.

If you only have time for one monastery excursion outside Lhasa, Ganden would probably be the best choice. Samye is also a strong contender, but it is more time consuming to reach. Ganden, just 40 km east of Lhasa, with its stupendous views of the surrounding Kyi Chu valley and the air of feverish excitement that accompanies the rebuilding work, is an experience unlike the other major Gelugpa monasteries, Dreprung and Sera, in the Lhasa area.

There is a Y10 admission charge for Ganden, but it is not collected very scrupulously and there is no one checking tickets.

The Monastery

Ganden is an interesting place to wander aimlessly about in. The sheer ochre walls of many of the buildings make great backdrops for photographs, there are always streams of friendly locals treading lightly uphill loaded down with stones and planks of wood and there is usually a yak or two lurking in the shadows.

Buses and rented vehicles stop in a car park to the south of the monastery. From here there are good views. There is a restaurant to the left as you face Ganden and dormitory accommodation is available just north of the restaurant.

Descriptions of the main points of interest in the monastery follow.

Nagam Chö Khang There are several buildings being reconstructed on the right after the car park before you reach this small temple. It may be possible to enter them by the time you have this book in your hands. Otherwise, head from the car park to Ngam Chö Khang. It is built on the site of Tsongkhapa's original assembly hall, and has a small shrine with images of Tsongkhapa and his two principal disciples who were responsible for elucidating on and distilling his thought into the body of beliefs that would become the basis of the Gelugpa order. On the left is a protector chapel that houses four protective deities. The largest image is of Yamantaka.

Debating Courtyard The debating courtyard is also on the right, behind a building that serves as living quarters for monks. There is often debating here in the afternoons. You should be able to hear the clapping of hands as you pass if there is a debate in progress.

Golden Tomb of Tsongkhapa The red for-

tress-like structure of Tsongkhapa's mausoleum is probably the most impressive of the reconstructed buildings at Ganden. Look for its inclining walls and the four highly placed windows.

The entrance leads into an open courtyard. The chapel straight ahead is the domain of the protective deity Dhamarja. Women are not allowed in to this chapel for fear the god's wrathful appearance might disturb their tender sensitivities.

Tsongkhapa's tomb is a silver and gold chörten on the 2nd floor. The original was destroyed by Red Guards. The new chörten was built to house some fragments of Tsongkhapa's skull that were salvaged. The images seated in front of the chörten are of Tsongkhapa flanked by his two principal disciples.

Golden Throne Room On the other side of the road from the Golden Tomb of Tsongkhapa, the Golden Throne Room is a narrow, red building that houses the throne used by Ganden Tripas. The cloth bag on the throne contains the yellow hat of the Dalai Lama. Evidently he forgot it when he fled to India; if you are heading to Dharamsala, you might offer to drop it off to him...then again, maybe not.

Residence of the Ganden Tripa Close to the Golden Throne room, the Residence of the Ganden Tripa contains another, lesser throne used by the Ganden Tripa on its 2nd floor. The 1st floor houses four chapels, all of which are worth visiting. The room with just a bed and a seat marks the place where Tsongkhapa, founder of the monastery, is thought to have died.

Amdo Khangtsen The 'Amdo' of Amdo Khangtsen's name refers to the Tibetan province that is now Qinghai. Tsongkhapa himself was from Amdo, and many monks came from the province to study here. There are some interesting chapels to the rear of the building and many thangkas and paintings on the walls. To the left are paintings of the 35 Buddhas of Compassion.

Ganden Kora

The Ganden kora, around one to 1½ hours, is a simply stunning walk and should not be missed. There are great views along the way and there are usually large numbers of pilgrims and monks offering prayers and prostrating.

From the car park bear left for the trail that heads up to the top of the ridge behind the monastery. The trail winds around the back of the ridge past several isolated shrines, a sky burial site and rock carvings. There are superb views of the Kyi Chu Valley on the left. The sky burial site is reached shortly after the path begins to descend. Some pilgrims undertake a ritual simulated death and rebirth at this point, rolling around on the ground.

Towards the end of the kora is Tsongkhapa's hermitage, a small building with a relief image of Tsongkhapa and two rock Buddha images that are believed to have the power of speech. Above the hermitage is a brilliantly coloured rock painting that is reached by a narrow, precipitous path. It is well worth climbing up to take a look at.

Places to Stay & Eat

The monastery guesthouse to the north of the car park has basic dormitory accommodation for Y10. It is used mainly by travellers who are planning to do the Ganden to Samye trek. A couple of minutes up the road from the car park is a well-stocked shop with everything from sweets and candles to instant noodles and beer. The restaurant is above the car park. It has thukpa (almost inedible unless you are *very* hungry) and nothing else.

Getting There & Away

Ganden is one of the few Ü sights that is connected to Lhasa by public transport. There is a small tin shack on the southern edge of the Barkhor circuit selling tickets for a minibus service that leaves from in front of the Barkhor square at 6.30 am. The bus takes around two hours to get out to Ganden and hangs around until about 2 pm. Tickets cost Y16 return and should be bought on the afternoon of the day before you visit.

If you can get a group of people together, Ganden is worth visiting in a rented vehicle. You can stop for photos on the long, panoramic haul up to the monastery itself and you have control over when you leave. A minibus or landcruiser for the day trip should cost around Y450.

GANDEN TO SAMYE TREK

The Ganden to Samye monastery trek has emerged as the most popular trek in the Ü region in recent years. The trek takes around four days, though some travellers prefer to take it easy and spread the sometimes difficult walk over five days or more. You should definitely be equipped with a tent. Even though there are several nomad encampments and small villages along the way where you might seek out accommodation, it is safer to be self reliant.

If you have your own tent and cooking equipment, you are pretty much free to do the walk as you like. Hiking six to seven

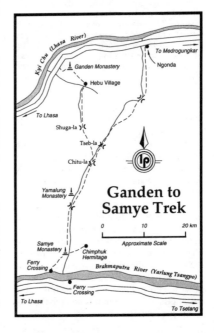

Ganden to Samye Trek

hours a day will see you at Samye monastery in four days. Assuming you do it this way, a day-by-day account of the trek follows.

Day One

There are two possible destinations for the first day of walking, depending probably on how late in the day you start. If you are planning to complete the trek in four days, you should aim to reach the foot of the **Shuga-la pass** (5210 metres), which is around seven hours from Ganden. Those with more time on their hands, might like to spend the night at or close to **Hebu** village, which is around three hours from Ganden. It may be possible to hire yaks or ponies at Hebu.

Unless you are one of those rare types who are lucky enough to have oodles of patience, it will not take you long to figure out that camping near Tibetan villages is not a particularly good idea. Lovely people, the Tibetans, but the sight of a few foreigners putting up a tent is enough to bring the whole village out in force for a few happy hours of vacant staring. The kids are the worst. They will happily sit around a tent all night waiting for the foreigners to appear dishevelled and sleepy-eyed the next morning. Most trekkers in Tibet elect to stay as far away as possible from villages – which in any case are often the domain of vicious dogs.

From the car park at Ganden Monastery, take the path on the left as you would for the kora of the monastery. About 15 minutes onwards the path forks. Take the left fork. This path descends and climbs over a couple of lower passes, before reaching the Hebu Valley below. The walk to Hebu takes around three hours.

From Hebu, it is a walk of around two to three hours to the foot of the Shuga-la pass, where there may be a small nomad encampment. Whether there is or not, this is a good place to camp for the night. After crossing the stream on the southern side of Hebu (it is not always easy to find a crossing), follow it downstream and look out for the trail at the base of the ridge. From this point to the foot of the pass is fairly obvious.

Day Two

Day two involves a long haul up to the Shuga-la pass. Give yourself at least four hours to make it to the summit. There are a couple of points where you think you've made it, and then discover that you have still further to walk. The summit appears suddenly, crowned with fluttering prayer flags.

At times the trail becomes difficult to follow, but providing you stop and survey your surroundings it should not present any major problems. The trail follows a creek gully initially, before climbing above the creek and then descending down into another gully. When the trail seems to disappear, keep to the east side of the valley and look out for the piled rock cairns guiding the way. From the pass itself, it should take around 1½ hours to make the descent into a valley with some good grassy spots for camping.

Day Three

From the south base of the Shuga-la pass, as you look up the valley, you can see a side valley ahead on the left. This valley leads up to the Chitu-la pass and from there down into the Samye Valley. From the valley floor to the top of the pass – just over 5000 metres – it should take around three hours of walking. It is not as difficult as the Shuga-la pass.

From the top of the pass, an indistinct trail through a moraine of boulders and rocks follows the western edge of two lakes for about an hour and passes a nomad encampment after another hour. Shortly after, you enter a ravine and from here an area of meadows that provide good camping. If you have energy you can walk on, as there are numerous places for camping along the way.

Day Four

The final day is a long one if you want to reach Samye. Realistically you can reckon on eight or more hours of walking. It would be a good idea to cover as much distance as possible on the third day.

Depending on how far you travelled on day three, the trail follows a stream for between an hour and two hours, before bearing to the right at a wooden bridge.

About two hours from here you pass a village. Just over half an hour from here is a good area for camping. At this point, you might consider camping the night and making it a five-day trek. Otherwise it is still over three more hours of walking to Samye.

There are a couple of bridge crossings from here, and within an hour the terrain starts to become more arid and sandy. Before too long the golden roof of Samye Monastery comes into view. From here it is another hot couple of hours trudging through the sand.

TSETANG རྩེ་ཐང་

Tsetang (3550 metres), 183 km south-east of Lhasa, is the second largest town – after Lhasa – in the Ü region. It is the capital of Shannan prefecture and is a good jumping board for exploration of the Yarlung Valley area.

The town itself is a hell-hole. At least it was in mid-'94, when it looked like downtown Sarejevo. All the roads had been torn up in preparation for a civic beautification job, but seeing as the roads had been torn up all the way to Gonggar and work was proceeding at a very leisurely pace it is anyone's guess when the job will finally be completed.

Tsetang is a tatty, decrepit town where the locals are guaranteed to linger listlessly in dark doorways and gaze vacantly at any foreigners that stray into town. Every Chinese male in town will probably hail you with a silly, strangulated 'hellauooo'.

Like Lhasa and Shigatse, Tsetang divides into a new Chinese town and an old Tibetan quarter. The Tibetan quarter is in the east of town, clustered around Gangpo Ri, one of Ü's four sacred mountains. All accommodation and restaurants are in the Chinese part of town. The Tibetan quarter of Tsetang is a shabby, dispirited affair compared to its equivalent in Lhasa. Most of the town's immediate sights are scattered around the outskirts of Tsetang but can be reached on foot.

Tsetang Monastery རྩེ་ཐང་དགོན་པ་

Tsetang Monastery suffered badly in the Cul-

tural Revolution and it is arguable whether it is worth the effort of visiting today. There is not a great deal to see besides ruins. The monastery dates back to the mid-14th century and was originally a Kagyupa institution. By the 18th century the Gelugpas had taken over the running of the place, and in the 20th century it appears to have become an artillery target-practice site for the Chinese.

Reach the monastery by walking up through the market street into the Tibetan part of town. At the end of the road is a kind of cul-de-sac. The crumbling walls of the monastery are to the left.

Sang-ngag Zimche Nunnery གསང་སྔགས་ཨ་ནེ་དགོན་པ་

Close by Tsetang Monastery and at the foot of Gangpo Ri is Sang-ngag Zimche Nunnery. It was spared the outright destruction suffered by Tsetang Monastery and has some important images in its main chapel. The principal image is of Avalokiteshvara, and dates back to the time of King Songtsen Gampo – according to some accounts the statue was fashioned by the king himself. The walls are draped with some fine old thangkas and there are a couple of small chapels with more images to the rear of the building.

The nunnery is well worth visiting. You should get a friendly reception, and it is a very short walk from the centre of town. From Tsetang Monastery, bear right up the hill. The path leads directly to the nunnery. The nunnery and Tsetang Monastery may also both be visited by way of an easy inner kora described below in the entry on Gangpo Ri.

Gangpo Ri གངས་བོ་རི་

Gangpo Ri mountain (approximately 4130 metres high) has a special significance for Tibetans as the legendary birthplace of their people. The story goes that Avalokiteshvara, the Bodhisattva of Compassion, descended from the heavens to the Land of Snows long ago in the form of a monkey. He meditated in a cave on the slopes of Gangpo Ri, before

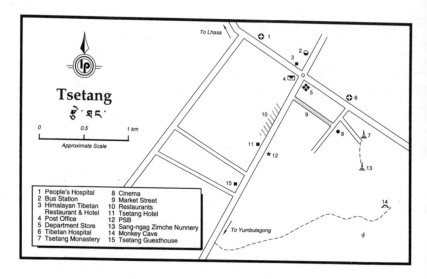

Tsetang
རྩེ་ཐང་

0	0.5	1 km

Approximate Scale

1	People's Hospital	8	Cinema
2	Bus Station	9	Market Street
3	Himalayan Tibetan	10	Restaurants
	Restaurant & Hotel	11	Tsetang Hotel
4	Post Office	12	PSB
5	Department Store	13	Sang-ngag Zimche Nunnery
6	Tibetan Hospital	14	Monkey Cave
7	Tsetang Monastery	15	Tsetang Guesthouse

being drawn from his solitude by Sinmo, a white demoness. It seems she got his attention by sitting outside his cave and weeping – oldest trick in the book, but one that is especially effective with a Bodhisattva of Compassion. One thing led to another and before too long they had six children – the beginnings of the Tibetan race.

The **Gangpo Ri Monkey Cave** where the monkey meditated can be visited near the summit of the mountain. The walk there and back will take close to a full day. Do it in the spirit of a day walk in the hills, rather than as a trip specifically to see the Monkey Cave. The cave itself is rather disappointing, with a few wall paintings of monkeys. Around two km south of the Tsetang Guesthouse is a trail that leads up the slopes of Gangpo Ri for around three km (an altitude gain of around 550 metres) to the cave.

There is a pilgrimage circuit around Gangpo Ri but it is a walk that will probably require two days. Very fit walkers can do it in one day, given around 11 hours. An easier inner kora can be completed in around two hours with a couple of visits to monasteries en route.

To take the inner kora, walk east from the Tsetang traffic circle in the centre of town and look out for an alley on the right a few minutes before km marker 1. This alley takes you into the Tibetan part of town, a maze of streets that makes navigation to Ngachö Monastery, the first sight on the kora, quite difficult. Assuming you stumble across Ngachö, however, the rest is fairly straightforward. A trail goes around the monastery and over to Sang-ngag Zimche Nunnery. From here, the trail descends to Tsetang Monastery.

The First Field of Tibet

A highly dubious excursion, this one, and quite likely apocryphal. What's known as Zorthang in Tibetan, is purported to be Tibet's first cultivated field. The exact location is disputed. It might be around 30 minutes' walk north of Tsetang; it might be in the vicinity of Yumbulagang; it might not be worth the effort of finding out.

Tsetang Market

If you are really stuck for something to do in Tsetang, you might wander down to the market near the Tsetang traffic circle. It is Chinese-run for the most part. The mornings see the place at its most lively and colourful. It is a pale shadow of the Barkhor market area of Lhasa, however. It closes reasonably early at around 6.30 pm.

Places to Stay

About 10 minutes' walk south of the Tsetang traffic circle is the *Tsetang Guesthouse*. It is a drab Chinese-style establishment with dorm beds for Y15. There is a reasonably good restaurant (though no better than the ones out on the street) and a well-stocked shop. It has little else to recommend it.

Down on the traffic circle itself is a Tibetan-run establishment, *Himalayan Tibetan Restaurant & Hotel*. Check to see if they are still taking foreigners. Dingy, dorm-style accommodation is available for Y10. Needless to say, there are no showers. Another drawback is the video room downstairs which blasts out the soundtrack of the current movie being shown with loudspeakers placed over the doorway. It runs late and starts early. Do not expect much in the way of peace and quiet.

Tsetang's premier lodging is the *Tsetang Hotel*, just down the road from the guesthouse. It is a tacky attempt to create a tourist-class hotel, but you have to give them credit for trying – in Tsetang of all places. Economy doubles are Y110 per person. Are they worth the expense? Arguably, yes. This is one of the few hotels in Tibet with a 24-hour hot-water supply, the Cantonese-style restaurant is excellent, I for one enjoyed the beer garden (only open in the summer months), and the staff – believe it or not – were very friendly. If you have not seen a shower for a couple of weeks and you feel like treating yourself, this is a good place to do it.

Places to Eat

The restaurants at the *Tsetang Guesthouse* and the *Tsetang Hotel* are both good. The Tsetang Hotel in particular has excellent Cantonese and Sichuanese fare that is not that expensive – reckon spending on around Y15 to Y20 per head without drinks. The beer is cold too.

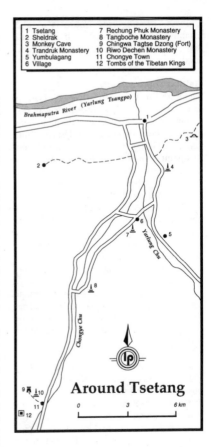

1	Tsetang	7	Rechung Phuk Monastery
2	Sheldrak	8	Tangboche Monastery
3	Monkey Cave	9	Chingwa Tagtse Dzong (Fort)
4	Trandruk Monastery	10	Riwo Dechen Monastery
5	Yumbulagang	11	Chongye Town
6	Village	12	Tombs of the Tibetan Kings

Around Tsetang

Outside the hotels, the street with both the Tsetang Guesthouse and Hotel is the best place to seek out restaurants. North of the Tsetang Hotel all the way to the traffic circle the road is lined with Chinese restaurants. The flashy places serve hot-pot and are generally expensive – it is notoriously difficult to keep track of the price when eating hot-pot and it is easy to get ripped off. There are a number of humble-looking places that serve up typical Chinese fare for prices of around Y10 to Y12 per dish. None of them have English menus – you will have to pick and choose in the kitchen if you do not speak

Chinese. *Yarmingoring House* is a small establishment on the left with an English sign. It serves coffee, snacks and Chinese food.

Getting There & Away

There are direct buses from Lhasa to Tsetang, though most travellers make their way first to Samye, spend a day or so at the monastery, and then travel on to Tsetang. The road from Lhasa to Gonggar airport is fine, but from this point on it becomes one of the worst in Tibet. There are a multitude of scenic detours to avoid members of work teams sprawled out amongst the rubble of the former road smoking cigarettes and kicking the odd rock about in boredom. My bus jolted through fields, through the shallows of the Brahmaputra River and even through a schoolyard at one point.

Transport out of Tsetang is fairly minimal. Buses to Lhasa (and the Samye ferry) leave between 7 and 7.30 am and take around seven or eight hours, depending on the condition of the road. There is no public transport out of Tsetang to the sights of the Yarlung Valley.

Some travellers band together in Lhasa for a three or four-day trip out to the Yarlung Valley by way of Tsetang. This way it is possible to visit Samye for four or five hours, drive on to Tsetang, spend the night there, visit the Yarlung Valley sights and head back to Lhasa via Mindroling Monastery and possibly Gonggar. The total cost for a landcruiser on a trip of the sort is around Y1700 to Y2000.

Getting Around

Most of Tsetang's immediate attractions can be reached on foot. Ask at the Tsetang Hotel for information on hiring vehicles to get out to Yumbulagang and Chongye. If there happens to be a small group of you in town, hiring a vehicle for a day excursion out to the Yarlung Valley should be fairly economical at around Y400. There is little in the way of other kinds of transport available in Tsetang. Bicycle hire is not available, but again the staff at the Tsetang Hotel may be able to

rustle something up for you if you ask nicely and offer to pay Lhasa rates of around Y2 an hour.

YARLUNG VALLEY ཡར་ཀླུང་

Yarlung is considered the cradle of Tibetan civilisation. Creation myth locates the valley as the origin of the Tibetan people (see the Gangpo Ri entry for Tsetang above), and it was from Yarlung that the early Tibetan kings unified Tibet in the 7th century. The massive burial mounds of these kings can be seen in Chongye. Yumbulagang, another major attraction of the area, is perched on a crag like a medieval European castle and is considered the oldest building in Tibet.

The major attractions of the Yarlung Valley can be seen in a day or two, but it is worth giving yourself some extra time here. Transportation in the area is something of a problem, but it is a beautiful part of Tibet for some extended hiking and day walks. Yarlung sees a lot less foreign travellers than the other major destinations of Ü and Tsang.

Some travellers have spent a week or more hiking in the Yarlung Valley region, and have successfully stayed with Tibetan families in the villages. If you opt to do this, always offer a gift or some money in return for the favours given by the locals and try to make sure that the reception for future travellers remains a welcome one.

Sheldrak ཤེལ་བྲག་

Sheldrak is the preserve of hardy hikers and Tibetan pilgrims. It is a tough six-hour climb to the west of Tsetang with an altitude gain of around 1000 metres.

For Tibetans, Sheldrak is one of Tibet's holiest pilgrimage destinations. It is the site of Guru Rinpoche's first meditation cave. At the invitation of King Trisong Detsen, Guru Rinpoche came to Tibet to exorcise the land of demons and the influence of Tibet's indigenous Bön faith. According to legend, it was here in the Crystal Rock Cave that he got the job done.

The cave is reached from the road that heads out to Chongye from Tsetang – it runs parallel and to the west of the Tsetang Hotel.

About three km from the centre of Tsetang, a trail heads west from the Chongye road up the Sheldrak Valley.

Unless you have a keen interest in Tibetan pilgrimage sites, this is another attraction that it would be best to treat as a strenuous hike. The cave itself has a small chapel and provides great views of the surrounding countryside.

Trandruk Monastery ཁྲ་འབྲུག་དགོན་པ་

Around seven km south of the Tsetang Hotel, Trandruk is one of the earliest Buddhist monasteries in Tibet, having been founded at the same time as the Jokhang and Ramoche in Lhasa. Dating back to the 7th-century reign of Songtsen Gampo, it is one of the 'Demoness Subduing' temples of Tibet. King Songtsen Gampo's Chinese wife, Princess Wencheng, divined the presence of a subterranean demoness in Tibet. Only by pinning this demoness down, it was felt, could the Buddhist faith take root in the high plateau. The location of Trandruk – which is one of 12 such subduing temples that ring the Jokhang in concentric circles like a mandala – corresponds to the demoness's left shoulder.

Trandruk has undergone numerous enlargements and reconstructions over the centuries. It was significantly enlarged in the 14th century and again under the auspices of the 5th and 7th Dalai Lamas. The monastery was badly desecrated by Red Guards during the Cultural Revolution, and extensive restoration work has been carried out since 1988. Monks at the monastery will solemnly point out wall paintings that were defaced and still await restoration.

The entrance of the monastery opens into a courtyard area ringed by cloisters. The building to the rear of the courtyard shares a similar ground plan to the Jokhang in Lhasa, and indeed shares the same Tibetan name: Tsuglagkhang. The room in the centre is the main assembly hall, and surrounding it is a walkway with chapels off to the sides. As is the case with the Jokhang, the principal chapel is the one to the rear centre.

Most of Trandruk's valuable images and murals were damaged during the Cultural Revolution and have been replaced with new ones. Images of note include those in the north and south chapels of the Tsuglagkhang. The northern chapel contains a fine 1000-armed Avalokiteshvara, while the southern chapel has a huge image of Guru Rinpoche.

Trandruk is a significant stop for Tibetan pilgrims, and the monks seem genuinely glad to welcome foreign visitors and show them around. It is a lively place and well worth a brief visit en route to Yumbulagang. Theoretically, there is an entry charge of Y10, but the monks do not seem particularly concerned about collecting it.

Getting There & Away Trandruk is in a small Tibetan village around six or seven km south of the Tsetang Hotel. It is possible to walk there in around two hours, but there is also a steady stream of tractors plying the road between Trandruk and Tsetang. Getting a lift should only cost one or two yuan. One possibility is to hitch as far as Trandruk and then walk out to Yumbulagang, which is another five km down the road.

Yumbulagang ཡུམ་བུ་བླ་སྒང་

This fine, tapering finger of a structure that sprouts from a craggy ridge overlooking the patch-work fields of the Yarlung Valley is reputed to be the oldest building in Tibet. That is, the original structure was at least. Most of what can be seen today dates from 1982. It is still a remarkably impressive sight, and should not be missed.

The founding of Yumbulagang stretches back to a time of legend; myths converge on the structure in bewildering profusion. The standard line is that it was built to accommodate King Nyentri Tsenpo, a likely historical figure who has since been swallowed up by the mythology of Tibet. Legend has him descending from the heavens and being received by the people of the Yarlung Valley as a king. Buddhist holy texts are also thought to have fallen from the heavens at Yumbulagang at a later date.

There has been no conclusive dating for the original Yumbulagang, though some accounts indicate that the foundations may have been laid more than 2000 years ago. They are probably inaccurate. It is more likely that it dates back to the 7th century, when the country first came under the rule of Songtsen Gampo.

The design of Yumbulagang indicates that it was originally a fortress and probably much larger than the present structure. Today it serves as a chapel and is inhabited by a few monks. Its most impressive feature is its tower, and the prominence of Yumbulagang on the Yarlung skyline belies the fact this tower is only some 11 metres tall. It is possible to climb up to the top, third storey of the tower via a couple of rickety step-ladders and a wonky bridge.

The ground-floor chapel is consecrated to the ancient kings of Tibet. A central Buddha image is flanked by Nyentri Tsenpo on the left and Songtsen Gampo on the right. There is another chapel on the 2nd floor with an Avalokiteshvara image.

It does not take all that long to explore Yumbulagang. Perhaps the best part is to take a stroll up along the ridge above the building. There are fabulous views of Yumbulagang and the Yarlung Valley from a promontory topped with prayer flags. It is an easy 10-minute climb.

Getting There & Away Unless you have hired transport, you will probably have to walk from Trandruk Monastery (see above) to Yumbulagang. There are plenty of tractors on the road between Trandruk and Tsetang, but very few between Trandruk and Yumbulagang. It is a walk of around five km, and for the most part it follows a shady, tree-lined stretch of road.

Rechung Phuk Monastery
རས་ཆུང་ཕུག་དགོན་པ་

The remains of Rechung Phuk Monastery are really only an attraction for serious pilgrim types or those with time to spare in the Yarlung Valley region. It is easily accessible on foot from Trandruk Monastery or from Tsetang, but little remains of its former grandeur.

Rechung Phuk is associated with the illustrious Milarepa (1040-1123), founder of the Kagyupa sect and revered by many as Tibet's greatest song writer and poet. It was his foremost disciple, Rechungpa (1083-1161), who founded Rechung Phuk as a cave retreat. Later a monastery was founded at the site, which eventually housed up to 1000 monks. Some buildings have been reconstructed around the cave, which can still be visited. The newly constructed chapels here contain images that are also of recent provenance.

To get to Rechung Phuk, follow the road between Trandruk and Yumbulagang and take the road to the west (right) about two km after the former (about three km before Yumbulagang). A couple of km along this road is a village. You can see the ruins of the monastery up on the ridge that divides the two channels of the Yarlung Valley. It is a steep 30-minute walk up from the village to the monastery.

Tangboche Monastery
རང་བོ་ཆེ་དགོན་པ་

Around 15 km south-west of Tsetang on the road to Chongye, Tangboche is not an important sight and should not be too high on most travellers' itineraries. Nevertheless, the monastery was less badly damaged during the Cultural Revolution than many of the other monastic sites of Ü and some highly rated murals have survived intact.

The monastery is thought to date back to 1017 and was instrumental in the revival of Buddhism in central Tibet. Atisha, the renowned Indian scholar stayed here in a meditation retreat. The murals, which for most visitors with an interest in things Tibetan are the main attraction of the monastery, were commissioned by the 13th Dalai Lama in 1913. They can be seen in the monastery's main hall – one of the few monastic structures in this region that was not destroyed by Red Guards.

Tangboche is easily visited if you are travelling by rented transport between Tsetang and Chongye. You should be able to see the building on the left around 15 km out of

Tsetang. You have to look carefully, as it is partially obscured by a village. There is a short trail from the road to the village and monastery. It is a dusty 12-km walk from Trandruk Monastery to Tangboche.

CHONGYE VALLEY འཕྱོངས་རྒྱས་

Most visitors to Chongye go there as a day trip from Tsetang, and combine the visit with seeing attractions in the Yarlung Valley. It is possible to stay in the town of Chongye, but for the average traveller there probably is not enough of interest to warrant a stay of more than a day or so. The huge burial mounds of the ancient kings of Ü are, pretty much as their name suggests, mounds, and not particularly exciting for anyone without a degree in archaeology.

Like the Yarlung Valley, Chongye is a beautiful valley enclosed by rugged peaks. The views from some of the burial mounds are superb. It is also well worth climbing up to Riwo Dechen Monastery and the ruins of the old *dzong* (fort) behind it for more views of the mounds themselves.

Chongye Town

Chongye town is a dusty street, lined with the occasional shop and restaurant, that culminates in a T-junction. To the far right of the junction as you come from Tsetang there is a basic guesthouse with beds for Y10. It is not a town to linger long in, but it makes a good base for hikes in the Chongye Valley area. It is around 27 km south of Tsetang and is not that easy, though by no means impossible, to hitch to. If you can get hold of a bicycle it is possible to ride out to the town in a few hours.

From Chongye town, most of the important Chongye sights are easily accessible on foot.

Chongye Burial Mounds
འཕྱོངས་རྒྱས་བང་སོ་

The Tombs of the Kings at Chongye in some ways represent one of the few historical sites in Tibet that give evidence of a pre-Buddhist culture in Tibet. Most of the kings interred here are now firmly associated with the rise of Buddhism on the high plateau, but the methods of their interment point to the Bön faith. It is thought that the burials were probably officiated at by Bön priests and accompanied by sacrificial offerings.

Burial of the dead is a practice that disappeared from Tibet after the fall of the Yarlung kings. Sky burial became the standard means for disposing of the dead for most people, while important lamas were interred in a chörten. Recent archaeological evidence seems to suggest, however, that burial might have been quite widespread in the time of the Yarlung kings, and may not have been limited only to royalty.

Accounts of the location and number of the mounds differ. Erosion of the mounds has also made some of them difficult to identify positively. It is agreed, however, that there is a group of 10 burial mounds just south of the Chongye river.

The most revered of the mounds, and the closest to the Chongye Bridge, is the burial mound of Songtsen Gampo. It is the largest of the mounds and has a small Nyingmapa

Remains of a stone lion in the royal cemetery at Chongye

temple atop its 13-metre summit. The southernmost of the group of mounds, high up on the slopes of Mt Mura is the tomb of King Trisong Detsen. It is about a one-hour climb, but there are superb views of the Chongye Valley from up here.

Chingwa Tagtse Dzong
འབྲི་ང་བ་སྟག་རྩེ་རྫོང་

The dzong, or fort, can be seen clearly from Chongye town and the Chongye burial mounds, its crumbling ramparts straddling a ridge of Mt Chingwa. It was once one of the most powerful forts in central Tibet and dates back to the time of the early Yarlung kings. The dzong is also celebrated as the birthplace of the 5th Dalai Lama. There is not a great deal to see in the fort itself, but again you are rewarded with some great views if you take the hour or so walk up from Chongye town.

Riwo Dechen Monastery

Riwo Dechen Monastery sprawls across the lower slopes of Mt Chingwa below the fort. It is well worth visiting this active Gelugpa monastery. The monks are friendly and there are surprisingly large numbers of them. Extensive restoration work has been carried out here, making this one of the largest monasteries in this part of Tibet.

Riwo Dechen Monastery can be reached by a half-hour climb from Chongye town.

LHAMO LA-TSO LAKE ལྷ་མོ་བླ་མཚོ་

Around 115 km to the north-east of Tsetang, Lhamo La-tso lake is one of Ü's most important pilgrimage destinations. The *la* of La-tso is a Tibetan word that means 'soul' or 'life spirit'. La resides in both animate and inanimate forms such as lakes, mountains and trees. The two may sometimes be connected, as in the Tibetan custom of planting a tree at the birth of a child – such a tree is known as a *la-shing*. In the case of Lhamo La-tso lake, the la here is identified with the spirit of Tibet itself.

The Dalai Lamas have traditionally made pilgrimages to Lhamo La-tso to seek visions which appear on the surface of the lake. The Tibetan regent journeyed to the lake after the death of the 13th Dalai Lama and had a vision of a monastery in Amdo that led to the discovery of the present Dalai Lama.

Lhamo La-tso lake is difficult to reach and receives very few foreign visitors. You should come prepared with your own food supplies and a tent if you want to hike in the region. Be prepared for cold weather – the lake is at an altitude of over 5000 metres.

The nearest accommodation to Lhamo La-tso is at Chökorgye Monastery, which is around four hours' walk from the lake. Nothing is charged for staying at the monastery, but it is appropriate to make a donation when you leave. Do your best to keep the monks well disposed to the occasional foreign visitor.

Getting There & Away

It is possible to hike all the way from Samye or from Tsetang to Lhamo La-tso. From Samye it is a taxing seven to eight-day walk; those considering it should refer to Victor Chan's *Tibet Handbook – a pilgrimage guide*, which has full details of the hike. From Tsetang, it may be possible to hitch to Gyatsa town, from where it is a two-day walk up to Chörkorgye Monastery.

Most travellers approach Lhamo La-tso by rented vehicle from Lhasa or Tsetang. Landcruisers should complete the road between Tsetang and Gyatsa in around five hours – reckon on around seven hours in a Chinese truck. In mid-'94 the bridge at Gyatsa was too unstable for vehicles to cross and it was necessary to proceed on foot over it. On the other side a truck was available to ferry pilgrims and travellers up to Chökorgye Monastery. It would be wise to check on the current situation before heading out there.

SAMYE MONASTERY
བསམ་ཡས་དགོན་པ་

Samye is deservedly the most popular destination for travellers in the Ü region. Samye, in the middle of the sandy Samye Valley and approached via a beautiful river crossing, has a magic about it that makes many travellers stay longer than they had intended to. No journey in Ü is complete without visiting Samye.

History

Samye, with a history of over 1200 years, was the first of Tibet's monastic institutions. It was founded in the reign of King Trisong Detsen, though the exact date is unknown and subject to some debate – probably between 765 and 780. Whatever the case, Samye represents the Tibetan state's first efforts to allow the Buddhist faith to set down roots in Tibet. Shortly after the founding of the monastery, Tibet's first monks were ordained by the monastery's Indian abbot, Shantarakshita, and Indian and Chinese scholars were invited to the monastery to assist in the translation of Buddhist texts into Tibetan.

Before long disputes broke out between followers of Indian scholarship and Chinese. The disputes culminated in the Great Debate of Samye, an event that is heralded by Tibetan historians as a crucial juncture in which the future course of Tibetan Buddhism was decided. The debate, which probably took place in the early 790s, was essentially an argument between the quietist Indian approach to bodhisattvahood via textual study and scholarship and the more immediate Chan (Zen) influenced approach of Chinese masters, who decried scholarly study in favour of contemplation on the absolute nature of Buddhahood.

The debates came out on the side of the Indian scholars. The reasons for this are complex and also of fairly dubious significance. Tibet was technically at war with China at the time, and this may have been a factor. There is also the fact that the Indian emphasis on a gradual approach to the bodhisattva ideal was an orientation that found favour with the Tibetan court due to its emphasis on Buddhist morality. Either way, both sides of the debate found their niche in Tibet.

Samye has never been truly the preserve of any one of Tibetan Buddhism's different orders. The influence of Guru Rinpoche, however, in establishing the monastery has meant that the Nyingmapa order has been most closely associated with the monastery. When the Sakyapa order came to power in the 15th century it took control of Samye, and Nyingmapa influence declined, though not completely.

Samye has been damaged and restored many times throughout its long history. Inevitably, the most recent assault on its antiquity was by the Chinese during the Cultural Revolution. Many of the monastery's structures, including the all-important, gold-topped Ütse, were badly damaged and vast numbers of relics and images stolen or destroyed. Nevertheless, Samye did not fare as badly as Ganden and some of the other minor temples in Ü. Extensive renovation work has been going on since the mid-'80s.

The Monastery

Samye's overall design was based on Odantapuri Temple of Bihar, India, and is a mandalic representation of the universe. The central temple represents Mt Meru, and the temples around it in two concentric circles represent the oceans, continents and subcontinents that ring Mt Sumeru in Buddhist cosmology.

At the centre of the monastery grounds is the Ütse, the most impressive of the monastery buildings. Directly to the north is a Moon Temple and to the south a Sun Temple. Ringing the Ütse are four large stupas, which are named after their colours: red, black, green and white. These were destroyed in the Cultural Revolution but have been rebuilt recently – they look decidedly new and slightly out of place. Surrounding the stupas are 12 ling chapels, four major ones and eight minor ones. The major ling chapels represent oceans, the minor ling chapels continents and subcontinents.

The Ütse The central building of Samye, the Ütse comprises a synthesis of architectural styles. The first two floors were originally Tibetan in style, the 3rd floor was Chinese and the top floor Indian. There is much scholarly debate on this issue and without a

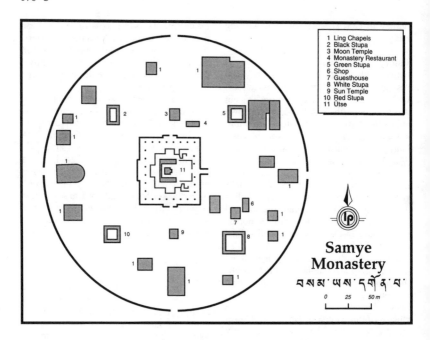

1 Ling Chapels
2 Black Stupa
3 Moon Temple
4 Monastery Restaurant
5 Green Stupa
6 Shop
7 Guesthouse
8 White Stupa
9 Sun Temple
10 Red Stupa
11 Ütse

Samye Monastery

བསམ་ཡས་དགོན་པ་

0   25   50 m

trained eye there is little way of telling anyway.

Just to the left of the entrance is a stele dating from 779. The elegant Tibetan script carved on its surface proclaims Buddhism as the state religion of Tibet by order of King Trisong Detsen. From here the entrance leads into the first of the ground floor chambers: the **Assembly Hall**. To the right of the Assembly Hall is a small chapel that stores important images salvaged from other chapels in the Cultural Revolution's assault on Samye.

To the rear of the Assembly Hall are some steps leading into Samye's most revered chapel, the **Jowo Khang**. On either side of the stairs are rows of statues depicting historical figures associated with the early years of the monastery. On the left are statues of Vairocana, a translator; Shantarakshita, Samye's first abbot; Guru Rinpoche; Trisong Detsen and Songtsen Gampo. On the right are two groups of three statues: the first

group are associated with the Kadampa order; the second group is multidenominational, including lamas from the Nyingmapa, Sakyapa and Gelugpa orders.

You enter the **Inner Chapel** via three doors – an unusual feature. They symbolise the Three Doors of Liberation: those of emptiness, signlessness and wishlessness. An inner circumambulation route around the Inner Chapel follows at this point.

The centrepiece of the Inner Chapel is a four-metre statue of Sakyamuni. Bodhisattvas and protective deities line the side walls of the chapel, and the walls themselves are decorated with ancient murals. Look also for the panelled ceiling – each of the panels is adorned with a Tantric mantra.

The main feature of the 2nd floor is an upper extension of the Inner Chapel. This houses an image of Guru Rinpoche in a semi-wrathful aspect. Some of the 2nd-floor murals are very impressive. Also on the 2nd floor are the Quarters of the Dalai Lamas.

The three rooms include a small throne room and a bedroom.

The 3rd floor is a recent addition to the Ütse. The original is thought to have been Indian in inspiration. It should be open by the time you have this book in your hands.

The Ling Chapels & Stupas As renovation work continues at Samye, the original ling chapels and the coloured stupas are gradually being restored. The four major ling chapels are Jampel Ling, Aryapalo Ling, Jampa Ling and Jamchub Semkye Ling. For the most part, the interiors have been desecrated and robbed of their statuary.

The minor ling chapels are usually closed and many of them have been badly damaged and still await restoration. They served many purposes when Samye was completely functioning: centres for translation, for training monks in meditation and for printing tantras among other things. Take a wander around and see which ones are open.

Chimpuk Hermitage མཚམས་ཕུ་རི་བྲོད་
Chimpuk Hermitage is a warren of caves that was once a retreat for Guru Rinpoche. It is a popular day hike for travellers spending a few days at Samye. The walk takes around four or five hours up and around three hours down. Take some water with you.

Chimpuk is to the north-east of Samye. If you head out of the monastery in this direction you should be able to find a path leading east through some fields. Keep following this track, bearing left. The path crosses through desert-like territory for a couple of hours before ascending into the surprisingly lush area in which the caves are.

Many of the caves are occupied by hermits – do not just go barging into them – and there is a small monastery up above the caves. There are splendid views of the Samye Valley from up here.

Places to Stay & Eat
There is only one place to stay and one place to eat. The *Monastery Guesthouse* is inside the Ütse compound – it is easy to find. It has basic dorm beds for Y8.

The *Monastery Restaurant* is just to the left after the west exit of the Ütse compound. Do not expect anything very appetising. Basically all they have is thukpa with meat and vegetables. Occasionally rice is available. It is not uncommon for the kitchen to run out of vegetables, in which case it is just plain thukpa. Food here is cheap at least.

Just outside and to the left of the guesthouse is a shop that is reasonably well stocked with instant noodles, sweets, biscuits, candles, cigarettes, beer (essential for any monastic sojourn) and so on.

Getting There & Away
Buses for Tsetang all pass by the Samye ferry departure point, which makes getting to Samye from either Lhasa or Tsetang fairly easy. A cheaper alternative to the Tsetang bus is a Samye bus service which leaves from the bus station just south of the Barkhor square in Lhasa. See the Ganden to Samye trek section above for information on a popular trek between the two monasteries.

Buses to Samye (the Tsetang bus) leave from Lhasa's main bus station at around 7.30 am. The cost is Y97 or Y47 for students. Do not buy a return ticket – it may not be possible anyway – as the return bus to Lhasa should only cost Y40. Buses from the small bus station south of the Barkhor square are much cheaper at around Y25 and also leave at around 7.30 am. You might try getting tickets the day before, but the best course of action is to get there before 7 am on the day you want to leave and ask around for the Samye bus.

Hopefully the road between Gonggar airport and Samye will have improved by the time this book is out. At the time of writing this road was a mess, and buses were taking anywhere from between seven and 12 hours to do the trip.

Buses drop off Samye passengers at the ferry crossing. River crossings are irregular (operating whenever there are enough people – about 30 seems the average) in flat-bottomed boats powered with a small motor. There is generally no problem paying what the locals pay, which is Y3, though some travellers have reported being stung for Y5. Anyone who turns up with a guide, can expect to be charged Y25. Hiring a whole boat costs Y60, though you can only expect to get this price after much haggling – travel agents in Lhasa were telling travellers that boats cost Y140 to hire.

The river crossing, one of the few in Tibet, is a fantastic ride. It takes a little over an hour, and much careful navigation around the sandbanks. On the other side, you hop across other boats moored against the banks of the Brahmaputra to avoid getting your feet wet.

It is a long walk from the ferry to Samye and almost everyone – Tibetans included – jumps on a truck or a tractor for the ride. The cost is Y3 and you can expect a crowded, bumpy ride – lots of fun if you are in the mood for it. The tractors take around 25 minutes to get up to the monastery.

MINDROLING MONASTERY
སྨིན་གྲོལ་གླིང་དགོན་པ་

Mindroling Monastery is a very worthwhile detour from the Lhasa-Tsetang road between the Samye ferry crossing and Gonggar. It is the largest and, along with Dorje Drak, the most important Nyingmapa monastery in Ü. Parts of it were dynamited during the Cultural Revolution, but most of it has been beautifully restored.

Although a small monastery was founded at the present site of Mindroling as early as the 10th century, the usual date for the founding of Mindroling is given as the mid-1670s. The founding lama, Terdak Lingpa, was held in high esteem as a scholar and counted among his students the 5th Dalai Lama. The monastery was razed during the Mongol invasion of 1718 and later restored.

The central building of Mindroling is on the left as you enter the monastery courtyard. It is an elegant brown stone structure. Note in particular the impressive masonry – the fit between the many different sized stones used in the building is near perfect.

Immediately inside the entrance to the main building of Mindroling is a hall with chapels along its walls. The most important chapel is the one to the rear, where you can

see a large Sakyamuni image. In the hall itself is a statue of Terdak Lingpa, the founder of Mindroling, in a glass case. There are more chapels on the 2nd floor.

Getting There & Away
There is no direct public transport to Mindroling. One possibility is to take the Lhasa-Tsetang bus and get off at km marker 81. The monastery is around five km south of the road, and the last section involves an uphill climb – it is not too punishing, however. You cannot see the monastery until you round a ridge and are below it – it appears on the right.

Mindroling is easily slotted into a Yarlung Valley excursion if you have a rented vehicle. It should add very little to the cost of your trip, as it is only a 10-km detour all up.

DORJE DRAK MONASTERY
རྡོ་རྗེ་བྲག་དགོན་པ་

Dorje Drak, along with Mindroling, is one of the two most important Nyingmapa monasteries in Ü. It is less accessible and not as well restored as Mindroling, and consequently gets few Western visitors. The monastery, on the north bank of the Brahmaputra, can be reached via a ferry from km marker 48 on the Lhasa-Tsetang road. Some trekkers approach Dorje Drak from Lhasa, which is a hike of around four days.

Another trekking destination in this area is the Drak Yongdzong cave complex, about 15 km to the north-east of Dorje Drak Monastery. There are ruins of hermitages here, and the chief cave is one of Tibet's most important Guru Rinpoche caves.

GONGGAR གོང་དཀར་

Gonggar's main claim to fame is its airport. There was once a fort here – Gonggar Dzong – but it now lies in ruins. A few km back on the road to Lhasa is Gonggar Chöde Monastery. This small Sakyapa monastery is by no means an important sight, but is worth wandering down to if you are stuck with a whole afternoon or morning in Gonggar.

Places to Stay & Eat

Many travellers are forced to stay overnight in Gonggar, as airport buses for Chengdu and Kathmandu leave on the afternoon of the day before the flight. The officially sanctioned abode for foreigners is the *Airport Hotel*, where surly staff will demand that you stay in a double room for Y50 per bed. Theoretically, triples are available at Y40 but these are usually 'full'. Evening meals are served at the hotel at between 7 and 8 pm – if you are late you miss out.

Outside the airport are a few other guesthouses and restaurants with cheaper prices than the Airport Hotel. They do not exactly jump out at you, but if you ask around you will find one of them. The *Gatoling* has triples for Y12 per bed. There is reportedly also a Tibetan guesthouse with doubles for Y20. The main Lhasa-Tsetang road running through Gonggar is the best place for restaurants. The food is fairly average Sichuanese fare.

Getting There & Away

Airport buses run from the Lhasa CAAC booking office to Gonggar every afternoon between 3 and 5 pm. The cost is Y15, though if you are unlucky there is always a chance that you will be charged the official foreigner's price of Y30. Return buses to Lhasa are timed to coincide with the arrival of flights from Chengdu and Kathmandu. The price is Y30.

Netang Drölma Lakhang

 སྣེ་ཐང་སྒྲོལ་མ་ལྷ་ཁང་

As you take the Lhasa-Tsetang road out of Lhasa, you will pass a Buddha carving at the base of a cliff and fronted by a pond about 11 km out of town. Five km further is Netang, with the small but significant monastery of Drölma Lakhang.

Drölma Lakhang is associated with the Indian master Atisha. Atisha came to Tibet at the invitation of the king of the Guge kingdom in Western Tibet and subsequently travelled extensively in Tibet. His teachings were instrumental in the so-called second diffusion of Buddhism in the 11th century. Drölma Lakhang was established at this time by one of Atisha's foremost disciples, Drömtonpa. Drömtonpa was the founder of the Kadampa order, to which the monastery belongs.

For those with an interest in Tibetan Buddhism the principal interest of Drölma Lakhang is that it was spared desecration by the Red Guards after a direct request from Bangladesh (Atisha's homeland) that the monastery be left untouched. Apparently, Zhou Enlai intervened on its behalf.

The entrance and exit of the monastery are both protected by two guardian deities. They are very ancient, and may even date back to the 11th-century founding of the monastery. From the entrance, pass into the first chapel. There are a number of chörtens in the chapel. They contain the relics of former Kadampa teachers. Statuary includes an image of Atisha and the Eight Medicine Buddhas.

The middle chapel houses a number of relics that are purported to be associated with Atisha. The central image is an 11th-century image of Sakyamuni from India. The rear chapel is said to be where Atisha himself once taught. It is dominated by the Buddhas of the Three Ages and the Eight Great Bodhisattvas.

Ratö Monastery ར་བ་སྟོད་དགོན་པ་

Really keen gompa stompers can plod out a further hour from Drölma Lakhang to Ratö Monastery. This Gelugpa institution is renowned for its fine wall murals. It is reached via a track that heads south from the Lhasa-Tsetang road just after Drölma Lakhang.

Tsang གཙང་

The traditional Tibetan province of Tsang lies to the west of Ü, the province with which Tsang has long shared political dominance over the Tibetan plateau. With the decline of the Lhasa kings in the 10th century, the next major regime was centred in Tsang's Sakya under Mongol patronage from around the mid-13th to the mid-14th centuries.

After the fall of the Sakya government, power shifted back to Ü and then back to Tsang again. But until the rise of the Gelugpa order and the Dalai Lamas in the 17th century neither Tsang nor Ü effectively governed the whole of Central Tibet, and the two provinces were usually rivals for power. Some commentators see the rivalry between the Panchen and Dalai Lamas as a latter-day extension of this provincial wrestling for political dominance.

The two major urban centres of Tsang are

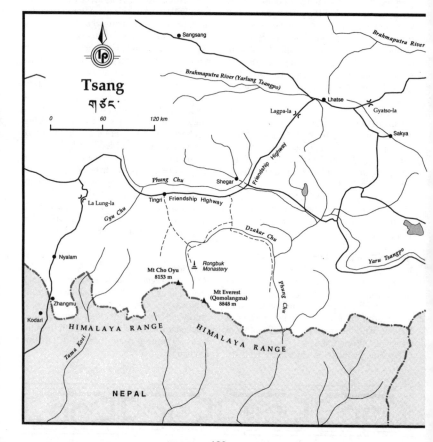

Shigatse and Gyantse. Both contain important historical sights and have emerged as popular destinations for travellers.

A large number of travellers make their way through Tsang from Lhasa to Kathmandu – usually in rented vehicles – via Yamdrok-tso lake, Gyantse, Shigatse, Sakya, Everest Base Camp, Tingri and Zhangmu. It is a convenient route that takes in Tsang's most important attractions.

The entries in this chapter follow a southwest route through Tsang from Lhasa to the Nepalese border, taking in the main attractions of the area on the way.

FRIENDSHIP HIGHWAY

Cutting through the centre of Tsang is the Friendship Highway, the 725-km stretch of road that connects Lhasa with Zhangmu. Most of Tsang's sights involve detours from the highway. Yamdrok-tso lake and Gyantse are now bypassed and best visited with rented transport, though some travellers make the trip by bicycle or even on foot

Sakya is a 21-km detour from the highway, close to Lhatse, while Everest Base Camp is a 71-km detour from Shegar by vehicle or a three-day trek from Tingri.

Although most travellers traverse Tsang in

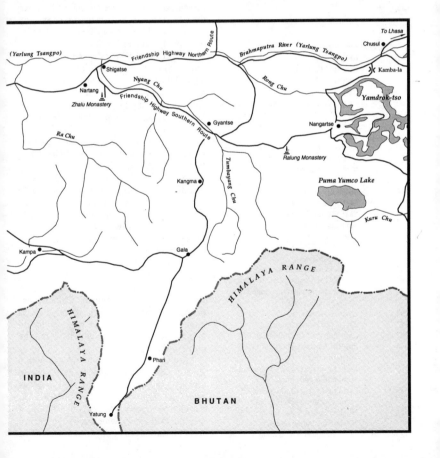

rented vehicles, there is still a sizeable number of people cycling, hitching and trekking sections of the Friendship Highway. Listed following is a selection of points of interest, towns and geographical features on the route along with their appropriate km markers. One point worth bearing in mind is that the km marker system changes at some points and in certain regions the markers have disappeared – sometimes turning up as doorsteps in new buildings. There are enough of them left, however, for you to be able to keep a fairly accurate track of your progress and identify turn-offs to places of interest.

Km Marker	Description
1	Lhasa
11	rock Buddha carving
17	Netang Drölma Lhakhang (see Central Tibet chapter)
60	Chusul (Qushui) (accommodation); turn-off for Chusul Bridge, after which are the turn-offs for Gonggar airport and Tsetang, and for the old road to Shigatse via Gyantse
60 +	new road to Shigatse, follows the bank of the Brahmaputra; flat, easy cycling
260	Shigatse (accommodation)
363	Gyatso-la pass (4950 metres)
377	Sakya turn-off (accommodation); Sakya is 21 km away
401	Lhatse (accommodation)
407	turn-off for Western Tibet (Kailash and Ali)
432	Lagpa-la pass (5250 metres)
482	turn-off for Shegar (accommodation)
489	Shegar checkpoint (accommodation); no permits required
494	Everest access road
543	Tingri (accommodation)
581	army barracks (accommodation)
614	turn-off for Saga; short-cut to Western Tibet
625	La Lung-la pass (5120 metres); first section of double pass
638	La Lung-la pass (5200 metres); second section of double pass
682	Nyalam Pelgye Ling Temple
693	Nyalam (accommodation)
724	Zhangmu (accommodation)

YAMDROK-TSO LAKE ཡར་འབྲོག་མཚོ་

On the old road between Gyantse and Lhasa, Yamdrok-tso lake (4488 metres) springs dazzlingly into view from the summit of the Kamba-la pass (4974 metres). It lies several hundred metres below the road, and is a fabulous shade of deep turquoise. For Tibetans, it is one of the four holy lakes of Tibet (the others are Lhama La-tso, Nam-tso and Manasarovar), the home of wrathful deities. The Chinese, on the other hand, have a more pragmatic interest in the lake as the potential site of a hydroelectricity generating station. This is a highly controversial issue not least because of the reverence Tibetans have for the lake. Yamdrok-tso is a dead lake and any water drained from it for generating electricity cannot be replenished.

Yamdrok-tso lake is a coiling, many-armed body of water that doubles back on itself at its south-west extent, effectively creating a large island within its reaches. Devout Tibetan pilgrims and the occasional Western trekker circumambulate the lake, a walk of around seven days. Most Western travellers, however, are content with a glimpse of the lake from the Kamba-la pass. For those interested in a day walk on the shores of the lake, see the following entry on Samding Monastery. Trekkers who want to hike around the lake should pick up a copy of Victor Chan's *Tibet Handbook – a pilgrimage guide*, which has detailed information on the various approaches to the lake and hiking around it.

Getting There & Away

There is no public transport to Yamdrok-tso lake. Those with Tibetan or Chinese language skills may like to ask around in Lhasa about the existence of a bus service to Nangartse (Langkazi), which is on the western shore of the lake.

Most travellers visit Yamdrok-tso with a rented vehicle en route from Lhasa to Gyantse and on into Tsang. For trekkers there are various approaches to Yamdrok-tso. One possibility is to head out to Gonggar (see the Ü chapter), which is easily reached from Lhasa and only a day's hike north of the

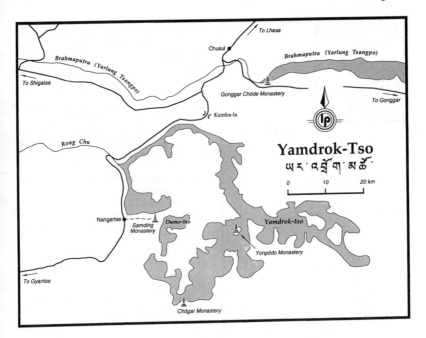

northern shore of the lake. With reasonable mapping, it should be possible to hike west from the Yarlung Valley (Chongye would be the logical starting point) in a couple of days to the eastern shore of Yamdrok-tso. Victor Chan recommends starting the lake pilgrimage from Nangartse, on the Lhasa-Gyantse road – see his *Tibet Handbook – a pilgrimage guide* for more details.

SAMDING MONASTERY
བསམ་སྡིངས་དགོན་པ་

Samding is a monastery on the shores of Yamdrok-tso lake, around eight km to the east of the town of Nangartse (4500 metres). Sited on a ridge that separates the southbearing northern arm of the lake from Dumo-tso lake (a smaller lake that intervenes between the northern and southern arms of Yamdrok-tso) the monastery provides excellent views of Yamdrok-tso.

The founding of Samding probably took place in the mid-14th century. It is associated with Bodong Chokle Nangyel (1306-1386), a monk who founded an obscure, syncretic sub-order derived from Nyingmapa and Sakyapa teachings. The order never prospered and was for the most part restricted to Samding and other smaller monasteries in the Yamdrok-tso area. The monastery is noted for the unusual fact that it has traditionally been headed by a female incarnate lama.

Not surprisingly, the monastery was sacked in the Cultural Revolution. Restoration work is being undertaken at a reasonably slow pace.

GYANTSE རྒྱལ་རྩེ་

Gyantse (3950 metres), in the Nyang Chu valley 254 km south-west of Lhasa, is one of the least Chinese-influenced towns in Tibet and is worth a visit for this reason alone. The town's principal attractions are the Gyantse Kumbum, a magnificent tiered structure that is now unique in the Buddhist world, Pelkor

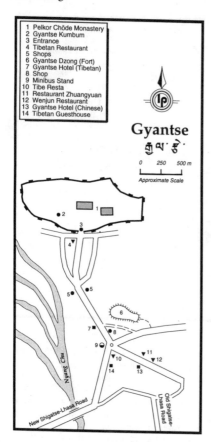

1 Pelkor Chöde Monastery
2 Gyantse Kumbum
3 Entrance
4 Tibetan Restaurant
5 Shops
6 Gyantse Dzong (Fort)
7 Gyantse Hotel (Tibetan)
8 Shop
9 Minibus Stand
10 Tibe Resta
11 Restaurant Zhuangyuan
12 Wenjun Restaurant
13 Gyantse Hotel (Chinese)
14 Tibetan Guesthouse

Gyantse
ক্রুন'ই'

0   250   500 m
Approximate Scale

The monastery compound in the far west of town, which houses both Pelkor Chöde Monastery and the Gyantse Kumbum, once contained 15 monasteries. Little remains of them today. They were a particularly interesting collection, however, in that they brought together three different orders of Tibetan Buddhism in the one compound – a rare instance of multi-denominational tolerance. Nine of the monasteries were Gelugpa, three Sakyapa and three belonged to the Bupa, an obscure order whose head monastery was Zhalu near Shigatse.

Gyantse's historical importance declined from the end of the 15th century, though it continued to be a major town – the third largest in Tibet at the time of the Chinese takeover. In 1904 it became the site of a major battle during Colonel Younghusband's advance on Lhasa, and the British troops spent a month here in the Gyantse Dzong before continuing to Lhasa.

Orientation in Gyantse is a fairly straightforward affair. Buses stop at the town's only major intersection. To the west is the Tibetan part of town. It is concentrated around the main road leading to Pelkor Chöde Monastery past the dzong, which looms over the town on a high ridge. To the east is an incipient Chinese quarter, with some government buildings, shops, restaurants and a couple of hotels.

Gyantse Dzong

The 14th-century Gyantse Dzong is worth the 15-minute climb to its upper limits, less for what is left of the fort itself – not much, though renovations proceed apace – than for the amazing views of Gyantse, the monastery compound at the end of town and the surrounding Nyang Chu Valley.

Some of the fort's buildings can be entered and explored, sometimes to upper floors by means of rickety wooden ladders. There is generally very little to see however. About midway up through the fort complex is a small temple that was being renovated at the time this book was researched. It is possible that work on restoring the temple and its

Chöde Monastery and the Gyantse Dzong. It is easy to spend a couple of days in Gyantse.

If there was a settlement in Gyantse prior to the 14th century, there are no positive records of its existence. But between the 14th and 15th centuries the town emerged as the centre of a fiefdom with powerful connections with the Sakyapa order. It also became an important link in the wool trade route between Tibet and India. By 1440 Gyantse's most impressive architectural achievements – the Kumbum and the dzong – had been completed. Pelkor Chöde Monastery also dates from this period.

murals will be completed by the time you have this book in your hands.

Entry to the dzong is via an alley that runs from the left of the northbound road from the roundabout. A couple of locals lounge by the entrance all day to nab the occasional foreign visitor for a Y10 entry charge. They do at least issue a ticket, and hopefully some of the money goes towards the ongoing renovations. They are not interested in student cards.

Gyantse Kumbum

Commissioned by one of the early Gyantse

Bayonets to Gyantse

The Younghusband Expedition, as it came to be known, is one of those controversial moments in the history of the British Empire when superior technology and military tactics were used to expedite business and political interests in borders far remote from those of the British Isles. In this case the main contenders for the much coveted jewel of Lhasa were the Russians.

Wild speculation of Russian designs on Tibet had reached epidemic proportions by the turn of the 19th century. And with Tibetans thumbing their noses at the British drafted Sikkim-Tibet convention of 1890, which allowed the free exchange of goods between India and Tibet, the British decided it was time for more persuasive tactics. Francis Younghusband, an army officer with rich experience of Central Asia, was the man chosen for the job. In 1903, Younghusband was instructed to advance on Gyantse from Yatung with an expeditionary force of some 1000 troops and gain 'satisfaction' from the Tibetans.

Despite previous brushes with British firepower, the Tibetans seemed to have little idea what they were up against. Not far from the village of Tuna (around halfway between Yatung and Gyantse) a Tibetan army of some 1500 troops armed with swords, matchlock rifles and a motley assortment of foreign firearms confronted the British force armed with light artillery, Maxim machine guns and modern rifles. The Tibetan trump card was a charm marked with the seal of the Dalai Lama himself which each of the troops had been given with the assurance by monks that it would protect them from British bullets. In the event, despite British attempts to achieve a peaceful solution and disarm the Tibetans, the bullets killed 700 Tibetans.

After setting up a field hospital to treat the Tibetan wounded, the British continued their advance on Gyantse. On arrival they found that the Gyantse Dzong had been deserted by its troops. Curiously, rather than

Francis Younghusband

occupy the dzong, the British camped on the outskirts of Gyantse. After a month in Gyantse waiting for officials from Lhasa to arrive (they never came), a force of 800 Tibetan troops reoccupied the dzong under the cover of darkness.

In early July, over six months after setting out from Yatung, and after nearly two months in Gyantse waiting for Lhasa officials, the British troops received permission from Britain to take the Gyantse Dzong and march on Lhasa. The assault on the Gyantse Dzong involved a diversionary attack on the north-east front while the real attack took place on the south-west. Shelling was used to make breaches in the walls, and when one of the shells destroyed the Tibetan gunpowder supply (and much of the dzong with it) the Tibetans were reduced to throwing rocks at their attackers. The dzong fell in one day, with over 300 Tibetans dead and just four British casualties.

The fall of the Gyantse Dzong was the last straw in Tibetan attempts to repel the British incusion. Tradition had it that if ever the impregnable fortress of Gyantse fell to foreign aggressors then Tibet would be defeated. The British proceeded to Lhasa without further incident. ■

princes in 1440, the Gyantse Kumbum is rated by many as Gyantse's foremost attraction. The stupa rises over four symmetrical floors and is surmounted by a gold dome that rises like a crown over four sets of eyes that gaze serenely out in the cardinal directions of the compass. Unfortunately the top of the Kumbum was marred by shoddy scaffolding in mid-1994 – hopefully this stuff will come down soon.

A clockwise route spirals up through all four floors of the Kumbum taking in the chapels that line the walls of the stupa. There are two sets of four central chapels which extend to the floor above from the 1st and 3rd floors, and each of these is surrounded by smaller chapels in diminishing numbers and size as the floors ascend.

Much of the statuary in the chapels was damaged in the Cultural Revolution and has only recently been restored. The murals, however, have weathered the years very well. They are of 14th-century provenance and if they were not executed by Newari (Nepalese) craftspersons they are obviously influenced by Newari forms. Experts also see evidence of Chinese influence and, in the fusion of these Newari and Chinese forms via Tibetan sensibilities, the emergence of a syncretic but distinctly Tibetan style of painting.

Whatever the case, there are an awful lot of murals to look at, and unless you have a particular interest in the evolution of Tibetan Buddhist art it is difficult not to hurry through the last two floors. Lingering in a few of the chapels and having a close look at the wall frescoes is enough to give you an idea of what is on offer in other chapels. Depending on the position of the sun, certain chapels are sometimes illuminated with a warm, soft light that allows flashless photographs. There do not seem to be any restrictions on photography in the Kumbum.

The eight main central chapels are listed here in a clockwise fashion from the first next to the front entrance of the Kumbum:

Sakyamuni Chapel The beautifully executed image of Sakyamuni that dominates

this chapel can be seen turning the Wheel of Dharma. Guru Rinpoche and the Eight Medicine Buddhas also share this chapel.

Sukhavati Chapel Sukhavati is the Pure Land of the West, home of Amitabha. Amitayus, a bodhisattva manifestation of Amitabha, is the central image.

Chapel of the Buddha of the Past As you might expect, the Buddha of the Past dominates this chapel.

Tushita Chapel Tushita is another Pure Land and is the home of Maitreya, who is the central image in the chapel.

Uppermost Chapels The 3rd and 4th floors are dominated by four main chapels. The first has an image of Sakyamuni. The second contains the Buddha of the Lion's Roar. The third contains a female deity turning the Wheel of Dharma. The last contains the Buddha Who Illuminates All Things. A single chapel can be found at the top of the Kumbum. It was not possible to visit this at the time of writing due to renovations, but these may be complete by the time you visit. The chapel is dominated by a Tantric manifestation of Sakyamuni.

Pelkor Chöde Monastery
དཔལ་འཁོར་ཆོས་སྡེ་

Founded first in 1418, Pelkor Chöde was once a multi-denominational complex of monasteries. Today much of the sprawling courtyard, enclosed by walls that clamber up the hills that back on to the monastery, is bare and the remaining structures are attended by Gelugpa monks. The best way to get an idea of the original extent of Pelkor Chöde is to view it from the Gyantse Dzong.

Pelkor Chöde Monastery is a dark, gloomy place and if you want a good look at the various murals and thangkas it is a good idea to bring a torch. The main chapel is to the rear of the assembly hall, the cavernous room just past the entrance. There is an inner circumambulation route around the chapel lined with murals. Inside, the central image is of Sakyamuni, who is flanked by the Buddhas of the past and future. Other bodhisattvas line the walls.

To the left of the main chapel is another chapel worth taking a look at. It is crowded with images, some of them particularly noted for their artistic accomplishment. There are a couple more worthy chapels back inside the main assembly hall.

There are also a number of interesting chapels on the 2nd floor. Some of the statuary may be of Indian origin, but whatever the case there are some beautiful images here with startlingly vivid and lifelike facial expressions. The first chapel to the left after you mount the stairs is noted in particular for a three-dimensional mandala that dominates the room, paintings of the 84 Mahasiddhas that adorn the walls and clay images of key figures in the Sakyapa lineage. Take a look at the 84 Mahasiddhas, each of which is unique and shown contorting itself in a yogic posture.

There is a Y15 entry fee for the Pelkor Chöde Monastery complex and this includes entry to the Gyantse Kumbum. There is no ticket office, but you will probably be waylaid by a monk after you have entered. Ask for a ticket.

Places to Stay

Gyantse has become a popular place to stay overnight and many travellers stay longer. Just to confuse things there are two guesthouses called the Gyantse Hotel in town (some travellers have reported a third on the outskirts of town). One of them is to the east of the main intersection, and is a Chinese place; the other is to the west, on the road that heads down to Pelkor Chöde, and is Tibetan. Most travellers stay at the latter.

The Tibetan-style *Gyantse Hotel* is built around a large compound and has dorm accommodation for Y10. There are no showers available and toilet facilities are very primitive – the sort of thing that you become accustomed to quickly in Tibet.

The Chinese-style *Gyantse Hotel* attempts to offer a bit more comfort, but falls short of succeeding. Doubles and triples with attached bathrooms cost Y25 and Y20 respectively. The showers in the bathrooms do not work, however, and the staff provide a big bucket of water for washing and flushing the toilets with. Cheaper five-bed dorms are also available for Y15.

On the southern corner of the main intersection is the *Tibetan Guesthouse* – there is a fading English sign over a shop next door that has been taken by some to read as the 'Hotel of Shower'. If that is how it is intended to read, it is a false claim. The Tibetan Guesthouse provides very basic accommodation in dorm rooms for Y10. The Tibetan-style Gyantse Hotel is a better place to stay.

Places to Eat

Dining out options in Gyantse have improved immensely in recent years, though unfortunately this is due to Han immigration. Most restaurants are concentrated in the stretch of road opposite the Chinese Gyantse Hotel. The best of the bunch is probably the *Restaurant Zhuangyuan*, a snazzy little joint complete with a cute concrete path leading to the door. Prices are a little expensive, averaging at around Y10 to Y12 per dish. The *Wenjun Restaurant*, close by, is also OK.

Over by the intersection are a number of other restaurants with slightly cheaper prices and lower hygiene standards. The *Tibe Resta* – as the English sign declares it – is a grotty little establishment recommended by a couple of travellers, though they did confess to spending the next couple of days after eating there rushing to the toilet. A Muslim restaurant almost next door to the Tibe Resta may also be worth trying. There are several Tibetan restaurants on the road down to Pelkor Chöde and, if you have not had your fill of momos and thukpa yet, they might be worth checking out.

Getting There & Away

All public transport to Gyantse nowadays is by way of Shigatse. It probably makes sense to at least overnight in Shigatse seeing you have to go there first, but if Gyantse is your destination and you do not want to bother with Shigatse it is usually possible to get from Lhasa to Gyantse in one day. Minibuses leave from Lhasa around 7 am and arrive in Shigatse around 2 pm. There are usually minibuses running from the minibus stand in front of the Shigatse bus station until around 4 pm. The trip takes from three to four hours and costs Y18. Minibuses from Gyantse back to Shigatse leave on an irregular basis through the day from the main intersection.

Most travellers heading to the Nepal border with hired vehicles pass through Gyantse. Many only give the place a few hours (including lunch) before travelling through to Shigatse for an overnight stop. It is worth considering overnighting in both Gyantse and Shigatse, however, as both have more than enough in the way of sights to keep you busy for a day.

Organising vehicle hire is not as easy in Gyantse as it is in Lhasa and Shigatse. The best advice would be to ask at the Chinese Gyantse Hotel, the staff of which seem to have their fingers closest to the pulse of happening Gyantse.

Getting Around

All of Gyantse's sights can be reached comfortably on foot, which is just as well because there is nothing in the way of bicycle hire or public transport.

YATUNG & THE CHUMBI VALLEY
ཡ་རུ་དུང་ ཆུམ་བི་

The Chumbi Valley is where Tibet dips a cautious toe into the Indian subcontinent between Sikkim and Bhutan. The lower-altitude subtropical scenery here differs immensely to that on the higher Tibetan plateau. Unfortunately, the Chumbi Valley and Yatung, the county seat, have been decidedly off limits to foreigners for the last few years. There are large numbers of Chinese troops in the area, and the last thing the authorities want is foreign backpackers snooping about. It may also be that Chinese authorities have woken up to the perennial travellers' fascination with illicit border crossings and have closed the area for this reason.

In mid-1994 two travellers made their way down to Yatung on Chinese bicycles travelling largely under the cloak of darkness. One of them, exhausted, gave himself up to the authorities on arrival. Not sure what to do with him, after much consideration he was simply asked 'well, where would you like us to take you then?'. He got a free lift back to Lhasa in an army jeep. The other traveller, who planned to slip into Bhutan, was not heard of and has melted into the mythic realm of travel folklore.

Getting There & Away

Unless the situation changes, you can not travel on from here. That is it. The Yatung road travels south from Gyantse for around 210 km. The main checkpoint is at Gala, 94 km south of Gyantse. The only way through this checkpoint is around it – not a recommended course of action.

SHIGATSE གཞིས་ཀ་རྩེ་

Shigatse (3900 metres) is the second largest town in Tibet and the traditional capital of Tsang. Around 250 km to the south-west of Lhasa (via the new road), Shigatse is one of the few places in Tsang with reliable and frequent transport connections with the capital.

Shigatse has long been an important trading town and administrative centre. The Tsang kings exercised their power from the once imposing heights of the Shigatse Dzong – the present ruins only hint at its former glory – and the fort later became the residence of the governor of Tsang. Since the ascendancy of the Gelugpa order with Mongol aid, Shigatse has been the seat of the Panchen Lama, who is traditionally based in Tashilhunpo Monastery. The monastery is Shigatse's foremost attraction.

Like most modern Tibetan towns Shigatse divides into a distinct Tibetan quarter and a newer Chinatown. The Chinese part of town comprises wide, dusty boulevards lined with building-block concrete cubes of the style beloved by Chinese town planners. The Tibetan part of town, which is for the most part clustered higgledy-piggledy between Tashilhunpo Monastery and the high ramparts of the Shigatse Dzong, is on the other hand a delightful place to be based for a few days.

Far too many travellers speed through Shigatse on their way to the Nepal border, giving the place just one afternoon to poke around Tashilhunpo and a night to rest up. This is a pity as Shigatse is one of the few urban centres in Tibet that has amenities – as the Americans put it – and is well worth staying in for a few days.

Shigatse may not be exactly brimming in sights, but it is a good place to hang out, kick back and enjoy a few beers on the roof of the Tenzin Hotel gazing across at the ruins of the fort.

Finally, one interesting feature of Shigatse is that it has two distinct populations, each with its own domain and sphere of activity. By day the town is largely human in character; by night it is decidedly canine. The dogs begin to assert themselves with a few stray yelps and howls at around 11 pm.

By midnight, however, the night air is static with a cacophony of blood-curdling canine cries of attack and wild retreat. Silence falls on Shigatse early in the morning

Shigatse
གཞིས་ཀ་རྩེ་

0   400   800 m
Approximate Scale

Market

1   Shigatse Dzong (Fort)
2   Tenzin Hotel
3   Shops
4   Yuanfu Restaurant
5   Skating Rink
6   Clinic
7   Sanzhuzi Hotel
8   Curtain Restaurant
9   PSB
10 Tashilhunpo Monastery
11 Orchard Hotel
12 Red Cross
13 Tibet-Shigatse Regional
    People's Hospital
14 Department Store
15 Post Office
16 Transport Hotel
17 Main Bus Station/Minibus Stand
18 Cheap Hotel
19 Restaurants
20 Shigatse Hotel
21 Bank of China

– that is until the propaganda speakers on the fort crackle into life with an anthemic version of Michael Jackson's *Bad*.

Orientation

Shigatse is not a particularly big town, but orientation can initially be a bit confusing. Tashilhunpo Monastery effectively marks the western extent of town – beyond it is a nomad encampment – while the Shigatse Dzong does the same thing to the north. The two main Chinese streets run north-south parallel to each other. One of these is where you will find the Main Post Office and the other has the Shigatse Hotel and the Bank of China.

The Tibetan quarter is around the Tenzin Hotel and the market. From the Tenzin Hotel and the market the road runs westward, quickly narrowing into a dirt track that threads its way between Tibetan homes to join up with the Tashilhunpo kora.

The Panchen Lama

Frequently rivals to the central authority of Lhasa and often pawns in Chinese designs on the high plateau, the Panchen Lamas, traditional abbots of Tashilhunpo Monastery, have often been the focus of decidedly unspiritual squabbles. The 9th Panchen Lama (1883-1937) ended up spending the last of his days in the clutches of a Chinese Nationalist warlord after attempting to use the Chinese as leverage to gain greater influence in Tibet during a disagreement with the 13th Dalai Lama. His reincarnation grew up in the control of the Chinese.

The Chinese connection hung over the 10th Panchen Lama like a grim cloud, and he was regarded with suspicion by his own people for much of his life. Even his authenticity was subject to doubt. There had been at least two other candidates for the position in Tibet itself, but the Chinese had forced Tibetan delegates in Beijing in 1951 to endorse the Chinese choice. It is said that in 1949 the 11-year-old Panchen Lama had written to Mao asking him to 'liberate' Tibet, although, to give him credit, it is unlikely he did it of his own volition. When the Panchen Lama became joint chairperson (with the Dalai Lama) of the Preparatory Committee for the Autonomous Region of Tibet (PCART), it was commonly felt that he was a mere Chinese puppet.

By the time he died of a heart attack at Shigatse in 1989, however, the Panchen Lama was regarded throughout Tibet as a hero. From his triumphant arrival at Tashilhunpo Monastery as the Chinese trump card in 1951, the Panchen Lama had become by 1965 a 'big rock on the road to socialism' according to Chinese authorities. What happened?

It seems likely that the Panchen Lama had a major change of heart about his Chinese benefactors after the 1959 Lhasa uprising. In September 1961, the Panchen Lama presented Mao with a 70,000-character catalogue of the atrocities acted upon Tibet and a plea for increased freedoms. His answer was a demand that he denounce the Dalai Lama as a reactionary and take the latter's place as spiritual head of Tibet. Not only did the Panchen Lama refuse, in 1964, with tens of thousands of Tibetans gathered in Lhasa for the Monlam festival, he announced to the assembled crowds that he believed that Tibet would one day regain its independence and that the Dalai Lama would return in glory as its leader.

It must have come as a shock to the Chinese to see their protégé turn on them so ungratefully. They responded in time-honoured fashion by throwing him into jail, where he remained for 14 years, suffering abuse and torture. His crimes, according to the Chinese, included participating in orgies, 'criticising China' and raising a private insurrectionary army. A 'Smash the Panchen Reactionary Clique' campaign was mounted, and those close to the Panchen Lama were subject to struggle sessions and in some cases imprisoned.

After emerging from prison in early 1978, the Panchen Lama rarely spoke in outright defiance of the Chinese authorities, but continued to use what influence he had to press for the preservation of Tibetan cultural traditions. Shortly before his death it is believed that he again fell out with the Chinese, arguing at a high-level meeting in Beijing that the Chinese occupation had brought nothing but misery and hardship to his people. Accordingly, many Tibetans believe that he died not of a heart attack but by poisoning. Others maintain that, exhausted and perhaps despairing, the Panchen Lama came home in 1986 to die as he always said he would on Tibetan soil. Whatever the case, the Panchen Lama was a man who spoke up bravely from within the ranks of a regime that was and is cruelly intolerant to dissent. ■

Information

It is possible to change money and post letters in Shigatse, but not much more than this. The Bank of China is next door to the Shigatse Hotel and has irregular opening hours. Basically it should be possible to count on from 9 am to noon and 2 to 5 pm on weekdays, 9 am to noon on Saturday, but this is by no means guaranteed – the bank was closed for a whole week when I was last in town. Travellers' cheques and cash in most currencies can be changed with a minimum of fuss, but it is not possible to arrange credit card advances – you will have to wait until Lhasa for this service.

The Main Post Office follows vaguely the same opening hours as the bank. It is possible to send international letters and postcards here, but *not* international parcels.

The Shigatse PSB is on the road that leads diagonally from the centre of town to the entrance of Tashilhunpo Monastery. It has the same opening hours as the bank. It is a friendly place and the staff seem quite happy to arrange any permits that they have power to grant. The standard permit fee is Y10. Visa extensions were only possible for a 15-day period in mid-1994 and could only be organised within five days prior to expiry.

Tashilhunpo Monastery

བཀྲ་ཤིས་ལྷུན་པོ་དགོན་པ་

Tashilhunpo is associated with the Gelugpa order and is one of the six great Gelugpa institutions along with Dreprung, Sera and Ganden in Lhasa and Kumbum and Labrang in Amdo. The monastery gets mixed reports from visitors. It is probably the largest functioning monastic institution in contemporary Tibet and is an impressive place to explore. On the downside, the monks here are sometimes unfriendly and there is conjecture that many of the English-speaking monks are in cohorts with Chinese authorities. There is no direct evidence of this, but it would pay to be careful about voicing controversial opinions and handing out Dalai Lama pictures.

Opening and closing hours at Tashilhunpo are fairly arbitrary. It is closed Sunday, and on other days is theoretically open from 9am

to noon and 2 to 5 pm. In practice, it is not uncommon to be told by monks at, say, 4 pm, after you have already bought your ticket, that the monastery is already closed. If this happens, try smiling and showing them your ticket – getting annoyed only serves to deepen their conviction that the monastery is closed. There is a Y15 entry charge.

There are severe restrictions on photographs inside the monastic buildings. The going cost for a photograph is Y50. This may be negotiable and once paid should cover more than one photograph, but do not count on it.

History Tashilhunpo Monastery was founded in 1447 by a disciple of Tsongkhapa, Genden Drup. Genden Drup was retroactively named the 1st Dalai Lama and he is enshrined in Tashilhunpo. Despite its association with the 1st Dalai Lama, Tashilhunpo was initially isolated from the mainstream of Gelugpa affairs, which were centred in the Lhasa region. The monastery's standing rocketed, however, when the 5th Dalai Lama declared his teacher – then abbot of Tashilhunpo – to be a manifestation of Amitabha (a deification of Buddha's faculty of perfected cognition and perception). Thus Tashilhunpo became the seat of an important lineage line: the Panchen Lamas.

The title Panchen means 'great scholar' and was the title traditionally bestowed on abbots of Tashilhunpo. But with the establishment of the Panchen Lama lineage of spiritual and temporal leaders – second only to the Dalai Lamas themselves – the spectre of possible rivalry was introduced into the Gelugpa order. Naturally it did not take long to emerge. The next Panchen Lama was declared ruler of Tsang and Western Tibet by the Qing Dynasty in China, a move that has been seen by many as part of a continuing effort by the Chinese to manipulate a schism between the Panchen and Dalai Lamas.

Of course it is arguable that such a schism did not require much prompting on the part of the Chinese. There have long been disputes between Lhasa and Shigatse over the autonomy of Tashilhunpo. In the early 1920s

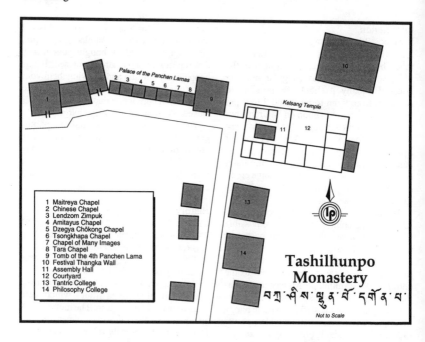

1 Maitreya Chapel
2 Chinese Chapel
3 Lendzom Zimpuk
4 Amitayus Chapel
5 Dzegya Chökong Chapel
6 Tsongkhapa Chapel
7 Chapel of Many Images
8 Tara Chapel
9 Tomb of the 4th Panchen Lama
10 Festival Thangka Wall
11 Assembly Hall
12 Courtyard
13 Tantric College
14 Philosophy College

Palace of the Panchen Lamas

Kelsang Temple

Tashilhunpo Monastery

བཀྲ་ཤིས་ལྷུན་པོ་དགོན་པ

Not to Scale

a dispute between the 9th Panchen Lama and the 13th Dalai Lama over taxes – and ultimately Tashilhunpo's right to self rule – led to the flight of the Panchen Lama to China. He never returned to Tibet. His successor, the 10th Panchen Lama, in turn never escaped Chinese clutches and was largely kept in Beijing, only occasionally visiting Tashilhunpo. He died in 1989.

The Monastery Tashilhunpo is one of the few monasteries in Tibet that weathered the stormy seas of the Cultural Revolution relatively unscathed. It is a real pleasure to explore. Go to the monastery several times if you can – there is really too much to see for a single visit.

From the entrance to the monastery visitors get a grand view of the complex. At the base of the ridge which the monastery ascends is a huddle of white buildings that serves as the monastic quarters. Above this is a crowd of ochre buildings topped with

gold. To the left and higher still is the great white wall that is hung with massive, colourful thangkas during festivals. The entire complex is surrounded by a high wall.

Walk up through the monastery and bear left for the first and probably most impressive of Tashilhunpo's sights: the **Maitreya Chapel**. An entire building is hollowed out to house a 26-metre image of Maitreya, the Future Buddha. It was made in 1914 under the auspices of the 9th Panchen Lama and took some 900 artisans and labourers four years to complete.

The impressive, finely crafted serene-looking Maitreya looms over the viewer. More than 300 kg of gold went into coating the Maitreya, much of which is studded with precious stones. On the walls surrounding the image are a thousand more gold paintings of the Maitreya against a red background. There are also numerous smaller chapels on two floors in the Maitreya Chapel, but it is difficult to give them attention; you'll tend

A: The Jokhang with pilgrims, Lhasa (CT)
B: Yarlung Valley (CT)

A: En route to Mt Kailash, near Lhatse (CT)
B: Mt Kailash with prayer flags (CT)
C: Bön pilgrims, Mt Kailash (CT)
D: Scene on southern route to Mt Kailash (CT)

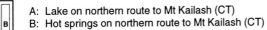

A: Lake on northern route to Mt Kailash (CT)
B: Hot springs on northern route to Mt Kailash (CT)

A: Group of monks, Sera Monastery (RI)
B: Crowds leaving assembly hall, Dreprung Monastery (CT)
C: A Rinpoche (reincarnate lama) near Mt Kailash (CT)

to keep returning for one more look at the huge central image.

East of the Maitreya Chapel is the **Palace of the Panchen Lamas**. The palace itself is the white building that rises over the red buildings in front of it. The palace has been the residence of the Panchen Lamas since the 1st Panchen Lama, although the present structure was built during the time of the 6th Panchen Lama (1738-80). It is not open to the public. It is possible, however, to enter a series of chapels in the anterior buildings.

Briefly, these chapels are, from left to right: the **Chinese Chapel**, noted by a Chinese shrine built in respect for the Chinese emperor Qianlong; **Lendzom Zimpuk**, a reception area for visiting dignitaries; the **Amitayus Chapel**, which is dominated by an image of Amitayus, the Buddha of Limitless Life; the **Dzegya Chökong Chapel**, a protector chapel that houses the wrathful female deity who guards over Tashilhunpo; the **Tsongkhapa Chapel**, in which Tsongkhapa and two of his principal disciples preside; the **Chapel of Many Images**, which as its name suggests has many images; and the **Tara Chapel**, a chapel with the 21 manifestations of Tara, a meditational deity associated with the enlightened activity of the mind.

Next to the last of these chapels is the **Tomb of the 4th Panchen Lama**. Entry is either via the Tara Chapel or through a door at the front of the building. There is not a great deal to see inside. The main feature is the 11-metre silver and gold funerary chörten of the 4th Panchen Lama.

The next sight, to the far east of the complex, is Tashilhunpo's largest structure: **Kelsang Temple**.

The centrepiece of this remarkable collection of buildings is a large courtyard, the focus of festival and monastic activities. Entry is via a narrow passage which leads into the courtyard from in front of the Tomb of the 4th Panchen Lama.

The flagged **courtyard** is of interest in itself. A huge prayer pole rears up from the centre, while the surrounding walls are painted with Buddhas. There are also splendid photo opportunities of the surrounding buildings.

There are so many chapels and points of interest in the Kelsang Temple that attempting to list them all would simply be confusing. Tibetan pilgrims generally walk to the opposite side of the courtyard and visit a series of chapels that lead back to the assembly hall, which is just to the left after you enter the courtyard.

The **assembly hall** is one of the oldest buildings in Tashilhunpo, dating back to the original 15th-century founding of the monastery. The huge throne dominating the centre of the hall is the throne of the Panchen Lamas. The hall is an atmospheric place, with rows of mounted cushions for monks and impressive thangkas depicting the 17 incarnations of the Panchen Lama suspended from the ceiling.

At this point, if you are not being shepherded around by a monk, you can explore the remaining maze of chapels on your own. There are dozens of them on the floors above and in the buildings that surround the courtyard. It is probably best to return to the Kelsang Temple several times. Attempting to see everything in one hit is to risk sensory overload and tedium.

As you leave Tashilhunpo, it is also possible to visit the monastery's two remaining colleges. They are on the left hand side as you walk down towards the entrance/exit. The first is the **Tantric College** and the second is the **Philosophy College**. Neither is particularly interesting, but you may be lucky and be in time for debating, which is held in the courtyard of the Philosophy College.

Tashilhunpo Kora The kora around Tashilhunpo takes just an hour and provides photogenic views of the monastery. Like on most walks in Shigatse, you should keep an eye out for dogs – keep some stones at the ready.

From the entrance, follow the monastery walls in a clockwise direction and look out for an alley on the right. The alley follows the western wall for a while before opening out into a wider trail that leads into the hills above Tashilhunpo. The walk is fairly straightforward. One diversion of note is a side trail that leads from the kora above the large white wall used to hang a giant thangka during festivals. This path leads along a ridge to the ruins of Shigatse Dzong, a walk of around 15 to 20 minutes.

For those staying at the Tenzin Hotel, the kora can also be approached by turning left out of the hotel and following the road past Tibetan homes and bearing left at the walls of the monastery. This path leads down onto the main road and on to the entrance of the monastery, where you can continue the kora finishing back on the trail that leads back to the hotel.

Shigatse Dzong

Once the residence of the kings of Tsang and later the governor of Tsang, very little remains of the dzong (fort). It was destroyed in the popular uprising of 1959. Pictures taken before the Chinese occupation, however, show an impressive structure that bears a remarkable resemblance to the Potala, though a smaller version.

The main attraction of the Shigatse Dzong today are the views it commands over Shigatse and the surrounding valleys. One approach is via the Tashilhunpo kora (see above). The other is to turn left out of the street with the Tenzin Hotel and market and look for an alley heading north on the left. Watch out for dogs. The walk takes around 20 to 30 minutes.

Places to Stay

Unless you are a tour-group traveller, there is really only one place to stay in Shigatse: the *Tenzin Hotel*. OK, it is not perfect. The hot shower, when it works, is an eccentric device that drips you with scalding water – that feels *gooood*; the staff are not to be trusted with hiring vehicles; and the hotel gets a full-frontal assault of propaganda from the fort in the mornings. But apart from this, the Tenzin is a delightful little inn. The upstairs veranda is a great place to lounge

around in the late afternoons and evenings, and they even keep cold beer in the fridge.

Beds cost Y15 in the dorm rooms, Y20 in the doubles or Y40 in the Dalai Lama suite. Check out the latter even if you do not stay there. The Tenzin was in the process of building an extension when I was last in town, so there should be new rooms available before too long.

Just down the road and around the corner from the Tenzin is the mock Tibetan-style *Sanzhuzi Hotel*, an uninspiring place to stay that are a reminder of guesthouses in China. Dorm beds here range from Y12 to Y16 and doubles are available for Y30 per bed. Hot showers are available at the Shanzhuzi, and are more reliable than those at the Tenzin Hotel.

The other hotel that sees a fair number of foreign guests is the *Orchard Hotel*, opposite the entrance to Tashilhunpo Monastery. It is basically a Chinese-style guesthouse with Tibetan staff and really has very little going for it. Dorm beds are Y15. The main reason for its popularity in mid-1994 was that a couple of travel agencies in Lhasa demanded that travellers using their services stay here. This scam was being investigated by the PSB and has hopefully been put to a stop. You are free to stay wherever you choose in Shigatse.

There are other options around town, but they are all depressingly dirty and noisy. If you are really stuck, try the *Transport Hotel* near the bus station. This decrepit joint has a pool table in the foyer, and the check-in staff shelter behind steel bars. Dorm beds are Y10. Opposite the bus station is another cheap, Chinese-style hotel. Avoid it unless you have to go there.

Finally, the lap of luxury in Shigatse is the *Shigatse Hotel* (☎ 22519), inconveniently located in the far south of town next to the Bank of China. It is worth going out there just to have a look at the place. Giant, ineptly painted Tibetan landscapes adorn the walls. A profusion of fairy lights flicker and blink erratically, and every available nook and cranny is piled with unconvincing plastic pot plants. Hats off for trying to create an oasis of sophistication and modernity in downtown Shigatse; but sorry guys...it does not quite hit the spot.

Prices here are reasonably negotiable, as occupancy rates are likely to be always lowish. Standard doubles with attached bathrooms (24-hour hot water!) cost Y280, and economy triples are available for Y270. High-fliers might like to enquire about the Tibetan suites: they range from Y480 to Y600.

Places to Eat

Shigatse is swarming with very good restaurants. Many travellers find the food better here than in Lhasa, though prices are slightly higher.

The best area for restaurant hunting is the road that runs north-south just down from the Tenzin Hotel. The restaurants here are all Chinese run, and most of the signs are in Chinese. It is difficult to make recommendations, but at the time of writing the most popular place was the *Yuanfu*, on the left of the arched doorway that leads into a deserted skating rink.

This place has an English menu, and the house speciality is the fish-tasting eggplant – an amazing dish that some travellers were ordering twice a day. Also popular is the place up on the far end of the road next to the intersection of the road heading out to Tashilhunpo. Look out for the curtain outside.

Out near the Shigatse Hotel are a number of other restaurants, some with English menus. Heading back into town from the hotel, there are a couple of Tibetan and Chinese restaurants on the left. There are also some dumpling shops next to the bus station, a good place to grab a snack while waiting for a bus.

Entertainment

Most visitors make their own entertainment on the roof of the Tenzin Hotel, and to be honest there is not much of an alternative to this. There are a number of karaoke bars scattered around town and numerous video rooms.

A few intrepid – desperate? – types have wandered into the Dynasty Club, a karaoke-cum-disco, next door to the Shigatse Hotel

Most of them seem to have had problems with the local PSB and were told to go to a foreigner's entertainment venue – umm, where? Unfortunately, the Oxygen Bar, next to the front entrance of the Shigatse Hotel has been gutted and is now derelict.

Getting There & Away

Between Lhasa and Shigatse most travellers use the minibus service that costs Y30. This is a big saving on the slower and less comfortable public bus service which runs from the main Lhasa bus station for Y95. It remains to be seen, however, whether the authorities will continue to turn a blind eye to this situation. Chinese government officials have little understanding of the idea of market competition, and some of the minibuses have been stopped and the drivers told that they are not to take foreign passengers

Minibuses for Shigatse leave between 7 and 7.30 am from in front of the Kirey Hotel in Lhasa. From Shigatse they leave from in front of the Shigatse bus station also between 7 and 7.30 am. Lhasa-bound minibuses also generally go to the Tenzin Hotel to pick up foreigners heading for Lhasa, which saves walking down to the minibus stop.

From the main bus station there are also three buses a week for Sakya – check at the Tenzin Hotel or the bus station for times. The cost is around Y40, or less with a student card. Buses go to Lhatse once a week for around Y50. The Lhasa-Zhangmu bus should pass through Shigatse three times a month, but it is often full and rarely arrives when it is supposed to.

Those heading out to the Nepal border or Tingri really have very few options. One possibility is to enquire at the Shigatse Hotel for minibuses or landcruisers heading out to the border to pick up tour groups. The cost for hooking up with one of these is around Y200. You will probably need to go out to the hotel three or four days in a row before you get lucky, and there is always the chance that you will not.

Rented Vehicles Renting vehicles in Shigatse is more difficult than in Lhasa and prices are not as competitive. The few agencies operating in town all have a reputation for ripping travellers off and should be treated with caution. The Tenzin Hotel, in particular, always falls through on its side of the bargain, and the agency at the Orchard Hotel is even worse. Upstairs at the Tenzin is a branch of CITS and, surprisingly, this was the most honest outfit around when I was last in town. Take care and ask around before you commit yourself to anything.

Getting Around

Shigatse is not that big and can be comfortably explored on foot. For trips out to the Shigatse Hotel, however, you might want to use the rickshaws or the tractors, which are abundant – there is usually a small crowd of them on every corner. Prices are negotiable, but should work out around Y3 per head after a little haggling.

Unfortunately, there is no bicycle hire in Shigatse yet, though it is probably just a matter of time until there is.

AROUND SHIGATSE

There are a number of sights around Shigatse, though few of them are visited by Western travellers, mainly because of difficulty of access. Those with time on their hands might want to consider doing some trekking in the Shigatse region. For detailed information on treks, see Gary McCue's *Trekking in Tibet*, which has details of a three-day hike between Zhalu and Narthang monasteries as well as day hikes around Zhalu.

Zhalu Monastery ཞ་ལུ་དགོན་པ་

Zhalu Monastery is around 19 km south-east of Shigatse, just off the Shigatse-Gyantse road. The monastery, which dates back to the 11th century, rose to prominence in the 14th century, when its abbot, Büton Rinchen Drup, emerged as the foremost interpreter of Sanskrit Buddhist texts of his day. A suborder, the Büton, formed around him.

Zhalu divides into sections, a Tibetan-style monastery founded in the 10th century and the Chinese-influenced Serkhang, which was founded in the 15th century. The former was destroyed in the Cultural Revolution, but the Serkhang has survived reasonably well.

Zhalu is noted for its murals but also houses some impressive statuary. The best murals line the walls of a corridor that rings the central assembly hall and the chapels that surround it. Zhalu was also a centre for training in skills such as trance walking, made famous as the flying monks of Alexandra David-Neel's in *Magic & Mystery in Tibet*.

Getting There & Away

Zhalu is one of the more accessible sights around Shigatse, as it is around four km south off the main Shigatse-Gyantse road. If you take a Gyantse-bound minibus from Shigatse, get off at km marker 19 and look out for the turn-off a couple of hundred metres beyond the km marker sign. The ride will probably cost around Y5, though it is negotiable and the driver may ask for more.

SAKYA ས་སྐྱ་

The monastic town of Sakya (4280 metres) is one of Tsang's most important historical sights and, even more than Gyantse, is very Tibetan in character, making it an interesting place to spend a day or so. The principal Sakya attractions divide into a northern and southern monastery on either side of the Trum River. The fortress-like southern monastery is of most interest. The northern monastery has been mostly reduced to picturesque ruins, though restoration work is ongoing.

Sakya is a small town, making orientation a simple affair. The main town is clustered to the east of the southern monastery, and this is where you will find Sakya's few hotels, restaurants and shops.

Do not expect too much of Sakya in terms of basic comforts – food is minimal and accommodation very basic. But if you are doing the Tibet grand tour – Lhasa and environs, Gyantse, Shigatse, Everest and the border – Sakya offers the opportunity for an overnight stay or longer in a town that has suffered little from the encroachments of the modern Chinese world.

One interesting feature of Sakya is the colouring of the buildings. Unlike the standard whitewashed effect that you see elsewhere in Tibet, in Sakya the buildings are grey with white and red vertical stripes. The reason is variously thought to be religious or perhaps a mark indicating the authority of the Sakya municipality – it is probably both.

Permits

There is much debate as to whether a permit is required for Sakya. If you are worried about this, you can pick one up with no hassles for Y10 in Lhasa or in Shigatse. On the other hand, if you simply turn up without one no one seems to care in the least. Those coming by rented vehicle from Lhasa will be told that a permit is necessary.

History

Sakya Monastery was founded in 1073 by Kön Könchog Gyelpo, a member of the influential Kön family. The 11th century was a dynamic period in the history of Tibetan Buddhism, due largely to renewed contacts with Indian Buddhists. The Kagyupa order was founded by Marpa and his disciple Milarepa at this time, and in Sakya the Kön family established a school that came to be called the Sakyapa.

Unlike most other schools and monasteries, which were headed by a succession of incarnate lamas, the abbotship of Sakya was hereditary and restricted to sons of the Kön family.

It is thought that in the early days of Sakya at least one Kön son would marry in order to perpetuate the Kön line, but later abbots of Sakya themselves married.

By the early 13th century Sakya had emerged as an important centre of scholastic study, much in the manner of Indian Buddhist universities that were destroyed in the Mongol invasion of India.

This was initially aided by the assistance of Indian translators such as Shakya-shribhada, who came to Sakya in 1204. But before long Tibetan scholars began to make their own unique contributions to Buddhist scholarship.

The most famous of these was a Sakya abbot, Kunga Gyaltsen (1182-1251), who came to be known as the Sakya Pandita, or the Scholar from Sakya.

Sakya Pandita wrote influential texts on perception and logic, and his learning gave rise to his being identified as a manifestation of Manjushri, the bodhisattva of insight.

It was no doubt Sakya Pandita's scholastic and spiritual eminence that led to his representing the people of Tibet to the Mongol prince Godan when the Mongols threatened to invade Tibet in the mid-13th century. Sakya Pandita made a three-year journey to Mongolia, arriving in 1247, and after meeting with Godan offered him overlordship of Tibet. Sakya Pandita defended his actions by noting that resistance to the Mongols was pointless.

After Sakya Pandita's death in 1251, one of his nephews became the abbot of Sakya, and, under the Mongol overlordship of Kublai Khan, the ruler of all Tibet.

It was the first religious government with a lama as head of state, thus setting an important precedent for Tibetan government.

The relationship between Tibetan lamas and the Mongol masters, which the Tibetans characterised as one between religious teacher and patron, set yet another important precedent; one that was open to various interpretations, would trouble the Tibetan state for centuries to come and, to the Chinese, justified their claims over the high plateau.

As it was, Mongol overlordship and Sakya supremacy were relatively short-lived. Mongol corruption and Sakyapa rivalry with the Kagyupa order led to the fall of Sakya in 1354, when power fell into the hands of the Kagyupa and the government moved to Neudong in Ü.

Sakya was to remain a powerful municipality, however, and like Shigatse enjoyed a high degree of autonomy from successive central governments.

Sakya Monastery ས་སྐྱ་དགོན་པ་

The immense, thick-walled structure of the Sakya southern monastery is Sakya's main attraction. It crouches grim and forbidding amongst the cluster of Tibetan houses that make up Sakya township. For good views of the monastery, climb up into the northern hills on the other side of the river.

The southern monastery was established in 1268 and is designed defensively, with watchtowers on each of the corners of its high walls. There may once have been further walls intervened by a moat in times past, but no trace of them remains today.

Entry to Sakya Monastery is via the east wall, though it is sometimes also possible to enter via the south wall – no one seems to mind.

Directly ahead of the east-wall entrance is the entrance to the central courtyard of the monastery, an impressive area with a towering prayer pole surrounded by chapels and the Main Assembly Hall to the west.

The **Main Assembly Hall** is a huge structure. It also tends to be very dark, though morning sunshine lights the place up with a diffuse ambience. It is still a good idea to bring a good torch with you if you have one. The hall's ceiling is supported by massive pillars, and the walls of the hall are lined with larger-than-life statuary. Uniquely, many of the images here also serve as reliquaries for previous Sakya abbots. Identifying them, however, is strictly a task for committed Tibetologists; refer to Victor Chan's *Tibet Handbook – a pilgrimage guide* if you are really keen.

To the north of the courtyard is a chapel containing 11 silver chörtens, again reliquaries for former Sakya abbots. A door leads to another chapel with more chörtens. There is more statuary and a library of Buddhist texts in the south chapel off the courtyard.

On either side of the east-wall entrance are stairs leading up to 2nd-floor chapels. Neither of them is of immense interest and

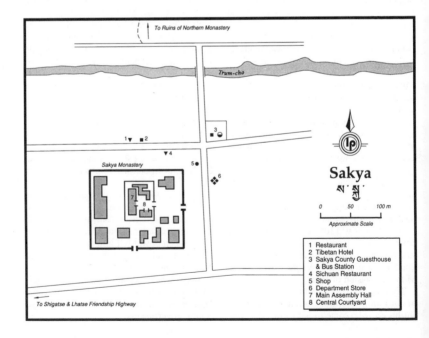

To Ruins of Northern Monastery

Trum-cho

Sakya Monastery

Sakya
ས་སྐྱ་

0   50   100 m

Approximate Scale

1 Restaurant
2 Tibetan Hotel
3 Sakya County Guesthouse
   & Bus Station
4 Sichuan Restaurant
5 Shop
6 Department Store
7 Main Assembly Hall
8 Central Courtyard

To Shigatse & Lhatse Friendship Highway

they may not be open. Finally, climb up onto the walls of the monastery for superb views of the surrounding valley and the interior buildings of Sakya Monastery.

Northern Monastery

Very little remains of the monastery complex that once sprawled across the hills north of the Trum River. It is still worth climbing up through the Tibetan town and taking a walk around what remains. Aim for the white stupa, which is a reconstruction of a stupa that held the remains of Kunga Nyingpo, the founder of the Sakyapa order and the second Sakya abbot. Above the stupa is a small recently reconstructed monastery. Particularly ferocious Tibetan mastiffs made it impossible to enter this monastery when I visited – enter with caution.

The northern monastery predates the southern monastery, and in its time is alleged, like Ganden, to have contained 108 buildings. It may once have housed some 3000 monks.

Places to Stay

There are definitely two places to stay in Sakya and according to some rumours there may be a third. If you come into Sakya by bus or rented transport you will inevitably be dropped off in the courtyard of the *Sakya County Guesthouse* (no English sign). This decrepit, Chinese-style hotel is a depressing little institution, and when the staff drop your bottle of hot water off and close the door as they go it is difficult not to get the sinking feeling that you have been incarcerated. The 'good' rooms cost Y16 per bed in a four-bed dorm; the economy suites (slightly filthier, and the windows are more likely to be broken) cost Y10. Finally, a tip – the women's toilets are marginally cleaner than the men's which should be avoided at all costs.

The official line is that foreigners are required to stay at the County Guesthouse. In reality, however, there is no reason not to give the place a miss and walk over to the *Tibetan Hotel* just around the corner. Look out for the sign saying 'Sofia's Soda & Cigs'.

The hotel is next door. This place has atmospheric Tibetan-style rooms for Y10 a bed; hot water and bedding are provided. The staff here are very friendly too, which is a lot more than can be said for the guesthouse. Even the toilets are cleaner at the Tibetan Hotel.

Places to Eat

In the cuisine line, Sakya is upcountry Tibet: in other words, do not expect anything too palatable. The courtyard of the Sakya County Guesthouse has a small Muslim restaurant that looks highly suspect, but may well turn out a good stir-fry.

The best restaurant around is the one next to the Tibetan Hotel. You can pick and choose from the vegetables in the kitchen for a stir-fried dish or get a noodle soup dish – basic but not bad. Across the road and back towards the County Guesthouse is the *Sichuan Restaurant*. This place is fairly popular with locals and tends to sell out early in the evening. Again, the food here is not bad.

There are several shops about, where you can stock up on instant noodles and dry, crumbly biscuits. Watch out buying beer in Sakya: some of the beer being sold in Wuquan bottles is a rebottled local brew that tastes like cat's piss – it really is undrinkable. Go up-market and buy some of the canned Blue Ribbon if you do not want to be poisoned.

Getting There & Away

Bus services between Sakya and the outside world are irregular, and locals find it impossible to agree when they come and go. There should be at least two (possibly three) buses a week between Shigatse and Sakya The price is Y37. There is also a once weekly service between Lhatse and Sakya, if you are looking at making your way to the border or out to Kailash. Buses in Sakya run from the Sakya County Guesthouse.

From the Sakya turn-off on the Friendship Highway it is 21 km to Sakya, which means that if you can get a lift as far as the turn-off you could hike the rest of the way. The distance between Shigatse and the turn-off is 127 km (km marker 5028). Some travellers report that there is Tibetan-style accommodation at the turn-off for Y5 per bed – it gets good reports.

For those with limited time, it should be possible to hire a vehicle in Shigatse for a day or overnight trip to Sakya. Figure on spending around Y800 to Y1000.

LHATSE

Approximately 150 km south-west of Shigatse and some 10 km west of the Sakya turn-off, Lhatse (4050 metres) is essentially just a truck stop. It is a dusty little place that lines the Friendship Highway, but has some good restaurants, well-stocked shops and a few guesthouses. Most of the traffic here is en route to Zhangmu on the Nepal border, but some vehicles take the turn-off, five or six km down the road, for Ali in Western Tibet – see the Western Tibet chapter for more details.

If you get stuck in Lhatse for a day or so (perhaps trying to hitch out of the place) there are a couple of attractions in the vicinity that can be hiked out to in a day, but it should be emphasised that they are minor attractions and probably of most interest to archaeologically minded Tibetologists.

About one km short of Lhatse as you come in from Shigatse, at km marker 400, is a north-bound trail that heads out to the ruins of **Lhatse Dzong** and **Drampa Gyang Temple**. The latter is one of King Songtsen Gampo's Demoness Subduing Temples, in this case pinioning the troublesome demoness' left hip; there is little to see today. The ruins of the dzong mark the sight of the old administrative centre of Lhatse.

It is around 20 km to either the dzong or Drampa Gyang. The trail forks around eight km after the turn-off, with the left fork heading out to the dzong and the right fork heading out to Drampa Gyang.

Places to Stay & Eat

There are a few guesthouses along the Friendship Highway in Lhatse. They are all Chinese-style and have little to differentiate

them. The *Lhatse Guesthouse* is at the Shigatse end of town on the right, while further down is a place called the *Four Unities Hotel*. Prices of around Y15 per bed prevail.

Lhatse has numerous restaurants as it is a fairly busy truck stop – the food is surprisingly good. The eastern end of town is the best place to look. There are a number of places on either side of the road – wander in and take a look in the kitchen; no one seems to mind.

Getting There & Away

Almost all truck traffic stops in Lhatse, making it a good place to hitch from. Some travellers have even had help from Chinese soldiers and PSB officials. Foreign backpackers have become such a common sight that only Tibetan pilgrims and beggars pay them any attention. For information on hitching from here out to Ali and Kailash, see the Western Tibet chapter.

There is a once weekly public bus running from the Shigatse bus station to Lhatse. The Tenzin Hotel is the best place to ask for the departure times. The cost is Y47. There may also be a once weekly bus service from Sakya, but this is likely to be an irregular service – no one was willing to confirm it absolutely in Sakya. Ask at the Sakya County Guesthouse.

To hitch from Lhatse to Zhangmu should cost around Y100, though this will probably require some determined bargaining. It will probably also help if you have a travel permit for Tingri, Nyalam and Zhangmu, though this is by no means necessary. All officials want to see at the Shegar checkpoint is your passport. Those looking at hitching to Tingri or Shegar will probably have to pay around Y40 to Y50, but again this depends on how hard you bargain.

SHEGAR (NEW TINGRI)
ཤེལ་དཀར་ དིང་རི་ གསར་

Not so many travellers stop over in Shegar (4050 metres), around seven km off the Friendship Highway from km marker 482. This is probably fairly sensible, as there is really not so much to see. One possible attraction is the ruins of **Shegar Dzong**, once the capital of the Tingri region, which sprawls over an area of approximately 1000 sq km. Also of interest is **Shegar Chöde Monastery**, a small Gelugpa institution. Both are easily reached from the village of Shegar.

Places to Stay

Shegar is a possible last stop before the Nepal border, though most travellers spend the night at Tingri, which provides views of Everest.

There is a basic guesthouse with rates of around Y10 and a couple of restaurants in Shegar itself. Close to the Friendship Highway is the *Qomolangma Shegar Guesthouse*, a ridiculously expensive attempt to capture passing tour groups for the night. Economy doubles are Y110 per bed and the staff refused to confirm whether there were any dorm beds available – give the place a miss. Next to the Shegar checkpoint at km marker 489 is a basic truck stop with beds for Y10. This place gets very bad reports from travellers, but is probably the most convenient accommodation if you are intent on hiking to Everest from Shegar.

Getting There & Away

It may be possible to hitch from the Friendship Highway to Shegar, but the chances are you'll end up walking the seven-km stretch of road.

TINGRI ཏིང་རི་

Tingri (4390 metres), a huddle of Tibetan homes on a hill that overlooks a sweeping plain bordered by the towering Himalaya, is where most travellers spend their last night in Tibet en route to Nepal or their first night en route to Lhasa from Kathmandu. For newcomers from Kathmandu, the discomforts of the sudden altitude gain are likely to make it an unpleasant stay. Those planning on using Tingri as a base to trek into the Everest region should consult the Everest Region section following.

There is little in the way of sights around

Tingri, though views of Everest and the nearby peak of Cho Oyu more than compensate for this. Ruins on a nearby hill overlooking Tingri are all that remain of the **Tingri Dzong**.

This is a fort that was not blown up by Red Guards. It was destroyed in a late 18th-century Nepalese invasion. On the plains between Shegar and Tingri many more ruins that shared the same fate can be seen from the Friendship Highway.

One other possible sight you might want to hike out to is **Tingri Langkor Monastery**. It is around five hours' walk to the west of Tingri village, though little remains of this 11th-century monastery. It is associated with Padampa Sangye, an Indian ascetic who was an important figure in the 11th to 12th-century second diffusion of Buddhism on the Tibetan plateau. Restoration work has been undertaken at Langkor and it may turn out to be a real treat.

Places to Stay & Eat

Tingri is not far north of the Friendship Highway at km marker 544. Most travellers passing through in rented vehicles stay in the *Everest View Hotel*, a shabby little place in a compound on the highway itself. Beds are Y15 and basic food is available.

Up in the village itself there are a couple more accommodation options, and these are the best bases for those planning on hiring pack animals and assaulting Everest. Do not expect much in the way of comfort. Beds are Y10. There is also a simple, Sichuan-style restaurant between the two hotels.

Getting There & Away

Tingri is only a destination in itself for those planning on trekking to base camp and there is no public transport to the village. Hitching a lift with trucks bound for the border from Shigatse or Lhatse would be the best bet. You will have to pay for the lift. The sum is entirely negotiable, but do not be surprised if it is as high as Y100. With some persistence, you should be able to do it cheaper than this, however.

THE EVEREST REGION

The Tibetan approach to Mt Everest (8848 metres) provides far better vistas of the world's highest peak than those on the Nepal side.

Views of the mountain can even be had on the Friendship Highway in the vicinity of Tingri. But it is from Rongbuk Monastery and the Everest Base Camp that the true grandeur of Everest's sheer north face becomes apparent.

The Tibetan name for Everest is generally rendered as Qomolangma, and some 27,000 sq km of territory around Everest's Tibetan face have been designated as the Qomolangma Nature Preserve. Planning of the project was cooperative and included local Tibetan organisations, the Chinese Academy of Sciences and the Woodlands Mountain Institute of the USA.

The nature preserve aims not only to protect the environment of the Everest region, but also the cultural traditions of the local people, a sophisticated development in China's approach to its administration of the Tibetan plateau.

For foreign travellers, the Everest Base Camp has become the most popular trekking destination in Tibet. This does not mean that the region is exactly swarming with hikers, but it is also not realistic to expect that you will be the only one up there. In the warm summer months there might be anywhere between 10 and 20 travellers camped out around or staying in Rongbuk Monastery, close to the base camp.

While more and more travellers are setting their sights on Everest, a trek to base camp is obviously appealing as one of the ultimate caches of a Tibet adventure, but it is also worth emphasising that trekking from either Shegar or Tingri – the two access points – is no easy three or four-day stroll. Many visitors have no prior experience of high-altitude trekking in harsh conditions and set out ill-prepared for the very demanding trek. It is not unusual to meet travellers who have made it exhausted and slightly emaciated to

Everest's Name

In 1849 the Great Trigonometrical Survey of India was carried out to map the heights of peaks in the Himalaya range. The calculations were carried out from the Indian foothills of the Himalaya, and three years later the computed results showed a peak known to the West as Peak XV to be the highest mountain in the world. This came as a surprise, as until this time a mountain called Kangchenjunga near Sikkim was thought to be the peak whose head rose closest to the heavens. Peak XV was rather an ignominious name for the highest mountain in the world, and immediately a search began for its real name.

Western linguists working in Nepal and India reported various local names for the mountain. In Nepal, it was claimed, XV was known as Devadhunga, 'Abode of the Gods'. German explorers, on the other hand, reported that the Tibetan name was Chingopamari. In 1862, the Royal Geographic Society lumped for an alternative Nepalese name for the mountain: Gaurisanka.

In the meantime, Andrew Waugh, Surveyor General of India embarked on a mission of his own to have the mountain named after the head of the Great Trigonometrical Survey, Sir George Everest. He met with much opposition, largely because it was argued that a local name would be more appropriate. In 1865 the Royal Geographic Society decided to back the Everest contingent due to uncertainties surrounding Gaurisanka (in 1902 it was determined that Gaurisanka was another peak, some 50 km from Everest).

The Everest name stuck amid much controversy, not least due to the fact that there were probably no shortage of experts who knew the true Tibetan name for the mountain to be Chomolangma (or Qomolangma, as the Chinese have transliterated it), which can be translated as Goddess Mother of the Universe. After all, as early as 1733, the French produced a map in which Everest is indicated as Tschoumou Lancma.

The Tibetans and Chinese have no truck with the Westernised name of the world's loftiest peak. Trekkers who make it up to Everest Base Camp have to make do with a posed photograph in front of a slab of rock inscribed with the words 'Mt Qomolangma Base Camp'. What's in a name anyway? ∎

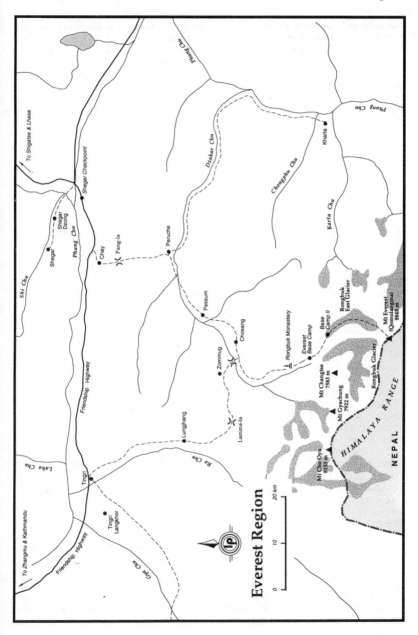

Everest Region

base camp and then become very depressed at the thoughts of having to trek back again. Counting on a lift back on the Everest approach road from Shegar is not realistic; some travellers have been lucky, but many more have not been.

This is not to douse your dreams of Everest with cold water, simply a suggestion that the trek should be treated with the respect it deserves. Go prepared. Seriously consider approaching Everest on the Tingri route, where yaks can be hired to carry supplies and backpacks. Do some easier treks elsewhere in Tibet by way of preparation and get thoroughly acclimatised. Whatever you do, do not attempt walking to base camp directly after arriving in Tingri from the low altitudes of the Kathmandu Valley. And finally, do not be tempted by the enthusiasm of others to climb any higher than you feel comfortable with. As base camp becomes more popular, many travellers are starting to set their sights at advanced base camp and higher. It is probably only a matter of time before some idiot decides to scale the peak itself and dies up there.

By way of compensation, for those who want to reach base camp the easy way, you can drive all the way to base camp from Shegar in a 4WD. It is a rough drive, but far less rougher than doing it on foot. Buy your 'Wimps Anonymous' T-shirt in Lhasa before you go and hold your head high as you wave to the real travellers you leave behind in a cloud of dust.

Permits

Permits for the Everest region are readily available in Lhasa, Shigatse and Lhatse. The cost should be Y100 per person, Y300 per vehicle. The big question is do you need one? Theoretically, yes. On the other hand, the only place it is likely to be checked is a nasty little checkpoint at the village of Chay, around two to three hours' walk from the Pang-la pass turn-off. This checkpoint is run by a few bored Tibetans in hand-me-down PLA uniforms, and they invariably demand payment of at least Y50 per person, whether you have a permit or not. At the time of writing, trekking from Tingri bypasses this problem, though there are rumours that the Chinese are looking at putting a checkpoint there as well.

A note of warning: if you trek via Chay, be prepared to pay your bribe with a smile. Some travellers have been beaten up and others threatened with electric cattle prods by the checkpost guards. It is really not worth it for Y50. If you have problems report them to the Shigatse PSB.

What to Bring

The usual rules for trekking in Tibet apply. Be prepared. Ideally, a good tent, sleeping bag and stove are basic requirements. Even in the height of summer, it is likely to get very cold at night. There is very little in the way of food en route, but there is usually somewhere to stay, particularly on the route from Shegar, less so from Tingri. Tibetan-style tents may be available for hire in Tingri, but again you *will* need your own sleeping bag.

Approaches to Everest

The two approaches to Everest are from Shegar, via the Pang-la pass, and from Tingri. The Shegar route is arguably easier since it follows a 4WD access road, but most trekkers choose the Tingri route. At Tingri it is possible to hire yaks and guides at very cheap rates, and not having to shoulder a pack the entire way to base camp makes a great deal of difference to your enjoyment of the trek. Even very experienced mountain hikers have complained about the hardship involved in carrying a heavy pack at the altitudes in this region.

From Shegar The Everest access road turns off the Friendship Highway around five km west of the Shegar checkpoint shortly after km marker 494, from which point it winds and climbs its way 63 km to Rongbuk Monastery and on to base camp. Unless you are driving to base camp, it is probably best to avoid this route in favour of the Tingri route. For one thing, this way you will not have to deal with Chay checkpoint; for another, it is much easier to hire pack animals at Tingri. Even if you are planning on using both routes in a loop – in on one and out on the other – it is still better to start with the Tingri route and exit back onto the Friendship Highway near Shegar. There is occasional truck traffic on the Everest access road, which means that if you are exhausted and fed up with walking you may be able to hitch a lift. The Chay checkpoint boys are also not going to fine you to leave the Everest region.

A good alternative to staying in Shegar (see the Shegar entry following) is to continue onto Chay (4300 metres), where there is accommodation for between Y6 and Y8. There is not much food available here, however. It is sometimes possible to hire pack ponies in Chay, but usually only as far

The Assault on Everest

There had been 13 assaults on Everest before Edmund Hillary and Sherpa Tenzing finally reached the summit in the major British expedition of 1953 led by John Hunt. Two of the expeditions were illicit solo attempts. In 1934, the first of these, Edmund Wilson, an eccentric ex-British army captain, travelled into Tibet in disguise with three Sherpas. He disappeared somewhere above Camp III, and his body was discovered in 1935 at 6400 metres. The second solo effort was attempted by a Canadian in disguise from the Tibet side. It was abandoned at 7150 metres.

From 1921 to 1938 all expeditions to Everest were British and were attempted from the north (Tibetan) side. In all, the mountain claimed 14 lives. With the conclusion of WW II and the collapse of the British Raj, the Himalayas became inaccessible. Tibet closed its doors to outsiders, and in 1951 the Chinese invasion wedged the doors shut even more tightly. In mountaineering terms, however, the Chinese takeover had the positive effect of shocking the hermit kingdom of Nepal into looking for powerful friends. The great peaks of the Himalayas suddenly became accessible from Nepal.

Much to their dismay, the British found that the mountain was no longer theirs alone. In 1951, Eric Shipton led a British reconnaissance expedition that explored the Nepal approaches to Everest and came to the conclusion that a Nepal assault might indeed meet with success. In 1952, however, the Nepalese issued only one permit to climb Everest – to the Swiss. The Swiss, who together with the British had virtually invented mountaineering as a sport, were extremely able climbers, and British climbers secretly feared the Swiss might mount a successful ascent on their first attempt; something that eight major British expeditions had yet failed to achieve. As it happened, the Swiss climbed to 8595 metres on the South-East Ridge – higher than any previous expedition – but failed to reach the summit.

The next British attempt was assigned for 1953. Preparations were particularly tense. It was generally felt that if this one were unsuccessful, any British hopes to be the first to reach the summit would be dashed. There was considerable backroom manoeuvering before the expedition set off. As a result, Eric Shipton, who had led three previous expeditions (including one in 1935), was dropped as team leader in favour of John Hunt, an army officer and keen Alpine mountaineer but relatively unknown amongst British climbers.

Shipton's 1951 expedition had at the last minute accepted two New Zealand climbers. One of them was Edmund Hillary, a professional bee-keeper and a man of enormous determination and seemingly unlimited reserves of strength. He was invited again to join Hunt's 1953 expedition. Also joining the 1953 expedition was Sherpa Tenzing, a Sherpa who had set out on his first Everest expedition at the age of 19 in 1935 and who had subsequently become infected with the dream of conquering the world's highest peak.

On 27 May 1953, Hillary and Tenzing made a precarious camp at 8370 metres on a tiny platform of the south-east ridge approach to the summit, while the other anxious members of the expedition waited below at various camps. The two men feasted that night on chicken noodle soup and dates. At 6.30 am the next morning they set out. Almost immediately they were in trouble, confronted with a vast, steep sweep of snow. It was the kind of obstacle that had turned back previous expeditions, but Tenzing agreed with Hillary that it had to be risked. It was a gamble that paid off. The next major obstacle was a chimney-like fissure which the two men squirmed up painfully. Struggling onwards they suddenly found themselves just metres away from a snow-clad dome. At 11.30 am, 28 May, they photographed each other standing at the closest point to the heavens it is possible to reach on foot. Everest had finally been conquered. ∎

as the top of the Pang-la pass. It probably depends on how much you are willing to spend.

From Chay, it is a long day of walking over the Pang-la pass (5120 metres) and down to the next settlement. Shortly after Chay, at a turn in the road is a local trail up to the pass that shaves at least an hour off the walk. This trail vaguely parallels the vehicle-access road to the east. It takes around three to four hours to reach the top of the pass. From the top of the pass it is around two hours to the small village of Holum or four hours to the larger settlement of Peruche. Consider staying the night in Holum rather than Peruche. Locals can arrange accommodation for around Y6 in the former and no one has a good word for Peruche. The Peruche 'hotel' is a noisy, dirty place which charges Y10 per bed. Check around the village for alternatives. There is very little food in either of these villages.

If you have stayed in Holum, it is a four to five-hour walk to the village of Passum. Consider spending the night here at the *Passumpembah Teahouse* (yes, there is an English sign). This delightful, cosy Tibetan home has a great little guestroom with five beds at Y15 each. Free tea is provided, the food is good and this is a good place to try the local chang, which is made by pouring hot water into a pot of fermented barley – suck the chang out with a wooden straw.

Passum is a good place to relax for an afternoon. It is a pleasant walk out into the valley, where you can laze around in the meadows next to icy streams admiring incredible views of the Himalayas. Unlike in some of the other villages in the vicinity, the locals around here are very friendly. Passum, along with the Samye Monastery guest-house, also has one of the most scenic toilets in Tibet – check it out.

Unless you've brought your superman suit with you, it is not possible to trek from Passum to Rongbuk in a single day. Chosang is around three hours from Passum, and from Chosang it is eight to nine hours up to Rongbuk. Most trekkers elect to stay at Chosang and if your schedule is tight it would be best to stay here rather than Passum, though it is not as pleasant as the latter. Several families offer accommodation at rates of between Y5 and Y10 – shop around a little, as sleeping conditions vary considerably. Many travellers have had problems with theft in Chosang.

From Chosang to Rongbuk is a long, steep day of walking – reckon on around eight to nine hours, possibly quicker if you are fit and not labouring under a heavy pack.

From Tingri Providing you are reasonably fit and acclimatised it is feasible to do the trek from Tingri to Rongbuk in three days. Ideally, you should hire pack animals and a guide in Tingri. Rates are very reasonable. Be warned, however, if you take yaks that they can be very frisky animals. Some trek-kers complain that they spent most of their trek chasing the yaks back on course.

A guide is useful on this trek because their are some sections which are potentially con-fusing. Unlike the route from Shegar there is no clear road to follow.

The first day of walking takes you to the village of Lungjhang (4510 metres), around five hours out of Tingri. This is the last village you will see for a while and it makes a good place to stay for the night. Usually villagers will rent out beds for around Y6, but this may require some friendly bargain-ing. Watch out for your goodies in this village. As in many villages in this region, travellers report problems with theft.

From Lungjhang the trail continues south. Bear right where the trail forks just after the village – the right fork is a longer route to Rongbuk over the Ding-la pass. After around three hours you should reach the second of two nomad camps. You might decide to stay here; the alternative is to push up to the summit of the Lamma-la pass (5150 metres), which is around 1½ to two hours' walk. There is a short cut over the pass that is used by locals. If your guide wants to use it, bear in mind that it is steeper and crosses the pass at a higher point; keep to the main trail if you do not think you are up to it.

From the Lamma-la pass it is a steep climb

down to the valley below, and a walk of around 1½ hours to the village of Zommug (4780 metres), which is north of the trail. It may be possible to stay with a family here, though it is preferable to camp somewhere in the vicinity.

There are actually two routes from Zommug to Rongbuk. Most groups take the lower, easier of the two. About three hours' walk and two river crossings on this route brings you to the Everest access road from Shegar, around three hours short of Rongbuk Monastery.

Rongbuk Monastery

Although there were probably monastic settlements in the area for several hundred years, Rongbuk Monastery is fairly recent. It was established in 1902 by a Nyingmapa lama.

Perhaps not of great antiquity, it can at least lay claim to being the highest monastery in Tibet, and thus the world, at 4980 metres. There were once 500 monks and nuns living here, but locals report that the number is now only 16. Another traveller, however, was told 100, a number that seems far-fetched.

Renovation work has been ongoing at the monastery, and some of the interior murals are quite stunning. The monastery itself makes a fabulous photograph with Everest thrusting its head skyward in the background.

Accommodation and very basic food are available at the monastery. The rooms are comfortable, heated with stoves and cost Y15 per bed. The only problem with the place is the hostility of some of the monks. Travellers have had stones thrown at them, been verbally abused and robbed at Rongbuk. It seems unusual monkish behaviour and may stem from bad experiences with travellers in the past, over-exposure to trekking groups and mountaineers or perhaps it is simply a side-effect of living in the world's highest monastery. Whatever the case, do not expect a friendly reception and keep a close eye on your belongings – one traveller had her money belt stolen while she was sleeping. Hopefully the situation will improve, and a night at Rongbuk will become the rare, magical experience one would hope it to be.

Rongbuk to Everest Base Camp It is just over two hours' walk from Rongbuk Monastery to the base camp. Vehicles do the trip in around 10 to 15 minutes. The walk is fairly straightforward, even if the altitude has you puffing within a few minutes of starting out.

The base camp is a dry, barren place, but the views of Everest more than make up for this. Have a photo taken at the base camp marker, which disappointingly does not even mention the word 'Everest'.

It reads: 'Mt Qomolangma Base Camp' and the Chinese below indicates 5200 metres above sea level. On a small hill to the left of the base camp marker are a couple of prayer poles. Clamber up for great views of the world's highest peak.

Snow leopard (JS)

Onwards from Base Camp Expeditions farther from base camp are only for very experienced trekkers or mountaineers. It is easy, once you have reached base camp, to succumb to the temptation to push just a little farther. Do not do it without adequate preparation. At the very least, spend a couple of days acclimatising in the Rongbuk area and doing day hikes to higher altitudes. AMS can strike anyone at these altitudes, and the nearest real help is far away in Shigatse.

Those contemplating pushing on to camps I, II or III, should come prepared with a copy of Gary McCue's *Trekking in Tibet – a traveler's guide*, which has comprehensive details on how to undertake such a trek as safely as possible.

Getting There & Away
The sections above have information on the logistics of hiking into the Everest region and visiting base camp. Not everyone wants to trek the entire distance, however, and it is perfectly feasible to hire a landcruiser in Shigatse or Lhasa to do the trip. Many travellers elect to include Everest as part of a 'package' of sights between Lhasa and the Nepal border. Landcruisers can lurch all the way up to base camp, but if you want to do some walking and turn up at base camp looking like you have trekked the whole way, leave the landcruiser at Rongbuk.

Hiring a landcruiser in Lhasa purely to visit Everest will cost almost as much as a border trip incorporating Everest – around Y5000 or more. Shop around. In Shigatse, prices for Everest with a stop-over at Sakya en route were between Y4000 and Y4500. Shopping around and some determined haggling can bring the price down lower than this, but be wary of deals that seem too good to be true.

NYALAM གཉའ་ལམ་
Nyalam (3750 metres) is a funky little town around 30 km before the Nepal border. It has been steadily growing in size and facilities have been improving over the last few years. This no doubt due to burgeoning trade opportunities with nearby Nepal.

Some tour groups coming up from Kathmandu spend the night at Nyalam, but most groups coming from Lhasa stay in Tingri, 150 km to the south. Even if you do not have time to spend the night, it is worth stopping for lunch in Nyalam and poking around. The Nepalese influence that is so prevalent in nearby Zhangmu can also be felt here.

For those who want to use Nyalam as a base for treks, Gary McCue has a section on treks around Nyalam in his book, *Trekking in Tibet – a traveler's guide*. The closest cultural sight to Nyalam is **Nyalam Pelgye Ling**, a small temple that is associated with Milarepa, the famous Buddhist mystic and composer of songs who lived in the late 11th and early 12th centuries. The temple is around 10 km north of Nyalam, and a path leads down to it from between km marker 682 and 683 on the Friendship Highway. It takes around three hours to hike here from Nyalam.

Places to Stay & Eat
Officially, foreigners are required to stay at the *Nyalam Guesthouse*, which is at the top (south) end of town. This place is very comfortable and even has TVs in the rooms. Hot showers will probably not be available, however. Beds cost Y25.

About midway up the hill through the township is a truckers' hotel on the right that has very basic rooms for Y10.

A few doors up from here is another hotel with an English sign outside simply indicating *Hotel*. Beds here are Y15 and they are sometimes willing to take foreign guests. If the Nyalam Guesthouse is full, they will have no choice.

The food in Nyalam is not bad, and there are a number of Sichuan-style restaurants lining the road. There is no point making recommendations.

ZHANGMU འཕམ་མོ་
Zhangmu (2300 metres) is a remarkable little town that hugs the rim of a seemingly never-ending succession of hairpin bends down to the customs area at the border of China and

A: On the northern route to Mt Kailash (CT)
B: Mt Kailash pilgrimage (CT)

Nomad woman from Western Tibet (IB)

Nepal. After Tibet, it seems incredibly green and luxuriant, the smells of curry and incense in the air are smells from the subcontinent and the babbling sound of fast-flowing streams that cut through the town is music to the ears.

Zhangmu is a typical border town and has a restless, reckless feel to it. The population is a fascinating mix of Han, Tibetan and Nepalese, the shops brim with goodies from India, Nepal and China, and in curry shops Tibetans watch videos of Indian soap operas. It is well worth spending a little time exploring the place.

Places to Stay & Eat

The main hotel in Zhangmu is the *Zhangmu Guesthouse*, right down in the south of town next to Customs. As you might expect of the last official foreigner's abode in Tibet, it is expensive and apathetically run.

Standard doubles cost Y80 per bed, and while the rooms are certainly luxurious there

1 Hotel
2 Post Office
3 Bank of China
4 Himalaya Lodge
5 Chinese Hotel
6 Tibetan-Nepalese Restaurant
7 Sichuan Restaurant
8 Zhangmu Guesthouse
9 Chinese Customs

To Nyalam & Lhasa

Zhangmu

ཞ་མོ་

Not to Scale

To Kodari & Kathmandu

is no hot water in the showers. Triples are also available for Y50 per bed.

Most travellers sensibly give the Zhangmu Guesthouse a miss in favour of the *Himalaya Lodge*, a great little hotel up the road before (south of) the bank and near a small stupa. It is run by a lively guy from Sichuan who speaks no English but really goes out of his way to please. Chinese, Tibetan and Nepalese food is available here until late at night and at very reasonable prices. This is also the place to change RMB and Nepalese rupees – very good rates are available. Comfortable doubles here cost Y10 per bed, and you can nod off to sleep to the sound of a stream that runs at the back of the lodge.

There are several other accommodation options in Zhangmu, though none of them match the Himalaya Lodge in warmth and atmosphere. Back down the road towards the Zhangmu Guesthouse, look out for a Chinese-style hotel on the right. This place has beds for Y25. There is another hotel further up the hill past the bank if all of these are full. It is less convenient for crossing the border or for picking up transport to Lhasa.

There is no shortage of restaurants in Zhangmu. There are a couple of very good options down by the Zhangmu Guesthouse. Next door to the guesthouse is a large canteen-style Sichuan restaurant. Across the road and slightly to the north is a good Nepalese restaurant. Look for it up a flight of stairs. The dahl baht here is excellent and the staff are super friendly. Wander further up the hill for a good selection of Chinese, Tibetan and Nepalese cuisine – for anyone who has come in from other parts of Tibet, it is paradise.

Getting There & Away

To Kathmandu Access to Nepal is via the Friendship Bridge and Kodari, around 10 km below Zhangmu. Traffic on the stretch of no-man's land between the two countries has increased over the last couple of years and it has now become quite easy to hitch a lift, though you will probably have to pay. Around Y15 should do the trick, but the amount depends entirely on who is giving the lift.

If you decide to walk, it takes a couple of hours down to the bridge. There are porters at both Customs points who will carry your pack for a few rupees or RMB. Look out for short cuts down between the hairpin bends of the road. They save quite a bit of time if you find them, though they put a real strain on the knees. For those looking at continuing straight on to Kathmandu, there are a couple of buses a day from Kodari that leave whenever they are full. The other option is to hire a vehicle. There are touts for vehicles to Kathmandu up at Chinese Customs. The cost is around R1500 to R2000. Most of the vehicles are private cars, and small ones at that; you will be hard pressed to fit more than three people into one, especially if you have big packs. Depending on the condition of the road, it should take around four to five hours from Kodari to Kathmandu.

Into Tibet It is very easy nowadays to get a lift from Zhangmu into Tibet. There are usually a number of empty landcruisers that have brought groups from Lhasa to the border waiting to make some extra cash by transporting new arrivals back. The going cost to Shigatse or Lhasa is between Y300 and Y400. Even if you are only going as far as Tingri, it will be difficult to get drivers to agree to a price below Y300 as they would probably prefer to wait for someone heading to Lhasa so they can earn a bit more.

Landcruiser drivers normally wait at Chinese Customs for new arrivals, but alternatively you can ask around at the hotels in Zhangmu.

Western Tibet མངའ་རིས་

Western Tibet is the most inaccessible region of the Tibetan Autonomous Region. The Chinese authorities do their best to make it even more inaccessible by putting as many hurdles as possible between individual travellers and the main attractions of the region: the sacred Mt Kailash, Lake Manasarovar and Tsaparang.

Until recently, Western Tibet has largely been the preserve of Western tour groups and the occasional intrepid traveller with a taste for adventure and plenty of time to spare. This situation, for good or for bad, is starting to change.

Over the last two years, it has become slightly easier to obtain permits for the region, and local authorities have become more relaxed about the arrival of individual travellers.

For non-pilgrims, the rewards of making the arduous journey out to Western Tibet are a little dubious. The journey from Lhasa is marked by stunning, if desolate, scenery, and Kailash and Manasarovar are two of the most remote travel destinations in the world. But, at the end of the day, the main attractions of what is likely to be a three-week trip are a mountain and a lake.

Visitors not overly fussed by the spiritual significance of Kailash are likely to come away with the feeling that it was one of those 'been-there-done-that' adventures, where the difficulty of access is as much an attraction as the destination itself.

HISTORY

Most histories of Tibet begin with the kings of the Yarlung Valley region and their unification of central Tibet in the 7th century. But it is thought that the Shangshung kingdom of Western Tibet probably ruled the Tibetan plateau for several centuries prior to this. According to some scholars, the Bön religion made its way into the rest of Tibet from here. The Shangshung kingdom may also have served as a conduit for Tibet's earliest contacts with Buddhism.

There is little material evidence of the Shangshung kingdom in modern Tibet. Khyunglung Monastery, around 95 km north-west of Lake Manasarovar, and ruins in its near vicinity are thought to mark the site of the old kingdom.

Those with a particular interest in this archaeological site and other remote monasteries in the area should go prepared with a copy of Victor Chan's *Tibet Handbook – a pilgrimage guide*.

The next regional power to emerge in Western Tibet was the Guge kingdom in the 9th century. After the assassination of the anti-Buddhist Lhasa king, Langdharma, one of the king's sons, Wosung, established the kingdom west of Manasarovar and Kailash at Tsaparang.

The Guge kingdom, via contacts with India, led a Buddhist revival on the Tibetan plateau and was home to over 100 monasteries, most of them in ruins now.

In the late 16th century, the Jesuits took an interest in the remote kingdom of Guge. From their enclave in Goa, rumours reached the Jesuits of a kingdom whose religion strongly resembled Catholicism – probably due to the monastic nature of Tibetan Buddhism.

Speculation that this was the long-lost Christian civilisation of Prester John – a legendary Christian priest and king who was believed to have ruled over a kingdom in the Far East – soon sparked enthusiasm for an expedition to this far-away community of lost Christians.

The first Jesuit expedition to set out for the kingdom ended in failure with the death of its leader in 1603. A second expedition, led by Father Antonio de Andrede in 1624, made its way to the head of the Mana Valley disguised as pilgrims and looked down on Tibet only to be turned back by heavy snows, snowblindness and altitude sickness. A

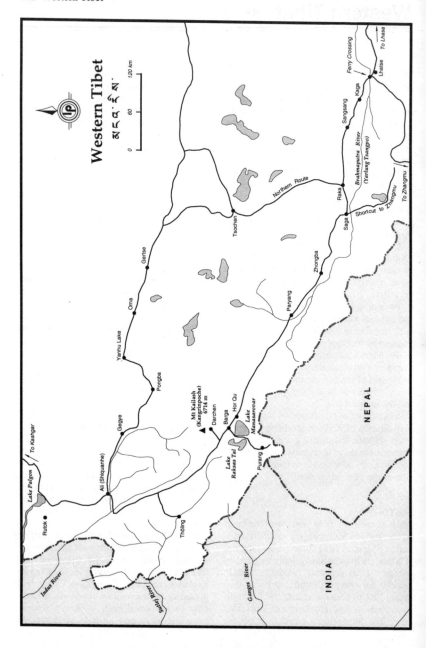

month later they returned and descended to the Guge kingdom.

If de Andrede had expected to find Christians waiting for him at Tsaparang, the Guge capital, he was to be disappointed. Nevertheless, he did meet with surprising tolerance and respect for the Christian faith. The Guge king agreed to allow de Andrede to return and set up a Jesuit mission the following year. The foundation stone of the first Christian church in Tibet was laid by the king himself.

Ironically, the evangelical zeal of the Jesuits led not only to their own demise but also to the demise of the kingdom they sought to convert.

Lamas, outraged by their king's increasing enthusiasm for an alien creed, enlisted the support of Ladhakis in laying siege to Tsaparang. Within a month the city fell, the king was overthrown and the Jesuits imprisoned. The Guge kingdom foundered on Christian zeal and factional manoeuvring.

At this point, Western Tibet became so marginalised as to almost disappear from the

Sven Hedin

history books – with one notable exception. In the late Victorian era, a handful of Western explorers began to take interest in the legend of a holy mountain and a lake from which four of Asia's mightiest rivers flowed. The legend, which had percolated as far afield as Japan and Indonesia, was largely ridiculed by Western cartographers.

But in 1908 the Swedish explorer Sven Hedin returned from a journey that proved there was indeed such a mountain and such a lake, and that the remote western part of Tibet which they occupied was in fact the source of the Ganges, Brahmaputra, Indus and Sutlej rivers. The mountain was Kailash and the lake Manasarovar.

PERMITS

In theory all foreigners travelling out to Western Tibet should have permits. In practice, however, many travellers – mainly those hitching – do not bother. It would be wise to check on the latest situation with other travellers, but in mid-'94 there was not a single checkpoint on either the southern or northern routes. On my legal trip through the region I was never once asked for my permit.

The catch with applying for permits and doing the trip officially is that the authorities only give out permits to tour groups with a guide, landcruiser and truck to carry supplies. On average, Lhasa travel agencies charge between Y20,000 and Y30,000 for a package of this sort. This fee will include the cost of permits for all group members. Those planning on doing the trip on their own will have no luck obtaining a permit from either the Lhasa or Shigatse PSB offices, and will be better off not drawing attention to themselves by trying.

Some travellers have found a loophole in this system by going to some of the smaller, privately run agencies in Lhasa and hiring just a truck for the trip. A group of seven or eight people can travel in reasonable comfort this way, and costs are reduced to between Y10,000 and Y15,000 for the whole package including permits. It is slightly illegal – the risk is the agency's not yours – and it is not possible to name agencies for fear of drawing attention to them. Ask around in the Tibetan quarter of Lhasa.

The only real danger spots for individual travellers are Ali and Darchen, where there are usually a couple of English-speaking PSB officers with a special interest in foreigners. But even here the general rule seems to be a fine of between Y100 and Y150, which then allows you to go on your way. Even if you pay the fine, you have got away with doing the trip a lot more cheaply than if you had done it officially. Some travellers go and give themselves up to the Ali PSB, an honest course of action that reportedly gives you a Y50 discount and a little goody-goody badge.

GETTING THERE & AWAY

Most travellers approach Western Tibet from Lhasa. There are other approaches of course – from Nepal or from Kashgar in Xinjiang – but for individual travellers Lhasa is the easiest place to organise permits and find travelling companions. In mid-'94 an increasing number of individual travellers were successfully taking the difficult road from Kashgar to Ali, but whether this will remain the case is anyone's guess. The Nepal-Western Tibet route is generally only used by tour groups.

From Lhasa

There are two routes from Lhasa to Western Tibet: a northern route and a southern route. The northern route is considerably longer than the southern route: approximately 1760 km as opposed to 1190 km. But, for those hitching, it is the northern route that sees the

---

Sven Hedin

Sven Hedin was born in Stockholm in 1865. From a young age he was inspired by tales of journeys to the empty spaces of maps. By the age of 15 he had already decided that he too would become an explorer, and undertook a fanatical regime of training that included learning languages (Russian, Tartar, Persian, Tibetan, Turkish and Arabic), naked romps in the snow (to improve his physical endurance), cartography and drawing. He was nothing short of a man obsessed, and at 21 he made his first long journey – 1500 km by steamer across the Caspian Sea, and on horseback across Persia, to the Gulf, to Baghdad and back through Persia. It established his reputation in Europe as a hardy traveller.

Hedin continued his travels, winning the approbation of other renowned explorers and, importantly, the Royal Geographic Society, which heaped him with honours. A close encounter with death in the Taklamakan desert of Chinese Turkestan made him more cautious, but it did nothing to dampen his enthusiasm. And having explored much of Central Asia, he turned his attention on Tibet and the forbidden city of Lhasa. Thwarted in his goal by zealous Tibetan border patrols and then beaten to the post by the British Younghusband expedition of 1904, Hedin suddenly lost interest in Lhasa and turned his gaze westward to the vast unmapped regions of Western Tibet.

The British Indian administration was none too keen on this idea. When Hedin arrived at Simla in early 1906, he received a frosty reception and was prohibited from continuing on to Tibet. For the next few months, with characteristic resolve, he played a cat-and-mouse game with the British authorities, finally breaking into Tibet in August 1906 from Leh in Ladakh.

Over the next two years, Hedin cut two great swathes across Tibet, filling in 100,000 km of blank spaces on maps of Tibet, discovering the sources of the Brahmaputra, Sutlej and Indus rivers, circumambulating Mt Kailash and returning with reports of a Trans-Himalayan mountain range that intervened between the Himalayas to the south and the Kunlun range to the north.

If Hedin expected to return to Europe a conquering hero, he was to be disappointed. Although his speeches at the Royal Geographic Society were received to fabulous applause, there were elements in the British geographical establishment who doubted some of his claims and acrimonious debate broke out. Not long after he published accounts of his journey (running to a massive 13 volumes in two works: *Trans-Himalaya* and *Southern Tibet*), he found a more welcome reception in Germany. His support of Germany in WW I led to his being struck off the membership of the Royal Geographic Society, and his similar support in WW II led to his being spurned by his own countrymen. His death went almost unnoticed in 1952. ■

most traffic. The southern route is generally deserted except for tour groups. The destination of traffic on the northern route is the Chinese town of Shiquanhe, or Ali, several hundred km north of Kailash.

Both the northern and southern routes follow the same road as far as Lhatse and on to the northern turn-off past Sangsang. Around six km after Lhatse, the road leaves the Friendship Highway and bears west. It is approximately 235 km from here to the northern road turn-off. The condition of the road shared by both routes is relatively good, and trucks generally average around 40 km an hour or more.

There is no public transport for either of these routes. The only options are to hire a vehicle or to hitch. Vehicle hire, along with permits, is best arranged in Lhasa, though Shigatse is another option. At the time of writing, Shigatse travel agencies – even more than their Lhasa counterparts – had a greater interest in relieving travellers of the contents of their wallets than in providing the services they promise. Ask around for the latest gossip before doing business in Shigatse.

Travellers planning on hitching out to Western Tibet should travel to Shigatse or Lhatse first. Lhatse is the better option. It is a small place and all the south-bound traffic is either heading for the Nepalese border or out to Ali. Some travellers hike from Lhatse for the Western Tibet turn-off six km out of town. Just after the turn-off is a ferry crossing. As all Ali-bound transport is compelled to stop here, it is an ideal place to begin hitching. Some travellers have managed to get lifts all the way to Ali from this point, some in landcruisers.

For more information on hitching see the Northern Route section following.

Northern Route The northern route is the more difficult and longer of the two routes from Lhasa to Western Tibet. Lhasa to Lhatse is a straightforward run, particularly since the construction of the new highway between Lhasa and Shigatse. The new road follows the Brahmaputra for 250 km to

Shigatse, and bypasses lake Yamdrok-tso. If you are keen to get a glimpse of the lake, you will have to take the old Lhasa-Shigatse highway, which travels via Chusul and Gyantse. The old highway is around 340-km long and includes a rugged haul over the Kamba-la pass (4900 metres) – there are stunning views of Yamdrok-tso from the top. It is much more time consuming than the new highway and will probably require an overnight stop in Gyantse or Shigatse instead of carrying on to Lhatse or further.

Hitchers will have no choice but to take the new highway between Lhasa and Shigatse, as for the most part only rented tourist transport takes the old road. The best option is to take a minibus to Shigatse (see the Shigatse, Getting There & Away section) and then take another minibus or hitch on to Lhatse.

From Shigatse to Lhatse is 157 km. Again, the road is in good shape and it is a smooth run. At this point, hitchers have the choice of hanging out in Lhatse to catch a lift or walking the six or seven km to the ferry crossing. The ferry crossing will be the easier of the two places to get a lift. Lhatse has several hotels with costs of around Y15, a couple of good restaurants (the best food you will come across until Ali) and some shops with instant noodles, sweets, biscuits and drinks – a good place to stock up on any supplies you forgot to bring along.

From Lhatse onwards there is little in the way of food or accommodation. There are truck stops strategically situated a day's travel from each other along the early section of the northern road, but all it takes is a breakdown (a frequent occurrence) and a delay of a few hours to fall completely out of synch with this arrangement.

From the ferry crossing, the road enters a surprisingly lush (well, during the summer at least) river valley, scattered with Tibetan villages. This is a beautiful area for photographs if your driver is amenable to the idea of stopping occasionally. Some 50 km onwards is the very small town of **Kaga** (Kajia). The Tibetan town is to the right of the road and there is a truck stop on the left a little further on. There is basic food, beer and accommodation here. The town is next to a very picturesque lake.

A further 65 km away is **Sangsang**, a slightly larger town with a restaurant, shop and basic accommodation. Expect to pay around Y10 for your accommodation both here and in Kaga.

From Sangsang, there is basically nothing in the way of accommodation before **Tsochen** (Cuojin), 370 km away. The northern route turn-off is 125 km from Sangsang and is marked by a weather-worn sign in Tibetan and Chinese pointing to Ali (those taking the southern route should turn to the Southern Route entry below at this point). The road deteriorates rapidly after the northern turn-off. The stretch of 436 km between the turn-off and the northern road proper is the worst piece of road on the entire trip. Road conditions from this point can easily slow your progress down to between 15 and 25 km/h.

The one compensation for the shocking state of the road after the northern turn-off is the frequently breathtaking scenery the road winds through. Look out for the hot springs and geyser to the right about 20 minutes after taking the turn-off. Not long after this, the road passes a series of lakes, their waters a miraculous shade of the deepest blue imaginable.

Tsochen, 242 km from the northern turn-off, is a pit of a town, a thoroughly depressing hybrid of both the ugliest of Chinese and the slummiest of Tibetan urban conglomerations. The best idea is to get there late and leave early. The *Gaoyuan Lüshe* (Plateau Hotel in English, not that there is an English sign) has basic accommodation at Y15. There is unlikely to be any food at the hotel restaurant, the only one in town. When I was there, the hotel restaurant was charging Y1 to pour some hot water into a cup of instant noodles. Diagonally opposite the hotel is a department store with basic food supplies.

From Tsochen it is 184 km to the northern

Pongba

I have fond memories of Pongba (what a great name!). We arrived after five gruelling days on the road, sleeping in the back of the truck and getting on each other's nerves. The driver had spent the whole day moaning about his back while we steadfastly ignored him and muttered 'drive on you bastard' under our breaths. But we'd made it to Pongba and were now only a day from Ali.

As we picked our way across the broken beer bottles, maintaining a vigilant eye on a nearby slavering pack of Tibetan mastiffs, we couldn't help but comment on the rustic charm of the quaint little Tibetan township we found ourselves in and lament the fact that there was no one selling postcards.

There were so many little endearing qualities about the place that we were loath to get up at the crack of dawn the next day and get the hell out. Efficiency for example: it only took 1½ hours to check-in, and we only had to walk from one end of the village to the other four times to do the paper work, get the keys and beg for some hot water. Of course they wanted to hold our passports overnight just in case we were tempted to make off with the dirty sheets and the adorable pillowcases covered in snot. But in the end they settled for my expired driver's license. I'm sure the scowls as they did so was just their way of saying 'have a nice day, sir'. That's the kind of people they are in Pongba.

Of course there was no food in Pongba, but by that time we'd developed such a taste for instant noodles that we'd probably have turned down a free serving of fillet mignon and a bottle of the best red in the house if they had been offered. And the beer...lots and lots of warm bottles of it. Interestingly, the locals have a quaint custom of throwing the empties at the dogs, which I recommend trying. It's more fun than being bitten by one.

Fondest memories, however, are reserved for the mad Tibetan who wanted to eat our empty noodle containers and kept bursting into the room through the night. I wanted to take him with us to Mt Kailash and have him eat all our rubbish as we went along, but I was out-voted on this one. ∎

route proper. It is a bumpy, arduous ride, but the last 40 or 50 km descends into a vast plain, where the going is much smoother. Just before the turn-off is a salt lake. Some trucks travelling the northern road come this far to collect salt that is mined here and then turn back to Lhasa or Shigatse.

It is 84 km from the turn-off to the next town with food and accommodation. **Gertse** (Gaize) has three or four Sichuan restaurants with surprisingly good food (even some fresh vegetables). Just wander into the kitchen and point out what you want. Accommodation is primitive and costs around Y10.

From Gertse it is 180 km to the next town of **Pongba** (Xiongba), a dismal little place populated by alcoholic Tibetans, mad dogs and broken beer bottles. En route the road passes two lakes. The second, **Yanhu**, has a small salt-mining community at its western end. Stopping here is probably not a good idea. It is another depressing little place populated by mad Tibetans, alcoholic dogs and broken beer bottles. From Yanhu the road turns up through a ravine and crosses a pass before descending to Pongba.

If you ever drag yourself away from Pongba, the last stretch of road between here and Ali is fairly good. An hour or so out of Pongba, the road enters a gorge and follows the Indus river.

The town of **Gegye** (Geji) is 105 km from Pongba and is a good place to stop for lunch or for the night. As you enter town, there is a road to the right that leads past several restaurants serving standard Chinese fare – which tastes very good after a couple of days of pot noodles. There is also a hotel with beds for Y10.

Ali is just 112 km from Gegye. The road deteriorates for the last 20 km or so, but until then it is fine. The main road of Ali has been covered with bitumen, and it is an amazing experience gliding smoothly into town after five or six days' of bone-jarring bouncing around.

Ali to Kailash From Ali to Darchen, the only town in the near vicinity of the Kailash

---

It's Kailash!?

All the literature about Kailash suggests a solitary peak standing in a vast plain, the holy lake of Manasarovar nestled at its feet. This was very confusing as we drove into view of the mountain that looked very Kailash-like huddled amongst a crop of other peaks. There was much argument about whether this was indeed Kailash – 'yes, it is', 'no, it isn't' and so on. I thought I had made a strong case of gainsaying the opposition, but my travel companion still insisted on stopping the truck and taking photos while I sulked in the cabin. The driver, who had never laid eyes on the sacred mountain before either, adopted a wise policy of neutrality and complaining about the condition of his back.

Of course it was Kailash, which just goes to show, I thought sagely to myself, that you can't believe everything you read in books. ■

---

pilgrimage circuit, is 331 km. The road is bad for the first 100 km or so, passing through a broad river valley in which there are many streams to ford. Most vehicles seem to get stuck in at least one of the streams. If your driver is not familiar with the road, have him drive carefully and stop at the streams to look for the best crossings. Deep ruts in the sand and gravel normally indicate where other vehicles have been bogged down.

This is quite a spectacular ride, but by no means outstanding in comparison with the rest of the northern or southern routes. Mt Kailash comes into view on the left around 30 or 40 minutes before reaching Darchen.

Providing there are no serious breakdowns and you do not spend too long languishing in a stream, there is no reason not to complete the trip in a single day. One last thing to be careful of just before reaching Darchen is a fairly deep river crossing. It comes up at the last minute before Darchen, around six or seven km after leaving the main road.

Southern Route If your objective is Mt Kailash and Lake Manasarovar, the southern route is the way to travel. The road is generally better and on a good run can be covered in four days from Lhasa, as opposed to six or seven (or more) on the northern route. The scenery, with its vast sweeping plains, sand dunes and the Himalaya range in the distance, is also more majestic on the southern route.

Apart from the fact that it is notoriously difficult to hitch this way (you are at the mercy of paying tourists who are generally not interested in freeloaders), the southern route is also subject to seasonal closure. From mid-to late July and through to late September, monsoonal rain usually makes the road impassable. Again, very few drivers are willing to attempt the route from January until the end of March. The best time to go is May, June and early July.

For information on the southern route as far as the northern turn-off, see the Northern Route section above.

From the northern turn-off it is 60 km to Saga (Sajia), the last town of any size. Turn left off the main road towards a vast Soviet-style people's hall and look out for the town's two hotels on either side of the road. The one to the right (it looks like a bus depot from outside) is the better of the two. Neither has an English sign and both charge Y15 for a bed. Just down from the hotel there are a couple of excellent Chinese restaurants and some shops.

Saga is also the turn-off for a short cut to Zhangmu on the Nepalese border – see the Nepal-Kailash section below and the Getting There & Away chapter for more information.

From Saga it is 145 km to Zhongba. The road is good, and most trucks can complete the trip in around four hours. Zhongba, a small dusty Tibetan town with a couple of shops, a restaurant and a hotel has little to recommend it. Given a choice, try and stay at Saga. There is a small gompa at the western end of town on a hill. It is not worth a special stop however.

Paryang (Paiyang), 110 km on from Zhongba, is the next town of any significance. It is a squalid place, littered with bones and broken beer bottles and infested with dogs. There are actually a couple of guesthouses here, though you would never believe it to look at the place. There are no signs. You find the guesthouses by standing in the main street and waiting for the manager of one of them to notice you – it does not take long. Both the guesthouses have basic meals available, but there are no restaurants as such.

From Zhongba onwards the southern road deteriorates. The section between Zhongba and Paryang is particularly bad for sand that has been swept down from the sand dunes on either side of the road. Many trucks get stuck briefly here – experienced drivers carry long poles which they wedge between both the twin rear wheels of their trucks for traction. You should not have any real problems with this section of road if you are in a 4WD however.

After Paryang, on the long haul to Darchen (around 300 km), the problem is not so much sand as river crossings. The first of these comes around an hour out of Paryang. The crossing here is fairly obvious, but it still pays to get out and have a good look before attempting it. A couple of hours on from here there are three tributaries of the same river to cross. It is not uncommon for trucks to get stuck in one of these for days at a time. The best crossing point is not obvious as there are tracks approaching the rivers in a multitude of directions. The best advice is to walk along the banks and look for the least sandy stretches of river.

There is yet another, very similar crossing an hour or so on from here. Again, you

The mantra Om Mani Padme Hum

should follow the same procedure and cross with extreme caution.

The section of the southern route from Zhongba to Darchen has some of the most panoramic scenery of either route. If you get an early start and do not get bogged in sand or a river, it should be possible to complete the Paryang-Darchen run in a long day.

Nepal-Kailash This short cut from Zhangmu to Saga saves at least a day of travel and is used by tour groups heading out to Kailash and by individual travellers who have hired vehicles and want to leave Tibet and enter Nepal after visiting Western Tibet.

The alternative to the Zhangmu-Saga route is to travel via the Friendship Highway to Lhatse and then turn onto the southern route to Saga, a total of 562 km. The short cut to Saga, on the other hand is a total of around 293 km.

From Saga the road leaves the southern route and crosses the Brahmaputra River via a ferry. Locals at Saga claimed that the ferry crossing did not start until 9.30 am, but when I arrived around 8 am they were already ferrying vehicles across. Ferry costs are for the vehicle only and not for passengers.

After the ferry crossing the road climbs steeply up and over a pass, before descending to follow a narrow gorge. Later the gorge leads into a vast plain with stunning views of the Himalaya. The road is very bad for most of the plain crossing, though it improves for the last hour or so. After rounding some hills at the far end of the plain, the road bears east and joins up with the Friendship Highway just before the ascent to the first section of the La Lung-la pass (5120 metres). The road drops from here, before ascending to the second section of the pass (5200 metres). From here it is downhill all the way to Kathmandu, providing breathtaking views as the scenery shifts from the windy barren pass to a luxuriant, deep gorge and on into the Kathmandu Valley.

In mid-'94 the authorities briefly opened another border crossing between Nepal and Tibet at Purang, very close to Kailash. The border crossing was open only to tour groups, who were reportedly being charged astronomical sums for the crossing. Within a month the crossing mysteriously closed again. Ask in Kathmandu or Lhasa for the latest on this crossing.

ALI ཨ་ལི་

Also known as Shiquanhe, Ali is the capital of Ali prefecture. There is nothing much to see, but it is a good place to clean up, have some decent food, do some shopping and rest for a day or so before heading off to the real attractions of Western Tibet.

The town itself is sited at the confluence of the Indus and Gar rivers, and is thoroughly Chinese in influence. There are plenty of Tibetans wandering the streets but, like you, they are probably visitors from farther afield.

Ali is basically one long street lined with shops, restaurants, the occasional department store and government buildings. The Ali Guesthouse is on the right shortly after you pull into town on the northern route from Lhatse. Turn left at the next crossroads for the road to Kailash and a cheaper guesthouse, officially off limits to foreigners.

Places to Stay

The official foreigner's abode is the *Ali Guesthouse*, a rambling, decrepit affair with dorm beds for Y25. Thermoses of hot water are available but there is no running water in the hotel. The toilets are a Tibetan-style pit out in the rear courtyard. Look for the suggestions box, perched so high on the wall next to reception that most Chinese and Tibetans would have trouble reaching it.

Permitless individual travellers should be warned that the Ali Guesthouse is also home to the local PSB officer in charge of foreigner's affairs. He was gracefully navigating the corridors of the hotel on a 12-speed mountain bike when I bumped into him, and seemed to be enjoying himself so immensely that he was quite happy to see another foreign guest en route to Kailash.

'Are you a group or an individual tourist?'

'I'm a group', I answered tactfully.

'Good, good, good', he said with a beam. And then he was off for another circuit of the hotel corridors. I never saw him again.

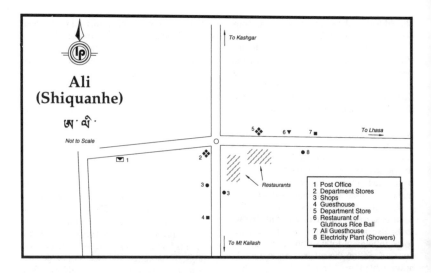

Ali
(Shiquanhe)

ཨ་ལི་

Not to Scale

To Kashgar

To Lhasa

To Mt Kailash

Restaurants

1 Post Office
2 Department Stores
3 Shops
4 Guesthouse
5 Department Store
6 Restaurant of
   Glutinous Rice Ball
7 Ali Guesthouse
8 Electricity Plant (Showers)

Travellers who have not yet gone completely native and are still partial to the occasional wash, can find hot showers in the electricity plant across the road from the hotel. Enter by a gate into a big courtyard, walk around the buildings on the right and look for a couple of attendants sitting beside an open door. Showers cost Y4.

There is another guesthouse around the corner from the Ali Guesthouse. This place charges Y10 for a bed. It is kind of off limits for foreigners, but it seems that if you pay your fine to the PSB they will let you stay there. This is a dubious saving in that your Y100 fine only gives you a Y15 saving on accommodation, but if you are forced to pay up ask about the *zhaodaisuo*, as it is known in Chinese.

Places to Eat

Food in Ali is expensive. This is hardly surprising given the town's remote location, but it still manages to surprise some travellers. The best hunting ground for restaurants is the area around the main intersection just down from the Ali Guesthouse. Sichuan fare is the standard cuisine available, and most places will let you pick and choose in the kitchen.

Just down from the Ali Guesthouse, on the same side of the road is the *Restaurant of Glutinous Rice Ball*. I cannot comment on the glutinous rice balls, but the other dishes (average Y12) I had there with a couple of friends were excellent. There is no English menu.

Things to Buy

It is not as if you are likely to leave Ali loaded down with souvenirs, but it is a good place, indeed the only place for hundreds of km, to stock up on some supplies. There is a small shop in Darchen, but prices there are higher.

There are at least three department stores in Ali and also a host of small shops selling basic supplies. The two best department stores are the one just down from the Ali Guesthouse and the one on the main intersection. Both have reasonably extensive supplies of cup noodles, biscuits, sweets and drinks.

Getting There & Away

See the routes entries above for information on getting to Ali from Lhatse and Lhasa and onward travel from Ali to Darchen and Mt Kailash.

Getting Around

There's no bicycle hire, no rickshaws – nothing; but then it only takes 10 minutes to walk from one end of town to the other anyway.

MT KAILASH གངས་རིན་པོ་ཆེ་

Throughout Asia is a myth of a great mountain, the navel of the world, from which flows four great rivers that give life to the areas they pass through. The origin of this myth lies in the Hindu epics, which speak of Mt Meru – home of the gods – as a vast column 84,000 leagues high; its summit kissing the heavens; its flanks composed of gold, crystal, ruby and lapis lazuli.

Early accounts of Mt Meru in the Hindu epics are thought to refer generally to a sacred mountain somewhere in the towering Himalayas. But, with time, Meru increasingly came to be associated specifically with Mt Kailash. The confluence of the myth and the mountain is no coincidence. There are

Mt Kailash Kora
གངས་རིན་པོ་ཆེའི་འཁོར་ར་

probably no gods at its summit, but Kailash does indeed lie at the centre of an area that is the key to the drainage system of the Tibetan plateau, and from which issues the four greatest rivers of the Indian subcontinent: the Ganges, Indus, Sutlej and Brahmaputra.

Mt Kailash, at 6714 metres, is not the mightiest of the mountains in the region but, with its hulking shape – like the handle of a millstone, according to Tibetans – and its year-long snow-capped peak, it stands apart from the pack. Its four sheer walls match the cardinal points of the compass, and its southern face is famously marked by a long horizontal cleft punctuated halfway down its traverse by a horizontal line of rock strata. This scarring resembles a swastika – a Buddhist symbol of spiritual strength – and is a feature that has contributed to Kailash's mythic status.

Kailash has long been an object of worship for four major religions. For the Hindus, it is the domain of Shiva, the Destroyer and Transformer. To the Buddhist faithful, Kailash is the abode of Samvara (Demchok in Tibetan), a wrathful manifestation of Sakyamuni thought to be an equivalent of Hinduism's Shiva. The Jains of India also revere the mountain as the site at which the first of their saints was emancipated. And in the ancient Bön religion of Tibet, Kailash was the sacred nine-storey Swastika Mountain, upon which the Bön founder Shenrab alighted from heaven.

Mt Kailash has been a lodestone to pilgrims and adventurous travellers for centuries. But, until recently, very few set their eyes on the sacred mountain. Even when tourism was jump started by the Chinese authorities in the mid-'80s, Kailash remained an inaccessible destination. This situation has begun to change in recent years, but tourist numbers are still thankfully low.

Mt Kailash Pilgrimage Circuit

The 53-km Mt Kailash kora is the holiest of all Tibet's pilgrimages. Like all other pilgrimage circuits, the kora describes a clockwise circumambulation of the mountain and includes various sites of religious significance along the way. If you meet pilgrims coming from the opposite direction, they are likely to be followers of the Bön faith, who make an anti-clockwise circumambulation of the mountain.

Most Western visitors complete the Kailash kora in three days. It is possible to complete it in two, but the last few hours of the second day are a real killer if you are not in reasonably good shape. This is not a walk to attempt before you are thoroughly acclimatised to the altitude. The kora commences at 4600 metres and climbs up to over 5600 metres before descending back to Darchen again. It is hard work.

Unlike their Western counterparts, many Tibetan pilgrims complete the Kailash kora in one long day of walking. Generally they aim to complete three circumambulations of the sacred peak, though for the hardy and determined 13 is a particularly auspicious number.

Ascetics with plenty of time on their hands sometimes go for the ultimate in circumambulatory glory: 108 circuits. It is said that a single circumambulation erases the accumulated sins of a lifetime, while 108 circumambulations are a one-way ticket straight to nirvana (do not forget to say goodbye to your folks before you leave if this is your plan).

The high altitudes involved make this a serious walk and it pays to be prepared. Some travellers who have completed the kora exaggerate the ease with which they did it and the availability of food and accommodation; others make a great deal of how difficult it is. In all honesty, it is neither. There is nothing much in the way of food en route – only some instant noodles at the two monastery guesthouses, but it would be risky to count on this. Accommodation at the guesthouses is very basic and, as there are limited rooms, may not even be available. It is a sensible idea to come prepared with a tent, a good sleeping bag and a stove.

The weather around Kailash is very fickle. Even in the height of summer, temperatures can plummet in the evenings, and when I was there in early July it snowed and hailed. This is not a place to sleep under the stars, no matter how good your sleeping bag is.

The kora begins in Darchen (see following), the closest town to Kailash. This is the place to stock up on last-minute supplies, write your will and perhaps hire some porters and a few dozen yaks.

The following describes the most prominent sights on a three-day circumambulation of the mountain. Over the centuries, the Kailash kora has accumulated a profusion of significant stops for the ardent pilgrim. Those with a real interest in such things would be best to do the kora with a copy of Victor Chan's *Tibet Handbook – a pilgrimage guide* (Moon, 1994) – hire a porter to carry it for you.

Day One The first day of the Kailash kora entails around six hours of walking from Darchen to Drira Phuk Monastery. With rest stops, the occasional prostration and visits to a couple of sights on the way, the walk can easily end up taking from eight to nine hours, however.

From the Darchen Guesthouse, there is a clear westward path that ascends gently for an hour or so to a ridge which is a prostration site and is marked with prayer flags and a small cairn of om mani padme stones. There are excellent views of the southern face of Kailash from here.

After the descent from the ridge, the path starts to bear northwards into the Lha Chu valley. In the distance is **Tarboche**, the site of Kailash's most important annual festival – Saga Dawa, which coincides with the full moon of the fourth lunar month. An enormous prayer-flag pole marks the spot. There are fabulous views here of the valley with Kailash in the distance.

Tarboche is a good place to take a break. At this point there are two options: to continue the kora or to take a detour up to the **Cemetery of the 84 Mahasiddhas**. The cemetery is on a flat ridge just to the northeast of the flag pole, and is worth the effort of climbing for those with a strong stomach and an interest in things morbid. The area was originally a burial site for monks and lamas, and thus sanctified has now become a popular sky burial site for ordinary Tibetans. There is a terrible odour of decay here, and an obvious shortage of vultures in the Kailash region means that the chopped-up bodies are left to wild dogs. Have some stones at hand for the latter, they patrol the ridge in savage packs.

From Tarboche, follow the Lha Chu valley for around an hour to a bridge. This is one of the most beautiful sections of the whole kora, with green meadows, streams and Kailash towering above. From the bridge, it is possible to see **Chuku Monastery** perched high up on the hills that rise from the left bank of the Lha Chu river. This monastery is probably the most worthwhile detour on the whole kora, but it is a fairly steep climb and, with a short tour of the monastery, a cup of tea and a rest on the monastery roof (amazing views of Kailash), will probably add an hour and a half to your walk on the first day.

Chuku was founded in the 13th century by Gotsangpa Gompo Pel, a devotee of the Kagyupa order. Monks at the monastery may show you his meditation cave, which is to the rear of the monastery.

After descending from Chuku Monastery, to rejoin the kora proper you should recross the bridge and follow the west bank of the river. This is slightly confusing as there is also a path that follows the east bank. As you continue, the valley narrows into a canyon with high cliff faces. Look out for some spectacular waterfalls. It is around 2½ to three hours from here, following the valley as it swings eastward and brings Kailash's north face into view, to **Drira Phuk Monastery**. Look for the monastery on a ridge above the west bank of the Lha Chu river.

The monastery dates back to the 13th century and has a few friendly resident monks. The staff at the monastery guesthouse just down from the monastery are not so friendly, however. Accommodation here is very basic and definitely not worth the Y15 that is charged for a bed. But if you do not have a tent, you will not have any choice. The area by the river down from the guesthouse is a popular camping site.

Day Two Day two of the kora is without a doubt the toughest. The major hurdle is the 5630-metre Drolma-la pass. The actual climb proceeds in three stages, all of which are very taxing, but the hardest of which is the final 200 metres to the top of the pass itself. Allow yourself plenty of rest stops.

From Drira Phuk Monastery the trail leaves the Lha Chu valley and enters the Drolma Chu valley. The upward climb begins shortly after you ford the Drolma Chu river – the best places to do this are upstream a little way. After about half an hour the trail flattens out and you have some level walking before ascending to the **Siwatshal cemetery**. Like the Cemetery of the 84 Mahasiddhas on day one of the kora, it is a grim, eerie place scattered with discarded clothing, hair and stone cairns. Pilgrims make an offering here to Jigje, the Lord of Death. And if all the unaccustomed exercise is getting to you, you can rest assured that this is considered a very meritorious place to lay down and die.

After the cemetery the path levels out once again and you have around half an hour of walking along a valley strewn with boulders before bearing right and making a final ascent to the summit of **Drolma-la pass**. This last, very strenuous ascent will probably take around an hour, depending on how fit you are.

The initial climb follows a steep series of switchbacks, before easing into a more gentle climb for the last 15 minutes or so. You know you are almost there when you see the prayer flag-festooned summit coming into view. Allow yourself a long rest at the top. There is no need to hurry as the rest of the day's walk to Zutrul Phuk Monastery is either downhill or level and should only take another four hours.

The descent from the summit soon brings you into view of **Thukpe Dzingbu lake**, one of the highest lakes in the world and often frozen over even in the summer months. The Lake of Compassion, as it is known, is a holy place: Tibetans pilgrims generally drink from its waters, while Indian pilgrims are required to bathe in it.

Pass the lake via a glacial moraine of shattered granite boulders. It is often necessary to hop across them and it is very difficult to keep track of the trail – which is to the right of the valley. The final descent is very steep and quite a strain on the legs. Beneath are fabulous views of the Lham Chu valley, with its green meadows. The entire descent takes just over an hour.

At the foot of the pass, you have a choice of fording the Lham Chu river to the east bank, where the walking is easier, or following the west bank. If you take the former course of action, you will need to keep an eye out for an appropriate place to reford the river at a later stage. If you leave this too late you will be faced with the prospect of a waist-level crossing in icy, fast-flowing water.

It is close on three hours from the foot of Drolma-la pass to Zutrul Phuk Monastery. The walking, however, is on level terrain and there are occasional views of Kailash's eastern face en route.

Zutrul Phuk Monastery is built at the site of a famous cave said to have been created as part of the contest between Milarepa and Naro Bonchung over whether Kailash would subsequently be the domain of Buddhism or Bön. Milarepa first brought the ceiling of the cave into being and left it suspended in the air; Naro Bonchung, too awestruck to complete the supporting walls, left the rest of the work to Milarepa. There is an image of Milarepa in the cave, and there are other meditation caves above the monastery. The monastery guesthouse below the monastery has better accommodation than at Drira Phuk and is run by a friendly old man who will supply tea even if you do not opt to stay at the guesthouse. A bed costs Y15.

Day Three The final day of the kora involves a walk of around 2½ to three hours. There are a few streams to ford in the initial section. The path then climbs gradually and follows the lip of an impressive gorge – look back for some fabulous views – before rounding into the Bharka plain. It is about an hour's walk through the desert from here to Darchen.

Darchen
Darchen is a forgettable little village strewn, as usual, with broken beer bottles and dotted around the outskirts with pilgrim tents. Most travellers linger here long enough to organise their kora of Kailash and then get out.

The *Darchen Guesthouse* is in a compound at the southern end of the village. Some travellers have a terrible time here, but as long as you are friendly everything should go smoothly. Beds are expensive at Y40 (Y80 for tour groups) and the same amount is charged to camp in the compound. Warm bedding and hot water is available. Meals are served in the restaurant at noon and 7 pm, but if you are extra polite and there is food left, they will probably cook something up for you. Belligerent visitors (or simply visitors the chef does not like the look of) are frequently refused service. This is the only restaurant in town.

In the compound of the hotel, a Tibetan woman has put up a tent and serves drinks and provides karaoke entertainment. She even has a CD player powered by a car battery, and when I was there she had a couple of early Talking Heads CDs – wonder where they came from? It is very tempting to listen to the Talking Heads, knock back a few beers and give the Kailash kora a miss.

The Darchen Guesthouse can arrange yak and porter hire. If you have a heavy backpack it is worth considering a porter. They are usually friendly young guys who know the circuit well. The guesthouse will take your money before you leave and pay the porter when he gets back. The cost is Y50 per day, but you can probably organise it yourself at a cheaper rate in the village if you have the energy and the time.

LAKE MANASAROVAR
མ་ཕམ་ཡུ་མཚོ་

About 30 km to the south of Mt Kailash, Lake Manasarovar (4560 metres) is the most venerated of Tibet's many lakes. It is divided from another lake, Rakshas Tal, by a narrow isthmus. A channel links the two lakes, and when, on rare occasions, water flows via this channel from Manasarovar to Rakshas Tal it is said to augur well for the Tibetan people. It's been long dry, but water has indeed been flowing between the two lakes in recent years.

According to Indian mythology, Manasarovar was formed in the mind of Brahma when his sons requested a place to bathe after having 'performed austerities' (whatever that means) on the slopes of Kailash. Accordingly, Indian pilgrims bathe in the waters of the lake and circumambulate its circumference. Tibetans, who are not so keen on the bathing bit, generally just walk around it.

The Hindu classical poet, Kalidasa, once wrote that the waters of Manasarovar are 'like pearls' and that to drink of them erases the 'sins of a hundred lifetimes'. Be warned, however, that the sins of a hundred lifetimes tend to make their hasty exit by way of the nearest toilet. On arriving at Manasarovar, the Tibetan pilgrims I was travelling with promptly emptied my canisters of water and filled them up with holy water from the lake

– with extremely discomforting gastrointestinal consequences for all of us.

Very few Western travellers undertake the 90 km, four-day kora of the lake. One of the main problems is the marshiness of the ground around the lake. But there are also many streams to ford, some of which become quite deep in the summer months. It seems that most groups and individuals base themselves at picturesque Chiu Monastery on the north-west shore of the lake, and use this small monastery as a base for day walks.

Lake Manasarovar Kora

Those planning to tackle the Manasarovar kora should be prepared for a tough four-day hike. Some groups set off and give up. A group of Indian pilgrims I met hired ponies in Darchen. There is food available in Barga, to the north of the lake, and in the village at the foot of Chiu Monastery, but it would be sensible to come supplied with whatever essentials you need.

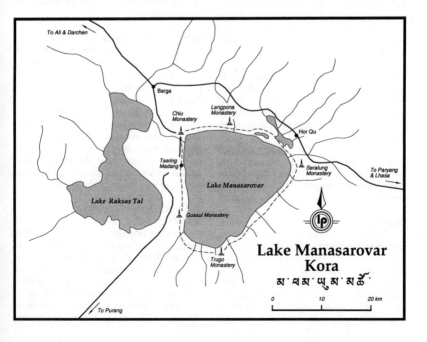

The obvious starting point is **Chiu Monastery** (around 30 km south of Darchen), a small monastery next to a hot spring that has become popular with individual travellers. There is a small, basic guesthouse on a hill opposite the monastery with earthen beds for Y10. There is no bedding available and you will have to pay Y1 for a thermos of hot water.

The monastery itself is picturesquely plonked on top of a craggy hill overlooking the lake. Climb up to the roof of the monastery for stunning views of Manasarovar. The hot spring is behind the monastery, and there is a small stone compound for bathing close to the village. The water is extremely hot, and unless you are Japanese it is unlikely that you will be able to wallow in it. You may have to content yourself with washing in the water that spills out from the compound while all the children in the village watch on with fascination.

The traditional starting point for the kora is the drab, dusty town of Hor Qu over on the north-east corner of the lake. Chiu Monastery is far and away a better place to spend a night before setting off, however. There is no accommodation in Hor Qu.

Day One From Chiu Monastery, the pilgrimage trail largely follows a ridge east along the hills overlooking Lake Manasarovar. If you try to walk along the shore of the lake you will find yourself frequently sinking knee-deep in mud.

After around five or six km, the trail dips down into a valley close to the lake shore, before climbing up into the hills again to **Langpona Monastery**. The total walk is around 15 km.

Day Two Day two involves a walk of around 25 km from Langpona Monastery to **Seralung Monastery**. From Langpona, it is not a particularly good idea to head back to Manasarovar and follow the shore line, as river crossings make this section very difficult. Rather, follow the trail inland, passing three lakes, to the north-east corner of Manasarovar. Towards the end of the day's walk there is a river crossing at Samo Tsangpo river – the water can often rise above waist level in the summer months. Seralung Monastery is around six or seven km from here.

Day Three Day three involves approximately 27 km of walking. Around four km south of Seralung is a bridge crossing, and from here the trail follows the shore of the lake down to **Trugo Monastery**.

Day Four From Trugo Monastery back to Chiu Monastery is around 23 km. Those with lots of time on their hands, might like to break the walk with an overnight stay at Tsering Madang, where there should be a guesthouse. Tsering Madang is two hours short of Chiu Monastery.

From Trugo Monastery the trail passes the small Shushup Lake, before heading north, roughly parallelling the Ali-Purang road. Around seven km north of Shushup Lake is Gossul Monastery, a small monastery of marginal interest.

Getting There & Away

See the Western Tibet Getting There & Away section above for information on the southern and northern routes to Kailash and Ali, and the road between Ali and Darchen at Kailash.

From Darchen to Chiu Monastery is a little over 30 km. There is no public transport and very little in the way of truck activity on this road. There may, however, occasionally be trucks on the main Ali-Purang road, around six km out of Darchen – be prepared for a long wait if you are hitching.

THÖLING & TSAPARANG
མཐོ་གླིང་   རྩ་བ་རང་

Thöling and Tsaparang are the ruined former capitals of the ancient Guge kingdom of Western Tibet. They are rarely visited by foreign travellers, largely because unless you have rented transport getting out to either of these historical sites is very difficult.

There is primitive accommodation in Thöling, or Zhada as it is known in Chinese, and at least one Chinese restaurant. Thöling makes a good base to explore the area.

Thöling

Thöling was once Western Tibet's most important monastic complex, and was still functioning in 1966 when the Red Guards shut down operations. Most of the complex is now in ruins, though some murals dating from the 15th and 16th centuries are well preserved.

The monastic complex at Thöling was founded by Rinchen Zangpo, a monk who, under the patronage of the Guge king, Yeshe Ö, spent some 17 years studying in India in the late 10th century. Rinchen Zangpo returned to become one of Tibet's greatest translators of Sanskrit texts and a key figure in the revival of Buddhism across the Tibetan plateau. It was partly at his behest that Atisha, a renowned Indian scholar and another pivotal character in the revival of Tibetan Buddhism, was invited to Tibet. Atisha spent some three years in Thöling before travelling on to central Tibet.

Most of the central chapel of Thöling Monastery has been reduced to rubble, its fine statues destroyed. The building was designed in the shape of a three-dimensional mandala. The last of the buildings on the left before the central chapel is the assembly hall. There are murals on the walls, but you will need a powerful torch to make anything of them. Opposite the assembly hall is the White Chapel. It may not be open but, if you can enter, it also has well-preserved murals.

Getting There & Away Thöling is to the west of the Ali-Purang road, and fairly inaccessible without rented transport. There are probably trucks leaving from Ali to Zhada (the new Chinese town at Thöling) from time to time and you might be able to get a lift with one of these. Alternatively, you might hitch to Nabuzhi (the turn-off for Thöling 136 km from Ali, 195 km from Bagar) and try hitching from there.

In a rented truck or landcruiser it should be possible to make it to Thöling from either Ali or Kailash in a single day, providing you get an early start.

Tsaparang

Tsaparang has been gracefully falling into ruin since its slide from prominence in the 17th century (see the Western Tibet History section above) and is perhaps of greatest interest to those with some knowledge of early Buddhist art. The ruins, which seem to grow organically out of the hills, make for a photogenically surreal landscape, but there are restrictions on photographs of Tsaparang's foremost attraction: its early Tantric-inspired murals.

The ruins of Tsaparang extend along a ridge with two main areas of interest: the Red and White chapels and the Tsaparang Dzong, all three of which are close to each other. The ancient summer and winter palaces are in ruins. The best of Tsaparang's murals are concentrated in the Red and White chapels.

The murals of the White Chapel (Lhakhang Karpo) are of debated antiquity, but probably date back to the 15th or 16th centuries. Their influences, however, extend back to 10th century Kashmiri Buddhist art, and for this reason are of particular interest to scholars of Buddhist art. With the exception of here in Tsaparang, very little material evidence of early Kashmiri art remains.

Above and just to the south of the White Chapel, the Red Chapel (Lhakhang Marpo) also has noteworthy murals, though they are thought to be more recent than those in the White Chapel.

The dzong is entered via a tunnel and stairway in the north-east section of the fortress complex which leads up to a platform with views of Tsaparang. The Mandala Chapel, immediately south of this area, has more murals.

Getting There & Away Tsaparang is about an hour's drive west of Thöling (Zhada), and the only way you will be able to get there is with a rented vehicle. At the time of writing a permit worth Y230 was required to visit Tsaparang. Check on the latest situation in Ali or Lhasa before you set out.

Glossary

Many of the terms in this chapter are of Sanskrit origin. Italicised entries in brackets indicate their Tibetan equivalents.

Akshobhya – the Buddha of the state of perfected consciousness, of perfect cognition; literally 'unchanging', the 'Immutable One'

Amban – Chinese representatives of the Manchu Qing dynasty posted in Lhasa from the early 19th century until the Chinese Republican overthrow of the Qing in 1911

Amdo – one of the three traditional provinces of Tibet, and now Qinghai province. The other two provinces are Kham (Sichuan) and Ütsang, which includes Central and Western Tibet

Amitabha – *(Wopame)* the Buddha of perfected perception; literally 'Boundless Light'

Amitayus – *(Tsepame)* a meditational deity associated with longevity; literally 'Limitless Life'. Amitayus is often featured in a trinity with the white Tara and Vijaya

Ani – Tibetan for 'nun', as in ani gompa, 'nunnery'

Apsara – a Sanskrit term meaning 'angel'

Arhat – literally 'Worthy One', the arhat is neither a Buddha nor a bodhisattva, but is one who has freed themself from the Wheel of Life and is free of hatred and all delusions

Atisha – (982-1054) an Indian Buddhist scholar from contemporary Bengal. His arrival in Tibet at the invitation of the king of Guge, in Western Tibet, was a major catalyst in the 11th-century revival of Buddhism on the high plateau.

Atman – a Sanskrit pre-Buddhist term that refers to a universal self in keeping with the beliefs of Brahmanism

Avalokiteshvara – *(Chenresig)* an embodiment of compassionate bodhisattvahood and the patron saint of Tibet. The Dalai Lamas are considered manifestations of this deity.

Bardo – as detailed in the *Tibetan Book of the Dead*, this term refers to the intermediate stages between death and rebirth

Barkhor – an intermediate circumambulation circuit, or kora, but most often specifically the intermediate circuit around the Jokhang Temple of Lhasa

Bhrikuti – the Nepalese consort of King Songtsen Gampo, an early Tibetan king

Black Hat – strictly speaking the black hat embellished with gold that was presented to the 2nd Karmapa of the Karma Kagyupa order of Tsurphu Monastery by a Mongol prince, and worn ceremoniously by all subsequent incarnations of the Karmapa – by extension, the Karma Kagyupa order

Bodh Gaya – the place in contemporary Bihar, India, where Sakyamuni, the historical Buddha, attained enlightenment

Bodhisattva – literally 'Enlightenment Hero', the bodhisattva is motivated by compassion for all sentient beings to stay within the Wheel of Life

Bö – the Tibetan name for their own land; sometimes written Bod or Po

Bön – the indigenous religion of Tibet prior to the introduction of Buddhism; a shamanistic faith associated with spirits, demons and exorcism among other things

Bönpo – the Bön faith as it has evolved into an organised school much influenced by Buddhism, in particular the Nyingmapa order of Tibetan Buddhism

Brahma – Hindu God, the underlying principal of the cosmos according to Brahmanism

Buddha – literally 'Awakened One', a being who through spiritual training has broken free of all illusion and karmic consequences and is 'enlightened'; most often specifically the historical Buddha, Sakyamuni

Büton – sub-order of Tibetan Buddhism associated with Zhalu Monastery, near Shigatse, Tsang

Chaktsal – Tibetan for the ritual of 'prostration'

Cham – a ritual dance carried out by monks and lamas usually at festivals; with the exception of the central lama, all participants are masked

Chan – Chinese for a branch of Buddhism more famously known in the West by its Japanese name, Zen

Chang – Tibetan barley beer

Changchub Gyatso – monk and official who ended the Mongol-Sakya hegemony over Tibet in the mid-14th century

Chang Tang – vast northern plains of northern Tibet extending into Xinjiang and Qinghai; the largest and highest plateau in the world

Chenresig – see Avalokiteshvara

Chömay – butter lamp

Chörten – Tibetan for 'stupa'; usually used as reliquaries for the cremated remains of important lamas

Chu – river, stream, brook, etc

Dalai Lama – one of 14 (so far) manifestations of Avalokiteshvara who, as spiritual heads of the Gelugpa order, ruled over Tibet from 1642 until 1959. The present 14th Dalai Lama resides in Dharamsala, India.

Deva – 33 gods of Brahmanism

Dharma – *(Cho)* sometimes translated as 'Law', this very broad term covers the truths expounded by Sakyamuni, the Buddhist teachings, the Buddhist path and the Buddhist goal, Nirvana; in effect it is the 'law' that must be understood, followed and achieved in order to be a Buddhist

Dölma – see Tara

Dorje – literally 'diamond' but by extension the indestructible, indivisible nature of buddhahood; also a Tantric hand-held sceptre symbolising 'skilful means'

Drigum – early Tibetan king whose name means literally 'Slain by Pollution'; his death marked the beginning of the practice of burying the Yarlung kings in funerary mounds which can be seen at Chongye, Ü

Drogpa – Tibetan for 'nomad'

Dromtönpa – 11th-century disciple of Atisha who founded the Kadampa order

Dungchen – long, ceremonial Tibetan trumpet

Dukhang – Tibetan for 'assembly hall'

Dukkha – Sanskrit for 'suffering', the essential condition of all life

Dusum Khenyapa – founder of Tsurphu Monastery and first Karmapa

Dzo – domesticated cross between a bull and a female yak

Dzogch'en – the Great Perfection Teachings associated with the Nyingmapa order

Dzong – Tibetan for 'fort'

Eightfold Path – one of the Four Holy Truths taught by Sakyamuni, this term refers to the path that must be taken to achieve enlightenment and liberation from the Wheel of Life

Eight Medicine Buddhas – *(Sangye Menlha)* the Buddha of healing, often depicted in a group of eight accompanying Sakyamuni

Four Guardian Kings – usually positioned on either side of the front door of a monastery or main assembly hall, these Indian kings guard Buddhist precincts from malevolent forces; each king is associated with one of the four cardinal compass points

Four Noble Truths – the first speech given by Sakyamuni after he achieved enlightenment: they are the truth that all life is suffering; the truth that suffering originates in desire; the truth that desire may be extinguished; and the truth that there is a path to this end

Gampopa – Milarepa's chief disciple and the founder of the Kagyupa order

Ganden – the Pure Land of Maitreya, the Future Buddha, and the seat of the Gelugpa order (Ganden Monastery, Ü)

Garuda – mythological bird associated with Hinduism; in Tibetan Tantric Buddhism it is seen as a wrathful force that transforms malevolent influences

Gau – an amulet or 'portable shrine' worn around the neck; contains the image of an important spiritual figure – usually the Dalai Lama

Gelong – the full indoctrinal vows of monkhood only achieved after many years of study and not necessarily by all monks

Gelugpa – major order of Tibetan Buddhism, associated with the Dalai Lamas, Panchen Lamas and Dreprung, Sera, Ganden and Tashilhunpo monasteries; founded by Tsongkhapa in the 14th century; also known as the Yellow Hats

Genden Drup – the 1st Dalai Lama

Genden Gyatso – the 2nd Dalai Lama

Genyen – one of the lesser ordination vows for monks

Gesar – a legendary king and the name of an epic concerning his fabulous exploits; the king's empire is known as Ling, and thus the stories, usually sung and told by professional bards, are also known as the *Stories of Ling*

Geshe – awarded on completion of the highest level of study, something like a doctorate, that monks may undertake after completing their Gelong vows; usually associated with the Gelugpa order

Getsul – one of the lesser ordination vows for monks

Gompa – Tibetan for 'monastery'

Guge – a 9th-century kingdom of Western Tibet

Guru – Sanskrit term for 'spiritual teacher'; literally 'heavy'; the Tibetan equivalent is lama

Guru Rinpoche – known in Sanskrit as Padmasambhava, Guru Rinpoche is credited with having suppressed demons and other malevolent forces in order to introduce Buddhism into Tibet during the 8th century; in the Nyingmapa order he is revered as the 'Second Buddha'

Gyeltsab Je – one of Tsongkhapa's chief disciples and the first Ganden Tripa, or abbot

Hayagriva – *(Tamdrin)* literally 'horse necked', a wrathful meditational deity and manifestation of Avalokiteshvara; associated usually with the Nyingmapa order

Hinayana – major school of Buddhism which follows the original teachings of the historical Buddha, Sakyamuni, and places less importance on the compassionate bodhisattva ideal and more on individual enlightenment; see Mahayana

Humours – underlying principle in both Hindu Ayuvedic and Tibetan medicine; the three humours are wind, bile and phlegm, and illness is seen as stemming from an imbalance between these

Jainism – an ancient Indian faith that like Buddhism believes in the cyclic nature of life

Jampa – see Maitreya

Jamyong Chöde – disciple of Tsongkhapa and founder of Sera Monastery

Je Rinpoche – an honorific title used for Tsongkhapa, founder of the Gelugpa order

Jigje – the Lord of Death

Jokhang – *(Tsuglagkhang)* the most sacred and one of the most ancient of Tibet's temples; in Lhasa

Jowo Sakyamuni – the most revered image of Sakyamuni in Tibet; it depicts the historical Buddha at the age of eight and is kept in the Jokhang

Kadampa – order of Tibetan Buddhism based on the teachings of the Indian scholar Atisha; the school was a major influence on the Gelugpa order

Kagyupa – order of Tibetan Buddhism that traces its lineage back through Milarepa, Marpa and eventually to the Indian Mahasiddhas; it divided into numerous suborders, the most famous of which is the Karma Kagyupa, or the Karmapa

Kangling – a ceremonial human thigh-bone trumpet

Kangyur – the Tibetan Buddhist canon; its complement is the Tengyur

Karma – action and its consequences, the psychic 'imprint' action leaves on the mind and which continues into further rebirths; a term found in both Hinduism and Buddhism, and which may be likened to the law of cause and effect

Karma Kagyupa – sub-order of the Kagyupa order, established by Gampopa and Dusum Khenyapa in the 12th century

Karmapa – a lineage of spiritual leaders of the Karma Kagyupa; also known as the Black Hat, there have been 17 so far

Kashag – Tibetan for the Cabinet of the Gelugpa lamaist Government

Kathak – prayer scarf; used as a ritual offering or as a gift

Kham – traditional Tibetan province; much of it is now part of Sichuan

Khampa – a person from the province of Kham

Khamtsen – monastic residential quarters

Khenpo – Tibetan term for 'abbot'

Kora – ritual circumambulation circuit

Kumbum – literally '100,000 images', this is a stupa that contains statuary and paintings; most famous in Tibet is the Gyantse Kumbum in Tsang

La – Tibetan for 'mountain pass'

Lama – literally 'unsurpassed', this is the Tibetan equivalent of 'guru' and is a title bestowed on monks of particularly high spiritual attainment

Lamaism – term used by early Western writers on the subject of Tibet to describe Tibetan Buddhism; also used by the Chinese in the term *lamajiao*, literally 'lama religion'

Lamrim – the 'Stages on the Path to Enlightenment', a graduated approach to enlightenment as expounded by Tsongkhapa; associated with the Gelugpa order

Langdharma – the 9th-century Tibetan king who is accused of having persecuted Buddhism

Lha – Tibetan term for 'life spirit'; it may also be present in inanimate objects such as lakes, mountains and trees

Lhakhang – Tibetan term for 'chapel'

Lhashing – a tree planted at the birth of a child and thought to harbour the 'life spirit' of the child

Lineage – an unbroken line of teachers who transmit oral instructions regarding sacred texts to their disciples

Ling – Tibetan term usually associated with lesser, outlying temples

Lingkhor – an outer pilgrimage circuit; famously the outer pilgrimage of Lhasa

Lönchen – government body of the Gelugpa lamaist state

Losar – Tibetan New Year

Lungta – prayer flag

Mahasiddha – *(Drubchen)* literally 'of great spiritual accomplishment', the mahasiddha is a Tantric practitioner who has reached a high level of awareness; there are 84 famous mahasiddhas

Mahayana – the other major school of Buddhism along with Hinayana, Mahayana emphasises compassion and the altruism of the bodhisattva who remains on the Wheel of Life for the sake of all sentient beings

Maitreya – *(Jampa)* the Buddha of loving kindness; also the Future Buddha, the 5th of the 1000 Buddhas who will descend to earth (Sakyamuni was the 4th)

Mandal – stones piled as offerings

Mandala – *(Kyilkhor)* a circular representation of the three-dimensional world of a meditational deity, and used as a meditational device

Manjushri – *(Jampel)* the Buddha of discriminative awareness; who is usually depicted holding a sword, which symbolises discriminative awareness, in one hand and a book, which symbolises his mastery of all knowledge, in the other

Mantra – literally 'protection of the mind', this is one of the Tantric devices used to achieve identity with a meditational deity and break through the world of illusion; a series of syllables which are recited as the pure sound made by an enlightened being

Mara – literally 'evil influences', mara stands between us and enlightenment

Marpa – an ascetic of the 11th century whose disciple, Milarepa, founded the Kagyupa order

Meditational Deity – a deified manifestation of the enlightened mind with which, according to Tantric ritual, the adept seeks union and thus experience of enlightenment

Merit – positive karma that accumulates through acts of compassion, through joy in giving

Meru, Mt – the sacred mountain at the centre of the universe; also known as Sumeru

Milarepa – 11th-century disciple of Marpa and founder of the Kagyupa order; renowned for his songs

Momo – Tibetan dumplings

Mönlam – a major Lhasa festival established by Tsongkhapa

Naga – *(Lu)* water spirits who may take the form of serpents or semi-humans; the latter can be seen in images of the Naga kings

Namri Songtsen – 6th-century Tibetan king, father of Songtsen Gampo

Nangkhor – inner circumambulation circuit, usually within the interior of a temple or monastic assembly hall, and taking in various chapels en route

Nechung – protector deity of Tibet and the Dalai Lamas; Nechung is manifested in the State Oracle, who was traditionally installed at Nechung Monastery, near Dreprung, Lhasa

Newari – Nepalese Buddhist kingdom

Ngari – ancient name for the province of Western Tibet; later incorporated into Ütsang

Nirvana – literally 'beyond sorrow', Nirvana is an end to desire and suffering, and an end to the never-ending cycle of re-birth

Norbulingka – the Summer Palace of the Dalai Lamas in Lhasa

Nyentri Tsenpo – legendary first king of Tibet

Nyingmapa – the earliest order of Tibetan Buddhism, based largely on the Buddhism brought to Tibet by Guru Rinpoche

Oracle – in Tibetan Buddhism an oracle serves as a medium for protective deities, as in the State Oracle of Nechung Monastery near Dreprung, Lhasa. The State Oracle was consulted on all important matters of state.

Om Mani Padme Hum – the mantra associated with Avalokiteshvara, patron deity of Tibet

Padmasambhava – see Guru Rinpoche

Panchen Lama – literally 'guru and great teacher', the Panchen Lama lineage is associated with Tashilhunpo Monastery, Shigatse, and goes back to the 17th century; the Panchen Lama is a manifestation of Amitabha

Pandita – a title conferred on great scholars of Buddhism, as in the Sakya Pandita

PLA – acronym for People's Liberation Army

PRC – acronym for People's Republic of China

Protector Deity – deities who can manifest themselves in either male or female forms and serve to protect Buddhist teachings and followers; they may be either wrathful aspects of enlightened beings or worldly powers who have been tamed by Tantric masters

Pure Land – other-worldly realms that are the domains of Buddhas; they are realms completely free of suffering, and in the popular Buddhist imagination are probably something like the Christian heaven

Qiang – proto-Tibetan tribes that troubled the borders of the Chinese empire

Qomolangma – Tibetan name for Mt Everest as transliterated by the Chinese; also spelt 'Chomolangma'

Qu – Chinese term for an administrative district, as in Shannan-qu

Ralpachen – 9th-century king whose assassination marked the end of the Yarlung dynasty

Rebirth – a condition of the Wheel of Life; the rebirths of all beings are limitless until they achieve enlightenment

Regent – a representative of an incarnate lama, who presides over a monastic community during the lama's minority; Regents came to play an important political role in the Gelugpa lamaist state

Rimed – a complicated movement that originated in 19th-century Kham; it was a multi-denominational movement and encouraged followers to study the thought of all schools of Tibetan Buddhism

Rinpoche – literally 'high in esteem', a title bestowed on highly revered lamas; they are usually incarnate, but need not be

Saddhu – an Indian ascetic who has renounced all attachments

Sakyamuni – literally the 'Sage of Sakka', the founder of Buddhism, the historical Buddha

Sakyapa – Tibetan Buddhist order associated with Sakya Monastery and founded in the 11th century; also known as the Red Hats

Samsara – the cycle of birth, death and rebirth

Samvara – a wrathful manifestation of Sakyamuni

Samye – the first Buddhist monastery in Tibet, founded by King Trisong Detsen in the 8th century

Sangha – community of Buddhist monks or nuns

Sangkang – pot-bellied incense burners

Sanskrit – ancient language of India, has a complex grammar and rich vocabulary; a classical mode of expression with the status that Latin had in earlier Western society

Shangshung – ancient kingdom of Western Tibet and origin of Bön

Shantarikshita – Indian scholar of the 8th century and first abbot of Samye Monastery

Shape – a member of the Kashag

Shenrab – mythical founder of the Bön faith

Shötun – the Yoghurt Festival of Lhasa

Siddhatta Gotama – see Sakyamuni

Sinmo – a demoness

Sky Burial – Tibetan funerary practice of chopping up the corpses of their dead in designated high places and leaving them for the birds

Songtsen Gampo – the 7th-century king associated with the first introduction of Buddhism to Tibet

Stupa – see chörten

Sutra – Buddhist scriptures which record the teachings of the historical Buddha, Sakyamuni

Tantra – scriptures and oral lineages associated with Tantric Buddhism

Tantric – of Tantric Buddhism; see Vajrayana

TAR – acronym for Tibetan Autonomous Region

Tara – *(drölma)* a female meditational deity who is a manifestation of the enlightened mind of all Buddhas; sometimes referred to as the mother of all Buddhas; she has many aspects but is most often seen as the Green Tara or White Tara

Tengyur – a Tibetan Buddhist canonical text that collects together commentaries on the teachings of Sakyamuni

Terma – 'discovered' or 'revealed' teachings; teachings that have been hidden until the world is ready to receive them

Terton – discoverer of terma

Thamzing – 'struggle sessions', a misconceived Chinese tool for changing the ideological orientation of individuals; ultimately a coercive tool that encouraged deceit under the threat of torture

Thangka – a Tibetan religious painting usually framed by a silk brocade

Theravada – see Hinayana

Thukpa – traditional Tibetan noodle dish

Trapa – Tibetan for 'monk'

Tratsang – monastic college

Tripa – the post of abbot at Ganden Monastery; head of the Gelugpa order

Tritsong Detsen – 8th-century Tibetan king; founder of Samye Monastery

Trulku – incarnate lama

Tsampa – roast barley flour, traditional staple of the Tibetan people

Tsang – traditional province to the west of Ü which has Shigatse as its capital

Tso – Tibetan for 'lake'

Tsongkhapa – 14th-century founder of the Gelugpa order and Ganden Monastery

Tsuglagkhang – 'grand temple', but often specifically the Jokhang of Lhasa

Tushita – Pure Land of Maitreya, the Future Buddha

Ü – traditional province to the east of Tsang which has Lhasa as its capital

Ütsang – the provinces of Ü and Tsang, also incorporating Ngari, or Western Tibet; effectively Central Tibet, or political Tibet

Vairocana – Buddha of enlightened consciousness

Vajrayana – literally the 'Diamond Vehicle', a branch of Mahayana Buddhism that finds a more direct route to bodhisattvahood through identification through meditational deities

Wencheng – Chinese consort of King Songtsen Gampo

Wheel of Life – often pictured in monasteries, the Wheel of Life depicts the cyclic nature of existence and the six realms that rebirth take place in

Yamantaka – a variety of meditational deity; Yamantaka comes in various aspects; the Red and Black aspects are probably most common

Yangsid – hereditary incarnation

Yidam – see Meditational Deity; may also have the function of being a personal protector deity that looks over an individual or family

Yigtsang – government body in the Gelugpa lamaist state

Yogin – Yoga in Sanskrit refers to a 'union' with the fundamental nature of reality; for Tibetan Buddhists this can be achieved through meditative techniques and through identification with a meditational deity; a yogin is an adept of such techniques

Appendix – Place Names (Chinese)

The following place names are listed with Chinese script to help travellers in Tibet to read maps and signs.

Ali
阿里

Barga
巴葛

Bayi
八一

Chamdo
昌都

Chongye
胼结

Chusul
曲水

Damxung
当雄

Dreprung Monastery
哲蚌寺

Everest, Mt
珠峰

Ganden Monastery
甘丹寺

Gegye
革吉

Gertse
改则

Golmud
格尔木

Gonggar
贡嘎

Gonggar Airport
贡嘎机厂

Gyantse
江孜

Hor Qu
霍尔区

Jokhang
大照寺

Kailash, Mt
神山 (冈仁坡齐峰)

Kangding
康定

Kashgar
喀什

Lhasa
拉萨

Lhatse
拉孜

Litang
理塘

Manasarovar, Lake
圣湖 (马旁雍错)

Markam
芒康

Mindroling Monastery
敏珠林寺

Nagqu
那曲

Nam-tso
纳木错

Nangartse
浪卡子

Norbulingka, the
罗布林卡

Nyalam
聂拉木

Paryang
帕羊

Pongba
雄巴

Potala
布达拉宫

Purang
普兰

Rongbuk Monastery
绒布寺

Sakya
萨迦

Samding Monastery
桑顶寺

Samye Monastery
桑耶寺

Sangsang
桑桑

Sera Monastery
色拉寺

Shegar
新定日

Shigatse
日喀则

Shiquanhe (Ali)
狮泉河
Tingri
定日
Trandruk Monastery
昌珠寺
Tsaparang
札达
Tsetang
泽当
Tsochen
措勤

Yamdrok-tso
羊卓雍错
Yatung
亚东
Yumbulagang
雍布拉康
Zhangmu
樟木
Zhongba
仲巴

Index

LONELY PLANET JOURNEYS

JOURNEYS is a unique collection of travellers' tales – published by the company that understands travel better than anyone else. It is a series for anyone who has ever experienced – or dreamed of – the magical moment when they encountered a strange culture or saw a place for the first time. They are tales to read while you're planning a trip, while you're on the road or while you're in an armchair, in front of a fire.

JOURNEYS books will catch the spirit of a place, illuminate a culture, recount a crazy adventure, or introduce a fascinating way of life. They will always entertain, and always enrich the experience of travel.

FULL CIRCLE
A South American Journey
Luis Sepúlveda
Translated by Chris Andrews

Full Circle invites us to accompany Chilean writer Luis Sepúlveda on 'a journey without a fixed itinerary'. Extravagant characters and extraordinary situations are memorably evoked: gauchos organising a tournament of lies, a scheming heiress on the lookout for a husband, a pilot with a corpse on board his plane . . . Part autobiography, part travel memoir, *Full Circle* brings us the distinctive voice of one of South America's most compelling writers.

THE GATES OF DAMASCUS
Lieve Joris
Translated by Sam Garrett

This best-selling book is a beautifully drawn portrait of day-to-day life in modern Syria. Through her intimate contact with local people, Lieve Joris draws us into the fascinating world that lies behind the gates of Damascus.

ISLANDS IN THE CLOUDS
Travels in the Highlands of New Guinea
Isabella Tree

This is the fascinating account of a journey to the remote and beautiful Highlands of Papua New Guinea and Irian Jaya. The author travels with a PNG Highlander who introduces her to his intriguing and complex world. *Islands in the Clouds* is a thoughtful, moving book, full of insights into a region that is rarely noticed by the rest of the world.

LOST JAPAN
Alex Kerr

Lost Japan draws on the author's personal experiences of Japan over a period of 30 years. Alex Kerr takes his readers on a backstage tour: friendships with Kabuki actors, buying and selling art, studying calligraphy, exploring rarely visited temples and shrines . . . The Japanese edition of this book was awarded the 1994 Shincho Gakugei Literature Prize for the best work of non-fiction.

SEAN & DAVID'S LONG DRIVE
Sean Condon

Sean and David are young townies who have rarely strayed beyond city limits. One day, for no good reason, they set out to discover their homeland, and what follows is a wildly entertaining adventure that covers half of Australia. Sean Condon has written a hilarious, offbeat road book that mixes sharp insights with deadpan humour and outright lies.

SHOPPING FOR BUDDHAS
Jeff Greenwald

Shopping for Buddhas is Jeff Greenwald's story of his obsessive search for the perfect Buddha statue. In the backstreets of Kathmandu, he discovers more than he bargained for . . . and his souvenir-hunting turns into an ironic metaphor for the clash between spiritual riches and material greed. Politics, religion and serious shopping collide in this witty account of an enlightening visit to Nepal.

LONELY PLANET TRAVEL ATLASES

Lonely Planet has long been famous for the number and quality of its guidebook maps. Now we've gone one step further and in conjunction with Steinhart Katzir Publishers produced a handy companion series: Lonely Planet travel atlases – maps of a country produced in book form.

Unlike other maps, which look good but lead travellers astray, our travel atlases have been researched on the road by Lonely Planet's experienced team of writers. All details are carefully checked to ensure the atlas corresponds with the equivalent Lonely Planet guidebook.

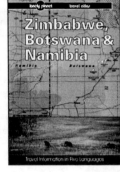

The handy atlas format means no holes, wrinkles, torn sections or constant folding and unfolding. These atlases can survive long periods on the road, unlike cumbersome fold-out maps. The comprehensive index ensures easy reference.

- full-colour throughout
- maps researched and checked by Lonely Planet authors
- place names correspond with Lonely Planet guidebooks
  – no confusing spelling differences
- legend and travelling information in English, French, German, Japanese and Spanish
- size: 230 x 160 mm

Available now:
Chile; Egypt; India & Bangladesh; Israel & the Palestinian Territories; Jordan, Syria & Lebanon; Laos; Thailand; Vietnam; Zimbabwe, Botswana & Namibia

---

LONELY PLANET TV SERIES & VIDEOS

Lonely Planet travel guides have been brought to life on television screens around the world. Like our guides, the programmes are based on the joy of independent travel, and look honestly at some of the most exciting, picturesque and frustrating places in the world. Each show is presented by one of three travellers from Australia, England or the USA and combines an innovative mixture of video, Super-8 film, atmospheric soundscapes and original music.

Videos of each episode – containing additional footage not shown on television – are available from good book and video shops, but the availability of individual videos varies with regional screening schedules.

Video destinations include: Alaska; Australia (Southeast); Brazil; Ecuador & the Galápagos Islands; Indonesia; Israel & the Sinai Desert; Japan; La Ruta Maya (Yucatán, Guatemala & Belize); Morocco; North India (Varanasi to the Himalaya); Pacific Islands; Vietnam; Zimbabwe, Botswana & Namibia.

Coming soon: The Arctic (Norway & Finland); Baja California; Chile & Easter Island; China (Southeast); Costa Rica; East Africa (Tanzania & Zanzibar); Great Barrier Reef (Australia); Jamaica; Papua New Guinea; the Rockies (USA); Syria & Jordan; Turkey.

The Lonely Planet TV series is produced by:
Pilot Productions
Duke of Sussex Studios
44 Uxbridge St
London W8 7TG UK

Lonely Planet videos are distributed by:
IVN Communications Inc
2246 Camino Ramon
California 94583, USA

107 Power Road, Chiswick
London W4 5PL UK

Music from the TV series is available on CD & cassette.
For ordering information contact your nearest Lonely Planet office.

PLANET TALK

Lonely Planet's FREE quarterly newsletter

We love hearing from you and think you'd like to hear from us.

When...is the right time to see reindeer in Finland?
Where...can you hear the best palm-wine music in Ghana?
How...do you get from Asunción to Areguá by steam train?
What...is the best way to see India?

For the answer to these and many other questions read PLANET TALK.

Every issue is packed with up-to-date travel news and advice including:

- a letter from Lonely Planet co-founders Tony and Maureen Wheeler
- go behind the scenes on the road with a Lonely Planet author
- feature article on an important and topical travel issue
- a selection of recent letters from travellers
- details on forthcoming Lonely Planet promotions
- complete list of Lonely Planet products

To join our mailing list contact any Lonely Planet office.

Also available: Lonely Planet T-shirts. 100% heavyweight cotton.

LONELY PLANET ONLINE

Get the latest travel information before you leave or while you're on the road

Whether you've just begun planning your next trip, or you're chasing down specific info on currency regulations or visa requirements, check out the Lonely Planet World Wide Web site for up-to-the-minute travel information.

As well as travel profiles of your favourite destinations (including interactive maps and full-colour photos), you'll find current reports from our army of researchers and other travellers, updates on health and visas, travel advisories, and the ecological and political issues you need to be aware of as you travel.

There's an online travellers' forum (the Thorn Tree) where you can share your experiences of life on the road, meet travel companions and ask other travellers for their recommendations and advice. We also have plenty of links to other Web sites useful to independent travellers.

With tens of thousands of visitors a month, the Lonely Planet Web site is one of the most popular on the Internet and has won a number of awards including GNN's Best of the Net travel award.

http://www.lonelyplanet.com

LONELY PLANET PRODUCTS

Lonely Planet is known worldwide for publishing practical, reliable and no-nonsense travel information in our guides and on our web site. The Lonely Planet list covers just about every accessible part of the world. Currently there are eight series: *travel guides*, *shoestring guides*, *walking guides*, *city guides*, *phrasebooks*, *audio packs*, *travel atlases* and *Journeys* – a unique collection of travellers' tales.

EUROPE

Austria • Baltic States & Kaliningrad • Baltic States phrasebook • Britain • Central Europe on a shoestring • Central Europe phrasebook • Czech & Slovak Republics • Denmark • Dublin city guide • Eastern Europe on a shoestring • Eastern Europe phrasebook • Finland • France • Greece • Greek phrasebook • Hungary • Iceland, Greenland & the Faroe Islands • Ireland • Italy • Mediterranean Europe on a shoestring • Mediterranean Europe phrasebook • Paris city guide • Poland • Prague city guide • Russia, Ukraine & Belarus • Russian phrasebook • Scandinavian & Baltic Europe on a shoestring • Scandinavian Europe phrasebook • Slovenia • St Petersburg city guide • Switzerland • Trekking in Greece • Trekking in Spain • Ukrainian phrasebook • Vienna city guide • Walking in Switzerland • Western Europe on a shoestring • Western Europe phrasebook

NORTH AMERICA

Alaska • Backpacking in Alaska • Baja California • California & Nevada • Canada • Hawaii • Honolulu city guide • Los Angeles city guide • Mexico • Miami city guide • New England • Pacific Northwest USA • Rocky Mountain States • San Francisco city guide • Southwest USA • USA phrasebook

CENTRAL AMERICA & THE CARIBBEAN

Central America on a shoestring • Costa Rica • Eastern Caribbean • Guatemala, Belize & Yucatán: La Ruta Maya • Jamaica

SOUTH AMERICA

Argentina, Uruguay & Paraguay • Bolivia • Brazil • Brazilian phrasebook • Buenos Aires city guide • Chile & Easter Island • Chile travel atlas • Colombia • Ecuador & the Galápagos Islands • Latin American Spanish phrasebook • Peru • Quechua phrasebook • Rio de Janeiro city guide • South America on a shoestring • Trekking in the Patagonian Andes • Venezuela

Travel Literature: Full Circle: A South American Journey

ANTARCTICA

Antarctica

ISLANDS OF THE INDIAN OCEAN

Madagascar & Comoros • Maldives & Islands of the East Indian Ocean • Mauritius, Réunion & Seychelles

AFRICA

Arabic (Moroccan) phrasebook • Africa on a shoestring • Cape Town city guide • Central Africa • East Africa • Egypt • Egypt travel atlas • Ethiopian (Amharic) phrasebook • Kenya • Morocco • North Africa • South Africa, Lesotho & Swaziland • Swahili phrasebook • Trekking in East Africa • West Africa • Zimbabwe, Botswana & Namibia • Zimbabwe, Botswana & Namibia travel atlas

MAIL ORDER

Lonely Planet products are distributed worldwide. They are also available by mail order from Lonely Planet, so if you have difficulty finding a title please write to us. North American and South American residents should write to Embarcadero West, 155 Filbert St, Suite 251, Oakland CA 94607, USA; European and African residents should write to 10 Barley Mow Passage, Chiswick, London W4 4PH; and residents of other countries to PO Box 617, Hawthorn, Victoria 3122, Australia.

NORTH-EAST ASIA

Beijing city guide • Cantonese phrasebook • China • Hong Kong, Macau & Canton • Hong Kong city guide • Japan • Japanese phrasebook • Japanese audio pack • Korea • Korean phrasebook • Mandarin phrasebook • Mongolia • Mongolian phrasebook • North-East Asia on a shoestring • Seoul city guide • Taiwan • Tibet • Tibet phrasebook • Tokyo city guide

Travel Literature: Lost Japan

MIDDLE EAST & CENTRAL ASIA

Arab Gulf States • Arabic (Egyptian) phrasebook • Central Asia • Iran• Israel & the Palestinian Territories• Israel & the Palestinian Territories travel atlas • Jordan & Syria • Jordan, Syria & Lebanon travel atlas • Middle East • Turkey • Turkish phrasebook • Trekking in Turkey • Yemen

Travel Literature: The Gates of Damascus

ALSO AVAILABLE:

Travel with Children • Traveller's Tales

INDIAN SUBCONTINENT

Bangladesh• Bengali phrasebook• Delhi city guide • Hindi/Urdu phrasebook • India • India & Bangladesh travel atlas • Indian Himalaya • Karakoram Highway • Nepal • Nepali phrasebook • Pakistan • Sri Lanka • Sri Lanka phrasebook • Trekking in the Indian Himalaya • Trekking in the Karakoram & Hindukush • Trekking in the Nepal Himalaya

Travel Literature: Shopping for Buddhas

SOUTH-EAST ASIA

Bali & Lombok • Bangkok city guide • Burmese phrasebook • Cambodia • Ho Chi Minh city guide • Indonesia • Indonesian phrasebook • Indonesian audio pack • Jakarta city guide • Java • Laos • Lao phrasebook • Laos travel atlas • Malay phrasebook • Malaysia, Singapore & Brunei • Myanmar (Burma) • Philippines • Pilipino phrasebook • Singapore city guide • South-East Asia on a shoestring • Thailand • Thailand travel atlas • Thai phrasebook • Thai audio pack • Thai Hill Tribes phrasebook • Vietnam • Vietnamese phrasebook • Vietnam travel atlas

AUSTRALIA & THE PACIFIC

Australia • Australian phrasebook • Bushwalking in Australia• Bushwalking in Papua New Guinea • Fiji • Fijian phrasebook • Islands of Australia's Great Barrier Reef • Melbourne city guide • Micronesia • New Caledonia • New South Wales & the ACT • New Zealand • Northern Territory • Outback Australia • Papua New Guinea • Papua New Guinea phrasebook • Queensland • Rarotonga & the Cook Islands • Samoa • Solomon Islands • South Australia • Sydney city guide • Tahiti & French Polynesia • Tasmania • Tonga • Tramping in New Zealand • Vanuatu • Victoria • Western Australia

Travel Literature: Islands in the Clouds • Sean & David's Long Drive

THE LONELY PLANET STORY

Lonely Planet published its first book in 1973 in response to the numerous 'How did you do it?' questions Maureen and Tony Wheeler were asked after driving, bussing, hitching, sailing and railing their way from England to Australia.

Written at a kitchen table and hand collated, trimmed and stapled, *Across Asia on the Cheap* became an instant local bestseller, inspiring thoughts of another book.

Eighteen months in South-East Asia resulted in their second guide, *South-East Asia on a shoestring*, which they put together in a backstreet Chinese hotel in Singapore in 1975. The 'yellow bible', as it quickly became known to backpackers around the world, soon became *the* guide to the region. It has sold well over half a million copies and is now in its 8th edition, still retaining its familiar yellow cover.

Today there are over 180 titles, including travel guides, walking guides, language kits & phrasebooks, travel atlases and travel literature. The company is one of the largest travel publishers in the world. Although Lonely Planet initially specialised in guides to Asia, we now cover most regions of the world, including the Pacific, North America, South America, Africa, the Middle East and Europe.

The emphasis continues to be on travel for independent travellers. Tony and Maureen still travel for several months of each year and play an active part in the writing, updating and quality control of Lonely Planet's guides.

They have been joined by over 70 authors and 170 staff at our offices in Melbourne (Australia), Oakland (USA), London (UK) and Paris (France). Travellers themselves also make a valuable contribution to the guides through the feedback we receive in thousands of letters each year.

The people at Lonely Planet strongly believe that travellers can make a positive contribution to the countries they visit, both through their appreciation of the countries' culture, wildlife and natural features, and through the money they spend. In addition, the company makes a direct contribution to the countries and regions it covers. Since 1986 a percentage of the income from each book has been donated to ventures such as famine relief in Africa; aid projects in India; agricultural projects in Central America; Greenpeace's efforts to halt French nuclear testing in the Pacific; and Amnesty International.

'I hope we send the people out with the right attitude about travel. You realise when you travel that there are so many different perspectives about the world, so we hope these books will make people more interested in what they see. These are guidebooks, but you can't really guide people. All you can do is point them in the right direction.'
– Tony Wheeler

LONELY PLANET PUBLICATIONS

Australia
PO Box 617, Hawthorn 3122, Victoria
tel: (03) 9819 1877 fax: (03) 9819 6459
e-mail: talk2us@lonelyplanet.com.au

USA
Embarcadero West, 155 Filbert St, Suite 251,
Oakland, CA 94607
tel: (510) 893 8555 TOLL FREE: 800 275-8555
fax: (510) 893 8563
e-mail: info@lonelyplanet.com

UK
10 Barley Mow Passage, Chiswick,
London W4 4PH
tel: (0181) 742 3161 fax: (0181) 742 2772
e-mail: 100413.3551@compuserve.com

France:
71 bis rue du Cardinal Lemoine, 75005 Paris
tel: 1 44 32 06 20 fax: 1 46 34 72 55
e-mail: 100560.415@compuserve.com

World Wide Web: http://www.lonelyplanet.com